Also by the Author

Treasury of Hunting (1965)

How to Shoot (1964)

Larry Koller's Complete Guide to Handguns (1963)

Treasury of Angling (1963)

Golden Guide to Guns (1961)

Fireside Book of Guns (1959)

Shots at Whitetails

Painting of Jumping Buck by Bob Kuhn

SHOTS
at Whitetails

by Lawrence R. Koller

with an Appreciation by
JACK O'CONNOR

Drawings by
BOB KUHN

Alfred A. Knopf, *New York*

1970

To

ALMA, my wife

whose great fund of tolerance and wisdom
befits her admirably for existence with
a hunter and angler

An Introduction

I READ AND ENJOYED *Shots at Whitetails* some years before I ever met the late Larry Koller. I liked the book because it was practical, well organized, and clearly and interestingly written from a wealth of practical experience and a great deal of enthusiasm, intelligence, and common sense. All too many books about guns, shooting, and hunting are hasty jobs by people who are shy on experience and have little common sense. But this book was solid. As I read it I realized that this was the best book on deer hunting since Van Dyke's *The Still-Hunter*. It never occurred to me that I would ever be writing an introduction to Larry's fine book!

When I first read *Shots at Whitetails* I thought I would like this guy Larry Koller, and when I did meet him a few years later I did like him very much. He was honest, forthright, fond of a drink and a humorous tale. We saw each other once or twice a year on the occasions when gun manufacturers wooed writers by plying them with food and drink and maybe giving them a shot at a bird or two.

The last time I saw Larry Koller was in Denver at the world premiere of a movie called *Stage Coach*. Winchester had a hand in its production, promotion, or something, so several gun writers, including Larry Koller and me, were invited to bring our wives along to Denver, to wet our whistles, eat some choice viands, see the movie, meet some of the actors, and gape at some of the fetching little actresses who had parts.

Shots at Whitetails came out in 1948. That is almost a generation ago, and the whitetail is still the furtive, wary, four-legged genius he was then. If anything, the race is considerably smarter—these lovely deer seem to get shrewder every year.

However, since the book was written there have been a good many changes in the rifle and ammunition field. Larry had intended to revise the chapters on guns and loads and on open, peep, and 'scope sights, but his untimely death prevented this. He, too, was aware, of course, that some of the cartridges used widely during the prewar and war years are obsolete. Also, favorite old models of rifles have been discontinued. New ones have come along. The .250/3000 Savage cartridge, which Larry liked so much, is just about dead, since no rifles are currently being made for it. The .30 and .32 Remington rimless cartridges are in even worse shape than the .250/3000. Furthermore, the Remington Model 141 pump-action rifle and the Remington Model 81 autoloader that fired them have long since been replaced by the newer and sleeker Remington Model 760 pump and Model 742 automatic for faster-stepping cartridges that mostly were not even manufactured when this book first came out—the .243, the 6 mm. Remington, the .280 Remington, the .308 Winchester among them. The .303 Savage is a just-about-forgotten orphan.

Likewise, other beloved models have been changed. The Winchester Model 94 is still manufactured, but in greatly changed form. The deer hunter's version of the Model 94—the Model 65—is now a collector's item. The old models of the Savage 99 have been replaced with newer ones easier to manufacture. They are still chambered for the .300 Savage cartridge, but they are also chambered for such new cartridges as the .308, the .284, the .243. Winchester's lever-action Model 88 is a fine whitetail rifle, and so are the Winchester Model 100 and the Harrington & Richardson autoloaders.

Larry Koller and I were in perfect agreement about deer rifles and their use. We both agreed that the hunter killed deer, or any other game for that matter, not by excessive power, not by blinding velocity, but by putting into the right spot a bullet that has been properly constructed to open quickly against the light resistance offered by the fragile and lightly constructed body of the average whitetail. We also agreed that of the various factors in killing power the most important was a hunter who didn't get buck fever and who could shoot well enough to hit. Larry Koller also said that the man who could shoot well enough to keep his shots in an eight-inch circle at fifty yards shot well enough for most whitetail hunting.

Since this book was written, American hunters have come down with a bad case of "magnumitis." All manner of powerful, high-velocity, hard-kicking magnum cartridges have been introduced. None of these has any place in the hunting of the whitetail. They are unnecessarily powerful; rifles for them are too heavy; and their recoil is disconcerting. For whitetails no one needs more power than that afforded by the .308—or for that matter by the .35 Remington or the .30/30.

Shots at Whitetails appeared before the postwar boom in the production and use of telescope sights for big-game hunting had really got under way. Since that time the scope has become the Number-One hunting sight, so much so that probably ninety-nine out of a hundred whitetail hunters who take their hunting and equipment seriously now use telescope sights and probably seventy-five per cent of all new big-game rifles suitable for scope mounting and for deer hunting are equipped with scopes within six months of the time they are purchased.

The material on iron sights for whitetail hunting is excellent, but the best of the open sights, that on the old Savage Model 99-T, has vanished along with the excellent rifle for which it was designed. The fastest aperture (peep) sights for woods hunting, the ones mounted on tang and cocking piece, are no longer manufactured. Iron hunting sights for hunting not only haven't improved since 1948, they have actually gone backward.

Material on specific models of scopes in *Shots at Whitetails* is, of course, obsolete. Of all the scopes mentioned, the only one still manufactured is the excellent Weaver K2.5, and it has been vastly improved since 1948. The companies that made the Noske and the Maxwell Smith scopes are no more; the firm that made the Norman Ford Texan is, I believe, still operating but under another name. Lyman, Weaver, Leupold-Stevens, and Bausch & Lomb, the great optical concern, all make quality scopes, as does the Redfield Gun Sight Company, which manufactured only iron sights when this book was written. In addition, some good hunting scopes are imported from Europe and from Japan.

In 1948 the first good American 4-power scope had been on the market such a short time that it is not listed in *Shots at Whitetails*. At that time the first American variable-power scope, the Weaver KV, was still in the offing. The scope sights listed were all from 2 to 2½ power, and such scopes are still the best for whitetail hunting.

The virtues of the low-power telescope sight for whitetail hunting in brush and forest are many. A good scope with a quickly seen reticle like a heavy crosswire makes accurate shooting possible in light too poor for iron sights to be used at all. A good scope is a very fast sight, since all the hunter has to do is to put the aiming point of the reticle on what he wants to hit and press the trigger.

The hunting scope also has the curious quality of enabling the user to "see through" brush. An animal completely or largely indistinguishable with the naked eye can be made out through the glass. Excellent scopes for the whitetail hunter are the Weaver K2.5 and K3, the Leupold 3X, the Lyman All American 2.5 and 3X scopes, the Redfield 3X, and the Bausch & Lomb 2½X scopes (one internally and on externally adjusted). They have wide fields and considerable latitude of eye relief—the two essentials for fast shooting. The 4X scope is superior for long-range shooting, but the field is smaller and the 4X is not as fast. The variable powers sacrifice width of field and are heavier and more complicated.

Today, most scopes for whitetail hunting are mounted on solid bridge-type mounts screwed to the top of the receiver. Good scopes are relatively if not absolutely waterproof and can be carried safely even in rain if waterproof lens covers are used. However, cautious hunters can use hinged mounts that swing the scope aside so iron sights can be used; Pachmayr, Redfield, and Weaver make these. Another solution is quick-detachable side mounts that permit complete removal of the scope. The Griffin & Howe side mount is an example.

Aside from product and equipment changes, Larry Koller's book is as instructive and valuable today as when it was written. The whitetail is still the same foxy creature now that he was in 1948!

—JACK O'CONNOR

New York
1970

Foreword

THERE ARE exceedingly few persons today who can (1) consistently outsmart a particular buck deer, (2) collect it with either a really good bow or rifle of his own manufacture, (3) properly dress and butcher the carcass, (4) concoct palatable dishes therefrom and (5) expertly mount the remains. Larry Koller can. Furthermore, he can write entertainingly of the whole operation. That last just about puts Larry in a class by himself. It puts this book in a class by itself, too, for in our decidedly humble opinion it is the most practical and comprehensive work on the whitetail deer and its by-products ever written. It should be standard for a long time to come.

There's one thing wrong with Larry's book: it's too enlightening. Its readers are bound to come out the other end more efficient hunters. Thus, the deer lose. That is bad. For under the present hunting system, there'll come a day when there'll be too many hunters to harvest too few deer. Then *bong* will go the gong proclaiming a deer bank holiday.

Here's what we mean: In 1932, New York State had about 68,000 licensed deer hunters. In 1948 — only sixteen years later — an army of more than 300,000 licensed deer hunters took to the tall timber.

To be sure, the nation's whitetail population has been increasing, too, simply by extending its range. Again using New York as an example, the legal deer-hunting territory in that state increased nearly 100 per cent in the last twenty years, while its take of deer increased 150 per cent. But the increase in the number of Empire State hunters was nearly 300 per cent during that same period. Also, the carrying capacity of the nation's whitetail deer range has been reached, or even exceeded, through much of the land.

So maybe we should consider a book like this too enlightening, although, of course, Larry Koller himself is as good a conservationist as he is a hunter. In any event, the book is bound to contribute substantially to the pleasure of the hunter, whether he gets a deer or not. That is good.

This is Larry Koller's first book. It is easy to predict that the public will not permit it to be his last.

CLAYTON B. SEAGEARS
Director of Conservation Education
New York State Conservation Department

Delmar, New York
1948

Acknowledgments

TO DEVELOP this book on whitetail deer it must be evident that a writer requires much more knowledge than that gained by a mere lifetime of deer hunting experiences. It is the author's good fortune to have been associated with some of the best of Eastern deer hunters throughout the past two decades; each of them has made his valuable contribution to ease the tortures of indecision along the trying, though exciting, path to whitetail hunting success. The author wishes to express his never-ending gratitude to all these firm friends and sturdy companions through the years that have brought him the tangible rewards gained in following the trail of the whitetail.

It must be equally evident that comprehensive knowledge of deer studies and habits lie far from the grasp of a single hunter's experience. For the information on deer research, distribution, and general life statistics, the author is deeply grateful to the Conservation authorities of New York, Pennsylvania, Maine, Wisconsin and Michigan. Their full co-operation in furnishing concrete facts and figures from files of many years' study has been of greatest help in preparing the text.

For the excellent photographs of deer and hunting scenes in this volume, full credit as well as much gratitude must be given the Department of Conservation Education, N.Y.S. Conservation Department; also to Ben Pearson, Inc., not only for the fine archery-hunting scene but for their aid in adding to the author's knowledge of beneficent archery legislation throughout the country. Remington Arms Co., Savage Arms Corp., Winchester Repeating Arms Co., also the W. R. Weaver Co., were kind enough to supply excellent photos of their products appearing in the text.

Last, but by no means least, the author wishes to express his deep appreciation to Clayton B. Seagears, a man who is a constant inspiration to all sportsmen who know him; a tireless conservationist, devoting his ample talents to bringing about a better understanding between the sportsman and those who hold the future of hunting and fishing within their hands. Also to artist Bob Kuhn, his many thanks for the faithfully accurate and artistic work on the line drawings and jacket painting, clear evidence not only of his skill but his interest in the whitetail deer. To his good friend, mechanical draftsman Ernie Russell, the author will always be indebted for the fine drawings in the gun-work chapter, which for him has been a labor of love.

It would be ungrateful of the writer not to express also his gratitude to Mrs. Koller for her gentle tolerance of his pecking at the typewriter during odd hours, not to mention her firm-handed help in keeping from underfoot the curious offspring.

Were it not for the warm sympathy and co-operation of all these wonderful people this, the author's first book, could never have been carried to a final curtain.

Contents

ON SNOW, AND THE VARIABLES IN DEER BEHAVIOR ON
SNOW ... CLOTHING AND FOOTWEAR FOR THE STILL-
HUNTER

Part Two—THE MECHANICS OF DEER HUNTING

Illustrations

PART ONE

The Sport of Deer Hunting

1/ *Perspectives*

AWAY BACK in the days when Old Dan'l Boone and Cooper's Leatherstocking roamed the timbered ridges and valleys of our great Alleghenies, the white-tailed deer was the support on which our pioneer forebears extended the western frontiers. To the whitetail they looked for their fresh meat, always easily available to these skilled riflemen and woodsmen. His dark red flesh formed the basis of their daily menus, varied only by occasional squirrel, grouse, wild turkey or fish. But the deer was always first choice, for it meant to them a maximum in food with the least expenditure of precious powder and ball.

Its tough, pliable skin clothed the settler in soft, warm garments — shirts, trousers, moccasins and even cap — clothed him almost entirely from head to foot. Sinews were used for laces and threads, bones went to make soap and needles; even antlers were fitted to knives and other simple tools, just as today. On long trips of exploration into new country where game might be scarce, no pioneer would be without his buckskin pack of "jerky" — smoked venison, hard as rock but capable of sustaining life for long periods in the wilderness. Even for more or less permanent camps sun-dried deer hides, coarsely thatched with their heavy hair, kept a waterproof roof over the settlers' heads.

Truly, then, we can well understand how much heavier would have been the burden of exploration and settling of new wilderness regions had these white-tailed deer not been a permanent and prolific resident of the forests.

Today, hundreds of years after the *Mayflower* first touched the rocky Eastern coast, we still have with us, keeping rapid pace with our growing civilization, "whitetail deer." These have not gone the way of many other vanished or vanishing Americans, and we must gratefully thank the Maker of All Things for bestowing on us so abundantly these splendid game animals in ever-increasing numbers.

Obviously, it is true that wise conservation measures and the never-ending search for new methods and ideas among our various state game commissions have made the present-day abundance of whitetails possible. Equally true is it that no other native game animal or bird has responded so well to intelligent conservation.

Encroaching civilization and the machine workings of man have failed miserably to daunt the spirit, and will to live, in the whitetail. Indeed, he thrives on these, it seems, growing more cunning with each generation, until now he puts to shame the sagacity of his pioneer-days ancestors. This deer lives and survives almost in the midst of the hum of cars and planes, raising his spindly-legged, spotted family in the best whitetail manner, well able to outwit all but the most careful sportsman.

Yes, if any of you who read this would gaze into the setting sun from the top of that great monument of stone and steel in mid-Manhattan, the Empire State Building, your eye would encompass lands now sheltering hundreds of wild whitetail deer — living now as they have before, a placid, almost abundant existence. Few elements disturb them other than the week or two each year when red-capped sportsmen take to the outdoors for that biggest of annual hunting events, the Open Season.

These magic words stir many thousands of hunters every fall. Year after year finds the number increasing, and their degree of success increasing in proportion — indicating that the whitetail deer is not only the most popular of our bigger game, but the most suited to sustain the casualties of heavy hunting in the thickly populated metropolitan areas.

During the past few seasons the licenses issued to New York State hunters alone have virtually doubled and doubled again. All other states where deer are hunted show also this tremendous increase in hunting pressure, particularly since the return of service men. It is, of course, fortunate that not every hunter kills his buck. Certainly there would be few left for posterity should this condition exist for a few years. There will ever be a high percentage of hunters who simply go deer hunting with little thought to the game as a specialized sport. This group will never menace our deer supply — bucks which they kill can be charged to Lady Luck.

On the other hand, there is an increasing number of sportsmen who have a sincere desire to learn enough about deer hunting to enable them to see their buck and dispatch it humanely with a well-

directed shot. The thousands of wounded deer which are never recovered each year show a dead loss on the sportsman's ledger — not
to mention the harried conservation officials. High quality sportsmanship demands of the hunter that he attain the prerequisite skill
both in hunting and shooting to make such losses each season a negligible factor. But careful checking of deer take against licenses issued each season shows that less than one hunter in every ten is successful in bagging his buck.

Attention to almost assumptive detail often means the difference
between the deer hunter and one who goes deer hunting. And,
oddly enough, few of our good hunters ever stop to analyze just
why they happen to return year after year with the proper spoils
of the hunt. All too often it is a single detail that makes or breaks
the whole season's setup for the shooter.

During the season of '39 I spent a few days in deer hunting with
a comparatively new deer hunter. This chap had already killed his
first buck — and with a single shot — so I couldn't classify him as a
greenhorn. He wasn't quite satisfied with his rifle though, after his
first year in the woods, and in the spring and summer of '39 I made
some changes for him. First I built a new stock and equipped the
rifle, a Krag, with ramp front sight and aperture rear. We loaded
plenty of shells and fired all of them at targets and woodchucks
during this off season, until he had reached the point of proficiency
where a target the size of a deer offered no difficulties.

Our third or fourth day in the woods gave him a wonderful shot
at a big buck; a standing, broadside shot at not over twenty yards,
with the deer totally unaware of his precarious position. At the report the buck reared high, reversed his field and abruptly vanished
in the laurels, in complete possession of his remarkable faculties, and
body and mind perfectly intact — in a word, a complete miss.

My partner's story was sad, but brief. He had raised his rifle,
squinted through the aperture, and could see only a dark, indistinct background filling the circle. The buck stood so close that he
completely filled the area encompassed by the peephole. He couldn't
tell whether his front sight was resting on trees, brush or deer. If it
were on the deer he couldn't tell just where, so he lowered his rifle
and tried again, with the same result, and then once more. At last
in desperation he threw the rifle to shoulder and fired blindly in
the general direction of his game. Net result was a bullet passing
somewhere under the buck's body where it promptly cut off a small
poplar on the far side of the deer.

The obvious answer to this maddening situation was simply this: he had unconsciously closed his left eye in squinting through his rear sight, shutting off the clear picture of his target and sight which he most certainly would have clearly seen had this left eye been open. His training in my hands had been in two-eye shooting, but under the stress of sighting at the all-important buck, he reverted to his days with a BB gun. Here the accepted mode of sighting, outlined graphically in Saturday-afternoon "horse operas," is to close tightly the left eye and leave the whole job of watching sights and target to *one* eye.

I wonder just how many bucks are missed each year for this one single reason. It seems such a simple detail, yet in my experience I know of at least ten deer missed or "creased" because sights could not clearly be seen in dim light against dark backgrounds, with the dark gray-brown of the buck's body subtly merging into shadows, sights and trees. In this situation two good eyes would have had trouble enough in directing the sights to the proper spot.

This business of sights being out of adjustment on deer rifles is one of the most common causes of hunting failures each season. An almost incredible number of deer shooters, beginners and experienced alike, do not know how to adjust their rifle sights; and with many of these same shooters, rifle sights could be far out of line without the hunter's knowledge.

Several years ago a close friend of this writer — an excellent wing shot, by the way — decided to hunt and kill his deer with the rifle rather than use the scattergun and buckshot with which he had managed to kill a couple of nice bucks. Acting on my suggestion he bought a Savage model 99 K in .300 caliber, one of the best models this outfit turned out, at least from the standpoint of price, and certainly a highly effective weapon for Eastern whitetail hunting.

This sportsman wasn't a rifle shot in any sense, so he spent a number of days afield with the new weapon, potting at 'chucks, crows, stones and what not, at all possible ranges. Just a day or two before the season opened he went out to get an hour or so of last-minute practice, just to reassure himself of his abilities. During this last outing, and after burning up most of his available ammunition, he decided to do some long-range work as a finale.

Directly across the little valley where he finally decided to take his last lesson stood a large white rock on the opposite hillside, offering a conspicuous target at a range of six to seven hundred yards.

His first shots of course dropped far short, so he started to move up the rear sight by adjusting the step elevator. At last he began hitting his target with the elevator raised to its highest notch. After firing his last cartridge and noting the satisfying spurt of white dust appear from the rock, he was well convinced of his prowess as a deer shooter, at least on a target the size of a deer.

Opening day found him standing the first drive, full of confidence and expectation. Appropriately enough, this first drive pushed out a fine buck directly toward him, offering a perfect standing shot at not over fifty yards. Still full of confidence, he held for the neck and squeezed off, but to his great surprise the buck showed no change in attitude whatever, but calmly began to walk along a small ridge of ground. Friend shooter then went completely haywire and dumped shot after shot at the buck, hoping only to hit him *somewhere*.

Emptying his rifle, he still had time to reload completely and finish this rapid fire round before the deer had passed from sight, still apparently much unconcerned, and injured in nothing more than feelings. Close examination of the ground covered by this buck revealed no indications of a hit, not even a hair, so this hunter headed right back to camp and offered his rifle for sale very promptly at a bargain price of five dollars.

Fortunately for him, all of his hunting pals were also his friends and none of them would take advantage of his generous offer under the circumstances. One of the more curious individuals in this group decided to look over the rifle carefully to determine, perhaps, "if the barrel was bent." No, the barrel was in perfect condition, but his rear sight was still carefully and tightly placed in the highest step of the elevator. None of the dozen-odd shots had passed even as close as six inches over the buck's back, with the sight in this position. The hunter had merely forgotten to drop his sight down to its normal position after his long-range target practice.

So much for sighting failures. We could talk about dozens of incidents where almost tiny details in sights and sighting have made a hunting trip a complete failure, so far as game is concerned, but these two will suffice.

Next in order of prominence is the malfunction of firearms. Firing pins break, actions jam, rifles won't fire or safeties confuse the shooter. Many of these functional troubles lie with the shooter alone and not with the maker of the arm; they may be caused by improper cleaning or lubrication, faulty loading, or abuse of rifle mechanisms.

Most of these troubles can be avoided if the shooter is well informed and careful.

Cold weather misfires are very common and are usually the result of excessive lubrication with heavy oil or gun grease. A few years back, in the middle of an unusually cold season, a deer hunter dropped into the shop with a new rifle of Remington design and make, a slide-action repeater. He loudly complained that the rifle wouldn't fire at all early in the morning, but seemed to work pretty well later in the day. He added, also very loudly, that the d——ed thing had robbed him of at least two bucks within the past two days.

Without comment, I dismounted the action and removed the breech block, a little task that had certainly never been done since this hunter had owned the rifle. The entire action was drowned in a heavy grease which subsequent check proved to be vaseline. In reply to my question, he blandly stated that he thought it was a good idea to keep his guns well greased, inside and out, so he had melted a large jar of vaseline and poured it into the action. It goes without saying that the early-morning cold had almost solidified the grease throughout the action, slowing down the spring and firing pin action to the point where it failed to strike the cartridge a hard enough blow to fire it. Added to this was the danger of grease running into the chamber and barrel, very likely resulting in a blown-up action if the rifle was fired in this condition. Proper cleaning with gasoline and a little lubrication with a light oil put the weapon in perfect shape for the woods, and as far as I know this hunter had no further trouble with the bucks.

Perhaps no single sport produces such a fund of improbable stories as deer hunting, unless it be that of Ike Walton. And even with this tough competition, deer-hunting tall tales and alibis will surely make a great showing. The tragic part of this situation is that deer-hunting tales need not be taken with such a large grain of salt as fishing stories, because in most cases they hold closely to facts. In deer hunting not only the big ones get away — there is no distinction of size. Bucks big and small get away, time after time, for no apparently sound reason. But such is deer hunting; and the fraternity increases year after year, regardless of the supposed danger hazard and the low average of successful sportsmen.

Safety in the woods is an important factor. No, not safety from the wrath of ferocious deer, although now and then a dying buck plants a sharp hoof somewhere on his captor's person. Rather, safety for the hunters from brother sportsmen, who sometimes, in their zeal to outshine their partners, will mistake a red cap for a huge rack of antlers. This little matter of danger in connection with deer hunting, while it must be considered, is highly overemphasized. Some hunters of small game won't even consider the grand sport of white-tail hunting because of the "danger" to deer hunters from their brethren. As a matter of cold fact, during the season of 1939 in New York State over 149,000 deer hunters took to the field and forest, and of this number only 5 were killed. In the same year in the same state, pheasant and duck hunting alone produced almost twice the number of fatalities — and no sportsman would ever consider pheasant or duck shooting dangerous to the hunter. These 1939 figures for New York State average out pretty well through the nation for the years since that date. Small-game hunting produces fully as many accidents each year, but of course there is a somewhat larger number of small-game hunters.

This writer is of the opinion that the automobile is a much more deadly weapon than the deer hunter's rifle, and the risk of a single Sunday-afternoon drive on our big highways is far greater than the slight risk involved in a whole season of deer hunting. Yet no one of us, sportsmen or otherwise, would consider driving exclusively on back roads or giving up driving cars altogether just to avoid being killed.

Good drivers are careful drivers, and seldom cause accidents or suffer injury in their cars. The same goes for deer hunters, with the possibilities of injury or death still far on the credit side of the ledger. Foolishness or carelessness in the woods reaps its own reward in bullets, but most of it can be avoided.

On our last deer drive of the 1940 season one of our bunch — a rookie hunter incidentally — carried a twelve-gauge shotgun well charged with big buckshot. We placed this chap well within the line of drivers, to forestall any chance of his straying in strange country, and the drive went forward in good style. All was going well, the drive was almost completed, with the drivers only a matter of two hundred yards from the standers. At this choice moment a grouse elected to flush wildly out in front of our shotgun bearer, and he just couldn't resist throwing his two loads of buckshot at the bird, even though the season was closed on grouse.

His buckshot swept the line of standers, Tommy-gun fashion, narrowly missing three of them and coming a bit too close for comfort to the others. I can't quite remember what became of this chap, but he must have stopped running at least by this late date.

All of these are deer-hunting problems, plus the failure of certain hunters to find and see deer even in country throughly populated with whitetails. The still-hunter has many factors to consider in his hunting; the club member who participates in deer drives exclusively also has an equal weight of details instinctively to remember. But the grasping of these details is only a matter of a little instruction and much practical application. More wounded deer should be recovered than are taken each year to date; fewer of these fine animals should be wounded, to stagger off into swamps and thickets and die slowly and miserably, alone, without comfort, not knowing why; with festering wounds, tongue and throat slowly burning for the water they cannot reach; with fever gradually consuming their great strength and vitality, and their blood slowly flowing to the forest floor, taking with it the final spark of vigor.

These whitetail deer are warm-blooded creatures, like ourselves. They must feel pain to much the same degree, perhaps even more, because of their extreme sensitivity. If we must kill them in the name of sport, let it be quickly and cleanly, without excuses. Paradoxical though it might seem, a sportsman, to enjoy his sport, must kill that which he admires. He must possess it, fondle it, show it to his friends; and to possess he must kill. No one can object to this, for it is the way of Nature; but in the name of this mother of all wild things, it should be a sudden, painless death.

It will be the privilege and purpose of this writer in succeeding chapters to carry the deer hunter through the many details associated with hunting the whitetail. We'll need to know a few of its life habits and queer traits, as they affect the hunter; its food, growth and mating practices. Methods of the still-hunter and group hunting will be detailed, and definite information on proper weapons and loads must be discussed.

Of all the deer hunter's equipment his weapon is, to him, the most important; it forms the connecting link between himself and his game. Many, many thousands of pages have been written about rifles and ammunition, much of it highly technical, some of it practical. Modern developments in weapons and loads have made it difficult for the deer hunter to sift this information to get the facts that he needs. The deer hunter is largely not a rifle crank, he doesn't have the time or interest to devote to careful study of ballistics and energies, and after wading through masses of trajectories and new calibers, he throws up his hands and decides to stick by his old thirty-

thirty. He doesn't know and doesn't care whether a Special .296 Magnum Flash is more effective on deer than an old .45-70 soft-coal burner. What he does want to know is how new developments in rifles, calibers and bullet designs are going to make it easier for him to bag his buck next season up in the spruce thickets of the Adirondacks.

His rifle sights, too, play a vital part, as the directing agent for the striking force of his bullet. It is still a fact that the only shot that counts is the shot that hits. . . . And to this we must add: the right spot. Sights must be selected to suit individual variances in vision, type of backgrounds and cover to be hunted, and the shooter's own capabilities.

To these ends, this book on whitetail deer will be devoted: that one or two points will be added to each hunter's store of woodcraft and knowledge, enabling him, perhaps, to add just one more buck to his list of lifetime deer-hunting experiences; that after the thrill of the supreme moment, when his game is down, he will be better prepared to bring out his game, properly dressed and ready for its last preparation — the banquet table. His trophy, too, he can prepare and mount with his own hands, making it ready to dominate gracefully his den or office, bringing back the ever-recurrent thrill of that grand day when the Red Gods smiled down on him at last.

More than this no one writer can expect: that he may again renew the urge to seek the whitetail deer in the often-disappointed hunter; that he may drop one hint, even only one, that will effect a clean kill, instead of a crippled and lost animal; and that in the final analysis he may gently stir a better appreciation of the great joys of deer hunting in the hearts of the novice and the old-timer alike.

If any or all of these aims are realized, then the labor in preparation of these succeeding chapters, plus the delights of this writer in setting them forth, will be amply rewarded to the end of his own deer-hunting days.

2 / The Whitetail at Home

REGRETFULLY we turned away from the river, to begin the two-mile return trip to our starting place at the bridge. We had been trout fishing, Earl and I, since early morning, wading and whipping the clear, boulder-studded waters of that most majestic of Catskill streams — the Neversink. The bright sun of mid-May had passed the peak of its ascent, to swing slowly toward the lofty ridges above Kitchen Eddy, bathing the valley slopes and their freshly budding hardwoods in an ever-growing golden light. Again it was a new spring and trout-time in Oakland Valley, and we had made our first foray up the river in the hope that the heavier browns would be ready to slash viciously at a big wet fly cast over the deep, rollicking runs. Odd that I cannot remember how many trout we caught or just how big was the heaviest; but I distinctly recall our meeting with the new fawn.

We had climbed out of the river at the head end of Long Eddy. Reluctantly, shoes and waders had been stripped off and light moccasins taken from our wading vests. Our weary legs welcomed the change from rushing rapids and heavy hobnails to the featherlight footwear springing our stride down the woods trail. Now as we swung down the bottom land it was easy to see the reawakening of the forest with the coming of the new season. A vigorous odor of new, living growing things filled our nostrils; the soft zephyr of a southern breeze swayed the tips of hemlock and poplar ever so gently. Bell-shaped blooms of dog-tooth violet poked above the snow-flattened dead leaves of a past fall, lone blooms on a bare forest floor save for an occasional bit of pale pink hepatica. The reedy, flutelike song of a hermit thrush filled the cathedral arches of big timber, now and then complemented by the rising crescendo of a drumming cock-grouse.

Perhaps the lethargic drowsiness of the late afternoon and the ear-filling roar of the river had dulled my senses of more acute perception. Certainly it was not until my companion, bringing up the rear, had hissed sharply, then again, that I became aware of the tiny new deer, lying by the trail. We had passed almost through a little glade in the small hemlocks when Earl had signaled. Turning, I discovered him pointing to the little bed of rooster-head ferns that lay between us and just off the trail. Momentarily I expected to find a coiled rattlesnake, just out of winter hibernation, and for an instant I failed to discern the white-spotted, red coat from the sun-specked dead leaves and winter-browned ferns covering the ground.

Here, lying still and quite hidden from a casual gaze, lay an infant member of Nature's most interesting and admirable family — the whitetail deer. It crouched snugly in its bed of tender ferns, tiny, dime-sized shining hoofs peeping out from under a delicately slender body, a well-molded head, with its translucent baby-pink ears laid back along a sleek neck, fully extended and pressed flat to the ground. Here the mother doe had left it in hiding while she fed along the river flats on tender new buds, and here it would remain, protected only by Nature's coloring, until she returned. I marveled at the rich red-brown shade of its coat; admired still more the blanket of scattered pure white spots covering its back and flanks, as though a heavy fall of outsized, puffy snowflakes had suddenly descended, then just as quickly stopped.

This miniature deer showed no fear, but a faint twitching of the moist nose, the overly bright gleam of its dark eyes, revealed the hidden inner conflict between its instinctive fear of the man animal and the knowledge that to lie quietly hidden would be the best security. At once I was overcome by the urge to creep up to this little fawn, snatch it into my arms, then, when its struggles had subsided, to put its tiny hoofs again to earth and send it off to the white birch and laurel thickets of its home. Many times before I had touched a whitetail deer, and known that mine was the first human hand ever to do so; but never had I been able then to say, "Off to the woods again and be more heedful of your mortal enemy!"

Although I tried, I didn't catch this little fawn. My clutching fingers grasped only dead leaves as the spotted form came quickly to life, bounding in a flash from the ground, then swerving off on wobbly legs to disappear within the thick hemlock screen. We could hear its tiny feet pattering through the dead leaves and the swish of hemlocks as it brushed by, long after it had melted from view; but for many moments we both stared after it, charmed first by its appearance then astounded at its sudden departure.

Often during the years which followed this incident have I wondered what became of the little fawn. How interesting it would have been to be able to follow its development through the years! Perhaps from this little spotted wood-nymph evolved a heavily antlered, broad-chested and thick-necked buck, a lord over all the deer tribe in the valley and the scourge of the younger spikes and fork-horns. Or the infant may have retained much of its sleek, delicate lines, its slender neck and neatly modeled head, to become a mature doe, the bearer of all the hunters' future venison and trophies.

Few men are privileged to find a newborn fawn. Were it not that the writer is trout fisherman as well as hunter, there would be but little opportunity for him to see the little ones in their home forests. But it is during this time of rising trout, fresh green leaves and early wild flowers that the doe retires to the seclusion of heavy thickets to bring forth a spindly-legged, dainty new deer or, as more often happens, a pair. Fortunately for the fawns the deer country of the East and North harbors few natural enemies at this critical period, so for the first few months after birth the little deer lead a placid, frolicking existence. They nurse at the mother doe's flanks for several weeks and then experimentally begin to nip at tender young buds and leaves.

When Jack Frost begins his landscape painting the fawn has his new coat. The white-flecked, fiery brown hair is shed, never to return, and in its place comes a tawny-gray winter coat of coarser, hollow hair to give insulating warmth against the chill winds of autumn and the icy blasts of dead winter. At this time the little bucks will have small skull buttons but, as a rule, no antlers. With the coming of the next spring the antler buds begin to form: downy blood-filled finger-size bulbs which by the following early fall will be hardened to small, sharp spikes. From now on the young buck must be on the alert for hunters — in most states he is legal game. And the young does, in some sections, will have given birth to their first single fawn by sometime in the latter part of the spring; most does will have it a year later. Thus the life cycle continues, season after season, with few disturbing elements other than the autumn meetings with red-capped Nimrods and the lean, hungry days of later winter.

* * *

The whitetail deer is far and away our most important larger game animal. With surprising tenacity and amazing fecundity, he has populated a great portion of our rolling hills and mountain lands; his forward-sweeping antlers and broad, white undercoated tail will be found flashing through much of our Eastern area, wherever food and cover are to his liking. He is as much at home in the dense wilderness of the Adirondacks, in northern Maine, and in Michigan's Upper Peninsula as he is within a few miles of New York City's boundaries. No other large game animal has the admirable versatility to so adjust itself to varying conditions of weather and environment. He is numerous in Florida swamp country and in the rocky ridges of northern Vermont, in the muskegs of Canada and in the Southern Tier farming belt of New York.

In fact the whitetail's ever-increasing abundance is a conservation headache in a dozen states. Herds have so increased in certain areas that they have eaten themselves out of house and home. Under these conditions, far from being rare, the deer starve during the severe winter months to die off by hundreds and thousands. Conservation workers are constantly harried by the nightmare of too many deer in some sections and comparative scarcity, so far as hunting pressure is concerned, in other areas.

As a trophy the whitetail leaves nothing to be desired. Cannily outwitting all but the best (and luckiest) hunters — many times, it seems, by divine guidance — when finally taken he should be highly prized. His dark red flesh is a table delicacy when properly handled and prepared; his tough, pliable hide makes the softest of gloves and outer garments; the head, with its neat antlers, becomes a favorite decoration for the hunter's den.

The whitetail deer is now, and we hope always will be, the big game of the common man. The machine operator and the office worker, the small businessman and the farmer, share equal opportunity to return with the spoils of a deer hunt. Perhaps in no other way is this better exemplified than in the taking of outstanding whitetail trophies. Most often it is the man of comfortable wealth, the hunter with ample funds and time to spare, who hunts for and bags the largest trophies of other species — moose, elk, caribou, mountain sheep and bear. But most of the prize whitetail heads adorn the homes of the butcher, the baker, the candlestickmaker. Outstanding whitetail trophies are not isolated in faraway, inaccessible areas. They exist near farm lands, in your own favorite deer country or right by your home; in short, wherever you are lucky enough to find one. Every man who takes to the woods has an equal chance at a record buck. Our present New York State record head was gathered under normal, almost casual, hunting conditions, and no doubt so were most "best whitetail heads" now on record.

Killing a record-head whitetail buck can be a simple matter. Certainly there is no positive method by which the expenditure of time and money can produce a record or near-record whitetail trophy. We cannot say the same for most other species of large American game. A good hunter with unlimited means and much time at his disposal could undoubtedly hunt any other of our big game with a reasonable expectation of bringing back a head of near-record size in one or two season's attempts. But not so with the whitetail. Many, many expert deer hunters have spent the better part of their lives in hunting deer, and only a favored few have gathered unto themselves large whitetail trophies. Big racks on whitetail bucks are a fortuitous combination of the right kind of food, a good growing year, proper minerals in the soil making up the buck's habitat, and a specimen of outstanding vitality, with the most active type of the correct hormone-producing glands. It is true that certain few areas throughout the country do favor the production of larger antlers, but big heads are spread throughout the land, each individual buck being a law unto himself.

There is no way that a hunter can plan to kill such a record deer. In the first place few whitetail bucks are seen in any one season by the hunter. And the big-racked bucks seldom wait for the hunter to count points and estimate size before bounding for the brush. Few men have a chance to pass up a smaller buck to wait for a larger one. As a rule the first legal rack to come before their sights is taken; and they are through for that season. The whitetail deer offers the greatest challenge to the trophy hunter, and most of these head-hunters will pass to the happy hunting ground before laying sights on that near-record buck unless Lady Luck guides a favored son to just the right place to meet his trophy of a lifetime.

Any man who hangs on the wall a prize whitetail can thank his lucky stars and not a superior grade of hunting skill. In the past fifteen years the author has taken two bucks with beam-lengths greater than twenty-four inches and with maximum outside spreads of over twenty-two inches, but believe it, this was plain, simple fool luck. I knew that both deer were large in body before getting a chance at either one. And reputation had given each a record head; but it was not until I had brought both to earth that I suspected they were this large in antlers. Neither, of course, is a record in any sense, but both are outstanding specimens of whitetail deer in any part of the country.

The antler growth and development of the whitetail buck is an absorbing study, but in spite of much published information on the subject, many hunters are ignorant of the actual facts about this intricate device of Nature. Everyone knows, of course, that the antlers are produced as an integral part of the male deer's mating processes. They develop concurrently with the increasing size of the testes, and are carried throughout the mating period to be used in warding off rival bucks from the desired does. When the rutting period is at an end, the useful life of the antlers has gone, so they drop off at varying periods throughout the winter.

Mr. Robert W. Darrow, Supervisor of Game Research for the New York State Conservation Department, describes the antler development as follows:

The antlers of the white-tail consist normally of one main beam on each side which extends upward from the skull and curves forward with branches (tines) coming off at intervals on the upper side. Typically these tines are not forked as in the mule deer. Except for an occasional "horned doe," antlers are a distinctive adornment of the buck. They first develop during the second summer of the buck's life and the following fall usually consist of slender twin spikes each several inches long. More mature deer grow heavier heads with longer beams, each having several points. A new set of antlers is grown every year, the previous set being shed during the winter after the end of the breeding season. The new antlers begin to "bud" in late April or early May and continue to grow during the summer. Throughout this period, when they are spongy and filled with blood vessels, they bear a protective covering called "velvet." Nevertheless, they are easily injured, which accounts for most of the deformities encountered. As Fall approaches the antlers harden and the velvet is rubbed off. . . .

Although their first set usually consists of spikes, the number of points on a buck's antlers is not a reliable index to his age. Many yearlings have no more than "buttons," while others may grow several points, as was demonstrated by a known-age buck, at the Department's Delmar Wildlife Research Center, whose first head was a 9-pointer. Then, too, spikes are often carried by old bucks which are past their prime but, in such cases, they tend to be rather long and unsymmetrical and are of comparatively large diameter at the base. Aside from spikes, by far the most frequent number of points on the bucks killed each Fall is eight. However, while there is no steady progression, as a buck advances in age and at the same time remains a vigorous animal, racks of ten, twelve or more points are grown more often. Also, the antlers of older deer are usually of larger diameter at the base than those of younger deer from range of the same quality.

The author would add to this that, in so far as the ratio of points-to-age theory is concerned, I had the opportunity to observe the successive antler growth of a game-farm buck over a period of several years. This buck developed very short, slender spikes in his first season, not over two inches long. The following year he again grew spikes, this time about eight inches long, somewhat heavier than the first set and with a slight outside curve. Then in the next year he jumped quickly to eight points and from this year until the time of his death he grew three more eight-point racks in succeeding seasons, never exceeding the eight-point development although the antlers became larger in diameter, longer in beam and spread, and at a lower angle to the skull with each year. This lowering of the angle of beam to skull is another characteristic of the whitetail's advancing age and is a much more certain indication than the number of points borne on the antlers. As an interesting sidelight in whitetail antler development, the New York State Delmar Laboratories have been experimenting for some time with hormones as antler producers. Bucks have attained tremendous antler growths here when fed the proper hormones, and antlers have readily been grown on the female deer by the forced action of such hormones. This summer I observed three of these antlered does at the Delmar Farm, but one had already dropped an antler and another had badly mutilated one of its branches. It seems likely that the females, unaccustomed to such headgear, have difficulty in preserving them in the final form. Another interesting fact in this connection is that of the number of antlered does which are killed each year, all show most of the velvet still remaining, indicating that the female has none of the male's interest or ability to remove the velvet before the mating season.

The whitetail's headgear is distinctive in that it definitely sets apart this species from the other native American deer — the mule deer and the Pacific Coast blacktail. Only the whitetail shows the

AGE INDICATIONS IN THE WHITETAIL

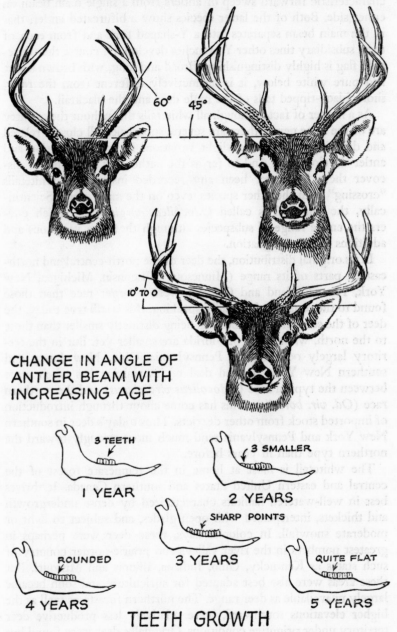

60° 45°

10° TO 0

CHANGE IN ANGLE OF
ANTLER BEAM WITH
INCREASING AGE

3 TEETH

1 YEAR

3 SMALLER

2 YEARS

SHARP POINTS

3 YEARS

ROUNDED

4 YEARS

QUITE FLAT

5 YEARS

TEETH GROWTH

characteristic forward sweep of antlers from a single main beam on either side. Both of the latter species show a bifurcated antler, that is, the main beam separates into a Y-shaped fork and from each of these subsidiary tines other Y branches develop. Of course the whitetail's flag is highly distinguishing. Broad and long, with brown above and pure white below, it is distinctively different from the ropy, short, black-tipped tails of the mule deer and the blacktail.

As a matter of fact, although all whitetails throughout the country are of the same genus, there are several subspecies, all closely related and differing only in size, slight variations in body coloration and antler development. And so far as the author has been able to discover there has never been any recorded instance of whitetails "crossing" with the other species, even on the same range. Scientifically, the whitetail is called *Odocoileus virginianus*, which covers the entire range of subspecies although there are variations and additions to this designation.

In its original distribution, the deer of the north-central and northeastern parts of its range (Minnesota, Wisconsin, Michigan, New York, New England and Canada) were a larger race than those found to the southward. Broadly speaking, this is still true today, the deer of the southern Appalachians being distinctly smaller than those to the north, while those of Florida are smaller yet. But in the territory largely occupied by Pennsylvania, Ohio, New Jersey and southern New York, a good deal of intermixing has taken place between the typical race (*Odocoileus virginianus*) and the northern race (*Od. vir. borealis*). This has come about through introduction of imported stock from other districts. Thus today's deer in southern New York and Pennsylvania tend much more strongly toward the northern type than in years before.

The whitetail is most at home in the temperate forest of the central and eastern United States and southern Canada. It thrives best in well-watered habitats characterized by dense undergrowth and thickets, interspersed with open glades, and subject to light or moderate snowfall. In colonial days, these deer were perhaps in greatest numbers in the river valleys and prairie-border country of such states as Kentucky, Ohio, Indiana, Illinois and Missouri. But these areas were also best adapted for agriculture and soon became largely unavailable as deer range. The northern forests, as well as the higher elevations southward, were relatively less productive deer territory under primitive conditions. Originally deer were found but little north of the St. Lawrence River, and were not recorded north of Lake Superior. In Nova Scotia and east of the Saint John River, in New Brunswick, they were unknown until after 1800.

Contrary to popular belief, the whitetail was not as abundant in Indian times throughout much of New York State as is generally supposed. During this period, before the white man spread out from the Hudson River Valley, deer were most numerous in the lowlands. Along the valleys of the Delaware, Susquehanna, Allegheny, Mohawk and Hudson, and in the Ontario-St. Lawrence plain, deer were fairly abundant, but elsewhere, in the extensive stands of big timber, they were less plentiful. This was particularly true of the whole Adirondack region, which at that time supported as many moose as deer.

As civilization entered, however, the entire picture underwent radical change. The deer, entrenched in the lowlands, were soon forced out by the tillers of the soil. These same early settlers depended principally on the deer for their fresh meat, and heavy hunting throughout each year soon virtually exterminated the large valley herds. On the other hand, civilization brought extensive lumbering activities to the Adirondack and Catskill forests, clearing out much of the virgin timber and opening up these areas into good feeding grounds for the deer. Then too, wolves and mountain lions, the principal deer predators, were soon exterminated and these areas more and more became the most favored habitat of the deer. Then followed a period of heavy market hunting which all but exterminated the Adirondack herd and completely decimated the Catskill deer.

Soon after, conservation measures and growing public sentiment put an end to the slaughter of deer throughout the state. In the Adirondacks for example, the establishment of many hundreds of lumber camps made it necessary to depend on the whitetail deer to supply fresh meat for the loggers. Other meats were not available due to transportation and preservation difficulties. But the senseless and indiscriminate slaughter was at last brought under control, and the passage of the "buck law" in 1912 saw the beginning of the return of the deer herds to New York State. This law has been in general force throughout the state with one exception: in 1919 the killing of both bucks and does was permitted and the results were disastrous. It is believed that more hunters were afield that year than there were deer in the state. The number of bucks killed exceeded the number taken in the "buck law" years, and the does taken exceeded the number of bucks. It was estimated that 20,000 deer were killed in that year and since then the state has adhered to the taking of bucks only, with some few exceptions. Today we have not only as many, but far more deer in the Adirondacks than ever before.

Deer were restocked on the Catskill area in this early period of conservation with a small herd of forty-five deer, maintained in an enclosed park. Each year the overflow was allowed to run free and largely from this small beginning do we have the present Catskill herd. Other deer were imported from Michigan and Virginia to improve the strain, however, and even now we can find the influence of these somewhat different species in occasional individuals.

In the early 1920's only a few counties in the state were permitted open seasons. The rest of the state was kept under strict control. As a result, the deer have increased in leaps and bounds throughout the Southern Tier farming area until at the present writing they represent the largest proportion of deer within the entire state. This agreeable increase has led to the establishment of open seasons in almost every county, and the deer now show no appreciable decrease in numbers despite the tremendous increase in hunters afield each season. The Southern Tier area, directly adjacent to Pennsylvania, shows a much larger number of deer taken in recent years than either the Adirondacks or the Catskill region. From this Southern Tier area in 1946 6609 deer were reported taken; the Adirondack region was second with 4897 head; the Catskill region reported 4361. Certainly this is a remarkable indication of the efficiency of present-day conservation measures and the outstanding ability of the whitetail deer to respond to such treatment.

The history of Michigan's deer herd closely parallels that of New York's except that the state is divided into two widely different areas, the Upper Peninsula and the Lower Peninsula. Here, as in New York State, the early deer population was most numerous in the more open, swampy marsh lands of the Lower Peninsula. In the Upper Peninsula the entire area was of virgin forest and harbored comparatively few deer. Then with the influx of logging operations the slashings created new "edge" growth for deer feed and the whitetail became numerous. In the Lower Peninsula, new agricultural activity created much of this same "edge" with resultant increase in the deer herd. However, the huge toll taken by farmers and the reduction of wild territory brought about the almost complete extermination of the herd by 1870.

In the Upper Peninsula the story was quite different. Extensive logging, begun about 1850 opened up the area for deer, so that about 1880 deer were numerous throughout the whole Upper Peninsula. But the opening up of the forests was overdone until by 1890 most of the big pine was gone and a reverse condition occurred. In the early days, deer were forced to "yard" during the winters under big timber, with little food and poor cover and little of the "edge" lands for feed. Now in 1890 we find little heavy timber and wide, open areas ravaged by forest fires which destroyed all small growth and seedlings. Soon the deer disappeared generally throughout the entire Upper Peninsula.

Also during this period of increase in the deer herd began the tremendous slaughter of deer for food in logging camps and for market. As railroads penetrated this territory, market hunters came in during the fall months and shipped hundreds of tons of "saddles" to commission houses in the cities. During the summer these same men turned to "hide hunting," killing many thousands of deer for hides and allowing the carcasses to rot.

By 1882 sportsmen were aroused, and some slight measures were taken to preserve the deer herd, but by 1890 the herd was on the downgrade because of a combination of market hunting, excessive logging and forest fire. Subsequent laws, passed by frenzied legislators, placed additional restrictions on hunting through the turn of the century, limiting the take per man severely and outlawing all market hunting. Between 1915 and 1920 the public became "fire-conscious," and a huge program of fire control was instituted. This, together with improved conservation measures, began to build up the herd until now Michigan enjoys some of the best hunting in the entire United States. However, the Upper Peninsula probably has not more than one half the deer population of the Lower, owing to its heavier snowfall — with the deer again "yarding" — and the increase in new large timbered areas discouraging the growth of small browse for deer food.

Michigan has done much to promote the present excellence of its deer hunting. Extensive research in deer foods, winter crowding and "overbrowsing" of certain areas has produced an intelligent approach to their deer problem, but of course in this age of increased hunting pressure, new problems constantly arise.

Almost every state in the northern section of the whitetails' range shows some similar condition — alarming decrease in deer population near the turn of the century, then a gradual up-trend until the early

1930's and the return of good deer hunting for all. Wisconsin and Pennsylvania have each experienced this decline, fall and resurrection of the deer population, to the extent that each of these states now offers some of the best whitetail deer territory in the nation. Pennsylvania has a tremendous herd, but Wisconsin's deer average quite a bit larger. At any rate the problem, now, seems to be not lack of deer but in many instances too many deer for the available feed existing on the available range.

Deer food has been the subject of colossal research by Game Commissions and Conservation Departments over the whole country. New York State, for example, conducted an extensive experiment at Willsboro in the effort to determine, under natural conditions, just what foods were most attractive to deer and which of these best sustained life during the winter months. In this experiment, conducted through two winters, deer were held in pens simulating conditions of the wild, but were so held that accurate observations as to food taken and physical condition, were possible throughout the entire period. An accurate and elaborate system of weighing the deer was devised, so that positive evidence of the nutritive value of the given foods was obtained.

The summary of the tests shows conclusively that the best natural foods for supporting deer in normal health and vigor are the various species of browse, notably white cedar, yellow birch and soft maple. Further it was shown that those animals which had suffered serious weight losses on such unsatisfactory foods as marsh hay and balsam, could be restored quickly to a satisfactory condition by being fed white-cedar and yellow-birch browse. Also, in the course of the studies it was learned just which food the deer preferred. The list on the opposite page should prove of some interest to the woodsman and deer hunter.

Alfalfa was fed also in conclusive tests and was found to be quite satisfactory, but owing to its weight and bulk and its low food value compared with concentrated foods such as grains, it was found to be much less desirable than other types of food for purposes of artificial feeding in winter yard areas where such food must be transported by conservation workers. Marsh hay was proven to be worthless as a nutritious food and was eaten only in small quantities, even though the deer were offered no other food. This is unfortunate because marsh hay is readily available for winter feeding. Balsam also was proved to be worthless as a winter deer food and to a lesser

Best Liked	Readily Eaten	Poorly Eaten
White Cedar	Apple Wood	Alder
Black Birch	Mountain Ash	Black Ash
Yellow Birch	Balsam	Aspen
Sumac Bobs	Basswood	Beech
Sweet Fern	White Birch	Butternut
Witchhopple	Buckbrush	Chokecherry
Ferns (many species)	Red Cedar	Ironwood
	Black Chokecherry	Blue Beech
	Elderberry	Leatherwood
	Ground Pine	Sugar Maple
	Hazelnut	Red Oak
	Juniper	White Pine
	Red Maple (soft)	Red Spruce
	Sumac Stems	Willow
	Hemlock [1]	

extent hemlock was found to be lacking in desirable nutritive qualities.

Subsequent studies at Ithaca, in the effort to find a satisfactory food in concentrated form for winter feeding, resulted in the development of the famous "deer cakes." These are a combination of soybeans and molasses, packed in a tin, and weighing approximately fifty pounds. Extensive field experiments with these cakes proved that they were readily eaten by the deer and one cake was adequate to provide nourishment to eight deer for a two weeks period. As an interesting sidelight on these supplemental foods it was learned that the deer consumed them rapidly so long as snow remained on the ground, but the day that bare ground appeared, the deer left the cakes untouched, preferring to forage for natural browse.

The aforementioned list of preferred foods includes only browse; the whitetail is also extremely fond of acorns, beechnuts, many types of mosses and other bare-ground foods. But in winter when the period of starvation and deep snow begins, such ground foods are not available. Deer as a rule are not grazers, although they have a liking for a farmer's young corn or wheat and in some areas will raise havoc with winter wheat during the cold weather.

The greatest mortality in deer herds takes place in those areas which are subject to heavy snowfall. When the snow becomes more than a foot deep the deer congregate in a cedar swamp or other

[1] Hemlock browse was eaten, when other well-liked browse was available, only at temperatures of near or below zero.

area of good feed, and mill around until the snow is packed to the ground, forming the "yard." Often several of these yards are made in a single area, connected by narrow trails through the deep snow. As the winter progresses and the snow becomes deeper, the herd clings together within the yard, eating off all the available browse, even down to branches an inch in diameter. With the feed gone, even to a point as high as they can reach by standing erect on their hind legs, the deer are faced with slow starvation. Nothing, not even the approach of a man, will induce them to leave the yard, at least for long.

Conservation workers carrying in food for the deer will rout them out for a short distance, but after a few bounds into the belly-deep snow they stand and wait for the intruder to leave, then bounce back into the safety of the yard. It becomes a questionable safety, however, for as soon as the food supply disappears, the weaker deer slowly die of starvation. This is the controlling deer-supply factor in every area of heavy snowfall. It is the unquestionable answer to the static state of the deer herd in the Adirondack region, Michigan's Upper Peninsula and other similar areas. No matter how large the fawn crop may be each season, only a certain number will survive the decimating effect of starvation in the yards, dependent from year to year on the severity and length of the snowfalls and snow covering. There are other limiting factors, of course, but this is the major control. It explains also why deer have made such remarkable increases in the areas of lesser snowfall — Pennsylvania, New York State's Southern Tier, Michigan's Lower Peninsula and many other such sections.

Strange it is that animals of such protective instincts should so trap themselves. Probably this is a carry-over from the early days when wolves and mountain lions made easy prey of deer caught in deep snow. Nevertheless, thousands of deer die annually in the confines of the foraged-off yards, with good food only a short distance away.

Throughout our broad expanse of deer country one of the greatest variables in whitetail characteristics is the body weight. In the deep South, a 100-pound dressed weight is extremely heavy for bucks; in Maine and Northern Michigan 200-pound dressed bucks are common. Arizona whitetails too are small; exceptionally heavy specimens will weigh not over 125 pounds, after hog-dressing. It's apparent that the further north we go in search of whitetail deer, the more likely are we to meet big ones. Yet the average whitetail buck is a much smaller animal than is generally supposed. Full-grown bucks seldom reach a height greater than 42 inches at the shoulder, and the average northern deer of the species will weigh from 150 to 180 pounds on the hoof. Such bucks will dress out from 120 to 150 pounds; any buck over this top weight can be classed as a large deer. Larger bucks are not uncommon, particularly where range conditions are highly favorable: 200-pounders are killed every year, and in Maine, Michigan, Wisconsin and the Southern Tier area of New York numerous bucks are taken which weigh over 250 pounds.

The heaviest authenticated whitetail deer ever taken in New York State was killed, in 1890, near Mud Lake in Warren County by Henry Ordway — who, at this writing, still lives in Glens Falls. This deer weighed 388 pounds about five hours after it was shot and *before* it was dressed out. Its head is now in possession of the State Conservation Department, and ranks tenth in the state list of record heads (based on size and symmetry) as of spring 1947.

In contrast to these exceptionally large deer, we find a much lower weight obtains as average throughout the whitetail's range. Most states have accurate data on deer weights, carefully checked from thousands of specimens taken during hunting seasons. Maine, for example, lists the weights and heights of its deer by counties, with the bucks averaging 145 pounds and standing about 38 inches high at the shoulder. Does average about 110 pounds, with a shoulder height of 36 inches. Somerset County shows the heaviest average deer: bucks scaling almost 200 pounds and does, 120 pounds.

Pennsylvania's deer average considerably smaller than this. Bucks average 115 pounds; antlerless deer, many of which are not adult, average 80 pounds. Here is a marked indication of the lower weights of deer that are subjected to overcrowding and overbrowsing, as well as the tendency toward smaller body size in the more southern subspecies of whitetails.

The natural tendency of a hunter is to exaggerate the size of his trophy. It's an understandable quirk in every man's make-up, but it leads to false impressions that become deep-rooted with repetition. Almost every hunter we meet will tell us about killing at least one 200-pound buck, yet inquiry reveals that none of these 200-pounders were weighed, just "guessed at." Seldom does a hunter encounter one of these big bucks in a lifetime of hunting experience, and when he does down a really big whitetail, the impartial verdict

of the beam-scales will most often throw the damper on his enthusiasm. In five years of hunting with one of the most consistently
successful Sullivan County deer clubs, the author never saw a deer
taken by this group which weighed over 164 pounds — actual
dressed weight. As a matter of fact I have seen in my lifetime of
deer hunting only four bucks which weighed-in at, or over, this
magic 200-pound mark.

Dressed weights and on-the-hoof weights of whitetail bucks
are something quite a bit different. Numerous formulas for obtaining live weight from dressed weight have been advanced; but
actually, there is considerable variation. The amount of herbage in
a deer's paunch at the time of death has a marked effect on the
accurate value of any of these, to the extent that any one can be
proved 50 per cent wrong with individual deer. Perhaps as accurate
a method as any is to take the deer's dressed weight, divide by four
and add the result to the dressed weight figure to obtain the live,
or on-the-hoof, weight. A hunter seldom has an opportunity to
check such formulas. When a man kills his buck, his major interest
is to dress his deer quickly, bleeding it well and cooling the body
cavity. Then with the "innards" removed the deer becomes a lighter
burden on the way out of the woods, but still a sufficiently heavy
one. However, on one occasion the author had the opportunity to
observe a large deer being weighed directly after taking. This buck
weighed-in at 246 pounds before dressing and 198 pounds after
the hog-dressing only had been completed.

For purposes of comparison the author has taken the measurements of a large, fat, Adirondack buck which weighed 212 pounds
dressed. From these figures any hunter can form an accurate estimate as to whether his buck will approach or surpass the 200-pound
mark. This particular specimen was not a heavily framed deer, rather
it was of normally large size, but the fattest buck this writer has
ever encountered. All measurements were, of course, taken over the
carcass with hide still on and with the tape pulled firmly taut. The
head measurements which are required in mounting are listed also,
for any hunter who might wish to compare them with his own
trophy.

Body Measurements

Length, nose to tail root	6 ft. 6½ in.
Height, hoof to withers	41½
Circumference, chest behind forelegs	43
Rump, largest diameter	46½
Overall length, nose to hindfoot	8 ft. 4½

Head and Neck Measurements

Length, withers to antler butts	23 in.
Right antler butt to nose	10½
Left antler butt to nose	10½
Eye corner to nose	8
Circumference, neck behind ears	22
Tip of right antler to nose	18
Tip of left antler to nose	17½

This buck was killed in Hamilton County in the Adirondacks on October 20, 1946; and while it was not an unusually large buck it represents a good model for a 200-pound animal. Any whitetail buck which compares with these figures can be well considered as an entry for the hallowed ranks of the 200-weight class.

Of perhaps more interest to the hunter in any discussion of deer habits and characteristics are the mating habits and occurrence of the rutting season. This period is always the most fruitful for deer hunting. It is then that the bucks lose some of their natural caution; in fact a rutting buck can at times be dangerous. Several instances have been recorded wherein a whitetail buck in the heat of mating frenzy has attacked men without provocation. Of course, this is rare but it serves to point out that the reproductive urge in the whitetail is so great that it transcends partially the normally greater instincts of self-preservation. Many a wise old buck would forever escape the hunter were it not for the occurrence of a heavy rutting period during the open season. And oddly enough it is the doe herself that sets up this mating time, rather than the buck.

Generally speaking, the buck is ready and willing for mating any time during the period between September 1 and the beginning of the next year. At the beginning of this period the velvet is dug off the antlers and the buck begins to prove his virility by rubbing bark from small saplings, and hooking brush. As October wears along, many of these "rubs" will appear in whitetail haunts, indicating that some of the does are beginning to accept service. This continues in ever-increasing frequency until at some time during November the rut will be at its height. This period varies with the locality, however, and as far as is now known, is connected in some way with the gradual diminishing in strength of the sun's rays as winter approaches. Once the doe is mated she will no longer accept the buck, which accounts for many of the does that a deer hunter sees running through the woods, with the buck in hot pursuit. Neither will the doe accept service except at the critical period of oestrus, and this period, late research indicates, may be of only a few hours duration.

If the doe is not mated and the embryo emplanted at this time, service will not be permitted until the next period of oestrus, which may occur within the next four weeks. In some areas the does may come into the oestrous or "heat" period three or even four times until pregnancy occurs, or the doe remains without fawn until the following season.

Much interesting research has been done on this fascinating study of the whitetail's mating processes. Many former theories have been discarded and much that is new has been brought to light, and at the same time new hitherto unknown problems have evolved. Dr. E. L. Cheatum, Senior Game Pathologist at New York's Experimental Game Laboratory, reports on the differences in regional breeding habits of New York deer in the *Conservationist*, the department's bimonthly publication:

The character of our wild and woolly Adirondack mountain country has long given the average sportsman sufficient reason to believe that it should be the best deer range in the State. But in late years he has seen the almost spectacular increase in deer herds in the central and southern counties and has begun to ask: "Why doesn't the same thing happen up north?"

He gets a lot of answers. Here are two most frequently given: "There is a shortage of breeding-age bucks, hence more fawnless does" — "Too many deer winter starve, and the annual fawn production hardly balances these losses and the kill by hunters."

Both explanations are premised on the idea that annual replacement of young stock is inadequate. There is a lot of truth in that, but it merely complicates the problem. . . .

During a Conservation Department study from the winter of 1938 to the spring of 1942, a large number of does from these two zones (the Adirondack area and the southern region of the Catskills and south border counties) were examined for the presence of unborn fawns. . . . From the Adirondack region we examined 158 does and from the rest of the state 258. The study included first-year fawns because we had previously discovered that, in the southern counties, does were frequently bred successfully at six or seven months of age.

Dr. Cheatum summarizes the results as follows:

1. Of the adult does from the southern zone, 92.3 per cent had

been successfully bred; of the Adirondack does, 77.9 per cent were with fawn.

2. Of the doe *fawns* from the southern area, 36.3 per cent were carrying embryos, while the figure for the Adirondacks was a mere 4.2 per cent.

3. Among the 144 pregnant does from the southern area, 48 bore singletons, 86 sets of twins, and 10 triplets. The 67 specimens from the Adirondacks carried 54 singletons, 12 twins and 1 set of triplets.

4. Among the 37 pregnant fawns from the southern zone, 35 carried singles, and two bore twins. The 3 Adirondack specimens carried singles alone.

5. The egg production rate of southern does was higher than that in northern deer, and percentage of eggs fertilized and successfully developed as embryos was much higher.

After gathering the facts, Dr. Cheatum turned to the "why." "The facts show no hereditary differences between the deer in the two zones . . . so it would appear that differences in living conditions are the controlling influences in fawn production. And there is every indication to believe that nutrition is a primary factor." Further study in this problem shows that not only do the long winter and deep snow contribute directly to the high number of starvation deaths, but adversely affect the incidence of doe fertility during the following breeding season, due to the results of malnutrition. . . .

As to the actual period of the height of the rutting season, extensive research indicates that the sexual season represents a brief terminal phase of the whole gradual increase of activity in the sexual organs, initiated by the increasing daylight of spring and summer, the fall rut ensuing under conditions of diminishing light. Captive animals kept in dim light, directly after the height of summer's solar activity had been reached, showed a definite disposition to breed much earlier than would be normal. Studies of Alaskan reindeer near the 64th parallel show that the rut began in the latter part of August, and continued through September into October. New York deer (42° – 44°) breed heaviest in November. Mule deer in the Yosemite Valley of California (38°) breed through the latter half of December and through January; further south the Arizona whitetail breeding season occurs most frequently between January 10 and the middle of February. Thus it would seem that some relationship exists between the progressively earlier breeding of the deer and increasing latitude.

Exhaustive study of New York State's deer indicates that in the Adirondack area the period of heaviest rut occurs from November 10 to 16; in the southern region from November 17 to 23. However, the actual period of the rut covers a wider span in the southern area than in the Adirondacks, indicating that there is a greater recurrence of the oestrous period in southern does than in the more northern regions.

In this study of breeding periods in New York State, considerable research was done on the male deer as well as the female. Testicles obtained from numerous bucks throughout the research period show a gradual increase in size concurrent with the development of antlers, ending with the greatest volume obtained at the end of November. It was learned also that, contrary to the findings with doe fawns, bucks apparently do not attain sexual maturity in the first year of life in this latitude.

For many years it has been thought that, because of the climatic differences in the Adirondacks and Catskill regions, the mating season in the Adirondacks would occur a full month before that in the Catskills. Accordingly, open seasons have been so established. But the results of new research conclusively prove that there is little actual difference in the mating periods in the two areas. If anything, the Catskill rut begins sooner and lasts longer than the corresponding period in the Adirondacks — the height of both periods is included between the dates of November 10 and 23. It does seem evident that in the areas of better wintering conditions the succeeding fawn crop each year is far superior to the fawn crop in areas of heavy snow, where deer are forced to the yards, thereby suffering the nutritional ravages of poor food. This, added to the number of yard deer which fail to survive through the winter, is evidence enough to account for the great increase in deer populations throughout most of our mild winter zones.

Another deer problem which vexes the hunter is the apparent scarcity of bucks in proportion to the number of does seen each season. However, this sex ratio is not nearly as unbalanced as the unsuccessful hunter would have us believe. Actual figures on deer census reports, conducted with a high degree of accuracy, bear this out. New York State reports that the ratio of bucks to does throughout the major deer-producing areas in the state is about

83 bucks to 100 does. However, in the Adirondack area the ratio
may be not greater than 38 bucks to 100 does. Even so, this is
definitely a large enough ratio of buck to doe to assure full mating
of all does in the area, provided contact is made at the proper point
of oestrus in the female. Any low fawn count among the does is
much more likely to result from lack of egg production in the
females, due to various factors, rather than from a shortage of bucks.

An interesting variation in the buck-to-doe ratio is reported by
Michigan. Here extensive live-trapping operations show a ratio of
1 buck to 5.8 does; observation throughout the year by competent
conservation officials indicates a ratio of 1 buck to 5.38 does. But
hunters' reports show a ratio of only 1 buck to 28 does — quite a
substantial difference. In the Upper Peninsula the ratio of bucks to
does was somewhat higher — 1 buck to 4.26 does. During the period
of the well-conducted C.C.C. Camp deer-census drives, the ratio
of bucks to does was reported as follows:

	Bucks	Does	Fawns
Upper Peninsula	19	49	52
Lower Peninsula	16	52	32

The census reports of this same period show the following interesting count of deer per square mile:

Upper Peninsula	18.05 sq. mi.
Lower Peninsula	45.60
State as a whole	32.59

Wisconsin, under much the same system of deer counting, shows
a ratio of about 1 buck to 3 does over an area of roughly 60,000
acres. However, depending on the section of the state, some areas
had a ratio of 1 to 5 while others graded all the way down to 1 to
1.5, all of this counting outside refuge areas. This includes records
not only of the Conservation Commission but of the Federal Forest
Service and the Federal Bureau of Agricultural Economics as well.
At any rate, in no instance of accurate counting does the ratio of
bucks to does appear as unfavorable as in the reports of deer hunters.
Every effort is made by conservation authorities to give accurate
information to the sporting public, and there is no reason to doubt
the overall accuracy of these figures. Undoubtedly the scarcity of
bucks reported by hunters indicates lack of both competent observation and hunting skill. There is no doubt that under hunting

conditions it is more difficult to detect the buck than the does, as every hunter knows, and these figures bear this out.

In regard to the taking of does via a legal open season, each state works out this problem for itself. It is only since the inception of the "buck law" that we have seen the remarkable increase in the nation-wide population of whitetails. It is obviously true, though, that in areas where deer have increased in such numbers that the carrying capacity of the range has deteriorated and in those regions where deer do considerable crop damage, an open season on doe deer will do far more good than harm. Pennsylvania was faced with this problem in the early '30's. Deer had increased to a point far beyond the forage crop of their range and it became mandatory to thin out the herd indiscriminately. Despite the howls of protest from "nature lovers" and "sportsmen," Pennsylvania put into effect a program of systematic reduction of its overpopulated deer herd. The result though succeeding years has amply borne out the original contentions of the Pennsylvania Game Commission to the extent that the state's deer herd is still ample to survive hunting pressure and the "overbrowsed" condition of its forests is gradually adjusting itself. This is the same problem facing every state with an overabundance of deer in certain areas; these deer are a crop of the land and must be intelligently harvested as such.

There will forever be a certain amount of public sentiment against the killing of does or antlerless deer. It is agreed among all conservationists that the reduction of the fawn-bearing does has a marked effect on the ensuing deer population in every section of the country. In heavily hunted areas a few years of indiscriminate killing of both sexes would materially affect the deer herd in reducing its numbers to the danger point. Every hunter will agree that the doe is an easy victim under all deer-hunting conditions. Most hunters who value the trophy above the mere collection of venison will never shoot the doe simply to fill a license. However it is true that the female makes the best eating and in those heavily overpopulated deer areas where available forage is being too rapidly reduced good judgment indicates that some thinning-out of the doe population is demanded. The argument has often been advanced that a buck will serve only a small number of does in any one rutting season, therefore in heavily populated areas the excess number of does should be killed off. This, of course, is pure nonsense. Any virile, normal buck can and will serve as many does as come to his attention, provided the females are ready to accept service.

The best research on the question tends to show that the number of barren does is the result of several environmental factors, chief of which is the very short period during which the doe will accept service, rather than the lack of willingness or ability on the part of the buck.

Clashes between bucks during the mating season seldom result in any injury to either contestant unless they are of equal size and antler development. As a rule the bigger bucks will ward off smaller rivals with a single shove and the duel promptly ends with the little fork-horn or spike slinking off into the brush. A bitter, long-fought engagement is a rare occurrence, though now and then two white-tail bucks have been known to fight until the antlers locked, resulting in a lingering death for both deer. John Shufelt, of Northville, N. Y., tells of coming upon two fighting bucks who were so bitterly engaged that they noticed neither himself nor his companion. John and friend thereupon quickly filled both their licenses, each with a nice buck. But it is seldom that a hunter is privileged to witness one of these little duels. Some years ago the author was still-hunting along the Shawangunk Mountain range when two bucks began to hit it off about a quarter mile down the mountainside. After slipping down to the spot, I discovered that the deer had finished the argument and had taken off, but it must have been a good scrap. The soft earth was torn up for a radius of thirty feet; small saplings were crushed to the ground, and scattered generously within this area lay big bunches of loose hair. No blood showed so the only damage done was most likely a small loss of prestige for the vanquished. I would have enjoyed a look at this battle, but it was all over before I arrived. I doubt if either deer could have heard my approach above the crashing of brush, the grunting impacts and clash of antlers; it was just my misfortune to arrive too late either to referee the bout or to bag one of the gladiators.

There is little doubt though that the smaller, less mature bucks have a good deal of respect for the long-tined heavy racks carried by the larger, more virile herd masters. This is just another method of Nature to ensure that the strongest specimens will sire the future generations of fawns. With the end of the breeding season the bucks begin to lose their headgear, smaller individuals losing antlers much sooner than the prime bucks. Pennsylvania hunters, during the latter part of their December season, occasionally drop a small buck only to discover that the antlers fall free from the skull when the deer collapses. I have seen a few of these bucks coming out on cars during the season, completely bald, and with the dropped antlers tied to the deer's head as evidence of legality. In New York State's lone December season, in 1939, two cases came to the author's attention wherein bucks had dropped their antlers after being taken. But in any case this incidence of early-dropped antlers is rare and occurs only with the smaller, less mature bucks — the spikes and small fork-horns. Many hunters complain that their failure to see bucks during the season's hunt is because the bucks have already dropped their antlers. So far as is now known, such a condition does not occur in any state during the regular open season with the possible exceptions mentioned. We can justifiably add this to the already long string of deer-hunting alibis.

Comparison of trophies is another sore spot among the deer-hunting clan. Now and then a lucky hunter kills a freak head, liberally studded with extra points, and immediately assumes that such a head should be included in the record class. Unfortunately for the man who kills such a head, it will be classed as simply a freak. The tendency in establishing whitetail head records has been to choose only those heads which accurately represent the antler development peculiar to the whitetail, discounting or penalizing the trophy for any extra points which detract from its character or symmetry. One of the author's friends, Joe Kelly of Pine Bush, New York, killed a many-pointed rack near Beaver Brook a decade or so ago. This buck carried something over forty points, but it was neither a large nor a handsome head.

The premium in whitetail trophies today is on both size of antler development and symmetry of form, with a perfect balance between the points on each beam. So far there is no system in universal use, but for many years the Boone and Crockett Club method has been generally accepted by most states throughout the country as a fair and representative means of establishing the merits of trophies. However, the Grancel Fitz system of point scoring is coming into use; New York State, for example, now lists its record heads under this latter system. Mr. Fitz apparently has devised a system which places greater emphasis on size *and* symmetry than even the Boone and Crockett Club's method.

Briefly, both systems involve the total, scored as points, of the measurements in greatest spread, length of each beam, diameter of beams, diameter of burrs, number of *normal* points and length of each point from the main beam. The essential difference in the two methods lies in the fact that the Fitz system calculates the greatest spread from *inside* the main beams and *subtracts* from the total score any point or points which mar the symmetry of the trophy by lacking a corresponding point on the opposite side. Under the Boone and Crockett Club method it is conceivable that a "freak" head, having abnormal points jutting out at right angles from either side of the main beam, could maintain a higher total score than other more representative heads which lacked such abnormalities. Then too, in this system, abnormal, unmatched points are included, giving greater value as trophies to these more or less freak heads.

Of the five largest New York State Record Heads, published in 1942 records not one appears on the state's present list. In 1942 the Boone and Crockett Club method was official, but today's state records are obtained under the Grancel Fitz system. These are the statistics of both record lists:

NEW YORK STATE RECORD HEADS – 1942

Length of Outside Curve R.	L.	Greatest Spread	Diam. of Beam R.	L.	No. of Points R.	L.	Killed	Year
28″	28″	23″	5″	5″	7	6	Adirondacks	1933
		Taken by Detrich Wortmann						
27⅛	27¾	26			11	10	Chenango Co.	1933
		Owned by E. E. Risley						
27¾	27½	20¼	4⅜	4½	7	11	Adirondacks	1927
		Taken by G. W. McEwan						
26¾	26¼	23½	5 1⁄16	5	4	6	Orange County	1933
		Taken by E. J. DeLin						
26¼	24¼	22¾	4¾	4⅞	10	10	Adirondacks	1919
		Taken by Russel Edick						

THE WORLD'S RECORD WHITETAIL (For Comparison)

30¾	27½	33½	4¾	4¾	12	14	British Columbia	1905
		Taken by J. G. Brewster						

THE AUTHOR'S BEST TWO HEADS (For Comparison)

26¼	26	22½	4½	4½	5	5	Sullivan County	1939
23¾	24	21	4½	4½	5	5	Ulster County	1938

All of these are scored according to the Boone and Crockett Club system of measurement.

Here is the record list of the ten largest New York State heads under the present Grancel Fitz system of scoring.

Taken by	*When*	*Where*	*Owner*	*Score*
1. Robert L. Banks	189–	Hamilton Co.	Fort Orange Club, Albany	198.3
2. Denny Mitchell	1934	Essex Co.	L. P. Evans, Elizabethtown	189.4
3. Sidney Mawson	1938	Cortland Co.	Same, Manlius	187.1
4. R. I. Page	1938	Steuben Co.	Same, Greenwood	186.
5. Henry Van Avery	1921	Hamilton Co.	Same, Mayfield	185.7
6. Lillian Trombley	1942	Genesee Co.	State Armory, Ticonderoga	183.1
7. Emilius Roberts	1906	Hamilton Co.	Same, Northville	181.2
8. John Galusha	1895	Essex Co.	North Woods Club, Minerva	178.5
9. Hans Oldag	1942	Erie Co.	Same, North Tonawanda	176.2
10. Henry Ordway	1890	Warren Co.	N.Y.S. Conservation Dept., Albany	175.7

[This tenth-place buck is the heaviest recorded taken in New York State.]

Briefly, here is the procedure followed in obtaining the total scores with both methods:

First, the Boone and Crockett method:

Length of outside curve is measured as follows: Establish accurately the center line of the main beam by making a series of lead-pencil dots along the entire outside length of the antler. Then draw a ruled line through all these dots, beginning at the tip. Start by laying the tape flat along the line as far as it is straight, and mark a cross where the line curves away from the tape. Begin again at this cross and continue the process until the base of the burr is reached.

Circumference of main beam is measured at the narrowest point between the burr and the brow tine, or first point; then at the narrowest point between the first and second points. Many authorities discount the measurement between the burr and brow points owing to the normal presence of irregularities or small protuberances which appear frequently in this section of the antler.

Circumference of burr is taken at the base of the antler where the antler joins the skull.

Greatest outside spread is the measurement between perpendicu-

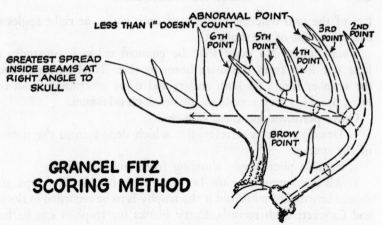

ABNORMAL POINT

LESS THAN 1" DOESN'T COUNT

6TH POINT
5TH POINT
4TH POINT
3RD POINT
2ND POINT

GREATEST SPREAD INSIDE BEAMS AT RIGHT ANGLE TO SKULL

BROW POINT

GRANCEL FITZ SCORING METHOD

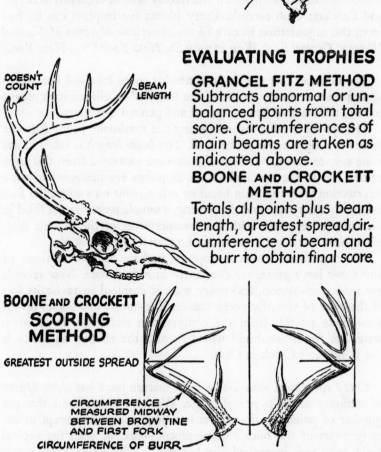

DOESN'T COUNT

BEAM LENGTH

EVALUATING TROPHIES

GRANCEL FITZ METHOD
Subtracts abnormal or unbalanced points from total score. Circumferences of main beams are taken as indicated above.

BOONE AND CROCKETT METHOD
Totals all points plus beam length, greatest spread, circumference of beam and burr to obtain final score.

BOONE AND CROCKETT SCORING METHOD

GREATEST OUTSIDE SPREAD

CIRCUMFERENCE MEASURED MIDWAY BETWEEN BROW TINE AND FIRST FORK

CIRCUMFERENCE OF BURR

lars of the two outermost points of each antler, at right angles to the center line of the skull.

Total Points. No point shall be counted unless it protrudes at least one inch from the main beam or tine. Total points include the number found on both antlers and those protruding from the burr, provided they accede to the one-inch minimum.

Other pertinent information includes:

1. Description of characteristics which depart from the normal of the species.

2. Suitable photographs showing front and side views.

3. All measurements must be made with flexible *steel* tape and should be suitably witnessed if the trophy is to be recorded in Boone and Crockett Club records. Entry blanks for trophies can be had from this organization in care of the *American Museum of Natural History, Central Park West at 79th St., New York City, New York.*

The Grancel Fitz system is somewhat more involved but represents a more accurate picture of the trophies' excellence with regard to size, thickness of beams, spread and general symmetry.

The spread is taken by measuring the maximum width *between* beams at a right angle to the skull. The *beam length* is taken in the same way as above, but *normal* points are measured from this same center line to the tips and *abnormal* points are measured to their intersection with the main beam or other point on antlers. To best exemplify the system and the scoring, a sample score sheet is filled in on the page opposite with the measurements of the present first-place New York State record head, taken by Robert Banks.

The records of whitetail trophies, perhaps more than those of any other large game, are constantly in a fluid state. New records are made each season, and every state is required to revise its lists at the close of virtually every season. The hunter can obtain up-to-the-minute records from the conservation authorities in his own state, but for national and world records the existing authority is the Boone and Crockett Club.

Every sportsman who kills a fully mature buck has some degree of curiosity as to its probable age. We have pointed out that the number of points on the antlers is a poor indication except in the early years of the buck's development — that is, until the typical eight-point rack is reached. But beyond this the antler points themselves have little value in determining age. A buck may grow two

Points of Measurement	Right Antler	Left Antler	Penalty
Length of main beam	25.0″	25.1″	.1
" " brow point	6.0	5.7	.8
" " brow point prong	2.5	2.1	.4
" " 2nd normal point	7.0	7.6	.6
" " 3rd " "	7.7	7.8	.1
" " 4th " "	9.7	7.4	2.3
" " 5th " "	8.4	7.7	.7
" " 6th " "	3.9	3.5	.4
Circumference of burr	6.3	6.5	.2
Circumference between brow and 2nd pt.	3.9	4.0	.1
" " 2nd and 3rd pt.	5.8	4.3	1.5
" " 3rd and 4th pt.	4.7	4.3	.4
" " 4th and 5th pt.	4.3	4.1	.2
" " 5th and 6th pt.	4.0	3.8	.2
Total length all *abnormal* points			4.1
Totals	99.7	93.9	12.1
Total for both antlers			193.6
Plus greatest inside spread			16.8
Total			210.4
Minus total of penalty column			− 12.1
Final Score			198.3

additional points each year up to twelve (in his sixth season) but he is much more likely to stop at the eight- or ten-point mark. However, the antlers become heavier in beam thickness and greater in length with passing seasons, and at the same time assume a progressively lower angle to the skull-line, until the buck reaches his peak of greatest vitality and virility. After this period, the antlers show signs of increasing senility. The points become less and less, shorter and stubbier, losing much of the graceful appearance of the long slender tines found on the best specimens. Finally, if the buck survives the winter periods and evades the hunter successfully, he may carry only spikes in his last year of natural life, although such senile spikes will be heavy at the butts.

The only accurate method for estimating a deer's age is by examination of the teeth and this requires expert observation, much as it does with horses and sheep. Up until the fifth year, however, a hunter with little experience can determine the age of his quarry by inspection of the lower molars. In the first year of life the deer carries but three molars; during the second year the full complement of six molars is reached, but the three first teeth remain soft and much more worn than the newer back teeth; the back tooth usually has barely come through the gum at this time. In the third year the six teeth are all fully developed, but the ridges and cusps are sharp and show little wear; fourth-year deer show some wearing of the ridges, but in the fifth year the teeth are worn uniformly flat, with no remaining high ridges of enamel. Beyond this fifth-year stage only competent observers can accurately judge the age of deer, by estimating the remaining height of the teeth above the gum line. This will vary with localities involved, because of the variation in abrasive nature of the herbage taken as food. Experienced observers can and do accurately determine age by this method, but it must be based on many years of observation.

All in all, the life span and biological characteristics of the whitetail should be of ever-increasing interest to the new hunter. Shifts in deer population, continued overbrowsing of range, and fawn production of favored areas all will affect his choice of a hunting ground. Paradoxical though it might seem, it has been definitely proved that the best way to maintain a healthy, well-proportioned herd is to hunt them and kill off the excess numbers within sensible limits. In the wilderness areas the influx of hunters tends to break up the large herds, so that there is less danger of overcrowding in yards with resultant decimation of the herds in far greater numbers than the hunter himself would legally harvest.

For the new hunter, the pursuit of deer can be a discouraging thing; he may walk the woods day after day and seldom see more than an occasional doe, never a buck. But of a sudden, one day he may encounter a sleek group of does, escorted by a majestic whitetail buck, and his chance will have arrived. What happens from this point forward is entirely up to his personal qualifications as a hunter, but in order to see his buck he must first make at least a rudimentary study of its habits. There is no magic in deer hunting. It is true that the element of luck is many times involved, but the young man who has yet to kill his first deer will fail to fill a license for many years if he must depend on luck alone. A good part of a deer hunter's share of woodlore must come from his study of the whitetail's home life, not alone his absorption of the limited knowledge in this field that he gains from his few days in the woods each season. All conservation departments publish detailed reports each year on the condition of their deer herds. These reports can be had for the asking in most instances, and those departments which publish monthly or bimonthly conservation magazines will supply them to the sportsman at a nominal rate. These reports keep a hunter posted on almost every detail of deer conditions throughout his own state, and form the basis of many a successful and enjoyable hunting trip.

At present the future of the whitetail deer is apparently secure for coming generations. Heavy increases in hunting pressure will make a few changes in local conditions, but the deer hunter's prospects look far brighter than those for many of the small-game hunting fraternity. The natural, God-given adaptability of the whitetail to fend for itself under all but the most adverse conditions, plus the more intelligent approach to conservation problems by our capable state organizations, has guaranteed solidly, for ourselves and our sons, the heartwarming thrills of many seasons to come.

3 / Woodcraft and Whitetails

OF THE MANY TALES that have been written around the drama of hunting the whitetail, each and every one tends to stress the importance of woodcraft to the success and enjoyment of the hunt. Aside from the deer taken each season by pure luck — and believe it, that number is substantial — a knowledge of woodcraft plays a most important part with every sportsman to a greater or lesser degree. The still-hunter draws heavily on his knowledge of the woods during his every moment on the hunt, for on this knowledge hinges the entire result of his trip. Even the deer hunters who gang up on deer drives, following the accepted practice of most club hunting, need to possess the fundamentals of deer tactics and behavior to qualify on the score sheet.

Perhaps the original interpretation of our word "woodcraft" goes back to pioneer days when its literal translation — craft of the woods — stemmed directly from its place in the economic picture of that day. During those times familiarity with the woods and its wild people had a direct bearing on the survival of early civilization. Food in abundance, clothing and shelter were provided for the woodsman with enough knowledge and skill to avail himself and his family of these benevolent gifts of Mother Nature, all there for the taking. Our present-day thoughts of woodcraft still swing back unconsciously to the early days; even though today's woodsman applies his knowledge only to increase his recreational pleasure and further appreciation of Nature's gifts, still here abundantly.

Much of the thrill and charm of deer hunting is influenced by our conscious knowledge of the whitetail's role in the romantic days of the Indian and buckskin-clad woodsman. Any glimpse of these splendid creatures along our wooded highways and parks will stop even the most blasé individual, sportsman or not, with a quickening of the pulse and a tiny thrill of secret pleasure, as though he had been favored by an intimate glance into the pages of Nature's book.

Much of this same effect is captured by the deer hunter. Of all our outdoor pursuits none is so wreathed by the aura of romance, none so connotative of our hidden pride in our American ancestry during its uphill climb for world recognition. The whitetail possesses every quality of a top-notch game animal — a position it undoubtedly commands — sufficiently to place it on the top shelf in every hunter's library of game birds and animals. No other game is so well able to adapt itself to changing conditions and the increasing spread of mankind's so-called civic improvements. The automobile and good highways, accused of ravaging the country of its small game and fish, seem to have simply awakened the competitive spirit in the whitetail — he flourishes now in many regions where he was unknown before the days of the machine age.

Our point is that the whitetail is so skilled in self-concealment and self-reliance that it requires the best of woods skill to beat him at his own game. In addition, most hunters of long experience agree that the deer of today is infinitely wiser than his ancestors of fifty or even twenty-five years ago. Just as the hunter has increased his knowledge of the hunt, successive generations have planted new, or newly sharpened, instincts in our present deer herd. Thus, we must indeed know our deer if we would eat venison.

The study of woodcraft in its general sense offers an enormously widespread field, of such scope that a lifetime of effort would scarcely scrape off the top surface of possibilities. Still, the richer we are in this knowledge, the richer we become. Each action and habit of wild creatures dovetails inescapably into the lives of its brethren, so that each new bit of information gleaned in trips afield adds immeasurably to what we have seen before. Unfortunately most of us are so situated that we can devote but little time to days in the woods and fields, spent simply in studying wildlife, however desirable this may be.

Our actual hunting trips, then, must be the sole means of enriching our knowledge of woodcraft; and fittingly enough it is this absorption of woodlore on our hunting trips that forms the major part of our deer-hunting pleasure. Action in deer hunting, unlike other sports, occurs quickly, exists for only a few seconds — thrill-packed though they may be — then it's all over, ending in a successful bag or a heartbreaking miss. These few seconds of action may have been days or weeks in preparation, for bucks aren't seen every day in the woods by even the best hunters. These days, though, should have been made profitable by observation of deer signs, tracks, runways, antler rubs and bed-downs, giving the hunter further information for subsequent days in the woods.

In this chapter we will confine our discussion to that branch of woodcraft which deals directly with deer and deer hunting. We shall attempt to interpret the signs and existing knowledge of whitetails to the hunter's advantage. We must qualify these observations by stating that the whitetail is often a most paradoxical animal. The one statement of fact that can be definitely and unequivocally made is that no one knows exactly what any one deer will do under any given set of conditions, not even the deer itself. The best that we can hope to do is anticipate probable reactions with knowledge gleaned from previous experiences.

In strange deer country both novice and expert hunter are faced with the problem of finding the deer. The novice usually elects to find a high spot overlooking as broad an expanse of territory as possible, in the hope that a deer will walk out within his line of vision if he waits long enough. If by lucky accident he happens on a spot near feeding grounds or a well-defined crossing he may get his shot — if he waits long enough. But as a rule this hit-or-miss method of deer hunting produces little results other than cold feet and discouraged impatience.

The deer hunter of experience wastes no time in watching barren ground. His first move in new territory is to locate feeding grounds, bed-downs, runways and crossings to the best of his ability. He understands that movements and behavior of the whitetail under normal conditions are influenced by just three factors: food and water; suitable cover for daytime hideouts and the process of moving from bedding grounds to food and returning once again to these bedding grounds. The logical course to follow is to locate these runways and feeding grounds and wait from some vantage point at those times when deer are most likely to be feeding. All this of course is under normal conditions but there are two factors which exist during hunting seasons that may induce some wide changes in whitetail behavior. These are the presence of heavy concentrations of hunters, and the rutting season.

With hunters tramping through almost all available cover and feeding grounds throughout the day, deer will be constantly on the move from one hideout to another, breaking their normal routine sufficiently that no rules of conduct apply. Then, during the height of the rut, all deer, bucks in particular, are constantly on the move, spending little time in feeding or resting. Any hunter who has killed a buck just after the rutting season can readily appreciate the tremendous amount of energy a buck must expend during this period, taking but little food in the process. Almost without exception, bucks taken after this period are exceedingly thin, almost to the point of emaciation, young bucks being affected to a greater degree than the older individuals.

The whitetail hunter must bear these two facts in mind, for they control hunting conditions to a great extent. However, there are many times when neither of these influences are present, and the hunter must employ straight woodcraft methods to find his deer.

First, the matter of feed. It's a recognized fact that deer feed very little, if at all, in heavily timbered areas, for the heavy top foliage discourages the promotion of undergrowth. Deer are browsers almost exclusively, feeding on the tender tips of second-growth timber and underbrush, although they're not adverse to grazing off a farmer's young wheat or rye. Whitetails don't favor any one type of food to the exclusion of any other, rather they select a varied diet from among the existing hardwoods and evergreens; among these are white cedar, hard or rock maple, black ash and black birch, white birch, scrub oak, ground hemlock, beech, poplar or aspen, yellow birch, dogwood and many others. The small, pyramid-shaped nuts of the beech and acorns of all species of oaks are especially favored by deer during the early fall, perhaps to the partial exclusion of other available diet at this time. The important point to bear in mind is that deer can only obtain good browsing on low second-growth stuff, regardless of its species. It's quite useless to look for feeding grounds in heavy timber, unless large numbers of acorns or beechnuts are dropping to the ground in these areas.

In looking for feeding grounds the deer hunter goes through all the heavy second growth bordering heavy timber or in locations that are close to good deer cover. He examines the tips of low-growing branches at about his waist level, which is the preferred browsing height, looking for freshly nipped-off ends, evidence of recent feeding. He goes through heavy timber areas looking for beech trees bearing nuts or oaks laden with acorns. If there is evidence to indicate that both nuts and acorns are dropping yet none can be found on the ground, this is also indicative of deer feeding but it's not conclusive. If these areas are well populated with squirrels it may be the squirrels and not the deer that are reaping the harvest. As a rule, though, the hunter can detect squirrel workings quickly by the breaking of the acorn shells and the pulverized results of nibbling. The feeding deer makes a thorough cleanup of acorns, shells and all.

These observations, plus fresh deer tracks on feeding grounds, are certain proof of recent deer activity; but the novice may have some trouble in determining just how fresh are the tracks. If autumn leaves are falling it's simple, for some of the older tracks will be covered with leaves; if the ground is mossy, none but very fresh tracks will show; in firm, moist ground the fresh track will show a glazed appearance at the bottom, old tracks will be dull. Almost the same holds true for deer droppings. These little, dark, elongated pills are dropped in bunches, and their freshness can be determined by their shiny surface coating. Old droppings are invariably dull on the surface and are firm and hard. It's good practice to pick up these little pills and squeeze them. If they're soft you can bet they haven't laid long on the ground.

Locating bed-downs is a somewhat tougher problem, for in most cases the terrain influences the deer's choice of a resting place as well as the weather. Normally the whitetail inhabiting an area of good feed and cover leads a well-ordered life. He feeds in much the same areas every day; low ground between ridges, valley slopes and along the edges of heavy timber. As a matter of fact the best all year round deer feed is found in low places, with the exception of scrub oak and acorns. Most whitetails prefer high ground for bed-downs — ridges, hillsides and knolls, where they can be sure of detecting the approach of danger well in advance of its arrival. Now this procedure of traveling down to feeding grounds, and back up to higher ground for bedding, is the most common of whitetail characteristics. It usually results in some well-defined runways connecting in some measure the two areas, for deer are creatures of habit. However, they seldom use the same spot twice running for a bed; but they frequently use the same general area, perhaps the same slope or ridge. These spots can only be found by the most thorough search of likely ground, and even then only the freshest beds will remain as evidence.

Fresh beds are well defined. Leaves will be pressed flat in an oval-shaped area about three feet long and two feet wide; fresh droppings are almost always found near the beds as well as fresh tracks. But after a day or two the leaves once again fluff up to their original shape, aided by wind and moisture, destroying all the evidence. Of course the easiest way to locate a bed is to jump a deer, but this requires some skill in still-hunting and approach, else the deer will sneak off without being seen.

With bedding grounds and feeding areas located it's a simple matter to find well-defined runways somewhere between the two. (Right here might be a good time to offer a little explanation of the difference in deer "runways" and "crossings." Deer hunters constantly use these terms interchangeably, yet they are not quite the same. A runway is a well-defined path followed by deer, whereas a crossing is a limited area where deer are likely to pass through.)

Whitetails, with customary caution, dislike traveling in the same beaten path day after day unless it is most convenient for them to do so. We find runways, then, through very thick cover — scrub oak, laurel, rhododendron, and other tough going where travel is almost impossible except on beaten paths. Runways often follow brooks hemmed in by deep gullies, or go under rocky ledges and through swamps where deer have little choice except to follow a single path. On the other hand, when more open timber or cover is reached, they will wander off a few yards on either side of the line of travel, still keeping within the limits of a crossing, but not following any definite line. These crossings are often found in ridge "saddles," below knolls, through narrow strips of timber between open fields or meadows, or between heavy swamps or dense thickets. At no time will a whitetail reveal himself completely in open fields willingly, unless it be after dark or near sundown or sunrise. When he approaches these clearings he skirts the edges, taking as much protection as the cover will afford.

Runways are easily found simply because they are more or less beaten paths. In heavy scrub oak or laurel they show up at once, in less dense cover they can best be located by watching for fresh tracks following definite lines. In soft ground along brooks or through swamps they are at once apparent, but on mossy ground or hard-packed soil it requires closer scrutiny to pick them out. As a rule though, deer keep their runways clear of twigs and branches by browsing as they travel, and this browse line is at once a dead giveaway.

Crossings aren't quite so easy. Perhaps the best plan for their location is to look over the territory for the spots previously mentioned — "saddles" over or between ridges, and such. Then minute examination of the ground in these areas should reveal clues: fresh tracks and old tracks in profusion, droppings, indications of feeding and, during the rutting season, antler rubs on saplings. These antler rubs are perhaps the most obvious hint of deer travel in any location, and usually they are numerous during the open season.

The general opinion on antler rubs is that the bucks use this method to remove the velvet after the antler has hardened and to polish and stain the antlers in the process. I cannot subscribe to this theory, for it is my belief that the rubbing occurs only when the rutting season is about to begin or has already started. The buck's antlers start to harden early in the fall, and by the end of September or early October are usually free of any signs of velvet. Yet the rutting may not begin until late October or November, and if the observant hunter takes a trip through the woods before the period begins he will find few, if any, rubs on the saplings and brush.

Later on, however, during the hunting season and after the rutting season, rubs will be noted in profusion through the same areas. I believe that this rubbing is performed by the bucks while leading up to the mating process, merely to show off their various good points to the courted doe. In much the same manner, the deer hunter will often see shallow holes about two feet round dug through the leaves down into the soil for an inch or two, with the leaves and soil thrown to one side and scattered for several yards. This the buck performs with his front feet, pawing at the ground like an angry bull, again to give himself a good build-up with the susceptible female.

Observations made at various game farms throughout the country indicate that the velvet is removed by the buck's digging it off with his hind feet. This velvet is attached to a thin skin and once this is broken through with a sharp hind foot it peels off quite readily. In my years in the deer woods I have examined thousands of these rubbed saplings and I have yet to find any trace of velvet or skin on the ground below, although plenty of the rubbed-off bark is present. As an additional point, every experienced hunter has noted flat spots rubbed on the antlers just forward of the burrs, indicating still further that all, or nearly all, of the rubbing is done with the bases of the antlers at or near the burrs. If removal of the velvet were the primary object, the antler would show no concentration of rubbing at one point.

Now if many of these rubs are noted throughout deer country it is almost conclusive evidence that the rut is on or has already past. This can only be determined by close observation of the peeled area itself and the condition of the peeled-off bark on the ground at the base of the tree. I usually peel some bark off the first rubbed sapling I see at the beginning of the season's hunt and leave it lying on the ground with the bark that has already been rubbed off. I come back to it in a day or two and compare its condition with the rub, and from this I can form a fairly accurate idea as to how old the rub may be.

All this may seem like unimportant detail in a small matter, but the success of a deer hunt often is made or broken by the rutting season. While the rut is on, deer are constantly on the move; bucks are chasing does over a wide area, and those does which have been already bred are running and hiding from the bucks. Likewise, the whitetail buck loses a great deal of his natural caution during this period and will blunder along runways and through crossings in pursuit of the doe with much less than his usual caution. A high percentage of the odd deer stories that come out of the woods each season can be directly attributed to the effect of the rutting fever when it is at its height.

With light snow on the ground all the problem of locating feeding grounds, runways and so on is at once simplified. It resolves itself into the single operation of finding tracks and following them, watching surrounding cover for evidence of feeding; and of course runways and crossings are at once evident. However, when snow covers the ground deer are much more on the alert; they realize that they can be seen more easily, so they take special pains to stay close to good cover in all their daylight movements.

In all our heavily hunted areas — which include most of our best deer-hunting territory — the larger bucks stay off by themselves. They find a safe hiding place for their daylight bed, usually on a ridge top covered with scrub oak or laurel, moving off this bed only after dark or at dusk. They travel down to low ground for their nocturnal feeding, then return again to the ridge for rest. These big fellows are lazy and unsociable throughout the year, with the single exception of the rutting season. At that time they single out one or two older does and stay with them for the greater part of the season, protecting them from the attentions of the younger bucks until their job is done. Then they retire to their old stamping grounds until the next season. Most of their travels are made after dark, regardless of moonlight or pitch-blackness, and as the restless urge of early fall seeps in they become more and more furtive until the mating season actually begins.

Throughout the year they permit no intrusions by young bucks into their chosen bailiwick and they demand no company of the opposite sex. All of these old bucks seem to realize that the often-careless female brings bad luck, and they fight any of the association except for the few weeks of the actual mating season. Needless to point out, these bucks carry the heaviest heads and often the fattest venison and are highly prized by the hunter. But it requires the best of skill and utmost patience to take these trophies by fair means. A "lone wolf" buck knows all the answers to a hunter's bag of tricks, but with a little luck on his side a good hunter can bring him to earth.

If a big buck is located in a given area much missionary work must be done before the season in the attempt to locate his habitat and feeding grounds. All runways and crossings must be carefully examined for the imprint of heavy feet. If the buck is a large one, he will have a much longer stride than the average deer as well as leaving a deeper impression of hoofs. This can only be determined by comparison with other tracks, but it's a good rule. When a definite runway is located somewhere near his bedding ground, a black silk thread can be tied across it at waist level. If it can be conveniently done, the thread should be examined every night and morning to determine whether he leaves his bed by that route or approaches by it, for often separate runways are used for coming and going. Of course, if the ground is soft enough a preponderance of tracks in one direction will give this information.

From then on, killing one of these big bucks is a matter of watch-ful waiting, taking a stand at daylight or moving in late in the after-noon, in the hope that he will leave his bed before dark or delay his return until after dawn. It may require much patient waiting, but these big fellows aren't taken every season and the time is well spent.

Discussing woodcraft and deer hunting at once brings up the sub-ject of the whitetails' powers of sight, scent and hearing. There is little doubt that their hearing and sight are better than our own, and their powers of scent very keen. The most careful observers agree though that the scent power of the whitetail is highly over-rated. Deer always seem to have trouble in establishing the identity of visible foreign objects unless these objects make some slight movement. In the case of a hunter on a stand, if a deer is within only a few yards even the winking of an eye is enough to start him off in a hurry. On the other hand, I have had deer approach within twenty-five yards and pass me by with hardly more than a glance, even though I was in full view, when I was virtually motionless.

The whitetail places little faith in any one of his several senses unless alarmed; that is, if he hears a strange noise he usually waits to see just what has caused it. If the wind brings him man-scent he bides his time until sight or sound confirms his suspicion. This natural curiosity has contributed directly to the untimely demise of more than one nice buck. Perhaps in strictly wilderness areas or regions rather remote from human activities the whitetail is much more conscious of man's intrusion and is alarmed more easily. But in those areas where deer are taken in cover near farm lands or in any populated section, the scent of man is so often in a deer's nostrils that he pays little attention unless the scent is accompanied by more tangible evidences of danger. In most cases, this is a matter either of territorial location or of one individual deer's previous experiences.

Any whitetail that has had a few close brushes with unfriendly Nimrods possesses a much higher I.Q. rating than his less sophisticated relatives. Such deer learn very rapidly with little teaching, with the result that their senses either become more acute or they develop a keener recognition of facts established by the life processes of seeing, hearing and smelling.

Five or six years ago I had located a nice buck by means of a little pre-seasonal work. I found that he bedded-down on the top of a densely thatched scrub-oak ridge. In that refuge he was completely safe from any still-hunter, for the most careful stalking couldn't bring an approach within a hundred years without alarming the deer. By a bit of good luck I found a well-defined runway approaching the bedding grounds, following up a tiny ravine, and it was here that I elected to head him off if possible.

I picked for myself a nice stand at the base of an uprooted red oak, giving me a view down the little ravine of about fifty yards and far enough off from its edge for any deer using the run to pass by with little possibility of spotting me. With a definite project in mind I quite eagerly awaited opening day, almost sure of a good shot; but my luck didn't hold out. Just the day before the season opened our deer-hunting territory was blanketed in a nice snowfall of several inches followed by a cold rain which quickly formed a most unsatisfactory crust over all. This made still-hunting in any form out of the picture entirely, and tramping through the woods rather a hardship.

Nevertheless, at daybreak of that first day I crunched up the hillside for a noisy half-mile to my chosen site. The dead air hung heavily over the hillside, sharply cold and pleasantly tingling on my cheeks. Hoarfrost formed lacy fringes on tree trunks and branches soon to sparkle with the first rays of the sun. Away off across the valley a blue jay sounded an early alarm as he policed his beat, his coarse, excited shrieking cutting crisply through the heavy silence and echoing among the white-bearded hemlocks along the slope. A beautiful morning to park quietly on a stand to listen and watch, I reflected, but that would be all.

On my stand, or seat — for I had snuggled down against the huge oak roots, well concealed — I amused myself by watching big clouds of vapor streaming out from my nostrils and lips. Trees were cracking and popping gently in the cold and a red squirrel chattered peevishly across my ravine. Soon the sun rose, spreading a deep pink over the white-blanketed forest floor, magically electrifying the frost-covered tree trunks and branches.

About half an hour after sunup I heard faint crunchings down in my ravine. As I listened they increased in volume and came nearer. Just a steady mixed crunch, crunch — sounding like a whole herd of deer in the quiet air. Then quickly they materialized into deer; first a sleek doe, head bobbing, ears waving an out-of-step beat as she daintily lifted a slim hoof for each quick stride. At her tail was another doe, somewhat smaller, just as sleek, just as dainty but with erect head and ears laid back. Steadily the procession grew until five tawny-coated does drifted by, closely followed by a tiny spike buck. Directly in front of my tree the leading lady stopped, halting the line momentarily. She swept me with a quick glance, then lifted a slim hind leg and scratched her right ear. The red disc of the morning sun behind them made a striking tableau, for each one had suddenly stopped all movement.

As I held my breath momentarily they all swung their heads over their shoulders and looked back down the ravine. Ah! I thought, here follows the object of my main interest. Then without another glance in my direction they moved by on up to the ridge. I waited with pounding pulse for my buck to make some sound to indicate his approach but after ten minutes had gone by, I gave up hope. Then I again heard the confident crunching step as my buck came up the ravine, but when he was almost within sight his footstep faltered, then stopped. I knew he couldn't wind me in that dead air, and I was sure he couldn't see me. I tucked my chin still farther into the collar of my coat to keep the telltale breath vapors from fanning out before me. Hesitantly now his crunching feet came on until I could just see a faint movement through the saplings, then he stopped. There he stood, stamping his feet, suspicious now but not quite sure just what to do.

My view offered no possibilities for a shot until he emerged from those saplings, so I resigned myself to rigid immovability, but it was of no use. He snorted twice, stamped his feet again, then turned and jumped down the runway.

I never saw that deer again, alive. But as a matter of record one of my hunting pals killed him two days later from this same stand. That morning had brought a gentle, warm rain and at about the same time this buck came up the little ravine without hesitation to meet his doom; he was a nice specimen carrying ten big points. To this day I am convinced that he could see my breath through those saplings and so took alarm, but he was an old-timer, wise in the ways of hunters and cautious in the extreme. This incident is unusual and proves nothing beyond the fact that the big bucks don't get that way by being careless.

It is quite possible that this buck was well aware of the noisy progress of his travels through that deep, well-crusted snow. Perhaps this alone made him doubly cautious; so cautious that his senses were more than usually alert to possible danger. He may have picked up a tiny wisp of man-scent drifting from my stand; may have seen some slight movement through the saplings caused by breath vapors. At any rate he was sufficiently alarmed, giving me no opportunity to place a shot. But two days later, when a warm rain had softened the crust, melted the snow and beaten down any possibility of drifting man-scent, he walked unconcernedly past this same stand, giving my partner a perfect, deadly, broadside shot through the neck.

The matter of the whitetails' keenness of vision is more closely associated with hunting methods than with woodcraft, yet it is sufficiently important for discussion here. It is hardly possible that their sight powers are more acute than the normal human animal's. It is more logical to attribute their ability to pick out a hunter quickly to their intense familiarity with their daily haunts. Any foreign object in their home woods and covers must be as apparent to them as would be a frog on our living room floor. Yet if the hunter remains quite still their attention will wander and they forget about the strange object.

Many authorities on the subject of deer maintain that deer are not color-conscious and that it does no harm to wear red clothing in the woods. This theory I personally reject. It is incredible to me that the creative force which so lavishly spreads such vivid coloring throughout the land could at the same time create any creature without inherent ability to absorb it visually. I do subscribe to the opinion that the wearing of red in any form has little effect in alarming deer, but not for the same reason. During our fall season the home covers of the whitetail deer are blotched in many ways with brilliant reds — the red oak and the sumach, to name two. What is more natural than to assume that a deer glancing casually at a hunter on his stand should mistake his red cap and coat for a scrubby red oak or a low sumach?

Deer are much more sensitive to alarming sounds than to the sight of unmoving strange objects. Many times I have had does stand, quietly watching me from distances of only a few yards. But a single snap of my fingers would be enough to produce a quick, frightened·reaction that would send them bounding and snorting to safety.

A decade or more ago, when old Abe Wykoff conducted the Buck Mountain Hunting Club in Sullivan County's Oakland Valley region, I was almost run to earth by two does. One morning Abe and I were hunting together, still-hunting the slopes on a long narrow hogback. Following our usual custom I was covering the river side of the slope, Abe the back side which sloped over to the Hartwood Club. I had just discovered a well-defined runway coming down the slope in a long angle and was investigating the runway at a point where it passed between two husky oak trees only about a yard apart.

At this precise moment Abe's rifle cracked once, then again, and in a matter of seconds two deer came over the hill in full flight, pounding down the runway toward my somewhat untenable position between the big oaks. My first glance labeled both deer as does, both badly frightened and in bounding high gear. When the leading doe was three jumps away I waved an arm enthusiastically, thinking this would shy her off. Quickly then I jumped behind one of my oak trees, barely clearing the run for the two deer as they bounced by.

I suppose that a good loud yell would have frightened them enough to swerve them off, but I didn't want to alarm any buck that might be following. Both these deer were blindly alarmed and might easily have knocked me down if I had stood in the run.

Minutes later I found that Abe had neatly dispatched the six-point buck that had been escorting these does, so my pains to keep quiet were unnecessary. Normally of course both these deer would have spotted me at once, but I am convinced that only a loud shout or a shot from my rifle would have swerved them from this runway. In like manner many frightened deer, both bucks and does, have been known to run headlong into danger even though such danger was visually apparent.

Inversely, though deer are highly sensitive to strange sounds, the usual woods noises bother them not at all. This too is fortunate for the still-hunter, else he would rarely get close enough to see a deer. Any deer must be hard put indeed to distinguish the step of the hunter's foot from the myriad rustlings of squirrels, the dropping of nuts and acorns and the clamorings of blue jays and crows. Such sounds of the hunter's progress as he must necessarily make to move at all in the woods are not in themselves alarming unless the deer can at once confirm them by seeing the hunter himself. Snapping of heavy twigs underfoot, breaking branches and rolling rocks are, of course, all taboo. Such noises form no part of the usual woods complement, and deer instantly detect them as foreign.

It is regrettable that of the hundreds of thousands of deer hunters spread throughout our whitetail deer country only a few spend sufficient time in the woods for absorbing some knowledge of deer habits. Most of the hunters of my acquaintance seem to be quite content with their knowledge after they feel that they can definitely establish the identity of the bucks' tracks from that of the does. And strangely enough, each hunter of some experience has decidedly definite ideas on this subject. For my part, although I have spent almost two decades in hunting the whitetail deer in some of the best covers of the East, I am never positive of the buck's track unless I have seen the deer making it.

Perhaps I have heard as much discussion of the subject from the hunter's viewpoint as any other individual in the East. Over the gun counter, in hunting clubs, at sportsmen's meetings, in the deer woods and in mountain taverns my ears have been bent with numerous positive rules for such identification. But still I remain unconvinced, for no two sets of rules seem to be the same.

It is this writer's experience and steadfast opinion that no man can by examining the single track of a deer thereby determine the sex of the deer making it. The best that we can hope to do is to make a reasonable deduction, considering all the factors involved, and then form an opinion. The shape of the foot alone is not enough. Neither is a large foot evidence of a buck. We have many does wandering our deer covers with feet as large as the biggest buck in the Catskills.

I have been told in perfect sincerity by certain of my deer-hunting friends that the buck always has a long slender foot. I have been told by fully an equal number of my friends that the buck has a short broad foot. Likewise I have been informed on numerous occasions that the toes of a buck always spread. Perhaps they do, but I have tracked numerous does which displayed this not too unique characteristic. There exists also a group of hunters who believe that the buck always leaves the imprint of dew claws directly behind the hoof. Perhaps no other item of deer lore carries more misinformation than this question of buck and doe tracks.

The best that any of us can hope to do to settle this problem of sex differential in the footprint is to observe all the visible evidence, then make logical deductions. Snow or soft earth is the ideal and perhaps only medium in which this can be done. It is absolutely necessary for the observer to find enough tracks in continual line to be able to establish a trend toward the identity of the animal making them.

First of all, the size of the track is no criterion. The larger females will most certainly have hoofs of greater length and width than the small bucks. Another factor is the type of terrain which the animal uses. Deer living in soft, swampy ground or an area of heavy coniferous timber will develop a larger hoof. Deer which climb rocky ridges and rock-studded slopes will have smaller, sharper hoofs. I have killed several large bucks on the Shawangunk mountain range in Lower Sullivan and Ulster Counties all of which had comparatively small hoofs. This mountain range is of heavy limestone with many jagged outcroppings and generally rock-covered. Deer living and feeding on this range keep their hoofs in a well-trimmed condition. In the swampy Wolf Pond area of Sullivan County, only a few miles north of the Shawangunk Range, the deer have somewhat larger feet.

During the latter part of December '46 one of my hunting friends and I skinned out our two bucks at the same time. One of these deer was unusually large, carrying a dressed weight of 212 pounds; the other was a normal eight-pointer which dressed out at 131 pounds. In the normal process of skinning and butchering we had disjointed the legs and thrown them into a single pile. Later, when we came to sorting out the respective feet, we would have been forced to pick at random were it not for the slightly longer and heavier leg of the larger deer. Certainly there was no apparent difference in the hoof sizes. In addition I have had ample opportunity during the past two decades to examine the carcasses of thousands of whitetail bucks. I am still unconvinced that the larger bucks carry the largest feet.

Depth of footprint is the more obvious indication of a buck's weight, plus the length of stride, both of which must be compared with other tracks made in the same vicinity by other deer. This gives an initial foundation for the hunter's deductions. Next, if the deer has been walking quietly, and a line of prints can be found, we must try to determine how closely each print will come to a center line, drawn lengthwise and between the tracks. The doe and young buck walk with feet placed close to this common center line, and are usually precise in placing the hind foot directly within the print of the front foot. Mature bucks are careless in this respect; often the hind foot is placed closer to the center line than the front footprint or fails to come quite as far forward as the location of the front print.

The fat and heavy buck shows a marked tendency to walk with front feet wider apart than the doe or small buck. Also these bucks usually show an inclination to toe-out with the front feet.

In following a group of tracks (in snow) there are some distinguishing characteristics which will help the hunter to pick out the buck's track — if there be one in the herd. The does have a tendency to wander aimlessly when the herd is moving; the buck is more purposeful and direct in his movements. The doe track will wander off the runway, then weave back. Often she'll playfully jump over a small bush or log, seemingly just for the fun of it. Her whole attitude as evidenced by the dainty hoofprints is much less concerned with a direct objective than is the buck. The buck seldom engages in the female frivolities. His walking stride is calm and purposeful; he seldom turns abruptly in his directional line to feed on a shrub just off the run. Rather he walks directly to the feeding spot. He engages in no playful antics such as the doe tracks indicate; there is little bush- or log-jumping to be found in the evidence of a buck's footprints.

Often the entire group of does in the herd will fan out through crossings, covering an area fifteen or twenty yards wide, as they precede the buck. The buck's track will usually be found, firm and purposeful, following up through the center of this welter of trails. Then again, the more wary old-timers will follow the doe herd but at a distinct distance apart. If the hunter discovers one of these lone trails showing a marked tendency to stray off a bit to right or left from the rest of the herd, he can bet his stack that there is a buck ahead.

In snow less than four inches deep the buck consistently will give away his sex by dragging his front feet. The doe lifts each foot daintily, then places it quite carefully down. A buck carrying heavy neck and shoulders will not trouble to lift his feet clear of the snow. His dragging forefeet leave a distinctive line behind each print. Of course in heavy snow any deer will drag its feet, so the hunter must use judgment in making a decision of this kind.

Much has been said about the spreading of a buck's toes as a distinguishing characteristic. To me a spread-toe print means only a heavy deer, whether it be buck or doe. Any running or loping deer will leave a spread-toe print, particularly in firm soil. Neither does the shape of the hoof itself have a definite bearing on the sex of the deer. Short, broad hoofs and long narrow hoofs will be found at random on both bucks and does. The nature of the terrain underfoot has much to do with slight differences in shape of hoofs. Hard rocky ground and generally rocky deer-areas contribute to wearing-off the front of the toes. The swamp areas and coniferous timberland allow the hoof to grow a much more pointed toe.

The woodsman who has opportunity to observe all the points we have mentioned will add up all of them before drawing any hasty conclusion. As a matter of fact the whole thing is not too important, because we must find the buck himself. Many times, though, we are forced to decide whether or not to follow a set of fresh tracks and we may be able to save a day's wasted hunt if we can make a logical and accurate interpretation. At any rate, the study of deer prints never loses its charm for a deer hunter. Rather it adds to the fun of a day in the woods.

There exists still another item of sex differential in deer which has caused many a clubhouse argument: the "snort" of the whitetail. Almost every hunter who spends much time in deer country has heard a deer snort. The sound is simply a whistling blast from a deer's nostrils and may be caused by the deer's alarm or anger. Of greater importance, it is often caused by the deer's effort to rid the nostrils of the nose-bot. The deer bot is one of the factors resulting in high deer mortality in certain areas. Commonly, it is the deer's ability to rid themselves of these bots by blasting them out through the nostrils that will mean whether or not the deer will be able to survive the vitality ebb of a hard winter.

However, it is a prevalent belief among hunters that only the buck snorts. As a matter of fact, this idea is so widespread that any snorting deer faces immediate danger during the hunting season.

During one of my still-hunting trips in the lower Catskills I was working a big beech ridge. I had been in the woods about an hour and had not yet heard or seen any other hunters, so I was unprepared for a sudden burst of rifle shots which crashed out directly ahead of me, farther along the ridge. Seconds later two does crashed by just below me, unaware of my presence. Just beyond me they stopped, looked over their backs in the direction they had left, then, shaking their respective tails, they quietly trotted off down the ridge slope to the valley below.

A light powdering of snow covered the ground, so soon I could see two red-capped hunters following along the trail just left by the two does. They were so occupied that neither of them saw me and would have passed me by if I hadn't whistled. I dropped down the hill then to talk with them.

"How long have you been standing there?" they both asked. "Didn't you see those two bucks go by?"

"Well," I said, "I certainly saw two deer go by, but if there had been any bucks you'd have heard some shootin'. Just what made you fellows think they were bucks?"

Both shifted their feet a bit and looked at each other before the older man spoke up. "Well, we had just come up on this ridge and these deer were bedded-down in some brush. When they heard us they both snorted and jumped on up the ridge. We could see their flags for quite a ways, so we started to pump it at 'em. We're glad that we didn't connect, but that's the first time either of us heard of a doe snorting." And so it goes. I have heard numerous incidents parallel to this one, and from widely separated whitetail regions, so the idea is by no means peculiar to a few deer hunters.

In this same connection, 'way back in the early '30's I had joined an Oakland Valley deer-hunting outfit called "The Beaverdam Club." On my first day's hunt, just after daybreak I had found a tiny scooped-out gravel bank up on the mountainside, near the camp. The boys had been taking gravel out to repair the winding wood road over the mountain to Beaverdam Pond. The bank was just so deep that I could barely look over the rim from a spot within the scooped hole.

I had a good view from this spot. With only my head exposed above ground level, I could cover the little ravine running down the steep slope to my left. The whole white-birch slope to my right and the valley below was in easy view for just a shift of the eye. This I decided would be a good spot to spend an hour while the deer still would be on the early-morning feed.

Hardly had I settled down to wait when two deer came into view, gently picking their way down the ravine edge toward the valley below. They were not alarmed, and would wander a bit from the ravine to the low second growth to nip off a tender bud now and then as they progressed, ever coming closer to my stand in the gravel pit. Finally they were only a few yards from my head, when the leading doe discovered me. At once her head was thrown erect, sensitive ears cocked in my direction. Then she lowered her head slowly and, at the close range, I could fairly see her nostrils quivering as they sucked in air, filtering it for a taint of danger.

But the wind was right and she could find nothing for fear. Still, she was mighty curious; so she raised a slim foreleg and stamped it to the ground with an audible thump. Finding that I could not yet be frightened into moving, she again stamped. Meanwhile her companion doe had inched forward cautiously until they were nose to flank. Then, incredible though it may seem, they each stamped and thudded their dainty forefeet into the hard ground, no doubt still expecting to frighten a move out of me.

At last, satisfied that no buck was tagging along behind, I broke the tableau quickly by yanking off my cap and waving it. The response was electric. Both does jumped into the air with loud snorts, reversing their field as they headed back up the slope, bounding as though they were on springs — tails flying erect — and snorting at every jump. At the top of the ridge they stopped, shook their heads, snorted a final blast and walked off into the white birches, snapping their flags in evident disgust.

Deer of either sex seldom make any vocal noises other than this common snort, yet there have been many instances of bleating deer recorded. Bert Sauer, old-time deer hunter and once charter member of the Iroquois Hunting Club in mid-Sullivan County, has reported to me that many times he has heard of female deer bleating, particularly when wounded. I have no firsthand knowledge of this, but I have heard the doe make tiny bleating noises to the fawns, as they nestled against her flank. I doubt if the noise could be heard, in this instance, at a distance of over twenty-five yards.

I remember a tender scene up in the Beaver River section of the Adirondacks. I had taken a stand at daybreak near the foot of a low spruce ridge. The morning was crackly cold; all was dead-still but for the chatter of chickadees and a red squirrel. After a while I became aware of slight rustlings that materialized first into a small fawn, just out of the spotted coat, then another fawn and the mother doe. The three stood at the edge of the birches, tiny wisps of steam fanning out from their shining black noses. The old doe then took the lead until she stood directly before my big spruce-tree stand, but the fawns hesitated. She turned her head and gave a little grunting bleat — almost a purring sound. I could see her flanks heave slightly and the vapor come from her mouth as she made this sound, so I could be certain that it was not a low snort. Then the fawns hopped over to her and one touched noses with the mother while the other nibbled playfully at her ear.

Again the mother gave this little purring bleat and the fawns moved off into the spruces, followed closely by their fond parent. Even after the little group had passed from my view I could hear the doe bleat gently now and then until at last all was still again.

In bringing out some of these more intimate details of deer behavior the writer has a definite purpose. There is a growing tendency among the great bulk of the deer-hunting clan to pursue the whitetail deer in a hit-or-miss manner. For any man to gain the fullest success and enjoyment from his hunting each year the whitetail must be made a hobby — a hobby of study which is as gratifying as the killing of the deer itself.

True, many men are fortunate enough to kill a deer the first time they set foot in deer country. This is not exceptional. Purely by the law of averages alone some small percentage of greenhorns will kill their buck, because with thousands of hunters in the woods each season some are bound to run across a deer. But the man who can kill his buck year after year is he who possesses a keen knowledge of woodcraft and deer behavior. No detail of deer lore is too insignificant to be overlooked. With the passage of years and the successive seasons no one more than the deer hunter himself will appreciate this fact.

There is much more to killing a buck than finding good deer

country and spending a few days hunting therein. Any woodsman worthy of the name covers his deer-hunting grounds with hawk eyes. He studies his topographical maps (in strange territory) and from these alone — virtually without seeing the land itself — he can often locate the sections where deer will cross from valley feeding grounds to hiding places in swamps and bedding grounds on ridges. These maps are invaluable to the deer hunter in familiarizing him with areas to be hunted. Such maps may be had from the United States Geological Survey, covering in quadrangle sections almost any area in the country. The maps show elevations as contour lines, and all roads, trails and streams in any given area.

It is a far cry from covering alder thickets with a good English setter or crouching in a duck blind on the Sound to the successful hunting of whitetail deer. The writer does not wish to disparage small-game hunting, for no one else enjoys that sport to a greater degree. However, I have always felt that such hunting calls more for good shooting ability and good dogs than for an abundance of woodlore. Successful deer hunting is the true test not only of a sportsman's shooting skill but of his specific knowledge of wood-craft and of his intelligent application of this knowledge.

A knowledge of woodcraft in deer hunting includes much more than a thorough understanding of deer habits and movements. The hunter himself must be at home in the woods, be able to detect good cover and feeding grounds at a glance, know his territory well enough to account for the movements of his pals, and above all be sure of his own position through every minute of the day. In small covers near farming lands and settled communities this is no problem. In the "back-country" and semiwilderness areas, it is not so easy. Individuals vary much in this quality of directional sense, but every hunter can acquire enough of it to give him perfect freedom of movement in any territory he might like to explore.

4 / Still-hunting the Whitetail

SUNUP was but moments away as I stood on the roadbank near the little old schoolhouse. Earl and Eddy had just dropped me off and had gone up the winding dirt road to the next farmhouse. They would park the car there and hunt up on the big hardwood ridge that parallels the course of the majestic Delaware River. I was to hunt on up this ridge, and meet them a mile or so beyond.

How quiet and lifeless were the slopes and valley below me! The quiet gray beeches stood like guardians among the little white birch and sumach by the roadside, gleaming damply in the early daylight. Now and then a heavy water drop would fall with a *thunk* on the dead-leaf carpet below. It had rained the night before — a soft, warm fall rain, bringing off the last reluctant leaves and opening the door to the hunter.

It was opening day some ten-odd years ago. We had decided to hunt here, in the Cahoonzie area of southwest Sullivan County, purely on my say-so . . . that it was good deer country. Of course all of us knew there were deer in this general area, but we had not yet hunted here for deer. I had, however, been over the section we were to hunt a few weeks before, with the setter. I had combined grouse-hunting with a little exploration, and had decided that the country offered good possibilities.

At that time I had been more or less driven out of my old stamping grounds near Wolf Pond by the heavy infiltration of new and reckless deer hunters. I had decided that this year I would seek new hunting fields, where still-hunting would once again be practical and enjoyable.

Perhaps no one can say just why he picks a definite spot for a new hunting ground. On my grouse-hunting trip I had found many tracks, some well-defined runs, and evidence of deer feeding on acorns and beechnuts up on the big ridge, now above me. But I knew many other places where signs were just as abundant. Perhaps on the day I had been here before, the beauty of the country impressed me and now had lured me there again.

It had been a glorious, golden fall day. Riotous color had filled the woods — the warm reds of the young oaks, the pastel yellows of the beeches. Waxy-orange bittersweet berries clung to the tumbledown stone fences and clambered over dark green cat-briers like living drapes. Here I had found grouse and the delicate heart-shaped prints of deer.

Topping the ridges were long lines of towering hemlocks, standing guard over their progeny in the struggle for sunlight among the heavy white birch. Groundpine and creeping hemlock carpeted the white birch grounds, almost concealing great beds of wintergreen and partridge berries. And over all was the heavy rich glow of October sunlight. In the valley below, the Shinglekill gurgled and chattered on its journey to the Delaware. Both brook trout and the heavier browns were even now lying in the gravel-bottomed riffles, ready to spawn. To me trout and whitetail deer have always been closely associated. Perhaps it is because many of my deer have been killed near trout waters, or perhaps because in both there breathes the never-ending beauty of the wilds.

The first pink rays of sunrise bathing the top of the ridge above stirred me from my reverie. It was time now to get up on that ridge and look for my buck. Behind the little school ran a low ridge, gently sloping upward to meet the big ridge that I felt should be the resting place of at least a few deer. Slowly, reluctantly, fearful of making any sound that might break the spell of silence, I began the climb.

My shoe-pacs fell softly on the sodden leaves — I brushed through little hemlocks whose evergreen feathers dropped tiny showers at my intrusion. Every half-minute or so I stopped to look down each slope of the ridge, watching for deer sign as I progressed. Soon I headed into the base of my big ridge. Now the timber changed abruptly from small white birch and poplar to the heavy-trunked red oaks and big beeches. The beech is ever a lovely tree. Its smooth gray bark gives an impression of quiet, firm dignity, a strong contrast to the rough, black trunks of oak and hard maple.

The woods were indeed quiet that morning. The air had but a touch of chill; no breeze moved the last remaining leaves of the aspens — nothing but a *put!* as an overburdened raindrop dripped from a high twig.

Now I struck a fresh track, and I stopped to study it. The prints were deep in wet leaves, wide-spaced and toed-out; they were heading for the ridge. It was apparent that this deer had spent the rainy night before down in the valley hemlocks, either feeding or in shelter from the rain, and was making for the ridge to bed-down.

I took the trail to the top; it was easy to follow in the sodden leaves. But at the top of the ridge, the trail became fainter as it led through long stretches of moss and over rocky ledges. Finally, I gave it up altogether to concentrate on covering the long hogback before me.

For an hour I carefully walked the ridge-top, swinging first right, then left, that I might watch both sides of the slope. Much of the time I stood to listen and watch, but I heard nothing more than the scurry of a gray squirrel as he dashed for a den tree, or the distant *Pow! Pow!* of a rifle. Then I turned to step around a big stump, and a movement in a white birch stand off to my left brought me to a halt. I could see moving bodies in the brush and now and then a slim foreleg, but no heads.

In a moment, though, two deer came out of the white birch and headed up the ridge. Both were does, or at any rate no antlers showed. I decided to wait right there for a bit and watch their back trail for any following buck. But for a quarter of an hour no other deer showed, so I took off again following the ridge and, in a sense, following the two does.

My route crossed many deer signs; fresh tracks coming up from the valley below and crossing over the ridge; many droppings sprinkled in the runs through laurel and rhododendron. Almost every visible track must necessarily be fresh, for the rain would have successfully obliterated all those before its coming. Here on a small poplar near a rocky ledge a buck had rubbed the bark — long shreds lay on the ground at the butt. No tracks were visible here; it must have been rubbed some days before. All these signs were heartening — perhaps this ridge would develop into a deer hunters' Utopia.

At last I reached the crest of the hogback. Beyond, the ridge sloped gently down to the valley of the little farm near where my pals were to be hunting. Quietly and slowly I worked down the slope, aware now of a gentle breeze fanning my left cheek and murmuring in the topmost hemlock boughs. The sun was much higher now — the early rose glow had changed to a pale yellow, penetrating to the forest floor in the beech and white birch stands, but failing to dispel the moist and morose shadows of hemlock and buck-laurel. Deer should be bedding now, I thought — not much chance to find any yet on the move.

In my musing way, I had passed a big windfall of white oaks, lying off the shoulder of the ridge, heavily leaved tops pointing down the slope. The uprooted trunks lay crisscrossed upon each other with the thick, brown dead leaves clinging to the branches in a high mound. I had stopped then for a moment, to wonder at the perversity of a flighty wind in singling out for destruction this particular clump of white oaks. And as I stood here my eye dropped to fresh deer tracks, tracks that headed toward this windfall.

Obeying the normal urge, my feet turned toward the fallen trees. No more than two steps did I make, when, with a bursting crash, a fine buck bounded out from behind the screen of leaves, high-tailing it for the crest of the hogback. As he jumped, his antlers had flashed in the sunlight, and even as my rifle came up, both antlers and long white flag were bobbing over the low brush.

My first fright over, I settled down to stopping him short of the ridge-top. Swinging with him, my front sight touched his knees as I tightened off the trigger. With the crash of the .250 his forelegs crumpled on that last bound; his nose slid to the leaves and his chunky body swept over in a high arching somersault. He made one game effort to regain his feet, but the second bullet threw a tuft of hair from the far side of his neck and he thumped to the ground again, stretched out in death.

As he lay on the damp forest floor, I marveled, as I do over every deer I have killed, at the dead-whiteness of his white hair and the tawny gray of his body coat, so like in color to the leaves in which he lay. His antlers shone dully, hinting of many rubbings on the soft-barked saplings on his ridge. The main beams swept forward and upward, topped with ten-inch-long tines. His was not a magnificent head of wide spreading beams and many points, but simply the grand, sturdy crown of an adult eight-point buck.

And now, I reflected, as I dropped down on a log to steady my quaking knees, my hunting was over and the hard work — yet a labor of love — must begin. I had to get him out.

An experience such as this is the deer hunter's dream. On the day that I have related, still-hunting conditions were ideal. Each circumstance had been in my favor — quiet, damp woods, a gentle breeze favoring my direction of hunting and the common, natural tendency of the whitetail buck to remain hidden even at the close approach of the hunter. It was mere chance that I discovered the fresh tracks, turning me towards the deer's hiding place; and at once he knew the jig was up — therefore his mad dash for safety.

It is in such a fortuitous hunt, when Lady Luck smiles, that the deer hunter reaches the greatest heights of hunting thrills and pleasure. True still-hunting will ever be a solitary effort, one in which the successful hunter can take the greatest pride of accomplishment. He has outwitted our most cautious and instinctively clever species of wildlife at its own game. The satisfaction of taking a whitetail buck by still-hunting methods alone can never be approached by killing a buck that has been driven to the stander to be killed.

Of course, still-hunting poses a myriad of problems. Much of our good deer-hunting territory is not well suited for still-hunting. For example, the heavy scrub-oak territory of many Pennsylvania counties makes a close approach to deer almost an impossibility. A large portion of New York's Sullivan County is heavily thatched with scrub oak, laurel and rhododendron, so the hunter can never approach deer without driving them ahead, far out of seeing or shooting range. Many sections of representative deer country abound in similar obstacles to the still-hunter.

The ideal type of cover for still-hunting is the rolling, many-ridged hardwood lands, where timber is heavy enough to discourage dense undergrowth. This is not to say that virgin-forest growth is good deer country, for generally it is not. Rather the best still-hunting country is a combination of big hardwood ridges and small valleys covered with good, low undergrowth for deer feeding grounds. An example of such country can be found in the Northville area of New York State. Here, in the southern foothills of the Adirondacks, at the northern extremities of Sacandaga reservoir lies just this type of rolling hardwood country. The tiny valleys lying within these hills are well thatched with small white birch, cedar, poplar and alder, as well as many other types of good deer feed.

The Catskill area offers many good still-hunting sections: Slide Mountain near Phoenicia; the Red Hill section farther south near Claryville; the whole Upper Neversink River Valley — just to name a few.

Heavy spruce areas such as we find in the western Adirondacks are difficult to hunt. Vision is limited to the extreme in such areas by the constant walls of evergreens. Under these conditions deer can gain a safe hiding place in a few bounds, in almost any direction, giving little opportunity for a shot.

But good still-hunting areas can be found in any state where the whitetail is numerous — Vermont, New Hampshire, Michigan or Maine, or whatever state happens to be the hunter's choice. In my own experience most of my deer country is discovered on my fishing trips, for actually a deer hunter never stops hunting, even on his summer jaunts. Many of my best hunting experiences have been enjoyed in areas that I scouted during the summer months. After arming myself with topographical maps of my chosen area I would be ready to hunt when opening day came around.

Another and perhaps more important problem for the still hunter is the abundance of other hunters in his area. Still-hunting is hardly practical when many hunters are tramping the woods in groups of two, three or even more. The deer become highly alarmed in any section where hunters are on the move all day; so much so that the slightest noise will tend to send them off at top speed. Deer under these conditions of heavy hunting have had their routine of natural habits broken. They feed little, if at all, during daylight hours and they bed-down in the heaviest thickets they can find.

There is a personal element too, under such a setup. It is hardly advisable for any hunter to go pussyfooting through deer country if there are many hunters strewn throughout the area. There is ever the thousand-to-one chance that a slowly moving hunter may be mistaken for a deer by one of his brethren. It is highly important, then, to pick your still-hunting grounds with a view to hunting pressure as well as abundance of deer and favorable terrain.

However, we do have many sections of good deer country where straight still-hunting methods are the only practical means to kill your buck. We speak now of the great wilderness areas of the Upper Michigan Peninsula, the North Woods of Maine, a great portion of the Adirondacks, or any true wilderness area accessible to the hunter only by trails or waterways. Here the deer live continually in a wild state, unfamiliar with the sight or scent of man. Perhaps many deer are born, live a normal span of existence and die without ever having seen a man. Hunting these deer successfully requires the best of woods craftsmanship.

It is just this type of hunting that the writer prefers, but unfortunately few of us have the time to devote to such a trip. Wilderness hunting involves considerable preparation, complete camping gear and a knowledge of woods lore in sufficient quantity to make an extended stay out of doors a pleasure rather than a hardship. Its great compensation rests in the hunter's opportunity to disassociate himself from the humdrum existence and the platitudes of normal living. Here the hunter must be virtually self-sufficient. He must walk many miles over dim trails, carrying his camping and hunting gear on his back. He must depend on his wits and ability to provide a good bed, good food and reasonable living comfort in camp. But most of all he must lean heavily on his still-hunting knowledge and ability to bag his buck. Any whitetail buck killed under these conditions will ever be the most highly prized trophy in a sportsman's collection.

And in these wilderness areas there is no other way to kill deer. No methods of deer hunting other than still-hunting are practical. The terrain is of great scope. There may be many deer but they are scattered over thousands of acres of timbered woodland. The still-hunter must seek until he locates his deer.

Many times I have thought that our deer hunters are becoming soft. Most of us can find deer within a few hours' drive of our homes. We drive into the deer country, park our cars and in five minutes are hunting in productive country. I must admit that this is good. In many cases it means that a man is able to hunt deer where otherwise he would never be able to enjoy this sport.

But in another sense, much of the true hunting spirit is lost if we hunt deer only under these conditions. The man who has the initiative to seek deer in the wilderness areas is the hunter who gains the most from his deer hunting. Still-hunting is becoming a lost art in many sections, primarily because of unfavorable local conditions but often because of general inertia on the part of the hunter. To those who say that there are too many hunters coming into their favorite haunts, or that the deer are being killed off, we can advise turning to wilderness areas. There still are many thousands of acres of wonderfully scenic forests, abundant with deer, that have scarcely felt the tread of a deer hunter's foot. Let these men get maps of the areas they would like to hunt, study them well, prepare the necessary camping gear, and when the season is at hand "go back in" for a week or two where there are still many wild deer for the taking if the hunter possesses the necessary skill and intestinal fortitude to make the grade.

"Still-hunting" is, as a term, slightly ambiguous. It is not to be confused with the common practice of sitting on a deer run all day

— day after day — hoping that a buck will come along, sooner or later. This method can be a highly successful one but it should never masquerade as still-hunting. Rather it might be more aptly named "ambushing."

This difference in terminology was driven home to me quite a number of years ago — during my early days of deer hunting. I had driven up to Wolf Pond, right in the heart of Sullivan County's best deer hunting, one morning in the early part of the open season. When I reached the old hand-laid stone dam, there was a large party of hunters gathered atop the dam, waiting for good daylight before taking to the woods.

Sitting apart from this group was another hunter — advanced in years and no doubt, I thought, well learned in the art of deer hunting. I struck up a conversation by asking him if he was hunting with the gang.

"No," he said. "This bunch are going up in the scrub oaks and drive the hell out of 'em. They've been doin' it all week. Guess they killed one buck so far. But I'm going to take it easy and do a little still-huntin'."

I looked him over pretty carefully after that remark. He was bundled up in a heavy sheepskin coat, covering layers of wool shirts and sweaters. His feet were well covered with a pair of huge felt boots into the tops of which were stuffed at least two pairs of trousers. He carried a huge lunch basket in one hand with a giant-size "Thermos" bottle resting upright in one corner; in the other hand hung a double hammer-gun of ancient vintage. Quite an outfit, I decided, for a still-hunter. Then I made off up the trail to do a bit of hunting myself.

Later that day I happened on this same character, sitting a few yards off the trail but not more than a hundred yards from the Wolf Pond Dam. I stopped to ask him if he'd seen anything yet and he told me, "Only a couple of does."

"Thought you were going to do some still-hunting to-day," I remarked casually.

"Well, by God," he replied, "don't you think for a minute that I ain't been. I been here all day — haven't moved a bit since sunup. This here's a mighty good run and I know I'll get a shot if I sit here long enough." So much for that brand of still-hunting.

This writer does not intend to ridicule those who prefer to hunt deer by careful watching and waiting near runways and feeding grounds. Many times it is the only way to kill a wary old buck that has been outwitting still-hunters and deer drives for season after

season. The true still-hunter, as a matter of fact, does a great deal
of watchful waiting as he moves over deer territory. Looking,
stopping, and watching with patience and care has many times
filled a deer license, oftener indeed than has barging through deer
country without regard or respect for a deer's keenness of vision,
hearing and olefactory senses.

The principal drawback in this ambush style of modified still-
hunting is that the hunter sees but little deer country. More valuable
in deer hunting than patient waiting is a true, firsthand knowledge
of the movements of deer in the area. This can only be gained by
moving quietly through the woods and swamps, studying tracks,
runs, bedding grounds and all the many signs that the experienced
woodsman can interpret in terms of deer lore. This is still-hunting's
greatest boon.

Add to this that in cold weather only the most Spartan courage
can keep a hunter on a stand hour after hour throughout even the
shortest fall or winter day. Such hunting limits the scope of a sportsman's knowledge. I know a goodly number of men who hunt deer
year after year and of this group none have yet seen for themselves
the telltale rub of a buck on a green sapling. These hunters lose
most of the charm of still-hunting. Deer hunting for them becomes
a battle with the elements — often highly antagonistic during the
open season in any of the northern zones of deer hunting.

Frankly, this writer lacks both the infinite patience and courage
to face a bitterly cold day on a runway stand. Feet become painfully
inanimate lumps of frozen flesh, fingers almost crackle with frost and
the entire human frame soon vibrates like a strummed harp. The
entire picture is out of tune with the normal theme of deer hunting
thrills and pleasure.

The hunter who follows the still-hunting game alone adheres to
a typical ritual. He works the lower feeding grounds during the
early morning and late afternoon hours. When the sun climbs above
the treetops he begins to look for bedded deer on ridge-tops or
along the edges of heavy swamp or thickets of evergreens. In any
case he covers ground slowly, traveling the route which will permit
motion through the woods with a minimum of noise. Feet are placed
carefully on moss or rock at every opportunity, keeping away from
the noisy rustlings of dead leaves. He travels wood roads wherever
possible to keep clothing from brushing noisily through the small
branches.

Many times a hunter will give up still-hunting entirely when the woods are dry and noisy. This can be a serious mistake. Deer are not instantly alarmed at the noise of a hunter's footfalls in dry leaves. Logically such a noise could be made by other deer, squirrels, partridge, wood mice or a myriad of other wood creatures. It is to be expected that deer will usually take off if they see the hunter after their attention is aroused by such noises. On the credit side of the ledger, we can say that a smart still-hunter will often spot his deer before their alarm sends them crashing away. Again, whitetail deer have a habit of standing quite still at the hunter's approach, if they feel that they are well concealed, or that the hunter will pass them by.

I recall an incident that illustrates this tendency to hide by remaining quiet in the hope that they would be undetected. I was not hunting deer at the time, for the season was still a few days away. Following one of my customs, I was hunting partridge in a favorite deer cover up on the Shawangunk Mountain range. It was a windy day with a decided fall bite in the air. The birds were wild, and my setter was ranging out a bit more than he would have been normally. Now and then he would pass completely out of sight and I would whistle him in. The air was filled with falling leaves, setting the whole mountain slope in motion. There were many deer signs, but so far I had not jumped a deer. Nor did I expect to, for I had taken no pains to conceal either my movements or the dog's.

At last there was a time when I failed to see Pep for several minutes. I found myself near a high ledge which dropped away below me for fifteen or twenty feet. I was not yet near enough to the rim of the cliff to see beyond, so whistling and calling as I went I came to the edge for a look below it. I searched the long slope stretching down through the big timber below for several minutes, still whistling and calling for the dog. Suddenly he appeared by my side and at once he stiffened and looked down over the cliff.

Following his lead, I too looked down, directly below the ledge. Right at the base of the rock lay two deer, a fat fork-horn buck and a doe, both flattened out on the leaf-strewn ground as though they would like to sink still further into concealment. For a space of several seconds they lay still, then in a single motion they leaped from their beds and disappeared along the ledge. The appearance of the dog was the factor that routed them out. I had stood for quite a bit just above them, shouting and whistling like a maniac, and there is no doubt in my mind that they would have remained right there in frozen immovability had not the dog suddenly appeared on the scene. I am certain that I would not have been aware of their presence if they had remained quietly huddled there at the base of the ledge and had not the setter come at that moment. At no time was I more than thirty feet from these deer while I was on the ledge-top calling and looking for the dog, but they managed to fight off any wave of nervous timidity with the knowledge that they were well hidden.

Deer continually follow this practice, of allowing the hunter to pass, and then making off quietly in the opposite direction. It is fully as important for a lone still-hunter to watch his back trail occasionally as it is for him to be alert for deer ahead. Every time the hunter passes a heavy thicket or clump of evergreens or rhododendron he should stop and watch behind for a glimpse of brown, sliding and shifting away through cover. And it's amazing to observe the ability of a sneaking deer to move with little noise, whether it be through scrub oak, tangled cat-briers or over crusted snow.

Weather has a direct bearing on a still-hunter's success. Ideal conditions are damp weather or the period immediately following rain or light snow. Dampness softens all woods noises and at the same time makes fresh deer sign more apparent. Connected also is the tendency of deer to hide away during periods of storm and to move about for feed directly after the storm has cleared. A quietly damp day with little wind and with all dead leaves fallen clear of trees and brush makes an ideal day for still hunting. I personally dislike still-hunting in windy weather. The thrashing of wind-whipped branches, the heavy sighing of evergreens and the constant motion and rustling of dead leaves fills the ears to the exclusion of all other noises.

Yet I have several highly successful still-hunting friends who much prefer still-hunting during periods of windy weather. They maintain that the noise of windswept forest effectively covers smaller noises made by their movements. Add to this the fact that with trees and brush constantly in motion the hunter's movements are more or less concealed or at least made less apparent. I can see the logic, but so far it has not worked out for me. I find that deer behavior on a windy day is skittish in the extreme and that often they dash off at any slight alarm.

In my mind the hunter who is most benefited by windy weather is one with defective hearing. Under normally quiet weather conditions such a man is at a disadvantage — the deer can hear him long before he can detect their movements by sound alone. But on a windy day every hunter must depend virtually on his eyes alone and this factor places the sportsman with poor auditory senses on an equal footing with those of us who are more fortunately equipped.

Old George Drake, well known to fishermen and hunters alike in the Lower Catskill region, had poor hearing during his last few years in the woods. But he continued to kill his buck with astonishing regularity. George was a woodsman of outstanding skill, carried over from his market-hunting days with the old muzzle-loader. Several times he confided to me that the wind had helped him get close enough to a buck to be able to get his shot. Until the time of his death a few years ago, his vision in the woods was of the best, even though he could barely read the local newspaper at a close range. Nature may have helped to balance the scales by enabling his old eyes to see well enough to overcome his other loss.

All other things being equal, the quiet day offers the best possible opportunities for the still-hunter. It is then that he may match wits with the whitetail on a more equal footing. I say "more" equal advisedly, for none of us can hope to be as familiar with any deer country as are the deer.

An intimate knowledge of the terrain to be hunted is mandatory if the still-hunter would kill his buck by not merely trusting to luck. In wilderness areas of wide scope no hunter will have the time to spend in making preseasonal trips to learn the layout. It is here that the topographical maps come into their own.

If the sportsman has a definite idea as to where he intends to hunt it is advisable to send to the *United States Geological Survey, Department of the Interior, Washington, D.C.* for an index map of his state or the state in which he intends to hunt. Then from this whole master layout he will be able to select the proper quadrangles to cover the area he plans to hunt.

I remember one of the incidents that proved to me the infinite value of these little maps. Quite a few years ago a friend took me on a deer-hunting trip up into Warren County in the Adirondacks. We planned a week's stay back in the woods, so we prepared our camping gear and started off. After getting in to the end of the road we packed in and made camp. We had a grand hunt; each of us had his buck at the end of the fourth day. We packed them out after breaking camp and started for home after a week of glorious weather and ideal hunting in some of the best still-hunting territory I have ever visited.

The years passed, and my partner of this trip had moved out to the Middle West. Once again I wanted to make the trip back to this hunting spot, but I had no accurate idea how to reach it. The topographical map came to my rescue. I picked out two quadrangles covering the general area and together with a state highway map I was able to locate accurately not only the exact route by car, but even the very trail which we had taken to the camping spot. Many times since I have had occasion to seek new hunting and fishing grounds with these maps. Indeed I am never without a complete set, covering most of my hunting and fishing grounds.

I believe that over half of the United States has been covered in this Geological Survey, begun some time back in the early 1880's. Most of the territory of interest to Eastern sportsmen has been mapped, and maps are available. Of course, many of the maps are not up to date as to highways, but the country is still just the same as it was the day it was mapped. By intelligent study of the individual quadrangles an accurate mental picture of the terrain can be visualized. Streams, lakes and swamps are accurately detailed; contour lines show every elevation. Valleys and ridges, steep hillsides and cliffs are graphically detailed. In a word, no area can be strange to the hunter who studies well one of these topographical maps.

Any still-hunter of experience can virtually pick out on these maps the areas to hunt. Crossings through ridge saddles can be determined, and swamp hiding places brought to light. Watering places and streams are of course at once evident, and if the still-hunter plans a camping trip he is able to pick out the exact trail to carry him to good water. The maps are roughly 16½ by 20 inches, and if they are to be carried on a trip, as they should be, they can be pasted on cheesecloth or muslin, rolled up and carried in a mailing tube. Reposing on my den wall is a large map of the Catskill area, made up by joining quadrangles together, the whole mounted on muslin. I have it covered with various colors of map tacks pointing out deer areas, trout and bass waters, and any other facts of interest to my sportsmen visitors. I consider it one of the most interesting additions to my equipment.

It has often been advised by authoritative writers that the still-hunter should always hunt upwind. The purpose, of course, is to prevent man-scent from reaching the game in advance of the hunter. No doubt a deer can pick up scent for two hundred yards if it's carried by a stiff breeze. Generally speaking it is good advice to keep downwind of any game, particularly deer. I fear, however, that in some areas the hunter will be hunting up hill and down dale all day long if he sticks to the letter of the rule. If the ridge we propose to hunt runs north and south and the wind blows east to west, we have little choice but to follow the ridge. Certainly we will never hunt straight up the side of the slope and down over the other side merely to keep head into the wind.

In every hunting problem rules must be tempered with good judgment, and in this matter of hunting against the wind there can be no hard-and-fast rule. A hunter's entire strategy is dictated for the most part by the lay of the land. And in rolling, hardwood whitetail country, the contours of the land are broken up in many ways by cliffs, ravines, pinnacles and knobs. Wind direction over such terrain is fitful and flighty. One moment we will feel a touch on the right cheek and as we move past a rock ledge the breeze will come directly toward us. In the mountainous areas the bright sunlight, beaming down on a southern slope, will create a heavy updraft, nullifying wind direction on this slope. Many times in a single hunt I have found the breeze shifting in every conceivable direction.

If the wind velocity is fairly stiff these modifying factors will be overcome, but in any case the hunter will abide by the influence of the terrain. He must keep a general upwind direction if possible, but it is not vitally important that he face forever into the wind. A good crosswind, either to right or to left, is every bit as effective in keeping away man-scent from the game, at least until the still-hunter is abreast of the quarry.

In hunting a ridge I prefer a cross-breeze, keeping on the downwind shoulder of the ridge as I move slowly along. Deer often keep constant watch along the very top of the ridge in both directions. They seem vaguely to expect a higher incidence of danger along the crest of a ridge. It is wise then to keep just far enough away from the top of the ridge to yet be able to see any movement upon it. In no instance however, will a still-hunter move in a deliberate down-wind direction — this simply advertises his presence to every whitetail in the area ahead.

The term "still-hunting" is in itself connotative of the hunter's actions while in the woods. Every effort must be made to move slowly, and with a minimum of noise underfoot. The cracking of dead branches, the rattling of loose rocks and other carelessly made noises are definitely foreign to the progress through the woods of any wild animal, except possibly a black bear or a frightened deer. Primarily, the still-hunter is most concerned with seeing or hearing his deer before the deer sees him. His every movement must be directed to this end.

The thought that much territory should be covered in a day's hunt must be abandoned. This single factor has contributed many an unsuccessful day to a deer hunter's season. No one, even the best woodsman, can cover five or six miles of territory silently and with caution and see the movements of game within his travels. The watchword must ever be: Move slowly, watch carefully and listen closely. Each time the hunter comes to a strategic spot where deer may cross, let him stop, first picking a suitable background where his silhouette will not stand out in bold outline. Deer are highly conscious of any new object in their home covers. If the hunter is foolish enough to permit his body to be seen against an open skyline or atop a rock-ledge or big boulder he cannot, in all honesty, complain if he fails to get a fair shot at his buck. The best policy is to stand against a neutral background — a scrub-oak patch, a big tree trunk or a boulder, first being certain that the background is large enough to cover his outline. Suitably placed, a passing deer may see him, but if he remains quiet and the wind favors him, there is every possibility that the deer will not be alarmed.

There is still another and important factor in watchful waiting. Often the most careful approach and intelligent observation will fail to give the hunter a look at his deer before it makes off. If the cover is good, and the buck has been making the area his regular hangout, the chance is great that he will return shortly. Any prime wise buck is ever reluctant to leave his home bailiwick unless he is badly frightened. The mere passage of an occasional hunter seldom routs a buck for long from his home coverts. The wise still-hunter who discovers fresh tracks leading away from an obviously good hideout will do well to spend a quiet hour waiting for the buck to come sneaking back home.

In any heavily hunted deer territory the older bucks have a habit of selecting a good high ridge, a heavy scrub-oak thicket or some other spot where a hunter cannot approach without the deer's being aware of the danger. When one of these bucks does locate such a safe spot for his hideout, it requires plenty of hunting to keep him away from it. He may be scared off by a still-hunter or driven out by a drive, but ten to one he will make every effort to get back again, provided always that the source of danger has apparently left the area. In my own experience, I have had the opportunity to kill several bucks in just this way, after locating their hideaways.

One of these deer bedded-down on a narrow scrub-oak ridge. Through the middle of the scrub oaks and lying along the crest of the ridge ran an old abandoned wood road. Many years of disuse had filled the road with tangled blow-downs and small brush, making quiet progress impossible. By the process of elimination, I discovered that this buck would take to this scrub-oak patch just as soon as the first rifles began to crack after the opening day sunrise.

Twice in as many days I jumped him out of the scrub but never caught a glimpse of him. Then I decided it might be good strategy to drive him out to a stand, giving someone a shot. I gathered together six of my hunting pals and mapped out a still-drive, thinking that he would run the top of the ridge, follow it to the end and give a shot to the standers I had posted at the top of the ridge where it sloped down to the creek bed. But he was too wise for us. Twice we jumped him but he failed to run the ridge. He went down the slopes to the nearest swamp, and of course there was never a stander near his route. He successfully eluded all our efforts that year, but I had decided to try for him again next season if he still used that scrub-oak ridge.

Before the season came around next year, I looked over the ground carefully for his tracks; they were sprinkled all over the ridge. I found two rather fresh beds in the scrub oak and near a well-defined run this buck had rubbed and gouged a small maple tree in pre-mating exuberance. There were many signs that he had been active on the ridge, but no tracks of other deer were evident. Apparently the ridge was not used by any other deer, or else this buck had driven off outsiders.

I decided to wait for him on one of his runways right after daylight on opening day. I waited and waited for two days but he made no appearance. I believed then that he was leaving the ridge after dark each night, feeding in the lower valley areas and then returning before daylight each morning. His fresh tracks were very much in evidence each morning so I could make no other deduction. Accordingly, at dark of the second day's hunt I tied my black thread across the runways in two different places. Next morning both threads were hanging limply.

By this time I was a bit desperate, so I decided that I'd jump him out of his bed anyway, just to make him "git." I swung up over the ridge, fighting my way down the wood road. I went through to the end of the cover — about a quarter of a mile; then I swung back through the scrub oak itself. At no time did I hear the buck leave but I found fresh tracks leading down toward the runway, and it seemed, from their appearance, he was in a hurry.

Satisfied that I had at least disturbed his siesta, I came out to the edge of the scrub and dropped down on a mossy patch near his runway for a little rest. Plowing scrub oak and brush for an hour had taken a little pep from my legs and shortened my breath to little pants. I soaked in a bit of November sunshine, listened to the red squirrels chattering and the little mountain brook gurgling below me. Suddenly a gang of blue jays set up a raucous chorus over on the next little ridge, and then just as suddenly flew off in silence. Disturbed by a hunter, I thought idly, wondering meanwhile if he had heard the buck come down off the ridge.

I passed many minutes in this fashion, planning new stratagems to outwit this deer, for by this time he had become a major obsession. In fact, I dreamed one night that I had killed him, but unfortunately I did not dream in sufficient detail, so it wasn't of much help. I had not yet set eyes on this buck, but I could easily visualize a great spread of antlers crowning a massive head and neck, an idea no doubt implanted by the deep gouges I had observed in the trunk of the little maple he had rubbed.

Somewhat lost in this haze of thought I gradually became aware of tiny noises, foreign to the normal sound pattern, filling my ears. I glanced across to the other ridge but could see nothing strange. Again I heard a mumbling footfall and rustling of twigs but could not make out any movement in the low second growth that separated me from the other hardwood ridge across the valley of the little brook. But quite without warning I saw the flash of sunlight on antlers as a buck moved slowly through the underbrush toward the brook, moving ever in the direction of the runway. He paused now and raised his head in my direction, lifting it until I could see the full wide spread of his long-tined antlers and the tips of his ears.

I waited, then, until he began to move again; I shifted my position slightly until I could bring the short-barreled Krag into line with his path. He was in no hurry. He stopped many times, probably to test the wind and listen for noises up on his scrub-oak ridge. Now he was quartering toward me, only fifty yards off, and still I could see no part of his body through the underbrush. Approaching the brook, he stopped dead-still in a little alder clump on the far bank. For many minutes he stood there, his antler-tips shifting to right and left as he looked over the area ahead cautiously. Then in a single leap he cleared the brook and walked into a big white-birch clump; and at the edge of the white birch lay his runway. My front sight rested on the runway where he should emerge, held at knee level; my breath again was short but for a different reason; my heart click-clicked in my throat. I thought he never would show himself — the suspense was frightful.

Slowly he poked a black nose out of the birches, head low now, as he sniffed at the runway. His front feet came into the opening and my front sight lifted to his neck as he quartered toward me. I squeezed off the shot. The muzzle blast blotted him out of my vision for just a fraction of an instant and then he lay across the runway, all four feet in the air, kicking out his last moments. He never regained his feet nor moved from the spot where he first came to earth. The open-point bullet had blasted a two-inch section from his neck vertebrae.

It was evident that this buck never moved far from his hiding place in daylight hours. When alarmed he simply moved off the ridge, crossed the brook and went up on another ridge, very likely staying there until things quieted down, when he would again carefully pick his way back to safety. He was a fine animal with long wide beams and carrying 8 long points; his dressed weight was just over 180 pounds. A splendid buck added to my list of trophies — simply by watching and waiting in the luckily chosen proper spot.

Often a buck will be aroused by a prowling hunter and his natural caution will dictate moving from the spot. But until he has precisely located the hunter he may remain hidden until he is certain in which direction the danger lies. On two occasions I have jumped whitetail bucks while still-hunting, bucks that jumped only at the noise of my approach and who then stood quietly waiting to spot the danger. One of these moved into a heavy spruce thicket and stood there for many minutes. When I alarmed this deer I had been fighting my way through some of this same spruce and any progress that I had made was far from silent. However, when I heard the deer jump just ahead I stood very still and watched carefully all about me on the ridge-top. I was aware that after the deer had jumped I had heard only a few bounds, then complete silence. I suspected that he might still be hiding in the heavy evergreens, so I waited for him to move out. The air was motionless, the day damp, giving any man-scent that may have carried from me, a limited range.

As I stood there in the quiet of the spruces I thought I could hear a faint sniffing noise. At first it puzzled me but it at last dawned on me that my buck was just a short way ahead, screened effectively and most likely wondering where I had gone. Perhaps a quarter hour passed before he decided it was safe to move on, and he chose to move out at right angles to his original flight. I could hear him moving through the heavy spruce off to my right and then I caught a quick glimpse as he crossed a small opening in the green curtain. He moved slowly, stopping often to listen and watch, but at last he came out of the spruce thicket, giving me a standing shot at its edge. This was another buck I did not have to trail after the shot.

Normally, of course, a buck fully aroused will move quietly away and will never be seen by the hunter, but every so often we'll run across one who pulls just such a trick as this. It pays then to play these little hunches when we're still-hunting.

In rainy weather many hunters are content to stay indoors and leave the deer hunting to the more hardy souls. But I remember vividly several occasions when I have been able to walk up on deer during a steady downpour.

The day that comes most clearly to my mind was in the Oakland Valley section of the Lower Catskills back in the early 1930's. At that time I was a member of a little group of good, old-time deer hunters who had a comfortable camp up on the mountainside above the Neversink River Valley. In those days, perhaps even more than now, my deer hunting was strictly secondary to making my living. I could hunt the opening day, perhaps, and a couple of week ends. That made up my deer-hunting season. My fellow club members were more fortunate. Deer hunting to them was a two weeks' vacation — the entire season — and how I envied them! For myself, I must hunt when I could find time, and had no choice about the weather.

Before daylight of this morning I had driven up into the Valley in a warm, steady fall rain. I was prepared to hunt, though, for I had brought oilskin trousers, laced rubber knee boots and a light rubber raincoat. When I hit the camp not a light showed. The gang were all still enbunked. I tried to rouse out a few, but I was turned down with much profane emphasis. The entire gang were in accord on late sleeping that morning. I gathered that they planned a leisurely breakfast, then a session with cards and a five-gallon demijohn of red Italian wine to keep up their morale. They graciously consented to give me the freedom of the entire mountain for my hunting.

I'll admit I was a bit downcast as I hit the long winding wood road leading to the top of the big hardwood ridge above camp. The gaunt black limbs of rock oak and hard maple dripped water steadily. The rain beat a steady tattoo on the flat dead-leaf woods floor. Tiny wisps of fog gathered in the tops of the big pines and beeches. Little rivulets slithered over the dead leaves, making their way down the mountainside. It was a dreary, dismal day, hardly one to fill a hunter's heart with the joy of the outdoors.

I managed to make the top of the ridge and here I encountered heavy patches of fog. I was carrying a 'scope-sighted .250 Savage, but I had the leather lens-caps in place to keep out the rain. However, I had mounted the 'scope high enough so that I could use the iron sights if need be. I had had this in mind when I picked this rifle for the day's hunt, rather than one of my other pets. I felt that I might have need of the 'scope's definitive qualities on such a gloomy day, but if the rain held on I could still use the iron sights below the 'scope.

As I reached the ridge-top I swung toward the west, heading for the big rhododendron clumps that I knew were sprinkled along the ridge-crest. I suspected that there might be a deer or two hiding in the shelter of the big flat, rubbery leaves, hoping to keep off some of the rain. I was not in the least concerned with walking quietly for the pelting raindrops covered any small noises I might have made.

I had covered only a few hundred yards when my eye picked out a slight movement at the edge of a laurel clump. The fog had again come down and it was difficult to make out anything over thirty yards away. But I stood quietly under a big, sheltering hemlock and waited for the concealing vapors to clear off. Again I saw that flick of motion — which evolved suddenly into a deer's tail, twitching now and then. The deer was headed away from me into the heavy laurels and it stood with its head down, much as cows will do out in an open pasture lot during a summer storm.

Carefully I removed the lens-caps from my 'scope and caught the deer in its field. Now I could see it distinctly but could not see anything but the hindquarters and that drooping tail, which still twitched every few seconds. At last when I saw that the deer had no immediate intention of moving, I put the 'scope post on its back and whistled sharply. At the sound the buck — for buck it was —

threw up a startled head, giving me a perfect opportunity for a *coup de grâce* through the neck.

Several times since then I have been able to approach to within close shooting range of deer during a fairly heavy rain. The drumming of raindrops effectively covers all movements of a hunter's approach and at the same time has the effect of dampening scents to a negligible factor. Deer hunting in the rain certainly is far from comfortable, but if the hunter equips himself with light waterproof clothing it isn't unbearable. We must concede that at many times it is highly effective. In such wet weather the whitetail moves around but little and if he does move he will skirt the heaviest covers, favoring the more open glades and bigger timber. Presumably the whitetail has no greater liking for traveling through the rain-sodden brush than does the hunter seeking him.

Thus far we have been still-hunting alone, but some of the finest days a man can spend in the woods will be with a well-chosen hunting partner — a man as well-versed in whitetail lore as is he himself. Two men hunting the ridges and slopes together in the right co-ordination can develop into a deadly deer-killing combination. Old Abe Wykoff, of the Buck Mountain Club, and I had some fine hunting days up along the rugged slopes of the Neversink River Valley. Abe knew the haunts of most of the deer in that area and soon I learned to match my pace to his, studying his movements and absorbing some of his skill. Together we jumped many a deer from the long slope above Kitchen Eddy and not all of them got away to safety in the scrub oaks of the high ridges.

Before Old Abe and I would start our hunt he invariably instructed me to take the high side or even the crest of a ridge. He himself would work the lower ground, knowing that a jumped deer most often runs uphill. He would insist that I keep about a hundred yards ahead of him as we moved along, and to help me keep his location he carried a crow call. Every few hundred yards he would give out with a few short caws and I never would be in much doubt as to his whereabouts. Each of us would follow the same hunting system — walk fifty yards or so, then stop to watch for several minutes. In this way I would have a crack at any deer moving out ahead of Abe as well as a jump shot in my own territory ahead. Often it worked out beautifully.

One time we started a still-hunt just above Barber's Eddy. Abe went down the trail to the river's edge and he left me to follow the old wood road crossing the face of the valley slope. I waited in the road until I heard Abe's call down by the river, then I moved in, watching carefully. This slope of cover between the river and the wood road which lay parallel to it along the mountain is thatched heavily with laurel and small hemlock. It's a great hideout for deer in the morning hours, before they have worked up from the river to the mountaintops.

Not long after we had started I heard Abe give a couple of short blasts on the call, quickly followed by two sharp reports from his little .32–20 Winchester. Then, with a great crashing of laurel and thumping of hoofs a whole herd of deer — seven in all — came bouncing up and across in front of me. A big doe was leading, followed closely by a small buck, with the rest of the herd right behind. I riveted my attention on the fork-horn and managed to throw three shots just ahead of him, piling him up a rod short of the wood road. The rest of the herd scattered off into the heavy laurel without my having been able to locate another buck in the bunch.

It developed that Abe had connected with this buck as the deer first moved off. His bullet had ranged up after entering the back ribs and no doubt would have dropped him shortly even if I had not luckily broken his neck with my third shot. Abe stoutly maintained that there had been another and larger buck in the herd and that he had taken a crack at this one too, not knowing that he had hit the fork-horn. But we went back to the spot and looked it over thoroughly without finding any evidence of a hit. There is no doubt in my mind that I would have seen this second buck if I hadn't been so intent on stopping the first one. But such is deer hunting.

We both were well pleased to have bagged this buck so easily, and within a matter of a few days I had killed mine, again with Old Abe's help. This time we were on the flats upriver, about a mile from Barber's Eddy. Here the river makes a wide sweep, leaving a flat several hundred yards wide between the foot of the steep slope and the roaring, boulder-strewn stream. The cover is good, mostly white birch and poplar. Again, Abe elected to work along the riverbank and I kept to the far side of the flat right at the foot of the slope.

We had almost completely covered this flat strip — about half a mile long — when I decided to stop under a big hemlock to watch for a bit. Glancing down through the white birch toward the river I saw the movement of two deer. They were sneaking through, stopping now and then to look back in Abe's direction. The cover was heavy and dark enough so that I failed to see antlers till the two deer were within forty yards. Then I could pick out the points on the second deer. As I raised my rifle, both deer spotted me but it was too late for the buck. My bullet struck him low in the chest. He made two bounds and collapsed; he was quite dead when I reached him. Abe had started these deer but had not caught a glimpse of them. They had started for the safety of the mountainside and it was my good luck to be in just the spot to intercept them.

In a like manner I have had some wonderful still-hunting trips with a partner in Pennsylvania's Pike County, on the ridges along the Delaware River. This lad had a full quarter-share of Iroquois Indian blood in his veins and his skill in the woods left little to be desired. His knowledge of deer behavior was uncanny. Many times he could call the spot where he would jump a buck and, even more remarkable, he would be able to tip me off to where the deer would run. If I followed his advice I soon would get a shot.

Strictly speaking such two-man hunting is not simon-pure still-hunting, but it produces good results. It is made to order for a couple of good friends who like to camp out in the wilderness, rough it for a week or two, and help each other to kill their bucks. And when it comes to bringing out that heavy old buck from over behind a small mountain, four hands are many times more efficient than two.

An additional point for the still-hunter: often in hunting over lowland country, where feeding deer may be wandering and browsing, it is good policy to hunt over small ridges and knolls. By this I mean to hunt up to the top of these high spots, then look over the little valleys in between for feeding deer, then move across and up to the top of the next little ridge. Feeding deer spend much of their time in such little valleys in low ground, and often it is easy to come up on them from over a slight rise. Under these circumstances a hunter has every advantage. He can approach unseen and virtually unheard until his head clears the top of the rise. Then, with only his cap visible, he can scan the whole terrain beyond with little chance of being seen by the feeding deer. Such "crossing" of the lay of the land produces excellent still-hunting results in the lower deer areas.

In wilderness sections, the still-hunter covers not only the slopes and ridges, looking for resting and bedded deer. The edges of slashings in heavy forest are always favored by feeding deer just after sunup and before sundown. In the heaviest of timber many deer find

all their available browse in these slashings — the big timber discourages the growth of small brush and offers little for hungry deer
except acorns or beechnuts. Cedar swamps are regular feeding
grounds too, and in deer country where high ridges are lacking any
swamp ground may be the hideaway of a resting buck. It pays off to
spend plenty of time in looking over these spots during the normal
daylight feeding hours.

Thus far, we have been hunting our whitetail buck on bare
ground. But in almost all of our great expanse of whitetail deer
covers, the magic of snow-covered ground can reasonably be expected during some part of the open season. Snow in deer hunting
changes many things; many a fervent prayer has been offered by
the deer-hunting fraternity that the all-revealing blanket of white
may cover the ground next morning.

How strange it is that a deer hunter can become so snow-
conscious that the first few flakes on his camp roof will strike a
hidden chord in his being! He will stir uneasily in his bunk or sleeping bag, get up and throw another stick in the fireplace; then,
prompted by some inner urge, he will throw open the door and
find the first crystal flakes sifting to the ground. I can offer no explanation but many times I have seen it happen. Its coming is un-
heralded; it drops softly and silently, yet seldom is a deer hunter
surprised at dawn by the nocturnal visit.

The snow transforms the hunter's familiar slopes and ridges into
a new world. Gone are the brown carpet of dead leaves, the gaunt
nakedness of leaf-stripped hillsides, the crisp cracklings and rustlings
of the fall woods. Instead, with the coming of the fresh, all-con-
cealing blanket, a new brightness and a tender hush sweep the deer
country. The deep shadows and gloom of dense poplar and birch
thickets are lightened by the new white base; the evergreen stands
are limed to overloading with the contrasting spread of puffy snow
on the outermost branches. The sweeping panoramic change
wrought overnight is miraculous.

Now is the time for the still-hunter to venture forth into this
revealing medium to read the pages of winter's new book. Every
movement of land animals and of many birds is at once apparent to
the woodsman who can read the signs. Here a squirrel has dropped
from his den-tree, making a lacy four-point pattern in the snow as
he searches for the acorns hidden early last fall. A ruffed grouse has
alighted from his hemlock tree roost, ready to try his new snow-

shoes along the hidden wintergreen beds. Now something has startled him — perhaps our approach. He bursts from the ground, leaving only a sweep of wing tips at either side of his trail's end to mark his flight.

The deer have been moving after the storm. Tracks fan out from the fringes of swamp and spruce thicket as the hunger urge prompts them to leave these shelters. The dainty heart-shaped prints move aimlessly here and there as the deer feed on tender buds of poplar and black birch. We can see the freshly nipped ends. Here three deer have been feeding; two sets of prints are much smaller than the third. It may be a doe and two first-year fawns; perhaps it is a trio of two does and a buck. At any rate we follow the prints for a while to detect indications of buck behavior in the larger prints. Thus we begin another interesting day in the deer woods, following and watching, anticipating the deer's movements, hoping to get a quick look at the game before it takes off in alarm.

The whitetail on the snow becomes almost a different animal. His senses, if anything, become keener. He is alert at all times for any danger approaching on his back trail. He stops frequently to scan the cover behind and in snow-filled woods his vision is as much improved as is the hunter's. Fortunately, the snow covering the earth deadens the noise of the hunter's footsteps and with proper caution he has a good chance of coming within shooting distance of the deer before being heard. The game resolves itself into a chess battle between the hunter and the hunted, anticipating each other's moves.

The problem, as always in still-hunting, is to see the buck in time for a shot. If the trailing hunter can keep always upwind of his deer he will in time get his chance. But as soon as a buck is aware of a following hunter he picks a good location to circle around, both to pick up a trace of man-scent and to throw the hunter off the track. A wise old buck is full of tricks to fool the tracker. He will often head for a small brook, follow it downstream for several hundred yards, then come out again to the same bank and circle back to some higher ground where he can watch the hunter following the brook. He may even lay a straight trail for several rods, then reverse his field, stepping carefully in each footprint of his back trail. Then with a tremendous leap he will leave the trail at right angles, often landing on a higher bit of ground. Many times the novice hunter will be fooled by the apparently abrupt end of such a trail.

Some years ago I followed a buck in a six-inch fall of snow for several miles. He tried several times to throw me off the track by heading into a herd of does, traveling with them for a while, then jumping off to the side, hoping that I would keep on after the does. He tried backtracking, going through the heaviest swamps and scrub oak, but always I was able to pick up his track and keep up the chase. Finally he headed for a heavy clump of rhododendron. This patch was almost round, covering at least an acre of ground. His track led directly into it, past a big yellow pine standing at the edge of the cover. Of course, I kept on his track even through this thick stuff. I knew that if I didn't overtake him soon, darkness would come to his rescue — there was but a short period of good light left for the day.

I had reached the middle of this heavy rhododendron thicket when I heard him moving ahead, perhaps forty yards off. He would move when I moved, stop when I stopped, but always kept a safe distance ahead. When I reached the edge of the cover his track swung around, circling the outer fringes, back to the big lone pine. He then had gone right in again over my tracks. This had me stumped. I knew he could keep this up forever and I'd never get a look at him.

I stood near the pine while I thought out a plan. Finally, I dug in the snow for some loose rocks small enough for throwing. I hung my rifle on a dead stub and began to heave rocks into the clump. I threw perhaps a dozen, then grabbed my rifle. With my back to the big pine I waited, watching his back track — and my own. Within two minutes I could see him picking his way around the fringe of the rhododendron, watching over into its center and looking behind him every few steps. Twice he stopped to listen, ears cocked in the direction of the noise he last had heard. Thus it was that he never felt or suspected the shot that dropped him with a broken neck.

The major problem in tracking deer through snow is to anticipate when they are preparing to find a resting place after feeding. When deer tracks have been meandering through heavy second growth in little valleys and ravines or in cedar swamps and open slashings it's a clear indication that they are feeding. Then when the tracks head for higher ground it's equally clear that they are looking for bedding grounds on a sloping sidehill or ridge-top. If the hunter has a reasonably accurate idea that his game will choose a certain ridge for a bed, then it is wise to leave the track and circle ahead and beyond the probable bedding spot. Quite often deer can be more easily approached by circling ahead rather than by following the trail directly. Again, if the hunter knows his country well, he may be able to determine just where his deer is heading and, by circling around behind a covering ridge or swamp, get into a good position to head off his buck. If no deer appears after a reasonable wait, then the hunter will again take the track, planning new strategy. It requires much hunting to head off a whitetail buck on the snow — for every buck killed there will be a dozen failures. This type of hunting demands the utmost in perseverance and patience.

Of all the advantages that snow-covered ground has for the hunter, undoubtedly its greatest boon lies in the reading of deer movements. The still-hunter who is willing to expend a little energy can, within a period of two days' exploring, uncover all the major feeding grounds, resting places and the connecting crossings and runways. Since these areas remain more or less unchanged from year to year in deer country such information gained in one season will form the basis of the hunter's strategy for years to come in such an area.

In the late '30's word came to me of a big buck that had been seen for several seasons in the Roosa Gap section of Sullivan County's Shawangunk Range. For two years I failed to gain an inkling as to just where this buck fed and rested, even though I spent several days each season in the region hoping to jump him or at least find a bedding ground that he used. He had been seen several times during the summers down in the valley, but so far as I knew no one had ever had a shot at him during the hunting season. Legend had given him a huge body and heavy, wide-spreading antlers, but for all I could tell he was due to die of old age.

One day in the early fall two young lads came into my shop and asked for a box of .38–40 cartridges. I had the shells but reluctantly I had to tell them they were both too young to buy ammunition. It was evident that neither of the two had seen more than twelve summers. I wondered out loud why two young lads would need a box of center-fire rifle cartridges of this caliber. So they told me that a big buck had been coming down through their Dad's meadow night after night just at dusk. They were going to be prepared for him when the season opened. After probing a bit more I learned that these boys lived quite close to the Roosa Gap road and their glowing description of the buck seemed to fit all the stories I had heard before.

Then I told them I would be glad to drive up to their farm with the ammunition and deliver it to their Dad, provided they would show me where this buck came down off the mountain. It was a deal. The following Sunday I went up into the valley to the farm, and after I had delivered the shells the boys guided me to the little ravine where a tiny mountain brook tumbled down the mountainside to the valley below. In the soft earth at the roadside were deep tracks, widely spaced in stride, indicating a really big buck. I thanked the boys and drove home, planning to make another visit a few days before the opening day of the season.

In that year our New York State opening Catskill date had been advanced to December first. On Thanksgiving Day we had a ten-inch snowfall, so on the intervening week end I went up to the mountain to do a little investigating. At once I found the big tracks coming down the mountainside along the little brook. They crossed the dirt road and went off down into the open valley fields. But here I could find no returning tracks, so rather than cover the whole valley by following his feeding trail, I walked the road hoping to cut his track on the return trip up on the ridge.

Only a hundred yards beyond, a rocky gulch butted into the road. And again here were his tracks, an identical set, heading up the slope through heavy alders and white birch. I took the track and followed it to the mountaintop about a mile off. At this spot the Shawangunk Range has a flat plateau for a crest; a plateau half a mile wide and every foot of this half-mile covered with the thickest sort of scrub oak, jack pine and laurel. Through all of this went the buck's track, heading for a swamp which lay in the middle of this flat plateau. The swamp was a forbidding place, filled with tangled cat-briers, piles of windfalls, thick, heavy swamp huckleberry and crowded stands of pin oak.

Just within the edges of the swamp I found beds — one for each day the snow had been on the ground. One bed fairly steamed — I had jumped the buck in my snooping! I took the fresh track and followed him throughout the length of the swamp; leaving the swamp he had circled and gone off into the scrub-oak morass surrounding the whole place. But I was satisfied — I had located this buck's hangout. On the way down the mountainside I picked up his coming-down runway. It closely followed the brook outlet of the swamp and continued all the way down the mountainside running parallel to the stream.

On the way up the mountain I had followed the buck's trail through the corner of a little clearing. Many years before there had been a house far up here on the mountainside but all that now remained was a crumbling foundation and the stumps of a few apple trees long since rotted away. Here, I thought, would be an ideal stand to kill this buck; I could crouch down against the old foundation and pick off the deer the moment he came near the clearing on his way up the mountain. But I had neglected to include Lady Luck in my plans.

Long before all this I had invited Jim Deren, of the Angler's Roost, to hunt with me that fall. The night before the season opened Jim hit the shop about eight o'clock, loaded down with baggage and prepared for a week's stay. I outlined what I had learned about this big buck, so together we planned to hunt for this deer alone, to the exclusion of any other deer that might be in the area.

The next morning dawned bitter cold — six above zero, with a gale whipping through the treetops. Jim decided not to climb the mountain so he waited on a good stand at the foot of the ridge while I swung up over in a wide circle, following a wood road.

I took my stand just at good daylight; I huddled down in the snow trying to gather as much protection from the wind as the old foundation would give. For an hour I sat and watched — the roaring wind precluded any chance of hearing a deer approach, so I had to keep both eyes riveted on the runway.

After an hour of this my feet were tingling bitterly. I knew I must move or once again suffer frozen feet. I headed for the mountaintop only a few hundred yards away; by the time I had plowed my way up to the top I was thoroughly warm. I turned around then and dropped back to my stand at the old foundation. Once again settled, I began to look around.

About thirty feet away I suddenly noticed a track that had not been there before. I rose and walked over, to discover that my buck had come up in my absence of a few minutes. He had stopped only thirty feet from my stand. From the nature of the tracks I could visualize him standing there, shifting his feet and testing the wind until he had located man-scent from my stand. Then with great leaps he had bounded down the slope and, making a wide circle, had gone up on the mountain to the safety of the swamp. I had missed my chance by a matter of minutes. I knew there was no further use hunting for him that day, so I went down the mountain to where Jim was shivering on his stand.

Daylight the following morning found me on the same stand, but as soon as it was light enough to pick out tracks I found that my buck had already made a safe passage up the hill. Again I brushed out the tracks and resigned myself to coming up the next morning.

Overnight the thermometer rose slowly. The first rays of the morning sun softened the top layer of snow. I had again taken my stand after learning that the deer had not yet come up the mountain, at least not on this runway. There were no fresh tracks leading up the mountain this morning, so this time I waited with high hopes. The day was Sunday and an army of hunters roamed the mountain-top and the valley below. From my stand I could hear talking and shouting above me and shots from widely scattered areas up and down the mountain slopes.

The sun rose high and still there had been no sign of my buck coming up the hill. I decided to walk across the ravine and look over his other runway, which up until now he had only used for coming down from his swamp hideout. But there were no tracks here going up the mountain. I decided then to swing down to the valley below and try to cut his track. There was now no doubt in my mind that the noise of many hunters on the mountaintop had kept him down in the lower ground where cover was good.

Halfway down the mountain I cut into his fresh track, heading up the ravine. I stopped then and watched above me but could see no movement. Slowly I moved up, following the trail until I came up over a little ledge. From here the timber above me was more open and as I glanced up the slope I saw a movement as the buck sneaked up through the big oaks and beeches about two hundred yards away. I knew then that I would never get a shot at him, for he had undoubtedly spotted me and would soon be within the safety of the screening scrub oaks.

Disappointedly, I stood there for a while looking at the depth and span of those big footprints, wondering if ever I would get a crack at the buck making them. Even as the thought crossed my mind, there was a staccato flurry of shots from just above me on the mountaintop. With the sound of the shots I was off like a sprinter at the starting gun. I raced across the ravine, jumped the brook and planted my feet in the runway coming down the mountain.

Hardly had I stopped for breath when, with a great clatter of rocks, my buck came crashing down the hillside directly toward me.

Now I could see the huge rack of antlers flashing over the tops of the underbrush. His feet hit the opening through the brush at the foot of the slope, thirty yards away, and my bullet met his chest as it emerged from the curtain of undergrowth.

Never did he falter in his stride. He made a mighty leap to my left, bounding over the brush. Fifty feet away stood a high stone wall; beyond, the ground sloped down to the valley. Frantically I threw the Krag bolt and as he left the ground in the last leap to clear the wall and to safety, my front sight swung with him. As the report cracked out there was a heavy thump; then all was still. I ran to the wall and looked over. There in a mass of bloody snow lay my buck, on his back, all four feet kicking. His wide-spreading antler points were buried in the snow — preventing him from turning his head in the least. The white throat-patch gleamed in the morning sunlight, offering my favorite target, so I ended his struggles quickly with a shot through the neck.

This was the largest buck — not quite the heaviest — that it has been my good fortune to kill. His antlers are wide, covering a 2-foot spread. The main beams are over twenty-six inches in length. His body was huge, but he was in extremely poor flesh, with hardly a bit of fat visible on the skinned carcass; yet he weighed-in, dressed, at 202 pounds. I doubt very much if I would have killed this buck had there been no lucky snowfall to give away his habits.

For several years Jim Deren had the mounted head of this deer hanging in the entry to the Angler's Roost. Of the many sportsmen who saw it and admired it none would suspect that such an innocent happening of Nature as a snowfall contributed to its capture. But without snow there never would have been an opportunity to learn that this deer followed such a precise routine to get from feeding grounds to his hideout in the safety of the mountaintop swamp.

From the viewpoint of the conservationist and true sportsman snow in hunting has a much more important value. Few badly wounded deer need ever escape to die a lingering death with snow covering the ground in hunting season. Any hunter with even a slight degree of woods skill can follow and find his wounded deer on the snow. It would be a highly conserving factor if all our open seasons in the Northern States would coincide with the first snowfall, but it would be a hopeless goal for legislators. I believe, too, that far fewer hunting accidents would occur under such conditions. The visibility of game is much more distinct in snow-filled woods.

*   *   *

The choice of clothing has a direct bearing on the still-hunter's comfort and success in the woods. It is impossible to recommend the exact outfit for a still-hunter, because of the wide variation in weather conditions throughout deer areas. Likewise there is always considerable variance in seasonal temperatures in any one section. I have hunted deer in the early part of the Adirondack season when the temperature at midday rose to eighty degrees. However, early morning hunting in the Adirondacks is always chilly, sometimes downright cold.

Sensibly, all garments worn in still-hunting should be of wool. There should not be any heavy, bulky overgarment to hamper freedom of movement or to load down a hunter who climbs the steep ridges of mountainous terrain. Two suits of wool underwear or a good Duofold garment are efficient, much more so than a shirt-and-shorts outfit covered over with sweaters and a blanket-type coat. As much wool as can be comfortably worn should be next to the skin. In warm midday, perspiration will be effectively absorbed and the wearer will still be comfortable after the late afternoon chill sets in.

If a still-hunter were constantly on the move throughout the day, proper clothing would be no problem. But a good still-hunter moves but little during the early morning hours when the air is cold. Then throughout the day he pauses many times to watch, wait and listen. During these periods of inactivity he must have sufficient wool clothing near the skin to retain body heat. So over the woolen underwear should go a pair of dark woolen trousers, or roomy hunting breeches. Trousers, however, are much to be preferred, for they give greater freedom of leg-action. A still-hunter does a good bit of climbing — up steep slopes, over windfalls and rocky ledges. Any confinement of leg muscles brings on quick fatigue. The trouser is much more comfortable in this respect, although if a pair of breeches are selected with wide, roomy knees and worsted cuffs they will be entirely satisfactory. Dark-red plaid makes a good color for hunting pants, but this writer prefers the Oxford gray. Woolrich makes a "felted" line of trousers and of hunting breeches in this Oxford gray; both are durable, warm and comfortable. By all means use a wide pair of suspenders to support trousers. If a belt is required, to carry a belt-ax, hunting knife or cartridge holder, then wear both. A full day's walk in the woods with only a belt holding up sagging trousers has left many a still-hunter with painfully sore hips.

A good solid wool plaid shirt is standard equipment. It should be a hard weave and all wool as heavy as can be found. Flannel shirts are much too light for woods wear, unless a hunter prefers to wear a heavy jacket over them. If the weather can reasonably be expected to be cold throughout the day, then a heavy sleeveless sweater should be worn over the underwear and under the wool shirt. Sheepskin vests under the shirt, too, are entirely practical. For normal temperatures — which, in most deer-hunting sections, means somewhere between freezing and forty above — the above outfit is sufficient for still-hunting comfort. In weather colder than this, add a light, short Mackinaw. It is of prime importance to have no more clothing than is required to keep comfortably warm. Too much causes excessive perspiration, so that as soon as a hunter stops for a while to watch a crossing he begins to freeze.

Another garment that this writer favors for still-hunting is the light, water-resistant parka. For windy weather or rainy, damp days the parka over proper underwear and wool shirt is extremely practical. Of course it will not keep the wearer dry in a steady rain, but for foggy, drizzly weather or during a light snowstorm it's a most effective garment. The close, water-repellent weave turns a good deal of moisture and gives comfort against a chilling fall wind. Another advantage: for those cold, early-morning stands the parka can be slipped on to take advantage of its heat-retaining close weave. Then when the hunter takes to the ridges and hills, he rolls up the parka and slips it under his suspenders behind his back. If he makes another lengthy stand he unrolls the parka, slips it on and is prepared to wait and watch, with some degree of comfort.

The most important item of wearing apparel in the still-hunter's duffel is footwear. Foot comfort is of the utmost necessity in still-hunting. Much walking over all types of terrain must be done — through swamps and slashings, over rocky ledges and steep slopes, crashing through scrub oak and laurel — and through it all the hunter must have both good foot protection and comfort. The soles must be sensitive, so that he can feel a dead branch underfoot soon enough to prevent cracking it. The uppers must be tough, to withstand the ripping, tearing action of briers and scrub. The entire shoe must be reasonably water-repellent, so that the normal amount of moisture encountered in a day's hunt will still not reach the feet.

Many hunters prefer the rubber-bottom, leather-top shoe-pac, the so-called "Maine Hunting Shoe." In most respects these are good. They are light, quite waterproof and fairly comfortable, but they have two objectionable defects. One, they do not offer good foot support to the man who is accustomed to wearing street shoes for fifty weeks of the year; they lack support to the arch, and are so soft in the foot that the foot lacks confining control. For the hunter who does much walking in rough country they are not as desirable as an all-leather shoe. Two, the full rubber foot in this style of shoe-pac causes excessive perspiration. To many hunters this contributes to extreme foot discomfort — among these is the writer.

The writer searched for a number of years before finding the ideal type of dry weather hunting shoe for still-hunting. My requirements were rigid. I needed an all-leather shoe to overcome any excessive sweating caused by rubber; I wanted a shoe-pac type for comfortable and quiet walking, with a sensitive sole yet one which gave good protection against sharp rocks. I wanted reasonably light weight so that I could cover plenty of ground without undue leg-fatigue. It was desirable, too, to use a boot sufficiently water-repellent for wading a small brook or hunting through swampy areas without soaking the feet. The entire boot should be tough, to withstand enough hard usage for the investment not to be lost in two or three seasons of hunting.

The first shoe that I found to meet these requirements was Russell's "Ike Walton." These have been so highly satisfactory during my last ten years of hunting that I have never had occasion to look further. There are other shoe-pacs which may meet my requirements, but so long as I am able to get Ike Waltons I will be content.

For hunting in rain or melting snow there is only one type of footwear that will keep feet dry — *all rubber*. Of the many types available the twelve-inch snug-leg or ankle-fit with the short lacing at the top is by far the most desirable. They should be purchased large enough, at least a full shoe-size larger than your size, in order to hold a light woolen sock and a heavy woolen sock easily. These boots are light and comfortable, but are not well adapted to long hikes over rough country. Neither do they give good foot support or adequate foot protection over rough, rocky ground. But they are the only medium for keeping feet dry under wet weather conditions. In wet weather the still-hunter does not cover much territory as a rule, so these boots will be practical for this type of hunting. I always throw a pair in the duffel bag when I plan a hunting trip for several days.

Further to assure foot protection the still-hunter must obtain boots — whatever the type — sufficiently large to accommodate a light wool ankle-sock and a heavyweight pair of full-length socks. Warmth is a reason for providing plenty of socks, but equally important is the cushioning effect that heavy socks give to the foot.

In cold weather, gloves are a problem. The all-leather, lined glove is too bulky to permit easy handling of the rifle. The unlined leather glove is hardly warmer than no glove at all. I have solved the problem — to my satisfaction at least — by using a light wool glove with full leather palm and finger facing. All-wool gloves are warm but are so slippery that handling the rifle and operating the action can be uncertain. Leather-faced wool gloves are both warm and sufficiently high in friction coefficient for shooting with them not to be much different from shooting with bare hands.

The still-hunter's headgear can be left to personal choice. By all means let it be red in color; likewise, the still-hunter should avoid any white in his clothing, even a white handkerchief. It's surprising how many hunters are ready and willing to blast a shot at a white flash in the deer woods. Better stick to somber grays and plaids for a general color scheme, and top it off with a red cap.

Add to the above outfit a small-bladed, sharp knife and a pair of rawhide shoelaces (for getting out your buck), and we are ready for a still-hunting trip. In wilderness areas we will need to add a small pocket ax, waterproof matchbox, and a floating dial compass (this we will deal with in a later chapter).

It is with some reluctance that the writer closes this chapter on still-hunting. No doubt a full book could be written about this one aspect of the deer hunting sport, but space limits such expansion. I have endeavored to show some of the thrill and satisfaction which lives forever in the mind and heart of the successful still-hunter. Deer driving and club hunting, while highly productive, never reap the reward of glowing inner satisfaction gathered by still-hunting.

There will always be, in the still-hunter's memory, the song of a little mountain brook, discovered in his wandering; the heart-stopping clutch as a magnificent buck bounds from a windfall hideaway; the triumphant moment when, by wits and woodsmanship alone, he has tracked down his whitetail buck and sent forth the well-placed shot that has brought his trophy to bag.

5 / Club and Group Hunting

A SINGLE RIFLESHOT cracked out sharply from the mountainside across the valley and below my stand, to send echoes rocketing back and forth from the rugged hillsides in diminishing volume until their last whisper was lost in the dim roar of the river. Expectantly, I waited for another but none came, so I fell to wondering whether or not another hunting brother had killed his buck. Perhaps, I mused, he had just taken a snap at a crashing, bounding deer in headlong flight up Old Baldy's gentle slopes, seeking security in the old mountain's scrub oak and laurel crown. Then again, he may have risked frightening a feeding deer by potting at a red fox, numerous in these hills. These scattered shots which come to every deer hunter's ears throughout a hunting day are always the cause of such wonderment.

In fact, on a deer stand we wonder about many things. There is little to do but listen, watch and wonder. Wonder if the boys have begun the drive — and if they've started, wonder how far they have worked their way along the mountainside. We wonder, too, if deer will be started; if they will break for our stand or come out to another watcher; if deer are jumped, whether there will be a nice buck trailing the does or a lone buck sneaking through the heavy white birch, skulking along the heavy rock-ledges, ready to break through the ranks of the drive.

This was one of those perfect mornings for a perfect drive. Air was celery-crisp; thick, crackly new-fallen leaves crunchy with lacy hoarfrost carpeted the forest floor. No steady breeze rustled scrub-oak leaves or sighed in the hemlocks. Only a faint zephyr lifted and rattled a singleton leaf high in the tips of bare red oaks. The *crush, crush!* of our own feet as we swung up the mountainside was the only disturbing and foreign sound.

Most of our little group of standers had dropped out one by one as we picked our way up, over ledges and washouts, following a wood road which carried on over the mountaintop. At last I was left to make my way alone, to take the highest stand on "Annemier Hill," a favored crossing on this drive, but one which the deer did not often use unless they were forced to the top of the mountain. Arrived at the little group of outsized anthills giving the stand its name, I picked a spot at the lower edge of a bluestone quarry, just a bit above the crossing. I buried my outline effectively in a huge pile of loose flagstone, facing downhill and across the direction of the coming drive.

On a deer stand only the mind is active. The enforced limitation of movement stimulates mental processes, heightening the expectancy of coming events. Nothing moves within the watcher's field of vision but a stray gliding leaf or a falling acorn, bouncing down among heavy branches to fall crisply into a leafy grave. A red squirrel, chattering peevishly, clings head down to the rough bark of a big hemlock, resenting this intrusion of ours into his normally quiet household. We wonder how he appeared so abruptly on the scene, and as we wonder, he whisks his pert tail and, turning, scratches his way up the hemlock to disappear into a tiny nest high up in a crotch. . . .

By now, I thought, the boys on the drive must have spread out around the old Paradise Quarry to begin the long trek up and across the slope. . . . As I waited I decided to shift my position just a bit so that I could bring my rifle to bear more readily on the crossing. I inched around to the right, facing now almost into the drive, so that the crossing below me lay fully at my left. This move placed a small branch into my line of vision, bringing it right across my rifle barrel when I mounted it to shoulder experimentally, so I reached up and snipped it off with my knife.

At this moment the thin, trailing whistle of the drive-starter came floating up from the valley below; the boys were on their way. In a matter of twenty minutes or so deer might be moving past my stand. But the action began much sooner than this. Just a few minutes after the whistle piped out came a staccato flurry of seven rifleshots; from the differences in the reports, I judged, fired from two different rifles. . . . Well, I reflected, the boys must have jumped at least a herd, to do all that shooting. . . . For the next few minutes, with nerves on edge, heart thumping audibly, all senses sharpened by the stimulant of anticipation, I waited tensely but nothing appeared. Then below me a shot rang out, then another and another as the first stander, far down at the foot of the valley slope, opened up on the deer. . . . That does it, I thought, sinking back against my flagstone back-rest; the deer took the lower crossing and George, away down at the foot of the slope, had the shot. No doubt the deer was hit by now, and would make for the lower valley to hide out in the heavy rhododendron bordering the Bushkill. At any rate the action was too far below to get me any shooting.

But I was wrong — dead wrong. Within a few moments two shots sounded off just below me. The next man to me was shooting at deer! Time to look sharp and prepare for action! Quickly then I could hear bounding, flying feet; the crashing of brush and rattling of rocks that spoke of frightened deer headed up to my stand. Then they appeared — two scared does, flags flying and hoofs flashing in the morning sunlight as they dipped and darted through the white birch, passing up the slope directly broadside to me.

No dice for me, I grunted mentally, George must have killed the buck. But wait, what was that crackle below to my left? I shifted my eyes from the spot where the does had disappeared and looked directly at a buck, showing small antlers, slowly sneaking through the small stuff, head bobbing as he pushed his way through. Quietly and slowly I brought the front sight up to bear on the edge of the thick brush, waiting until he should come clear. This he did, head down, all four legs bent in a gliding, slithering gait. He showed no disposition to stop, even though I knew he hadn't heard or seen me yet; I knew too that he was frightened and thoroughly confused and wouldn't tarry for a second if he did discover me. I shifted the sights then to a little opening through the heavier timber, and as his head appeared I held for the neck and squeezed the shot off.

Magically, the whip-snap report of my rifle pulled the string that threw the buck into a frenzy of action. He reared high, toppling over backward to land heavily on his withers. He thrashed and scrambled in the leaves, all four feet kicking furiously in the struggle to regain his feet. Anxiously I waited, with rifle ready for a finishing shot, but his wild movements made it impossible. Then for a brief instant his head lifted and held the pose and my bullet ended all movement save a last long shudder.

Once again I sat down among the flagstones, partly to regain my composure — my scalp still tingled, my hands were trembling and my ticker bumped furiously in my heaving chest — but principally to abide by the rules of the drive: never leave the stand until the drive comes through. Within five minutes I could see a tall, lumbering figure spooking through the tall beeches — Big Lew, the end man on the drive, coming up to see what the shooting was about. He spotted the buck almost as soon as he had picked me up and together we looked him over. He was a nice fat four-pointer, chunky and round, with the thickened neck of a rutting buck. My first shot had pierced the neck, but low, tearing out the windpipe and large veins; the finishing bullet had broken the neck vertebrae.

We set to work then to get our buck dressed out and ready to hit the downhill trail to camp. I wondered aloud as to all the shooting but Lew didn't know any more about it than I. He had been up the slope above all the commotion and hadn't seen a deer, but we wondered collectively how this little buck had escaped unhit to reach the top of the ridge at my stand. As we talked a bit and rolled our buck over to shake out the entrails, came the anticlimax.

We had laid our rifles off a bit, away from the blood-soaked leaves; I was up to my elbows in blood and Lew had the buck's head over his powerful shoulders, holding the forequarters high. I had the buck by the tail, shaking out the lower abdominal cavity. Suddenly a whistling snort blasted out below us, and, with the snort, a craggy-antlered buck wheeled and bounced down the slope, swinging around us and then heading for the mountaintop. He had caught us flat-footed and made an easy getaway; we had had no chance to reach a rifle, for within mere seconds he had flashed out of sight into the heavy laurel.

This big buck had hung back, sneaking broadside past the line of standers, until he had made the last ledge, then he had decided to cut over the ridge shoulder, following the old, familiar crossing through the anthill stand. No doubt he had stood watching us, concealed in the brush through which my buck had passed; momentarily he must have felt that he had stepped into a trap, with hunters below him and two more of the obnoxious creatures barring his way above. Then in anger and alarm he had snorted his disgust and swung around, heading up over the hill to his original destination.

Reluctantly we scored the first round won for this big buck, hoping that the second round would not be so heavily in his favor. We dragged our little buck down the slope to the next stander and here we found three of the boys preparing to drag out another buck — a little spike. With the deer in camp and the gang all gathered around we at last pieced together the whole tale of the drive.

At the very beginning, Cy — the first driver — had jumped a small bunch of deer directly after he had sounded his whistle and entered the woods. The deer headed right up the slope, crossing before the line of drivers. Two of the boys fired the first seven shots at two different bucks, splitting the herd into two bunches. Several does and the largest buck had turned down the hill, coming out just above the lowest stander, George, who had thrown three shots at the big deer, turning him back toward the drive. The second bunch, two does, the spike and my four-pointer, had swung up the hill heading for the mountaintop. The man on the next stand to mine killed the spike before he saw the four-pointer, and this had swung the herd directly up to my stand. But with all this shooting, and virtually surrounded by hunters, the biggest buck in the herd managed to escape. Such is deer driving, but two bucks among a group of ten men on the first drive of the season isn't too hard to take.

This drive — the "Paradise Drive," the gang called it — was always made in the same way and at the same time of day, early morning. It was based on a certain knowledge of deer runs from the valley floor up and across the face of the mountainside to the bedding grounds on the very top. The standers year after year took the same stands; the drivers began the drive in the same area — at the Paradise Quarry — and traveled the same route. The drive was useful only in the first hour after daylight, when the deer were moving out of the valley feeding grounds and before they had bedded for the daylight hours. Many deer have been killed on this drive season after season. Many more will be killed in years to come. The group which hunts this mountain know exactly, from long experience, the runs and crossings favored by the deer on their way to the mountaintop. It is only necessary to post watchers on these crossings and start the deer moving up.

The success of any deer drive is predicated on these two principal factors: the exact knowledge of deer crossings and runs in any given territory, and the normal movements of the deer in the area at any specified time. In general, deer drives can be classified in three wide categories: the morning drive, the late afternoon drive, and the drives which take place during the daylight hours between these two periods. Elementary, you say, this covers the entire hunting day. Indeed it does, but what the author wishes to point up is the distinction between the three types. As a rule it is useless to make a "morning drive" in midday, or an "afternoon drive" in the morning. Of course this does not apply to community drives, where a

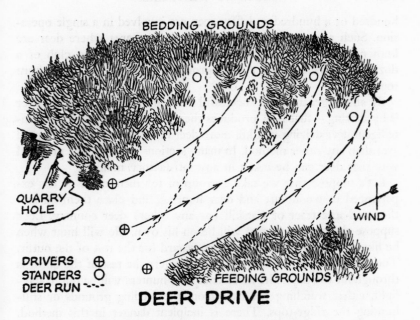

BEDDING GROUNDS

QUARRY HOLE

WIND

DRIVERS ⊕
STANDERS ◯
DEER RUN ----

FEEDING GROUNDS

DEER DRIVE

TRACK PECULIARITIES

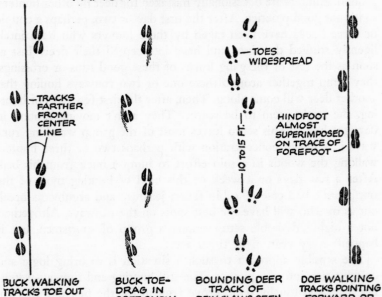

TOES
WIDESPREAD

TRACKS
FARTHER
FROM
CENTER
LINE

—— 10 TO 15 FT. ——

HINDFOOT
ALMOST
SUPERIMPOSED
ON TRACE OF
FOREFOOT

BUCK WALKING
TRACKS TOE OUT

BUCK TOE-
DRAG IN
SOFT SNOW

BOUNDING DEER
TRACK OF
DEW CLAWS SEEN

DOE WALKING
TRACKS POINTING
FORWARD OR
SLIGHTLY INWARD

hundred or a hundred and fifty men are involved in a single operation. Such a gang can drive out deer in any area where deer are known to be. But these affairs are not for the hunting club of a dozen or so men, or for a small group of friends who like to hunt together.

By and large, the most successful method of killing whitetail deer is by driving — that is, it produces the most uniform end-results. Intelligent deer driving will kill more deer in any given heavily hunted area than any other method. In many sections it is the only practical way that deer can be taken in any satisfactory number.

Let's suppose that we take a group of ten men, more or less experienced in woodcraft and deer hunting, and place them on any thousand-acre tract of Catskill (or any other) deer country. Let's suppose also that each man will be on his own. He will hunt when he likes and where he likes with no regard for the rest of the outfit. The result will be that no man knows where the rest of the outfit is throughout the day. The more energetic hunters will be out at daylight, either watching the runs from the feeding grounds or still-hunting the ridge-tops. There is incipient danger in this method, however — for any ten hunters to prowl any thousand acres of ground. Hunters are occasionally mistaken for deer by other hunters, so it's not good practice. After the first day or two, perhaps a couple or three bucks have been taken by those hunters who have intelligently studied the signs and have intercepted their deer. Just as soon as the rest of the gang learns of these good runs or crossings, they lump together around these one or two runways hoping that another deer will come along. Then, after the first few days of hunting, the bucks seem to be scarce. They aren't moving around in daylight hours. This setup leaves most of the group watching runways in a heavy concentration with perhaps two or three hunters walking the woods in a solo effort to jump a buck from his bed. After a few days or a week of this kind of hunting most of the outfit has a bad case of cabin fever; jealousy and arguments break out as to who will have the best spots on the runways. Altogether, not a highly desirable setup among a group of sportsmen, but it happens every year, many times over.

The sensible approach to such a situation is to bring logic and co-operation into the picture. The still-hunting and runway-watching may, and usually does, prove fruitful for the first day or two, but after this period the deer, bucks in particular, take to hiding, at least in heavily hunted areas. Logically then, for this group to get a crack at the deer, they must first locate the bedding grounds and hideaways, then attempt to move the deer out to where they can be intercepted by the watchers. This isn't as tough as it sounds.

In any sizable area of deer country, we will find specific feeding grounds and ridge-top or scrub-oak bedding areas or hideouts. Using the methods of the still-hunter, two or three of the more experienced men in the group will do the necessary missionary work to find these spots, together with the runways used by the deer in entering and leaving such spots. If it seems apparent from the fresh signs that deer are moving into any chosen spot directly before daylight, it's advisable to make an early-morning drive, posting watchers near the exit runways, with the drivers moving into and through the area on the incoming runways.

Deer are creatures of fixed habits. They approach bedding grounds and hideouts in much the same places, year after year. When some foreign element disturbs them they leave quietly over well-ordained routes. If they are intercepted by a hunter they usually attempt to go around, but will head for their original destination after by-passing the intruder. As the season advances and hunting pressure continues, the deer feed more and more after dark, moving toward feeding grounds only near sunset, then getting back to safety before daylight. Weather, of course, has much to do with deer movements as well as hunting pressure.

The three major factors controlling deer movements in any area are food, shelter and the mating habits. The weather will change both the place of shelter and the time of feeding. Heavy rains will keep deer from feeding at all and will usually induce them to find a better shelter than is normally used during dry weather. In periods of storm, deer will often lie down in the deepest valleys, provided there is sheltering timber or evergreen scrub for cover. They will wait for clear weather or a definite slacking in the storm before they seek the normally used, higher-level resting places. Directly after a storm then, large numbers of deer will be found on the way up to higher ground. Just before a storm deer will be moving down to lower ground.

There is no mystery involved in reading the deer signs which are found in every section of deer country. The evidence of tracks, droppings, rubbed saplings and nipped-off branches is all there for every hunter to see. The difference remains in the proper interpretation of the signs. In this the novice fails. Deer tracks taken by themselves have little meaning. It is in their relationship to the surrounding cover that their value comes forth.

Suppose we are scouting an area to find evidence for making a deer drive. We should know, first, how old are the tracks we find and whether they lead to bedding grounds or feeding grounds. We get out at daylight and walk the bottom edge of a ridge which might hold bedded deer, walking all along the foot of the slope where it joins the valley floor. We see a number of tracks concentrated in certain areas or "runs." The fresher prints will have a crumbling edge of moist earth, the older tracks will be rimmed with dried-out soil. If the majority of fresh tracks leads up the slope toward the ridge-top and we know that the valley area is a feeding ground for deer at night, then logically the deer are heading for the ridge in the early morning hours to bed-down for the day. The hunter then should scout the ridge itself, looking for beds, and, more important, runways which lead off the ridge, determined by the preponderance of tracks in that direction. It will be logical, then, to make a drive covering this ridge, placing the watchers near the runs leading off the ridge and making the drive on the runways which lead up to the bedding places.

If our group of ten hunters will locate these areas of resting places and hideouts, a drive can be organized in this way: by mutual consent or vote a man can be selected for the drive-starter, or hunt captain. He will select perhaps three men for the drive, then will select a hunter to place the standers. The standers will leave camp at daylight and trek off to the ridge, sweeping around it so as not to jump the deer before the drive begins. The standers drop out at the best crossings and take up their watch facing the coming drive. The three drivers and the starter will give the watchers half-an-hour's start, then move into their positions at the foot of the ridge. The starter whistles and the drive begins, with each hunter following a runway if possible, but in no case so far apart that any one man will not be aware of his neighbor's progress.

In a small group like this the best policy is the still-drive, in which the drivers actually still-hunt their way through the woods to the waiting standers. This system has one prime advantage over the noisy drive — it keeps the deer ahead constantly guessing as to the exact whereabouts of each hunter. As a result they tend to move ahead of the drive slowly and when they approach the stands the watchers will get a better shot. Often, quite often, if a driver advertises his exact location by shouting every few yards, a wary buck will hide, well concealed, until the drivers pass him by, then sneak off behind and never be seen at all. Again, the noisy drive will send the deer bouncing out past the standers, making a good shot almost impossible.

Proponents of the noisy drive maintain that by it deer can be driven toward the waiting standers with more accuracy than is possible by the silent method. This I doubt, in all sincerity. The author firmly believes that few, if any, deer can ever be driven to a desired spot. The best that any drive can do is to start the deer moving in the area and keep them moving until they themselves find their own way out, using the favored spots; then the standers will take up their posts near by.

With this group of hunters putting in three short drives a day, many more deer will be seen than if the day is spent idling time away on a runway, on the odd chance that a deer will come along. It does mean that the hunters must study their ground and apply woodcraft logic to each of the drives. But it will produce more venison than any other method of hunting for the group as a whole.

As a matter of fact it is this writer's guess that 60 per cent of the total take of deer in the East is taken in just this way. It is the only logical approach to deer hunting for the new hunter if he would gain deer-hunting knowledge and a shot at a buck for his first year or two in the deer woods. Much can be learned by the new hunter if he participates in a number of drives with seasoned men. If, after he has killed his first deer or two, he prefers to go alone on the more sporting still-hunting trail, he will be better prepared than if he steps into the woods the first season with no knowledge and little preparation.

Deer stands have a magnetic attraction for any deer hunter. He learns from his pals that many deer have been killed from Patterson's Rock or the Twin-Oak Stand or Skunk Gully; he swells mentally in anticipation as he approaches any of these hallowed spots, knowing that when the drive comes through his chances of killing that white-tail buck are better than those of the unfortunates who may be watching less favored areas. Every deer club has these sacred spots, and sacred they are, indeed. They have achieved reputations simply because deer favor these places for moving from hideout to hideout.

Up in one of the deer camps to which I belonged for a time was one of these favored spots; a huge boulder ten feet high, which the

Ice Age glaciers had stranded on an otherwise smooth, laurel-topped ridge. One year a new hunter climbed aboard this big rock and killed a buck and a big black bear — the next year, again aboard this rock, he killed another fine buck. Forever afterward, this rock bore the hunter's name, "Brazington's Rock" — and it will ever bear this name distinction long after we who have hunted there are gone. One year I stood with this big rock at my back, standing a drive, and had seventeen deer pour past me in the largest mass movement of deer I have ever seen on a deer hunt. There were at least four bucks in this herd. One of these bucks dropped at my second shot, and as the herd scattered away I saw the three others breaking out into the laurel. This would be a moment of tremendous thrill to any hunter — for a matter of seconds I had been completely surrounded by deer; deer large and small, does and half-grown fawns followed closely by the bucks. Many of these deer looked at me directly but were not alarmed, and as they swerved to pass the rock none gave me more than a glance. But when the rifle cracked they scattered off like scared rabbits, swinging around the rock in tremendous leaps, but all headed at last for their original destination, the Hartwood Club and game preserve. For a full minute after they passed my stand I could hear them crashing and rattling through the brush, snorting and blowing, the woods filled with bobbing, waving tails — truly an amazing experience and a never-to-be-forgotten sight.

The existence of such established stands at once simplifies the post for the hunter. Long experience has proved that these spots are located strategically both for seeing the deer for an advantageous shot and preventing the oncoming buck from picking out the hunter before it is too late. But in crossings and runs which enjoy no such traditional distinction a hunter must look over the ground carefully before choosing just the right place for his stand.

It's far too much to expect that a deer, when approaching a crossing or "run," will follow an exact path; rather it will pass through the crossing area somewhere within certain limits, be that a width of ten yards or a hundred. This will depend entirely on the limitations of the crossings geographically. However, at no time should a stander so position himself that the buck will come directly toward him. Better by far is it to be off a few yards to one side; the deer will have less opportunity to spot the stander and the chances of a good shot are somewhat better. It goes without saying that a deer passing a stander broadside offers a much better target than a deer coming in directly head-on. These head-on shots are critical in that the bullet must be placed precisely in the sticking place — neither too low nor too far to right or left — to make a clean kill.

For a right-handed shooter it is always advantageous for the hunter to select his stand so that the deer should pass on his left. This makes it possible to take the shot across the chest without any last minute shifting of the body. Many times this last shift has alarmed a wise old buck so that he never came out to the stander at all. Of course there are other factors to consider in selecting the spot for the stand. If there is a breeze blowing the stand should be taken on the down-wind side of the crossing; and if other conditions agree the spot chosen should be on ground higher than the run. Deer for some reason or other seem to pay more attention to the area below their position than that above it.

It seems unnecessary to mention that the hunter should pick his stand to get as full a view of the crossing as possible — and this means a full view, right down to the ground itself. Many times a hunter has posted himself near a shallow ravine runway, forgetting to give himself a full view right to the bottom of the depression. Then when a buck would sneak out on the drive he would get just a glimpse of antler tips or an ear with no chance for a fatal shot or even a hit.

In this connection it might be well to mention that many new hunters have only the haziest ideas as to how high above ground to look for a deer. Several times I have tried to point out a standing deer to new hunters — a deer that might have been standing in laurel or scrub oak — only to have them tell me they couldn't pick it out. Following their line of vision it was easy to check that they were looking too high above the cover, expecting to see an animal as tall as a horse. Deer are pretty close to the ground; even the biggest whitetail deer will seldom scale higher than forty-two inches above ground at the shoulders. To really be able to see a deer a man must, on level ground, look right down into the cover, considerably below his eye level. Beginners constantly see deer too late for a shot through this habit of looking over the top of normal deer cover at their own eye level. Often they hear a noise, but if it's a windy day the constant motion of leaves and branches will cover up a whitetail's movements unless the eye be dropped to the deer's level.

One day in the lower Catskills we were putting on a little drive through some fairly heavy undergrowth. One of the watchers was a brand-new deer hunter, spending his first day in the woods. We had dropped him at the first stand, then had gone on around the long strip of cover to begin the drive. Somewhere along the last half of the drive two deer broke out and headed toward the new man. We didn't hear any shooting so concluded that the deer were does, as they well might have been — we'll never know. After the drive had come through we wondered if any of the watchers had seen the deer. As a single man, all declared no deer had come through. Then the new lad spoke up saying that even though no deer had come out, two small dogs had sneaked past below him. He hadn't been able to see them clearly but he knew they weren't deer — too close to the ground! He wondered too, what dogs were doing 'way up here in the deer country.

During my early years of deer hunting it was considered taboo to smoke on a stand. Even though the author began to hunt deer before acquiring the smoking habit it was always advised never to give away the hunter's presence by filling the woods with foreign odors of pipe or cigarette. Once having acquired the tobacco habit it seemed impossible to get along without it even for a day in the woods, so I took up the gentle art of chewing, just for deer hunting. So far as I can determine now, some twenty-odd years later, all that this practice ever did for me in deer hunting was to inflict a day-long nausea and heartburn hangover. Finally I gave it up. Now I smoke just as much as I please while standing or watching and it has never had any apparent effect on my success or failure in taking deer. I doubt that any deer, even catching the scent of tobacco smoke, can or will associate it with the presence of man. It seems more likely that if the deer is alarmed by catching down-wind scent, it will be the man-scent and not the smoke which gives it the warning signal.

My original ideas in this connection changed abruptly some years ago. One late afternoon in the fall I was walking a wood road following the crest of the Shawangunk Mountain range in a pre-season inspection of the deer signs. I had spent the whole day in looking over the fresh signs — tracks, droppings and crossings. On the return trip I swung along the wood road making no attempt to move quietly. As I approached a sharp bend in the trail, a deer's hindquarters passed just off the trail beyond the bend and over to my right. At once I dropped to the ground, expecting to see another deer or two following. After a few moments' wait no deer had showed, so I moved quietly up the road to a huge uprooted oak, lying at right angles to the path. I sneaked up behind the log and looked over it into a little clearing in the timber.

Here stood seven deer — six does and a fine buck with wide slender antlers, gleaming white. He had not yet stained them by rubbing on the juicy bark of the saplings. None of the deer showed any alarm. They moved quietly, nipping browse. It so happened that I had lighted a fresh cigar just before sighting these deer; this was an opportune time for an experiment. A slight movement of air was stirring from my hiding place toward the clearing, carrying my cigar smoke right along to the deer. I puffed furiously, laying a virtual smoke line toward the herd, but it had no apparent effect on any of them. The buck glanced casually in my direction once or twice; perhaps he wondered about the trail of smoke rising from the log. At any rate the deer all fed quietly, slowly moving in the direction of a little gap in the ridge, on their way to the lower valley feeding spots. I watched them until the last twitching tail had disappeared into the white birches, fading now into the golden sunset. For several minutes more I could hear the whispered rustles and cracklings as the herd moved slowly along. Then I rose quietly from behind my log-blind and made my way homeward, satisfied that none of these deer had suspected my presence in the least.

To finish the story I could say that when the season opened I returned to this same log-blind by the little clearing and killed the buck, but nothing remotely like this happened. However, this little experience went a long way toward dispelling any preformed theory I may have had as to smoking in the woods. None of these individual deer were alarmed in the least and I had laid down a screen sufficient to fill every nostril in the herd.

Of far greater importance to the deer stander is his ability to conceal his presence from not only the buck but the does. Usually on a deer drive, if a buck is running with one or more does, the doe will take the lead. Invariably the buck, totally lacking in chivalry, will wait for the female to clear the way. If the leading does detect the stander on his post and become alarmed, instantly, by some animal telegraph, the buck will be alerted. If his instincts are the same as any normal whitetail buck's the stander will never catch a glimpse of him. When does come out to a stand the watching hunter must make every effort to avoid alarming them. If his outline is well blended into a suitable background this simply means that he must keep still, dead still, until they have passed him by. Any following buck, knowing that the does have gone quietly ahead, will not hesitate to continue through the crossing. He may hang back for fifty or a hundred yards or even farther, but if he is satisfied that no danger lies ahead he will eventually come on.

There is yet another angle in a stander's reactions to does on a drive. As the drive progresses, he hears the rustlings and snappings of coming deer. He tenses expectantly, facing the sound. He lifts his rifle, checking the visibility of the sights. Then the gray-brown forms approach, bobbing and gliding through the trees. He searches the bobbing heads for antlers, but none appear. Now the deer are close to the stand; still the heads are bare, and as they pass the stand he relaxes physically and mentally, disappointed that no buck has shown. To relieve the tension he rises from his seat, shifts his feet; perhaps he coughs nervously. Meanwhile a buck may have been following the does but at a respectably safe distance behind. If he sees movements on the stand, coupled with a strange sound, he will stop quietly, screened by brush or timber. Then if he suspects that the strange new moving object offers a possible threat to his well-being, the hunter will never catch more than a glimpse of him. He will sneak away, circling the stand, quietly keeping enough cover between his body and the watcher.

For a like reason, when a stander picks his spot he should stay away from openings in the natural cover. This means he should stay away from wood roads, open fields or clearings. Any driven buck approaching such an opening will pause, look over the open ground ahead, then flash across. It is far better judgment for the stander to take up a post a bit within the natural cover, quite away from the open areas which are certain to be looked over by any normal buck before he makes his way through. A buck may approach such areas on a trot, but invariably he will stop just before he emerges into the opening to be certain the coast is clear for crossing. Driven deer in heavily hunted areas are much more suspicious of such openings than are deer moving normally toward feeding grounds or bed-downs. Even so, any whitetail buck will use normal caution before showing himself in any opening, at least during the hunting season.

While the conduct of a stander is pretty well fixed, the drivers' actions are somewhat more fluid. The best hunters of my acquaintance make a drive in much the same manner as a still-hunt, except that they may often drive through areas which would hardly be called still-hunting territory. If four or more men are making a drive, some effort should be made by at least the outside drivers to maintain an even line throughout the drive. This will prevent in some measure a buck's sneaking around a driver who may have traveled too far ahead of the rest. One of the author's deer-driving gang would use crow calls for signaling. Two short caws would start the drive after the hunters had lined up; from then on, the two end men would sound off a single caw every hundred yards, keeping the men in between pretty much in line. At the end of the drive the starter would blow three caws, repeated twice, to bring both drivers and standers together for the next drive. This method has always worked out well. The drivers are always certain of their respective positions, and as the drive comes through the standers themselves will be warned to be alert for moving deer. The simulated calling of crows in the woods should never alarm deer unduly.

On a still-drive the driving hunters have almost as good a chance to kill a deer as do the standers. When deer are moving away from one driver they often will cross before the next man on either side, giving a good shot. Likewise it is never necessary for drivers to hoot and howl to make their presence in the woods known to the deer. Once deer are started it is the best policy not to let them know definitely just where each driver may be. A crafty buck, once he learns the positions of every man, will find a good spot to hide, allowing the drive to pass him by. Of course a buck will occasionally do this on a still-drive, but the best experience indicates that this latter method is more effective in keeping deer moving always ahead.

The big outfits putting thirty or more men in the woods on a drive might conceivably do a more effective job with a noisy drive, but it is the writer's experience that even these big drives fail to keep the larger bucks always going to the stands. One of my hunting club's grounds were joined by a large tract belonging to a big club of fifty members. Each morning twenty-five or more hunters would take a stand on a right angle line to our boundary. At the beginning of the drive, twenty or more paid drivers would enter the woods fully two miles from the standers, then set up a tremendous racket — howling, baying, banging on tins, blowing horns and ringing cowbells. This was carried out through the entire drive, until the drivers met the standers after a two-mile rumpus through the woods.

The odd thing about this deal was that our small group of hunters would kill more deer off these drives than the gang putting them on.

Time and again deer would be started, only to cut out the side of the drive and head for our grounds. I can recall distinctly that in one season this big group of hunters killed only three deer in all these long, noisy drives. During the same period, and as a direct result of this ill-directed commotion, our own handful of men killed seven bucks.

These big drives undoubtedly are useful in many sections where the cover is thick and the terrain more or less flat. New Jersey hunters take hundreds of deer in this way, but it requires many men, standing almost within view of each other, covering almost every avenue of escape. For the number of men involved the short still-drives, intelligently planned to take advantage of feeding habits at the right time of day, with proper runways picked for the standers, will produce many more deer per man than any other method.

Many odd experiences take place on a deer drive. The variable factors are two: the individual differences among whitetail deer, and the element of pure chance — Old Lady Luck. These two factors can and will keep anybody guessing as to the outcome of a drive. Perhaps the most outstanding of the whitetail buck's peculiar traits is his habit of breaking away from the confusion of a drive and hiding out near an open field, where nobody will look for a deer; then, when the tumult has passed, he sneaks back to his old hiding place. Another, and equally disconcerting trick, is for a buck to stay put until the drive is past or to pick his way carefully around the end of the drive, going back into cover around the end man.

Quite by accident I killed a small buck that had pulled this same trick on our gang for three successive days. This deer bedded-down on a laurel-topped ridge near an old abandoned apple orchard. Our drive would start at the orchard and carry through along the ridge-top to meet the watchers posted at the end of the ridge. It was a short drive, not over a third of a mile long, and each morning we would jump this deer within a minute or two after the drive began. Yet no one would get a look at him after he jumped. We had covered every discernible runway leading off this little ridge but the ground was so dry and hard-packed it was impossible to pick up any tracks to indicate which way he had sneaked out.

After circling the entire ridge and finding no fresh sign, I decided to walk along the lip of a fairly high rock ledge, lying parallel to the ridge and about fifty yards below the crest. As this ledge averaged ten to fifteen feet high for the full length of the drive, we had neglected to put a stander anywhere below it, in the belief that no deer would jump this height unless hard-pressed. While I walked the ledge I saw nothing unusual in the way of new signs until I reached a little cleft in the rocks. Running down through this cleft were the unmistakable marks of sliding hoofs, and below, in the softer earth, were deep, new tracks, three sets in all. Each of the clean, sharp hoofprints pointed back toward the orchard.

Next morning we started the drive as before, but instead of taking my position as end man on the drive, I dropped down below the ledge. Soon the starting whistle sounded and the drive began. As I waited my imagination almost led me to believe I could hear the boys jump this deer again up in the laurel. Within a matter of minutes I heard bounding feet and the rattle of a loose rock. And there, headed directly toward me, was this foxy little buck who had given us the slip for three days running. Needless to say, we had him hanging from an old apple tree near camp before noon.

Jim Deren and I, along with another half-dozen hunters, were completely fooled by one old buck — outwitted, when I was certain that we had him trapped. This buck — and he was a big one, with a heavy, high rack of antlers — hung out just above the head-waters of the lake at R. H. Macy's summer camp in Burlingham. Each night he would cross the road about a quarter-mile below our camp, leaving a big set of widely spaced footprints in the sandy soil by the roadside. Jim and I waited near this crossing each evening for five successive days, until darkness sent us back to camp, but he never showed. Then each night after dinner we would walk down to the crossing and find another fresh line of his prints. Evidently he bedded-down at the head of a ravine, coming out only after dark, then returning by some other route — we never learned where.

In desperation we decided to try to drive him out to a stander, and geographically we had a fair setup. I knew that he favored the far side of the ravine for his bedding ground, for I discovered him one morning on a still-hunt. I had climbed steadily up the steep sides of the gully, rifle slung over my shoulder, pulling my way up with anything that came to hand — roots, saplings and outcropping rocks. As my head cleared the upper edge of the ravine, I looked directly at a huge buck lying on a little raised mound in a thick poplar stand. He looked me right in the face and with the meeting of eyes he was gone beyond the mound in a single leap. He had been following my noisy progress up the ravine wall but had decided to lie low until I appeared. After I had scouted the area I found two more beds back in the heavy growth, so I felt reasonably sure that this was his favored bedding place. Now this ravine formed the base of a short triangle bounded on the other two sides by the dirt road he used for a crossing and another dirt road which intersected this one about two hundred yards from the ravine. Within the limits of the triangle lay a heavy mass of cover — big hemlock and small jack pines, white birch, poplar and small hardwoods.

We planned, then, to post all the available men — seven in all — along the two sides of this triangle. I would try to jump the buck and move him out over his regular crossing. Accordingly, the boys took their places and I crossed the ravine far below, to work it up. Carefully I crept through, stopping many times to look over the area ahead, but I failed to see the buck in time for a shot. Yes, I jumped him, just a short distance from where I first had seen him. I took the track, following the deep prints easily in the damp leaves.

The deer crossed the head of the ravine, then sneaked back down the far side, heading directly for the crossing through the triangle. Hot on his track, I kept him moving directly toward the waiting standers, none of whom were more than two hundred yards away. Once in the triangle the going was heavier but I managed to keep to the trail. Then, just as I could see the open area of the road ahead the tracks veered sharply left, continued on for fifty yards, then swung back toward the ravine once more. This buck had sensed something wrong and had made a full half-circle, going straight back to his old stamping grounds across the ravine. Every man watching had heard him coming through; but only one, the end man in the far corner of the triangle, caught a flash of antlers as he leaped down the ravine sides to safety. Never again were we able to drive this buck out. He had learned enough in that one lesson, even though not a shot had been fired at him. So far as I know now this buck has died of old age — more power to him!

On snow, driving deer is pretty much simplified. Once a track is taken a man or two can keep the deer going until they pass the stands. If a buck manages to slip out past or between standers the hunters can take up a new watch farther along in the effort to head him off, leaving one man on the track. With snow covering the ground any group of hunters can easily work out their own approach to the driving problem.

There is yet another method of taking deer on snow which is a modification of both driving and still-hunting. It's not a method in

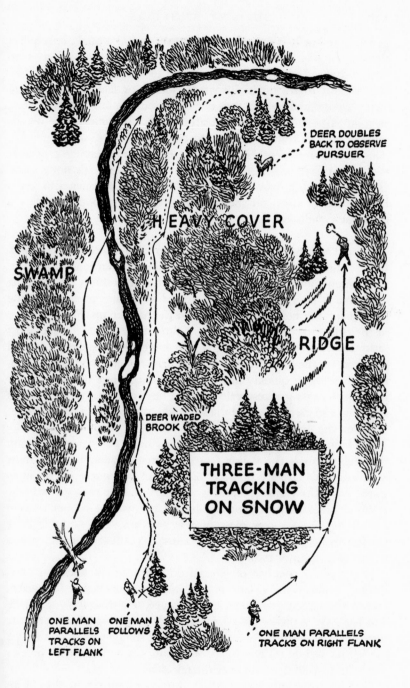

DEER DOUBLES BACK TO OBSERVE PURSUER

HEAVY COVER

SWAMP

RIDGE

DEER WADED BROOK

THREE-MAN TRACKING ON SNOW

ONE MAN PARALLELS TRACKS ON LEFT FLANK

ONE MAN FOLLOWS

ONE MAN PARALLELS TRACKS ON RIGHT FLANK

general use but it is one of the best ways to kill a buck. It requires
three men: one to take and follow the track and two others who
keep just ahead of the tracker and as far to the right and left as they
can be, still following his progress. Sooner or later the buck will
swing around and cross before one of the outside hunters. Any deer,
as soon as he is aware of being followed, will concentrate his attention on the tracker to the partial exclusion of other possible
danger. If the two other hunters have the same staying power as
the tracker they will in time get a shot at the deer. It's not a game
for greenhorns, however; but if three good woodsmen can get a
buck ahead of them on such a setup, the deer's doom is almost a
foregone conclusion.

In cold weather the big problem is to keep warm on the stand.
On the short still-drives the watchers rarely remain long enough to
become uncomfortably cold. If they do begin to shiver by the time
the drive is over, the usual practice of switching places with the
drivers for the next drive will warm them right up. For this type
of driving practice the regular still-hunting garments are most
satisfactory. Too much clothing will build up perspiration-soaked
garments on the drive; then when the driver changes off to standing
he chills through quickly in the damp clothes. Here the waterproof
parka proves its greatest value. It can be worn on the stand, then
rolled up and carried behind the suspender straps or in a game pocket
while on the drive.

For long watches, and if snow lies heavily on the ground, keeping
the feet warm is the major factor. If feet are comfortable, most
hunters can endure a little body discomfort, but when feet begin to
tingle the entire frame soon takes up the tune. The author finds that
a short sheepskin boot worn under a large pair of rubber-bottom
leather-top shoes solves most of this problem. The outfit is light
enough to be comfortable during a drive, yet warm enough for a
watch of an hour or two.

In the bitter weather of late fall in the northern zones or even
during Pennsylvania's late season, the best medicine for warm
feet is the twelve- or fourteen-inch laced felt shoe with stiff sole
and heel. Over this is pulled a pair of light four-buckle arctics or
overshoes. In dry, cold weather, the arctic should be the cloth type
for lighter weight. When soggy wet snow lies underfoot it's best to
wear the all-rubber arctic over the felt shoe.

Generally speaking, any clothing for deer hunting should not be so bulky as to impede quick movement. (One friend of mine piled on so many sweaters and jackets he couldn't get the rifle to his shoulder. And it was his misfortune not to discover this little but important detail until a buck came out to his stand. In the resulting confusion he did manage to get off one shot at the deer, but this bullet whistled quite harmlessly over the buck's head.) Garments of all wool are the best. Duofold underwear or two suits of under-garments, one of cotton next to the skin and heavy wool over this, will do more to keep a watcher warm than a heavy Mackinaw over shirts and shorts. Many of the alpaca-lined, water-repellent outer garments, both jackets and pants, which from time to time have been offered as armed forces surplus, are just the ticket for the deer drive. Light in weight, not bulky, they are just as warm as any garments of equal weight can be.

If a stander has tender ears and must wear ear muffs to ward off frostbite, let him punch holes through each one so as not to impede hearing. Many a bundled-up, ear-muffed stander has had a buck sneak up from behind, to crash away quite unharmed after he had all but walked over the watcher. In this connection the author be-lieves that of all the normal senses with which we are equipped, hearing is of the greatest value on a deer stand. Most often a deer will be heard coming long before it can be seen; if the hunter has trained ears he will be able to locate his deer's position almost as well as though he could see him. Good judgment in this sense of hearing will enable him to prepare for the coming shot. Best of all, to exercise the sense of hearing requires no conscious effort; but in-tense watching through heavy covers surrounding the stand, with the inevitable shifting of head and eyes in all directions, can be ex-tremely tiring. The trained hunter can learn to differentiate readily between the sound made by walking deer and the step of a hunter or the amblings of gray squirrels and partridge. A hunter can drive himself into a deep funk of excitement by listening to the rustlings of the forest creatures, until he learns to pick out the more distinc-tive noises made by moving deer. In any case, though, a full com-mand of all senses is vitally important to the watcher on a deer stand.

While driving deer may not appeal to every hunter, the cold fact remains that this is the most effective method of taking Eastern whitetails. Obviously, no man will achieve the same measure of satisfaction in killing a deer driven to him as will the still-hunter who outwits a whitetail buck by skill and woodcraft alone. The full glory of killing a driven buck will always be tempered in the hunter's mind by the fact that someone else had a large part in helping him to get his shot. Nevertheless, it's good fun. In no other phase of deer hunting do we encounter the same wealth of odd situations and humorous anecdotes emanating from the ranks of the deer-driving fraternity. Success in this method of taking deer requires a good fund of woodcraft to lay out the drive, a high degree of intestinal fortitude and patience to spend tense hours on a cold watch, and a thorough knowledge of firearms-handling to kill any buck driven to the stand.

6 / Hitting Your Buck

AFTER ALL, the primary consideration in deer hunting is to hit your buck. Weeks of anticipation, days of deliberation in choosing rifle, load and sights, plus plenty of shooting practice, all total zero if you fail to connect. Added to this is that sinking sensation in the pit of your stomach when your trophy vanishes in the timber, well under its own power.

Hitting your deer means not only planting a bullet somewhere between nose and tail; the shot must be planned to reach one of the vital areas, delivering such an explosive shock to nerves and muscle tissue that your buck will come crashing to the ground, either staying there for keeps or giving you an opportunity for a quick, final shot. Of course, not all shots into the vital area will immediately ground a deer. Heart-shot bucks will often run fifty, sixty, or even a hundred yards before calling quits, but recovery of these deer by the hunter is comparatively simple. They leave a heavy blood trail and in almost every instance are dead when they are reached.

Too many hunters are guilty of simply shooting "at" the deer. They seldom, if ever, make any conscious effort to drop their game at the first shot. Under some circumstances a snap shot at a rapidly moving target is all that the deer hunter gets, and if his mixture of luck and skill is in correct proportions, he'll bag his buck. We can't forget, though, that most shots like this are either graceful misses or the beginning of a long, hard trailing job, to end all too often with the unlucky hunter deep in a swamp or thicket several miles from his pals — and no deer.

There are just three portions of a deer's anatomy to reach with your bullet to bring about his quick demise: the neck, the chest and the spine. The head might also be included in these vulnerable areas, but no sportsman wants to risk ruining his trophy with a head shot.

Dividing these areas into their vital organs we find that the neck offers two good possibilities.

Any shot into the upper third of the deer's neck with a high power bullet of any expanding type is certain to break the neck vertebra and the spinal cord, producing instant death. This is without question the most effective shot that can be fired at a deer and is so decisive in result that this writer has yet to hear of a deer moving from its tracks after being hit in this area.

Still shooting at the neck, we find that a shot in the lower half of the neck, somewhere between the buck's jaw and shoulders, will succeed in severing either the windpipe or the jugular vein, or both. Such shots usually knock a buck down instantly and keep him down, because of the high degree of shock inflicted in this sensitive region. These lower neck shots seem to have much the same effect on deer as the quick removal of a head with ax has on the Thanksgiving turkey.

Some years ago I had a quick shot at a running deer, having time only to throw into an opening ahead of him, then snap off the shot just as his head appeared. He dropped at once, but almost as soon as he hit the ground he tried to get up. Staggering to his feet, he wobbled around crazily in small circles, finally dropping to the ground for good, with all four feet kicking and head thrashing from side to side. After a quick finishing shot through the neck, I made all haste to examine him for the location of the first bullet wound.

I found it directly behind the jaw, where it had passed through low down, completely cutting off the windpipe and large neck veins. This buck never at any time had moved more than twenty-five feet away from the spot where he first came to earth, and had completely bled out in a matter of a minute, more or less. That is the usual story with deer shot through the neck: instant death, or death within a matter of minutes.

Shots into or near the spinal column, too, have a quick stunning effect, and while not immediately fatal, they keep the deer definitely on the ground, permitting an easy finishing shot. Guard against hitting the spine far back in the neighborhood of the hindquarters. Any deer so hit will drop at once, but if you don't keep your eyes on him he'll drag himself away with his forefeet and may give you a few moments of anxiety before you can follow and finish him off. Such shots, we must admit, are far from humane in their effect on deer, but they certainly do produce results.

Ask deer-hunting friends where they try to hit a deer. Those who do indicate any definite point of aim, will probably say "through the shoulders." This is good, generally speaking, because it indicates that the shooter wants to reach the chest cavity with his bullet. Actually, if you did shoot a deer broadside through the *shoulders* you certainly wouldn't kill him quickly, unless the bullet went high enough to pierce the spine. The vital organs of the chest cavity, heart and lungs, lie much lower in the body than the shoulder blades. They lie on the ribs, directly between the points formed by the junction of the shoulder blades and the upper foreleg; so that if you are shooting directly at a buck broadside, your shot should land low enough almost to strike this joint, not more than six or seven inches above the buck's chest line.

A bullet striking the shoulder halfway between the back line and chest line will pass through the upper portion of the chest cavity, missing entirely the heart and lungs unless it be a very high velocity light-bullet type which expands rapidly on impact. A buck so hit with rifles of the medium-velocity heavy-bullet type can travel up to three miles before dropping from loss of blood, unless by lucky accident the shoulder blades are broken.

Standing deer offer no problem to an experienced rifleman and hunter. In his own words, "they're duck soup," yet many, many standing deer have escaped the fire of the red-capped Nimrod. It does seem odd that any buck standing for a shot within thirty yards of a hunter should ever escape being eaten; but it does happen year after year. There are many contributing causes, among them the hunter's own ignorance of where his shot should be directed. As a matter of record, standing broadside shots aren't too common, and some sportsmen will say that they *never* get a standing shot at a buck at all. Of this group, I can only say that they are poor woodsmen and, more than anything else, they should absorb enough woodcraft to enable them to see and hear their game before it spots them.

The broadside shot gives the hunter his choice of several marks — breaking the neck; cutting the jugular and windpipe, wrecking the heart and lungs; or breaking the buck's spine, at a high point through the shoulders. Any of these are easy kills on a broadside shot, because your bullet only has to penetrate three or four inches of flesh to reach its mark, and the job is done. Many times a hunter robs himself of a good broadside shot by shooting too quickly, before the deer has reached the right angle in his travel toward and past the stander. By plotting a buck's direction of movement, a stander

can pick his opening ahead of the buck and at just the right angle
to afford him the best shot.

I realize that this formula is a bit easier to talk about than to put
into actual practice under the excitement of your first glimpse of
an oncoming deer, but if your plan of action is worked out well beforehand it is much easier to put it into effect during those critical,
tense moments when game is first sighted.

Many bucks are killed as they approach a stander, giving a front
quartering shot which is sometimes tricky to make. Assuming that
the deer has stopped and is looking your way, you have two possibilities for a fatal hit. Again, if the range is short, your first choice
will be the neck, deadly from this head-on angle. The spot to pick
is the near edge of the white throat-patch, and in a line directly
under the eye, at once severing the neck veins and windpipe; and,
if the buck's head is erect, this will break his neck. Second choice is
low in the chest, exactly on the line where the shoulder meets the
neck, an almost certain heart shot. If it should miss the heart it will
clean house in the lung areas. If your buck's head is held low, this
neck-shoulder shot is your only chance, and this same shot should
be made if you feel that your holding may not be close enough to
make the neck shot.

The rear quartering shot is common with the still-hunter as he
approaches feeding deer, upwind and undetected; standers who discover that their buck has already sneaked past them get these shots
too, and they are quite easy to make. All that is necessary to down
a deer facing away from the shooter on this quarter-angle is to
judge the point of bullet entry well down in the side of the body
so that it will pass diagonally through the heart and lung cavity. The
shooter must try to picture the position of the buck's far shoulder
and direct his shot to pass through it or just beyond it. Stated
definitely, on a full-quarter rear shot this point will be halfway
between the point of the shoulder and the last rib. Neck shots from
this angle are rather difficult to make accurately, so they should be
passed up in favor of this shot through the back ribs.

Any shot directly from the rear, affording the hunter no view of
the target other than the hind quarters, is not feasible except with
a rifle of high penetration qualities carrying a heavy bullet. Such a
rifle is capable of penetrating completely through the paunch into
the chest cavity. Such shots cannot be recommended as at all certain,
but they have been made successfully on some occasions. However,
the chances of inflicting a painful, but not necessarily fatal, wound

from this angle are so high that no sportsmen will attempt it. Very often a deer standing at this angle to the hunter will turn his head and look back over his shoulder, offering a fine shot at the neck, which promptly dumps the deer.

If a shooter insists on taking a crack at a deer's hind quarters from this rear angle, then let him hold his shot low between the hind legs on the chance that it will travel through the paunch and diaphragm and still have enough punch left to blow up the chest cavity.

Deer hunting will afford shots at all angles from front and rear. The only point to keep in mind in all of these angle shots is to picture the path of the bullet as it travels through, adjusting its entry so that it will emerge or stop near the opposite shoulder.

One of the trickiest shots a deer hunter can get is the direct head-on shot, with the buck facing directly toward the line of fire. If the range is close enough and the deer holds his head erect, looking at the hunter, the best shot will be through the white throat-patch or just below it, giving us our favorite neck shot. But there is one factor to consider in this matter of a buck's holding his head erect and high enough for the shooter to make the frontal throat shot. During the hunting season, in most states, the larger and more mature bucks carry necks heavily swollen and enlarged, a characteristic of the "rutting" season. Any such buck will be unable to raise his head high because of this swollen neck, so that very little of the neck will be seen by the shooter, directly from the front at least.

The only alternative shot from this angle is straight into the middle of the chest, just above the brisket, actually hitting the junction of neck and shoulders, just between the points of the shoulders which are clearly visible from the front. We say that this shot is tricky because a deviation of two inches to the right, to the left, or below this point will result in a fluke hit — and here's why: the forward point of the deer's chest cavity is well protected with closely spaced ribs, well knit together at their lower points with tough cartilage. If the bullet strikes too low, it will glance down and off this cartilage or the rib ends, never entering the chest area at all and creating only a "crease."

On the other hand, if your bullet lands high enough but is not well-centered in the chest, it will glance off these same ribs to either right or left, and slide between the ribs and shoulder blades; doing at most no more damage than breaking the shoulder. And don't forget that your buck can travel almost as fast on three legs as he can on four. This shot, to be fatal, must be closely held, entering above the point of the brisket, where it will tear through and expand in the middle of the heart and lungs, doing a quick, thorough job of execution.

In all these foregoing explanations, we're assuming that the shooter is on the same ground level as the deer, but there are other angles of fire that the deer hunter will encounter, so let's be prepared.

There is the buck that walks out on a high cliff of rocks or the upper edge of a steep ravine well above the shooter; or the shot may have to be taken in the reverse position, with the point of fire well above the game. This is particularly true of deer hunters who like to watch runways during a drive from a seat high up in a tree. Occasionally the angle of fire is directly down, as will happen when the deer elects to walk right under your tree seat.

Everything that we have discussed so far in regard to angles of fire and vital areas still goes for these above- and below-level angles. The difference here is that the hunter's view of the deer is somewhat foreshortened, dependent directly upon the steepness of the angle. Broadside shots from below should be held still lower than before; the bullet aimed to enter the top of the foreleg, where it will range up into the vital organs. The above-angle is handled in much the same way, except that the bullet should strike about halfway up the deer's side.

One other point on these above-angle shots: the tree hunter and the hunter standing on a high cliff or ledge above his deer should never attempt a shoulder shot if the angle of fire is steeper than sixty degrees to the horizontal. There is a high degree of probability that when the bullet strikes the wide, tough shoulder blade it will glance to the right, left or low, making a mere flesh wound which won't even slow a deer down. The best *body* shot from these steep angles is the spine, just between the upper shoulder blades, not forgetting that the neck shot will be the best of all from above.

Head-on shots from below should be aimed directly at the center of the brisket or the white throat-patch; from above, drive your bullet directly between the withers (top of the shoulder blades) breaking the spine. Direct rear shots from above should strike this same point between the shoulders, and from below should strike the sternum, the junction of the last ribs, by being fired between the hind legs. This shot will range forward and up into the chest.

Slight changes in angle of fire will necessitate slightly different

VITAL
AREA

VITAL
SHOTS

LINES OF BULLET PENETRATION

holds on the body, but the single thought that should be carried is
to direct your shot to pass through the deer, to emerge somewhere
in the area of the far, or opposite shoulder. Angle shots from the
rear should emerge ahead of the shoulder; from the front, behind
the shoulder.

It is almost impossible to overemphasize to the novice deer hunter
the importance of the white throat-patch as a target. It stands out
very clearly against the gray-brown body-color of a deer, and is
large enough to make a good target if the rifleman is capable of
holding his shots within a six-inch circle at fifty yards.

My first buck dropped to a shot through this white throat-patch,
and since that day this white target has added a goodly number of
clean kills to the record. A year or two after this initial experience,
one of my regular fishing partners coaxed me to take him along on
a deer-hunting trip and start him off right on "big game" hunting.
Incidentally this chap was a fine wingshot and very handy with a
rifle, but he had never hunted deer.

As a matter of course, he wanted complete information on where
to hit his buck when the chance came. Now, frankly, my experience
at that time was limited to neck shots, so I advised the throat-patch
shot, never considering that such a shot might not be offered.

We still-hunted until late afternoon without sighting a deer, so
just before sundown I suggested a stand for him to take, near the
junction of two runways leading from a peat swamp. Not more
than a quarter hour later his rifle cracked — just once. Then a
moment later there was a steady roar of rifle fire from the same
spot. I waited a bit, then rushed over to see what was going on.

I came upon him standing in a grove of birches, pale and shaking,
totally incoherent, and pointing to the ground some yards away
where a nice six-pointer lay stretched out. Not much use talking
to him now, I thought, so I went over to look at his buck. Sure
enough, his first shot had slid through that white throat patch, breaking the neck. But, tragically enough, he had dumped the rest of the
gunload into the deer's belly as it lay dead in the ferns. He explained
later that the buck had made one kick after he dropped, so he
thought it would be a good idea to make sure of him. I was tickled
that he'd dropped this deer so neatly, but the unpleasant part of the
deal was left to me: dressing out a buck after five .303 Savage bullets
had riddled his paunch.

The point to be emphasized is that this chap, though a rank
greenhorn in the deer woods, had enough presence of mind and

ability with the rifle to follow instructions to the letter, killing his first buck with his first shot. Just what would have happened had the buck presented a different shot I don't know, but it serves to illustrate just how vulnerable this throat target is.

A great many experienced deer hunters will say that as a rule in deer hunting there isn't a chance of much choice in shots. To this I must agree. All deer, bucks in particular, take every possible advantage of cover and seldom offer a full view of themselves to the hunter. During daylight hours they stay out of the open places and when they are moving to or from the feeding grounds they sneak through second-growth stuff, thickets and heavy timber. They invariably skirt the edges of clearings and open glades, rather than risk showing themselves in the open. Driven deer will often dash across these small clearings and wood roads, but always at such speed that even a fair shot is virtually impossible.

Briefly, then, the whitetail hunter can't expect to get a full view of his game, much less an open shot. He must take his shots as they come, whether it's only a head peeking out from a clump of laurel or a few patches of hair showing through a screen of scrub oak or birch. He must study deer anatomy so thoroughly that he can estimate accurately just where the vital spots lie, even if he sees only a head or a hindquarter. Deer are adept at sneaking past the stander or still-hunter; one moment he'll see head, neck and shoulder through the trees and brush and at the next step his shot is gone. But he can judge from this one quick glance just what direction the deer's next move will take him. He must then align his sights at the right elevation, just where the deer will next offer a shot, and he must be ready to touch off his trigger. A slowly moving deer offers a constantly changing target — first the head and neck will be seen, then this area moves out of sight and the shoulder comes through. Decisions to shoot must be made quickly, or your chance is gone, and if you know what spot to hit, most of the battle is won.

Driven deer often spot or scent a stander ahead of them, long before this hunter sees or hears them. They're cautious and suspicious by nature — more so when the woods are full of man-smell — and they watch a wide area ahead of them as they move before the drivers, testing the wind very carefully. If they scent or sight a stander ahead they're caught between two fires. Usually, they elect to sneak around the stander, trying to escape notice and taking advantage of all cover.

On a deer drive one day up in the Oakland Valley region, my stand lay on the edge of a wide area of scrubby laurel, none of it over three feet high. As the drive approached my stand I thought I heard a deer walking through the big timber to my right, skirting the edge of the laurel. A few minutes passed without any perceptible action, until I chanced to notice a slight movement directly before me and about thirty yards off in the laurel.

For a few seconds I couldn't make it out, but it finally dawned in my mind that it was a deer's back just over the tops of the laurel scrub. This deer was so low to the ground that he must have actually been crawling. I couldn't see the head at all and could only catch an occasional glimpse of the back, but a sixth sense told me it was a buck.

I jumped up quickly to the top of my rock stand and from there I could see movements in the laurel, but no deer. I decided that if it were a buck I would have only a quick shot as he broke from the edge of the laurel into the timber again, so I lined the sights on the far edge of the laurel in the general direction of the deer's travel. My first view of him was a small head, neatly crowned with slender antlers, poking around the edge of the laurel. I shifted sights to the throat-patch and squeezed off the shot, then there was a heavy silence.

After the drive came through, I walked over to the edge of the scrub to look him over — a fat little six-pointer, victim of his own "last-look" curiosity. It was only by the merest chance that I discovered this deer at all, for he was almost past my stand before I had so much as a glimpse. Had he kept on going to the edge of the timber, without pausing to look me over, he would still be safe as far as I am concerned.

Hitting the deer in this instance meant being ready for his first appearance. Sights were aligned; all but the last few ounces of pressure were on the trigger, and getting off the shot meant only a slight shift in holding and a quick squeeze.

Rifle sights, particularly those of the open type, have a nasty habit of blending into the shadows surrounding the target. Flickering shadows and changing backgrounds make the front sight hard to see. The tendency here is to hold the front sight high above the rear notch — for easier visibility — causing a high shot over the target. To overcome this, the front sight should be quickly aligned in the rear notch, against a good background — offered perhaps by a tree trunk, a rock, or a snow patch. This elevation should be held

ONE-EYE SIGHTING

TWO-EYE SIGHTING

by pressing the cheek firmly against the comb of the stock. Then the sights can be swung on the target rapidly and smoothly and the shot released as soon as the front sight comes to rest on your buck.

Of greatest value to the deer hunter, whether his shooting be at moving or standing deer, is the well-fixed habit of shooting with both eyes open. Any rifle shooter using iron sights at once loses two vital essentials of good hunting marksmanship if he closes the "off eye" in sighting. In the first place, he can see only half as well with one eye as with two; closing one eye promptly robs him of the benefits of binocular vision. As everyone knows, a one-eyed man has trouble with perspective; precise judgment of distance is based entirely on the use of two eyes. The brain then, by rapid triangulation coupled with experience, calculates the distance from the eye to the object within view. This point is not of vital importance in deer hunting but it helps to explain why two-eye shooters are faster, more accurate marksmen in the hunting field.

More important to the deer hunter, particularly he who uses the open rear sight, is the fact that with the nonsighting eye closed all vision of target and terrain is blotted out by the outlines of the rear sight and the weapon. His view is confined to the area above the sights, but he sees nothing behind them. And the man using the buckhorn or deep-notch "Rocky Mountain sight" will find a large part of his deer completely obscured by the high side ears of the sight. With a deer moving in heavy cover a hunter needs both eyes to follow the movement and find an opening to slip his bullet through. The use of two eyes permits a man to cheek his rifle stock, align the sights with his shooting eye and still retain a clear view of target and terrain up to the moment that his chance for a shot appears.

One-eye hunters repeatedly raise and lower their rifles when a buck is passing through thick stuff. Here the shooting eye is overworked — it must pick out an opening for the shot first, then align the sights for the trigger squeeze. This takes time, perhaps only an instant, but many opportunities have been lost even in tiny instants. I suspect also that many of the bullets slammed into tree trunks every season would have found a better target if the hunter had been using two eyes for his shooting.

On deer drives most shots will be had at walking, trotting, or running deer. It's always to the hunter's advantage, of course, to have a standing shot, but few hunters ever try to make a moving deer stop for a second or two and so give them a better chance to plant the bullet where it will do the best job. There isn't much chance of stopping a frightened buck or a buck that has seen the stander, but if he doesn't seem to be alarmed and hasn't located the hunter, he can usually be stopped by a low whistle.

With most of us, though, the heart pounds too loudly and the mouth is too dry to allow even a faint whistle when a buck is nearing the stand. Often a slight movement, such as shifting a foot in the dry leaves, will stop a deer long enough for a quick standing shot. In any case the hunter should be well set and ready to touch off his shot before he decides to go about stopping his deer. Finally, of course, the best method of stopping your buck is with a well-directed shot.

The hunter who shoots at hard-running deer should be thoroughly familiar with his rifle before he even attempts it. This kind of shooting in normal deer cover is pointing rather than aiming, for the sights are never seen clearly, if at all, by the shooter. Any man who can be called a consistent shot on running deer has developed a smooth technique of so cheeking his rifle stock that he knows instinctively his sights are properly lined up without hesitating to check. For in running deer shooting, more than any one other field of sport, "he who hesitates is lost."

If we can state that there is any regular procedure of shooting at a running deer this is it: to swing the rifle with the deer's directional flight, finding an opening, if possible, ahead of the deer and when he appears there, letting him have it. The swing must be just like swinging a shotgun, smooth and steady, with the eyes watching the deer rather than the sights.

Such shooting is tricky to the nth degree and requires a highly developed skill with the rifle, produced by much handling of that particular weapon. Consciously leading a deer with the rifle, much as a bird shooter leads a grouse, is not necessary. The follow-through of the forward swing is enough, if the shot is fired when the eye signals that the sights are on the target.

Vital hits are hard to make on running deer, but it will help if the sights are kept low on the target and well ahead. I like to swing the rifle under the deer's forelegs, forward then, under the neck, and fire at this instant. This will always place the bullet somewhere in the neck or shoulder region and often grounds the deer at once.

Bounding or jumping bucks are something else again. To connect with these acrobats everything we have said in regard to running deer applies, except that some effort must be made to time the jumps and the shot should be released when the deer's feet hit the ground. The hunter has to estimate instantly just about where the deer is going to land on his next jump or two, throw his sights to this spot, holding well down toward ground level. Then as soon as those flying hoofs touch earth the bullet must be on its way. This low holding of sights is essential in this kind of shooting, for the deer's body is low to the ground in the middle of his spring. Misses at bounding deer invariably are high shots, as a matter of record, sometimes twelve or fourteen feet above the ground. A high average on bounding deer is one hit for every three shots, proof in itself that this type of work on deer requires the smoothest of gun handling, the best muscular co-ordination and keenest judgment in making quick decisions.

Not too much can be said for the hunter who shoots at "flags." These straightaway shots at running deer rarely produce a fatal hit except by pure luck, and in most cases the shooter can't tell whether his target is buck or doe, for the head is pretty well hidden from view. "Flag shooting" is excusable if a hit has already been scored on a buck and he is trying to make good his escape, but under other circumstances — never.

After your deer has dropped to your shot, whether well placed or not, it's the proper part of good sportsmanship to finish him off as quickly as possible. Some few of the old-time hunters will let a badly crippled deer linger in death, on the theory that the deer will bleed out better. This is not only disgusting, but heartlessly criminal in the extreme, and only serves to satisfy a sadistic urge that is planted in the black souls of a few gunners. Finish your buck — from a safe distance, bear in mind — with a single shot through the middle of the neck at the halfway point between jaw and shoulder. Better work around your buck and make this shot from an angle above the neck as he lies stretched out. Then the bullet will at once sever the jugular veins and arteries, bleeding the carcass well, and break the spinal cord, terminating the animal's agonies promptly. And don't worry about a bullet hole through the neck spoiling your trophy. The taxidermist can easily sew up such holes so that they won't be noticed.

Strangely enough, many deer hunters seem to feel that the traditional *coup de grâce* should be made with a knife. To this end we find that the less experienced grade of hunter carries a huge bowie-type knife — presumably for the above purpose of finishing off his buck. For my part, though I have killed many deer, I have yet to puncture a new buckskin with the knife until I prepare to dress the deer.

Some tragedies and more near tragedies have occurred — not to mention loss of deer — through this uncontrollable urge to use the knife. Hunters who should know better have been known to lay down their rifles, unsheath their knives and walk over to a wounded or dying deer. Sometimes the first prick of the blade brings a buck to sudden and alarming life, either to battle it out with the hardy soul or to escape to the nearest thicket if the knife wielder be of the more timid type.

My single experience in this connection took place during the season of 1938. I had walked up to a huge buck, feeding on the far side of a little knoll. My first glimpse of him showed just the tips of his antlers above the scrubby white birch. Either he heard my footsteps or sensed me, right at that moment. Raising that heavy rack for a better look, he offered me a clean, clear open shot at his throat. I was ready. At the shot he thumped heavily to the ground, as motionless as death itself. Confidently, for I knew my bullet had centered that white throat-patch, I approached him. His sturdy forelegs were stretched forward, cradling that massively crowned head. Eyelids were drooping in death and blood welled slowly from his nostrils. Fascinated, both by the heavy body and the magnificence of the antlers of this, my then biggest buck, I found myself standing almost over him. Suddenly I was aware that he was not yet dead. The flanks heaved gently, a wisp of steam flowed from the crimsoned muzzle. Hastily, I snicked back my bolt to reload for the finishing neck shot, for feeling certain that he would never move again, I had failed to eject the fired case and close the bolt on a new round.

With the click of the bolt the buck was instantly on his feet, sweeping those sharp hoofs and heavily tined antlers around and almost under my rifle muzzle. There was no semblance of attack, rather he wheeled as he left the ground, vainly trying to gain shelter in the birch clump behind. At his second leap my bullet smashed through ribs and chest, crashing him to the ground, this time for keeps.

This buck had definitely been hit neatly through the neck. But his head had been cocked around a bit on a quartering angle and the bullet had managed to sneak through without severing the neck vertebrae. Of course, all of the neck veins had been cleanly cut, and he would undoubtedly have expired on the spot if I had not alarmed him by my too close approach.

My imagination is just sufficiently vivid to paint for me a grim picture of the scene should I have attempted to stick this buck. He weighed, cleanly hog-dressed and on tested scales, a full 196 pounds. His antlers were of heavy beam, with a 23-inch spread carrying 10 perfect points. Tangle with such a buck with only a knife in my hand? No, thank you. I will continue to finish my deer off with the rifle.

Deer undergo a wide variety of reactions after being hit in a vital area. Spine and neck shots, of course, ground a deer at once, whether or not the buck is standing or running when hit. But many deer vitally hit will continue in their flight for varying distances up to a hundred or more yards before dropping. There is a difference, too, in reaction to a shot through the heart or lungs, dependent on the deer's activity at the time of impact.

A standing deer that has not been alarmed, unsuspicious of the presence of possible danger, goes down at once if hit anywhere in the body area. If the bullet finds the right area (lungs or heart) the betting is ten to one that he won't again reach his feet. The coming of the bullet has been a complete surprise and a terrific shock to a quiet nervous system, so much so that muscles won't react to the brain message.

Running deer, or deer that are alarmed, will often keep right on going, though their hearts and lungs may be shot to pieces. They are frightened: their nervous and muscular reactions are at such a pitch that the shock of the bullet doesn't have such a stunning effect. These deer, so hit, will run until the chest cavity fills up with blood, stopping lung and heart action until at last they can stand up no longer. They literally suffocate, rather than die from loss of blood or shock.

Modern science indicates that there is an additional factor in this connection. It is well known that among the higher mammals the adrenal glands immediately send into the bloodstream their charge of adrenalin as soon as fright, anger, or alarm stimulates them. It is this quick spurt of adrenalin that in many cases keeps that heart-shot buck on his feet until death overtakes him.

Only a couple of years ago I made an incoming quartering shot at a small buck, hitting him just at the junction of neck and shoulder with a bullet having a high degree of striking energy. The buck was

The hunter poses in classic Eastern deer cover. If that old coat is canvas, he might be better advised to wear wool the next time—it makes less noise on the brush.

The deer hunter seldom sees his game this clearly....

More likely he will glimpse his trophy through brush, often more dense than that partially camouflaging this sleek six-pointer.

The experienced whitetail hunter would spot the six-pointer and would seldom expect to see him as exposed as the little spike buck.

More and more women have taken up the sport. Here an eight-pointer has fallen to the wiles of one of these ladies.

More and more deer hunters are mounting 'scope sights on their deer rifles. This hunter has mounted one on his lever-action Savage. (Note the tang safety on this rifle, a useful and fairly recent departure from the old lever-blocking safety.) Most deer hunters in the Eastern woods use 'scopes of low magnification (2 to 2.5X) to provide the widest possible field of view—useful when the flags fly.

SAVAGE MODEL 99.
COURTESY OF SAVAGE ARMS.

WINCHESTER MODEL 94 CARBINE.
COURTESY OF WINCHESTER WESTERN.

MARLIN MODEL 336.
COURTESY OF MARLIN ARMS.

MARLIN MODEL 444.
COURTESY OF MARLIN ARMS.

WINCHESTER MODEL 88.
COURTESY OF WINCHESTER WESTERN.

Survivors of a grand tradition in lever-action deer rifles. Missing is the Winchester Model 71, .348 no longer manufactured but often seen in the deer woods. The Model 99 Savage, the Model 94 Winchester carbine, and the fine 336 Marlin are all rifles with notable, long-time reputations in the deer woods. The Savage and Marlin lever-action rifles are also available in carbine-length barrels.

REMINGTON MODEL 81.
COURTESY OF REMINGTON ARMS CO., INC.

REMINGTON MODEL 742.
COURTESY OF REMINGTON ARMS CO., INC.

WINCHESTER MODEL 100.
COURTESY OF WINCHESTER WESTERN.

BROWNING AUTOMATIC RIFLE.
COURTESY OF BROWNING ARMS CO.

Remington and Winchester now produce sleek autoloading rifles and carbines—svelte and trim compared to the old, once-popular Model 81 Remington Auto. Browning, long known for its reliable autoloading shotgun, offers a fine rifle which, like its rivals, is available in several good deer cartridges.

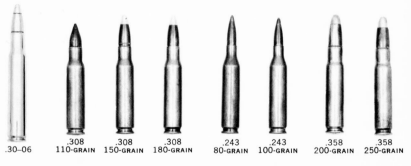

| .30–06 | .308 110-GRAIN | .308 150-GRAIN | .308 180-GRAIN | .243 80-GRAIN | .243 100-GRAIN | .358 200-GRAIN | .358 250-GRAIN |

This picture shows three fairly recent Winchester loads excellent for deer, with .30–06—on left—for comparison. The .358 Win., for which Winchester does not presently manufacture a rifle, did not catch on with deer hunters, yet it is an excelllent load and ideal for brush shooting. It is shown loaded with Winchester's Silver Tip bullet, 200-grain (left) and 250-grain (right).

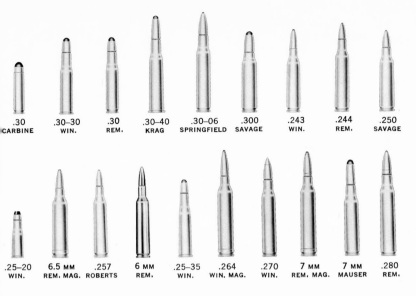

.30 CARBINE	.30–30 WIN.	.30 REM.	.30–40 KRAG	.30–06 SPRINGFIELD	.300 SAVAGE	.243 WIN.	.244 REM.	.250 SAVAGE

.25–20 WIN.	6.5 MM REM. MAG.	.257 ROBERTS	6 MM REM.	.25–35 WIN.	.264 WIN. MAG.	.270 WIN.	7 MM REM. MAG.	7 MM MAUSER	.280 REM.

Deer cartridges, old and new, from Remington. Note the scalloped soft points. These are Remington's time-tried Core Lokt loads, whose reliable mushrooming continues to make performance history. Such cartridges as the .264 Win. and the 7mm Rem. Magnum are not needed in the Eastern woods, where ranges are short, but are useful where the whitetail inhabits open, mountainous country that offers long-range chances.

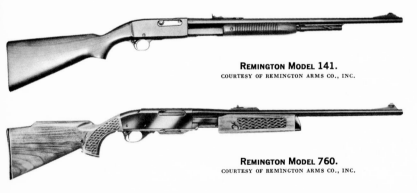

REMINGTON MODEL 141.
COURTESY OF REMINGTON ARMS CO., INC.

REMINGTON MODEL 760.
COURTESY OF REMINGTON ARMS CO., INC.

Only Remington now makes a slide-, or pump-, action rifle chambering big game loads. The old Model 141 (and the earlier but similar Model 14) made a great name for itself on deer in the still-useful .35 Rem. load. The Model 760 will handle such high-intensity loads as the .30–06, .270, and .308. Like its famous predecessor, the 760 comes also in carbine-length barrel.

Special archery seasons on deer in many states have increased the number of bow hunters. Fred Bear, Herter's, and other firms produce fine archery equipment. Here are some offerings from Browning: bow quiver, camouflaged thigh quiver, hunting bow (Cobra), arrows with fiberglass and wood shafts in various hunting broadheads.

Western archers get more open shots, but their chances are longer, too.

Does and fawns. Digging for sweet ferns?

The whitetail does occur in mountainous country in the West, where open, long-range shooting brings the high-velocity loads and the bolt-action rifle into their own.

The whitetail jumped while taking a drink on the edge of the lake and is heading into typical Eastern cover, where shots are fast and usually close.

Deer of the Southwestern brush country. The bucks dress out smaller than those from Michigan or Maine or Ontario, but they sport some surprisingly large antlers. Here in the foreground are typical Texas or Arizona bucks; the six-pointer has rather unusual "straight-up" antlers.

Jim Rikhoff, public relations director of Olin Mathieson, runs a cleaning cloth (Hoppe's No. 9?) through his Model 88 Winchester. The stove is typical of many to be found in such peeled-log deer hunting camps.

Two successful hunters carrying out their buck the hard way. But some hunters just don't like to scuff the hair by dragging out their deer. Snow helps.

running before a drive at the time of the bullet's impact, but he showed no ill effect; rather he increased speed. Thinking that I might have made a miss or a "fluke" hit, I swung on him again as he passed below me, luckily breaking his neck.

When I opened up the chest cavity for closer examination, the heart, intact, rolled out on the ground, completely cut off from veins and arteries, the result of the first shot. Further examination showed that the bullet had not come out, proving that this small buck had taken the full blow of twenty-five hundred foot-pounds of muzzle energy at a distance of thirty yards and had not even flinched! This deer, although not shot at before coming to me, had been thoroughly scared by drivers and standers and must have been under a high degree of tension.

Paunch-shot deer — that is, deer that have been shot through the body anywhere behind the diaphragm — usually are a problem in trailing for the hunter. Yet more deer are hit through the stomach region each year than are shot in any other body area, and a great many of these deer are lost. Deer rifles using cartridges of medium power and medium velocity don't deliver enough shock to put a deer down with a paunch shot.

It is true that high-velocity cartridges will often deliver the necessary shock to the animal to put it down for the count when struck far back, but we can't depend on it. Try always to keep your bullet well ahead of the stomach region if you really want to hang up some venison. Any deer shot in this stomach area leaves a very thin blood trail and after a short time the holes will close up, cutting off even that small amount of blood, so that there will be little chance of recovering that particular buck.

Trailing wounded deer brings up new problems under present hunting conditions. The advice of experienced hunters of the old days of deer hunting — still good advice — was to sit down for a half hour and have yourself a few pipes of tobacco, giving the deer a chance to lie down and stiffen up before taking up the trail. In wilderness country no better advice could be given. But today the great majority of our seasonal take of deer is killed in areas heavily populated with hunters.

Most of these hunters, unhappily, are all too ready and willing to claim wounded deer and there doesn't seem to be much that can be done about it. It is remarkable how many hunters will make a beeline for a spot where a shot or two has just been fired, on the off-chance that a wounded deer will run into them, either dropping dead at their feet or offering an easy opportunity for a finishing shot. Let me add, too, that sportsmanship seems to have little effect in these areas of heavy hunting, possession being *ten* points of the law. Many unpleasant scenes have been the result of this wounded-deer problem. The best advice is to follow your deer at once, under these conditions, and finish it off as soon as possible. Better than this, make your hit a clean one, dropping your deer for good, and the trailing worry will be over. If you are sure that your bullet has reached a vital spot then a quick follow-up is in order, for your deer won't go too far. Then too, as long as your deer is in sight, keep throwing lead at him; when he goes down, keep him down, if it means emptying your gun and reloading. No one dislikes to see a fine game animal mutilated by many expanding bullets more than does this writer, but all too often it is the only means of saving your deer.

When you are not sure just where your shot has landed even though you have scored, you can find some good information in the blood trail left by your wounded buck. Look for bloodstains on trees, brush and saplings along the path your deer has taken. From the height of these above the ground you can estimate how high or low your game is hit. Examine the color of the fresh blood and its quantity. If it's very bright red and plentiful your bullet has severed some large arteries and quick death will come to your buck. Further indication of large artery hits is indicated by blood squirting out and away from the deer's path to a distance of several feet.

When these signs are abundant, then it is in order to follow your deer at once, though he will probably be dead by the time you overtake him. Small quantities of dark blood found in the trail, with no evidence of artery squirts, are almost certain evidence that your deer is lightly hit, or paunched. In this case it's the better part of discretion to sit down for that hour or more, then take up the trail in the hope that some other hunter has not been ahead of you.

As an additional point: be most reluctant to credit yourself with a miss when your buck runs off after your shot. Often a deer will show little sign of being hit, particularly if the deer was running at the time. Old-timers will state with conviction that a buck always drops his tail when hit, but I am not yet convinced of this. I have had many reports to the contrary on just this point in my years of deer hunting.

Normally a deer will begin to bleed within a dozen yards of the spot where he was hit. However, a shot far back, even though the bullet may have ranged forward into the chest cavity, may not cause heavy bleeding within fifty or seventy-five yards. If your buck runs off, apparently unharmed, after your shot has been made, don't begin to run after him. And strangely enough this often happens when a new hunter shoots at his first buck.

The thing to do is to stand quite still and try to pick out the spot where your deer happened to be when your rifle cracked. Take off your cap and drop it on the ground on the spot where you were standing when you began to shoot. You may later want to know this. Then you can begin to look for signs of a hit.

Perhaps the most tangible evidence of a hit on a deer, other than blood, is a tiny tuft of deer-hair lying on the ground near the scene of action. I believe that it is virtually impossible to hit a deer in any portion of its anatomy without cutting off a bit of hair. Invariably you'll find the hair before you come across blood. Unless a rapidly expanding bullet rips right through heavy arteries a running deer will not bleed for its first few jumps. In any case be certain to spend all the time that you need to be thoroughly convinced that you did, after all, make a miss.

Back in the early '30's I jumped a buck off the top of a big beech ridge. I glimpsed antlers just as he cleared the shoulder of the ridge on his way down. In a few crashing leaps he had gained the top of the next adjoining ridge and was well on his way to be out of sight. I could do nothing but swing a quick snap shot just as he quartered over and down, flag flying and hoofs pounding.

Not willing to believe that I could have had such phenomenal luck as to hit him, I hunted on down the beech ridge as I had intended. I spent a quiet hour in working the end of this ridge, then I worked back. With nothing better to do I thought I might wander over to the little ridge where my buck had disappeared and look over his tracks.

I found tracks to be sure — great leaps that had carried him down the ridge slope and over the next, digging up the soft humus and scattering groundpine from his path. Just over the ridge where I had fired my lone shot I found a last bunch of four deep hoofprints — then, to my surprise, an upheaval of crisp leaves and sweet fern — changing quickly to a dragging path down the steep slope, and at its end — my buck. There he lay, head curled about his neck, with antlers tangled in a tiny hemlock.

The little .250 Savage bullet had caught him in the right flank, far back, as he quartered away and had passed through the diaphragm, blowing up entirely within the chest. The shock must have been terrific for he had not been able to regain his feet. How fortunate it was that I found him, for I was thoroughly convinced I had made a quite excusable miss!

By all means then, the deer hunter should follow up his shot with intelligent observation. Not all the misses that are told about each year are really misses. Many times, as a matter of record, deer have struggled off to die and rot in a near-by scrub-oak thicket or spruce swamp. Every effort should be made both for reasons of sportsmanship and good conservation to follow every shot, never leaving off until firmly convinced that your buck is still free to roam his range.

So far, everything we've said applies to the rifle shooter, but many deer hunters are not riflemen — either by choice, or through economic necessity, or because of unfavorable local or state legislation. Many deer are shot at and killed with buckshot each year and almost as many are wounded and *not* killed. Buckshot is a deadly load when it's properly handled and will kill any animal on the North American continent within the limits of its range. But that range is very short, because of the scattering tendency of the pattern. Therefore, the buckshot slinger should know not only when to shoot, but also when *not* to shoot.

I should place the outside limit of effect on deer with a charge of buckshot, regardless of size, at not over fifty yards, and clean kills cannot be expected at over thirty yards. Double o buckshot are large in size, but they scatter widely even at short range. The single o load is better balanced and holds a good killing pattern to a greater range, but even this range is not greater than fifty yards. It is quite true that now and then a deer will be dropped with buckshot at ranges of a hundred or more yards, but one buck doesn't make a summer. The buckshot shooter should make a series of pattern tests of his gun and load before going into the deer woods. Then and only then will he know how far to take his shot.

Whenever possible a load of buckshot should be directed at the neck of the deer. Shoulder shots will ground deer promptly at close range, but so will the neck shot. Under all circumstances, then, I would unreservedly suggest the neck shot only, in hunting with buckshot, wherever humanly possible.

A better load for the shotgun toter is the rifled slug — not the round single ball, which is hopelessly inaccurate. These slugs are fairly accurate at normal deer-hunting ranges. Because of slight in-accuracies in loads, as well as the coarse type of sights found on shot-guns, this rifled-slug load will be most effective aimed to strike low in the chest cavity, rather than to try for neck or spine shots. The terrific shock of these heavy-slug loads, with their high striking-energy, will do good work on whitetails if placed somewhere in that vital chest area.

With all kinds of rifles and every type of sights, many misses are made because of too much haste in shooting. Speed is necessary, but not undue haste, because this causes many high shots due to holding the front sight too high over the rear notch. This overshooting of deer is well marked in hunters who use the buckhorn, semi-buckhorn and other types of deep-notch rear sights. In his haste to shoot, the hunter quite unconsciously throws his front sight well above the notch where it can clearly be seen, and when his rifle cracks the bullet passes over his game's back.

The aperture rear sight eliminates this one cause of overshooting, because the front sight can only be held in one position relative to the rear sight: through the middle of the peep. It makes no practical difference in the size of the aperture; your front sight will be seen only through the center of the hole and the centers of all circles are the same regardless of their diameters.

Good telescope sights are a big help in hitting your deer in the vital spot. Their wide field and great light-gathering power makes it easy to pick out your buck under poor light conditions — not forgetting that antlers show right up on a buck's head when viewed through the 'scope.

An experienced 'scope shooter who knows his rifle can do re-markable work with the telescope in snap shooting at running deer at close range. The scope so magnifies the target at close ranges that the shooter needs only to catch the forequarters of the deer in the field of view of the scope to make a hit. After some practice with this kind of shooting a 'scope user can take running shots and score a high average of hits, merely by catching the moving deer some-where near the center of the field of vision.

It goes also quite without saying that a deer hunter equipped with the right kind of 'scope sight can not only pick the vital areas to hit, but can almost call his shot to a finger-breadth. Neck shots on stand-ing deer are simple with the 'scope and one of its best features is the user's ability to pick out openings through timber and brush to find his game and deliver the shot. Trees, saplings and other obstructions in the path of the bullet are clearly defined through the 'scope, to the extent that the shooter has little excuse for hitting intervening trees with his bullet.

At least three out of every ten hunters who take out deer licenses each year know where to hit their deer to kill it quickly and humanely. But unfortunately it is only one of the three who will be able to hit that spot at a fair shot. Practice with the rifle is what all deer hunters need, and this practice will eventually lead to bringing home the bacon in place of the usual alibis.

No deer hunter needs to be an expert shot, judged by the standards of the target shooter, but he must be able to lift his weapon, align the sights and squeeze off the shot, smoothly and effortlessly, in almost a single movement, without wasting any time in looking for sights or target after his rifle comes to shoulder. He must be able to hold *all* of his shots within an eight-inch circle at fifty yards in the standing, or offhand, position — and do it without regard to his own stance or the position of his target. Neither must he spend five to ten seconds in finding the target, but should be able to get all of these shots into the eight-inch bull within three seconds for each shot. *Any* shooter who can do this well with his high power will certainly never need to come out of the woods with a flock of excuses for his season's work.

Nor is this standard of excellence too difficult for any hunter of normal vision and average abilities. If anything, it is somewhat under par for a good rifleman.

Perhaps no weapon plays a more important part in the shooting skill of a game hunter than the .22 caliber rifle. Safe to use in settled communities, light in report and recoil, inexpensive to shoot and highly accurate, it gives the best opportunity for out-of-season deer-hunting practice.

No matter what type of high-power action the deer hunter uses in the woods, he can get its counterpart in a smaller .22 rifle — auto-loader, slide action, lever action or bolt action. Equipped with the same kind of sights as on his high-power, and with trigger-pull adjusted to equal weight and crispness, this rifle can almost duplicate the performance of his pet deer rifle. It will lack the weight, certainly, but this can be added to butt stock and forearm by the hunter himself or by any gunsmith, and then he has an arm for easy, cheap practice. It will have all the features he needs for intelligent rifle shooting except recoil, and that he is better off without.

This recoil plays an important part in a deer hunter's shooting, especially if the hunter spends little time in practice, because it is one of the major contributions to the flinching habit. No rifleman can ever expect to kill his deer if he is a flincher. The jerk that accompanies the flinch always throws the sights far off the mark before the shot is fired. A great deal can be done to prevent this flinching if the shooter will begin on a .22 caliber rifle, developing a good trigger squeeze. Then, after he has learned just how important a part good trigger squeeze plays in accurate shooting and "calling the shot," he'll apply it directly to the high-power rifle.

We might state here that no rifleshot will ever be worthy of the name unless he can call his shots with a certain degree of accuracy; otherwise he will never know whether or not his sights are correctly adjusted to the rifle. Calling the shot simply means the retaining of the image in the eye and mind as to just how the sights looked with reference to the target at the exact moment when recoil blotted out the shooter's vision of the target. Then from this retained picture the shooter will know just where the shot should have hit. If it hasn't, then the sights are not looking where the rifle shoots and should be adjusted to suit the line of fire.

Trigger-pulls on many rifles as they leave the factory are atrocious. They often pull as hard as eight to ten pounds, and will have creep, drag and rough places which can be felt distinctly as the trigger is squeezed. With such a trigger release, the shooter has no accurate idea as to just when his hammer or firing pin will fall, and if the pull is very hard, sights will be pulled off the mark, even though they might have been correctly aligned before the final squeeze.

All of these pulls can be greatly improved by proper stoning and should be reduced in weight to pull off at about five pounds. A clean, crisp trigger of five pounds' weight is just about ideal in the deer rifle; heavy enough to be absolutely safe against accidental discharge, yet light enough to permit quick, smoothly accurate shooting.

Even in this modern age there is no substitute for practice in developing a good degree of shooting skill. A fine rifle, carefully selected sights, and a good choice of ammunition will all fail to fill the license if the hunter does not possess a good sense of gun handling and the mechanics of shooting. Under the excitement and strain of sighting your buck all your book lessons will pass fleetingly from your mind. Instead there will remain only the burning urge to bring down that buck — a blinding urge that transcends reason. The hunter's entire being is concentrated on the game — he has no brain power left for coherent thought. At this critical period of the hunt only the mechanical training of body, hand and eye will support his desire to down his deer. The mechanics of shooting must be performed easily, smoothly, without conscious thought.

To this end, every sportsman who takes to the deer woods during the open seasons in our various states must find time and energy to develop a good grade of shooting skill. This he owes both to himself for the success of his hunt, and to the game for the sake of good sportsmanship.

Perhaps the best and most easily available shooting practice for whitetail hunting is hunting the gray squirrel — with a rifle, of course. Squirrel hunting develops both hunting technique and good rifle handling. Secondly, and available to perhaps more hunters, is woodchuck shooting. Either type of shooting is valuable in that it engenders a gradual familiarity with handling the rifle while under nervous tension. This is a most desirable result, never to be achieved by shooting at inanimate targets.

Smooth handling of the rifle comes only with much practice. Keep your rifle handy at home and whenever you think of it, pick it up, find some target in the room that can be seen distinctly and throw the sights on it just as quickly as you can. This kind of home practice, together with some field shooting with the .22 at informal targets — tin cans, bottles, blocks of wood floating down a fast-running stream — will do wonders for your gun handling and almost before you know it those sights will line up wherever you look just as soon as the rifle butt touches your shoulder.

Every group of deer hunters has its good shot; the instinctive type of shooter who never seems to take time to aim his rifle, but somehow or other always gets his buck with the least number of shots. Just remember that no man is born with this ability, and no matter how easily these instinctive shooters seem to hit their target, that ease is the result of years of steady practice and gun handling, not of favorable stars in their horoscope.

7 / Getting Out
Your Buck

LAST YEAR, the third day of the Catskill deer season ushered in a cold drizzly rain. The writer's hunting pals weren't enthusiastic about still-hunting or driving the heavily thatched ridges of the Shawangunk Mountain range which had been our stamping grounds for the first two days. In fact the best offer to hunt that anyone came up with was to take a runway stand — not too far from the road — and spend an hour or two waiting for a deer to come along. Accordingly, the boys moved off to favored spots atop the ridges to stick it out, for the morning at least.

I suspected that few if any deer would move at all in such weather, so on the off-chance that one of the gang would get a shot, I swung out of the heavy cover and took to the clearings for a half-mile. Then I cut back into the heavy white-birch stands lining the lee side of the ridge to begin a one-man drive, or still-hunt. The woods were soggy, every bush showered a deluge at my passage; all fresh signs had been erased by the night's rain. Nevertheless I worked my way slowly toward the spot presumably occupied by the last watcher, hoping to start something out in my wide sweep through the birches.

Two thirds of the way through, heavy crashings and waving tails signaled the rapid exit of three deer. They headed for a wire fence running diagonally toward our last stand. Moments later, four shots ripped through the drumming rain, not more than two hundred yards off. After waiting a bit, I moved over to the spot, to discover a strange hunter, highly excited, looking for some sign of his departed deer. Somehow or other this lad had managed to get into the middle of our party some short time after my gang had taken their stands, in just the right spot to intercept the deer. This, of course, was his good luck, but he said he'd failed to kill or even scratch the buck. I tried to learn from him whether he had scored a hit but he didn't know. I asked him in which direction the buck had gone and this he didn't know, also. Neither did he know that he had shot at a buck — he'd just shot at the biggest one of the three.

I decided then to look over the scene, knowing that it would be tough to find any blood still remaining in the downpour, but hoping to find some other indication of a hit. I asked the lad to take the same spot from which he had fired the shots and I would come through on the runway along the wire fence. Then he was to signal at whatever point the deer had reached when he began the barrage, at least as closely as he could tell. We carried this out; the tracks showed the deer moving along at a stiff trot, then at a point some yards beyond the area where my hunter friend believed the shots were fired, I found a fistful of hair and two sliding hoof prints, certain evidence that the deer was hit. He decided then that the bunch had scattered in three different directions — one had leaped the fence and gone over into a heavy slashing — the other two he knew not where. Nor was he sure which of the deer had been hit. He was inclined to follow the deer that had crossed over into the slashing, so off he went.

I continued on along the fence, picking up the track in the scuffed-up leaves. Fifty yards beyond, the fence abruptly ended at a wood road. Here in the middle of the road was a thin bloodstain, with more faint blood trail leading up to the ridge-top. I turned to look for my new acquaintance, but he was out of sight in the slashing. I carried on then, picking up the trail, which sloped up to heavy cover. I had moved perhaps thirty yards when, at a movement ahead, a small pair of antlers appeared, feebly hovering above the sodden leaves. Thirty yards off, the buck lay on his side, able to raise only his head.

Covering the deer, I yelled for brother hunter over in the slashing. The buck made one effort to rise, then fell back feebly. Within a moment or two the young hunter galloped over and, at my insistence, delivered the *coup de grâce* through the neck.

"Gee," he puffed, "what am I gonna do now? I never killed a deer before. I've got a knife but I don't know how to get his guts out. There's a certain way you're supposed to do it, isn't there?" I assured him that there was. He pulled out his knife and, strangely enough, it was a sensible-looking blade, about four inches long, with a good curved, skinning edge — but as dull as an Indian's stone tomahawk. I handed him my own knife and outlined the process. Together we had the deer dressed, skidded-out on the wet leaves and hung up to drain and cool out by his car within twenty minutes.

This year, and for many years to come, new hunters will take to the woods. Many will kill their first deer, many more will not. As this is written meat prices are the highest in history, making venison on the hoof a really valuable piece of property for the man taking it. Much of the good qualities of venison can be preserved by careful, intelligent handling of the carcass as soon as it comes into the hunter's possession. There are three important phases in this first handling of the carcass: quick, thorough bleeding; prompt removal of all the entrails and natural cooling of the body cavity by exposure to the air.

The whitetail deer has a thoroughly blood-filled body. It is the hunter's first obligation to remove as much of this blood as can be done under the circumstances of the kill. Nothing is more unpalatable than venison filled with settled blood. Sometimes it can't be avoided, but if the animal can be reached within a few minutes after death takes place there should be no excuse for blood-settled meat. That is, unless the carcass is riddled with expanding bullets.

The most efficient way to bleed a deer is to cut his throat or pierce his heart with your bullet, at your first shot. Most often we won't have too much choice in the matter, but neck and chest-cavity shots always will produce the neatly killed, well-drained buck.

When you make your first approach to a downed buck, stay out of reach until you can see his eyes. If they are glazed over, your buck is now venison; if the eyes are still bright or other signs of life are evident, place your finishing shot to both break the neck and sever the large neck veins. With modern quick-expanding bullets this is no problem. You may have to work around your dying buck for the right position to make this shot; but if you take your place directly above the deer's back (that is, if he were standing) you will be able to place a bullet which will enter the top of the neck, breaking the spinal column, then pass through the windpipe and neck to exit on the lower side, leaving a large exit hole for bleeding. This shot will instantly put an end to the buck's suffering and at the same time bleed him out. The expanding bullet will sever all the large lower neck arteries on its way through.

Sticking a deer is hardly to be recommended. In the first place it is a dangerous practice for the novice; the deer may not be quite dead and the prick of the knife will bring him quickly to life. Several hunters have been badly hurt by wounded deer. This author would never suggest that a hunter put down his rifle to tackle a deer with only a knife. Secondly, a good knowledge of the deer's anatomy is necessary for a hunter to stick a buck effectively. I have seen numerous deer carcasses badly incised throughout the chest region with little or no bleeding effect. At the same time many of these deer had the cape so badly cut that a taxidermist would have been hard put to make a presentable mount. Sticking a deer will do little good unless the large blood vessels connecting the heart are completely severed. To do this blindly, with the point of the knife buried deep in a deer's chest, requires more butchering skill than most hunters possess.

As a matter of fact the process of killing the deer normally will produce plenty of bleeding. Much better than sticking and certainly more effective, once your buck is quite dead, is to get the chest and abdominal cavity cleaned right out. Dressing-out the deer quickly will effect good blood drainage — as well as any other method, once the deer is killed.

To begin this unpleasant little task, the buck should be turned over on his back. Then, straddling the buck's chest and facing the rear, begin the cut by entering the point of the knife at the junction of the last ribs. As soon as the hide is pierced, turn the knife over so that the edge of the blade lies uppermost, then continue the cut straight back along the genitals to the straddle. The point of the knife should lie just under and ahead of the cut, as it moves back, to prevent cutting into paunch or intestines. Now cut a stick about an inch thick and twelve inches long. With this, wedge open the sides of the abdominal cut, giving access to the chest cavity. The paunch, liver and intestines can now be rolled back out of the way, exposing the diaphragm. This is a thin wall of tissue separating the chest and abdominal cavities and joined all the way around inside directly at the last ribs.

This should be cut through, close to the internal walls, all the way around to the backbone, on both sides. Now roll up your sleeves as far as they will go, reach up into the chest cavity and grasp the neck veins and windpipe just above heart and lungs, with one hand. Pull back on this handful as far as it will come; then with the other hand go in with the knife and cut the whole works off. This frees all the internal organs with the exception of the rectum.

Now with the sharp point of the knife cut entirely around the rectal opening, freeing the tube from the sides, until the rectum can be pulled out for a few inches. Tie this up tightly with a piece of string, rawhide or even a strip of narrow white-birch bark. Once tied, the rectal intestine is then pulled back through into the intestinal cavity and the whole set of "innards" can be dumped out by turning the deer over and picking up first his head, then his tail and shaking them out. This is all that is required to completely dress out a deer in the woods; no further cutting, hacking or chopping. The rectal tube is pulled out and tied before pulling back into the abdominal cavity simply to prevent droppings from lodging within the straddle opening, to contaminate the meat.

The only deviation from the foregoing method that might be required is if the hunter happens to be alone and with an exceptionally heavy deer to dress. Average to small-size deer can be dressed-out on the ground by a lone deer hunter, but really big deer might better be lifted off the ground to facilitate removal of the entrails. Of course, two men can dress-out the biggest buck without much difficulty, right on the spot.

If your deer is too much for you to handle alone on the ground, drag him over to a small sapling, about three or four inches at the butt — a white birch does very well. Fasten your rope or rawhide to his head by looping it around the antler butts. Make the abdominal incision, and tie off the rectal tube as outlined, before getting your buck up in the air. (It takes an expert to make the abdominal cut in a hanging deer without cutting through the paunch or intestines.) Now climb your small tree and bend it down to a point near your buck's head. Straddle the branch and cut the top off, then trim off some of the smaller branches to clear your way. Bend your springy pole down to the deer's head and tie it fast with a couple of half hitches. When you release the pole, if you've chosen a good stiff one, the buck's head and forequarters will be lifted partially clear of the ground by the spring of the pole. Cut now two crotched poles, fairly sturdy and about eight feet long. Place the crotches under your spring pole, right where the deer is hung, and jack up the carcass by shifting the butts, one at a time, toward the deer. As soon as the hindquarters are clear of the ground, dress him out as previously described, cutting loose the diaphragm and severing the windpipe and neck vessels from inside the chest cavity.

Irrespective of the method used, some effort should be made to keep the deer's carcass away from the blood or other drainage from the body cavity. The hair stains readily and if you would keep your trophy looking presentable, take some pains to avoid soiling the carcass. If possible, when you dress a deer on the ground lay him on a slope or bank, that the insides may be shaken free to roll downhill. It is advised too that some care should be taken to avoid touching the metatarsal glands while dressing the deer and handling the carcass. These glands are the little horny spots on the hind legs, surrounded by somewhat coarser and longer hair than is found on the rest of the leg. Personally the author has never paid any attention to the existence of these glands, so far as handling the carcass is concerned, but many authorities feel that the meat may be contaminated if these glands or their secretion makes contact with the carcass. Some hunters make a point of severing these glands as soon as a deer is down, thus eliminating any possibility of their contaminating the carcass.

With the deer dressed-out some attempt should be made to cool out the interior of the body cavity, before starting for camp. If you have hung your buck to dress him, simply prop open the sides of the abdomen with a stick, allowing the body heat to escape. If your deer is on the ground, the same step is in order, after turning the carcass on its back. It can be propped against a log or supported by a couple of stones, leaving the opened cavity uppermost for better dissipation of body heat.

While you wait for the carcass to cool somewhat you might pass the time in removing the genitals from the skin. Most states require that evidence of sex remain attached to the hide during transportation or possession. This does not necessarily mean that the organs remain fast to the carcass, for these parts spoil readily in warm weather. The sensible solution is to remove the testicles by squeezing or pulling them out of the hide covering and leave these hide pockets attached to the carcass. No game law official can dispute the sex of the deer, even with its head removed, if this is carried out.

Under no circumstances should a buck be hung by the hind feet for hog-dressing in the woods. In this "upside-down" position all the work involved in cutting and removal of the entrails takes place on the top half of the deer, out of reach of the hunter. When the entrails are finally loosened, they drop down into the chest cavity and must be lifted out by your digging right into them and hauling them out of there. In addition, all the remaining blood and juices from the abdominal cavity flow right down into the chest; the loose entrails always drop out over the head and neck of the deer, making an unsightly and smelly mess. If a hunter decides that he will, in spite of all logic against it, dress his deer in this head-down position, he must first lift the deer partially from the ground, in order to make the initial knife-cuts, then he must start to pull out the entrails, stop to jack the deer up a bit more, tie the head up out of the way of the descending intestines, and, in the process, get both himself and the deer thoroughly messed-up. To remove the lungs and heart without diving for them he must split open the chest cartilage all the way to the brisket — no little stunt in itself, unless the hunter is provided with a small ax or saw. He then must try to drag the chest entrails through the ragged edges of the cut so made, with the springy ribs always closing the opening like the jaws of a trap. Even after he manages to remove the entrails in this manner he must still hang the buck by the head if he would have it properly drained. Better to hang it this way in the beginning, if the deer is to be hung at all.

Actually, not more than once in a thousand times is it necessary to lift a deer from the ground to dress it in the woods. Mighty few deer attain so much weight that an average-sized man cannot effectively perform this simple operation entirely by himself. With a partner at hand the whole operation can be completed in five minutes or less.

With the deer cooling off a bit, the hunter can rescue the liver and heart from the steaming pile of "innards." He who likes the flavor of deer liver will provide himself with an empty salt sack or a square of cloth for wrapping it. Otherwise it will make a sorry mess in his hunting-coat pocket. If there is a surplus of hunters in the party, perhaps one man can be pressed into carrying out the liver, strung on a forked stick.

In this dressing-out of a whitetail buck the hunter must have a definite plan of action fixed firmly in his mind before his deer is downed. Then and only then can he tackle it quickly and complete it easily. All cuts should be made decisively and firmly. The belly cut can be made in one sweep with a small, sharp knife; the rectal tube can be freed in ten seconds, just like coring an apple. Normal care should be used to avoid cutting into any of the internal organs. Puncturing paunch or intestines makes it more difficult to perform a neat, clean operation. Don't fail to give the body cavity time to cool out. Body heat spells the beginning of spoiled venison, so don't too hastily throw your buck onto a fender for a quick triumphal trip home. This can wait until later, but cooling off of the carcass cannot.

Now that your buck is neatly dressed and cooled off a bit, you wipe some of the blood from your hands and forearms, then decide how you'll get him out to camp or your car. On light snow, wet leaves or if your way out is more or less downhill, dragging the deer will be the easiest, unless you have a long distance to go and you value the condition of the buck's hide and flesh. Ninety-five of every hundred deer taken each year are dragged out of the woods. This is ideal if conditions are suitable, but if a buck is dragged over rocky ground too far both the hide and the meat can be pretty badly bruised. Then again, if you kill your buck in heavy laurel or scrub-oak country it will be much more difficult to drag than to carry him. The nature of the terrain lying between your deer and your car or camp will be the deciding factor.

Although skidding your buck out is the widely accepted method, there are right and wrong ways to do even this. Any buck will slide fairly well on that coarse, heavy-hair body covering, but there are two factors in dragging which will make the job even more difficult. First, the antlers seem to reach out and grab every passing bush; secondly, all the weight of the buck's chunky body rests on the ground, building up the friction. We can partly reduce both of these factors in this way: When the rope is made fast to the buck's head, tie and hitch it to keep the nose in line with the rest of the body, throwing the antlers back and more or less out of the way. Then by using a short rope and tying it to the middle of a short heavy stick, part of the deer's weight can be lifted from the ground as it is dragged along.

The simplest way to make the head-hitch is as follows: Throw a loop around the deer's head, just behind the antler butts. Tighten the loop so that the knot lies under the throat, just between the jawbones. Then bring the rope forward under the chin and take a half-hitch around the nose. Now, when tension is put on the rope, the buck's nose, head and neck will lie in a straight line, with the antlers lying well back on the neck, as much out of the way as they can ever be.

Two men on a short haul need never touch a rope to the buck. Each can take an antler in hand and make the drag, but for any considerable distance this will be tiring. For a long drag, the rope should be tied to the middle of a stout stick, about three feet long;

then with a man on either side, the pole can be laid across the upper arms, giving maximum pulling efficiency with the least effort.

Alone, and with rough country to cover, the hunter must carry out his deer. There are two good methods, both involving a little preparation before the deer can be swung up for the carry. One way is by making a "knapsack" of your buck by connecting the forelegs with the hinds legs, forming two "straps" into which the hunter thrusts both arms for carrying. There are two or three methods for making the "knapsack," but the author will describe only the simplest. First, slit the skin through each hind leg just above the hock and between the large tendon and the leg bone. Through these slits insert the corresponding front leg, pulling it through up to the front knee joint. Make ready two short sticks half an inch thick and six inches long. Sharpen one end of each. Punch a hole through each foreleg, directly below the knee and close to the bone, insert the short stick through the hole making a lock within the hind leg.

To get into the "knapsack" grasp the buck by the hind feet and pull him up on his rump in a sitting position. Steady him thus, spread the hind legs apart and sit down between them. Lean back, grasp a foreleg in each hand and swing the buck up over your back; insert both arms through the loops formed by the joined legs. Now roll over onto hands and knees, throwing as much of the deer's weight as possible above your shoulders. Leaning forward now, bring up first one foot, then the other, and rise erect. Now the buck's head will be rolling out to the side, so reach out and hook your right arm into the near antler. With the buck high up on your back you can cover long distances without unhooking him for a rest. Every time you near a fair-sized log or a big rock, back up to it and rest the deer's weight thereon, while you have a quiet smoke and catch your breath.

Another good method is to "rump-pack" your buck. This involves a bit more preparation, but under some conditions makes a more comfortable burden. To do this skin the deer's legs up to the first joint of each. With your knife sever the tendons across the front of the joints and break off each leg. This leaves four straps of hide which are tied together with square knots. Tie the two front legs together and the two hind legs likewise, making the knots as close as possible to the ends of the joints. Sit down now with the deer at your back, slip into the shoulder straps and roll forward, then rise to your feet. You now have a fairly comfortable pack, supported on your shoulders by the straps and with much of the buck's weight carried just above the hips. Your buck's head will swing down to the side, so reach out and hook his neck with the crook of your arm, then carry your rifle with the other hand.

When carrying out a deer in heavily hunted areas, to maintain a state of good health it's advisable to hang your red cap or hand-kerchief on the deer's antlers. It's also in order to make plenty of decidedly manlike noises as you make your way out. Whistle, shout or talk to yourself — anything to make it impossible for a hunter to mistake your trophy for a buck still on the loose. The author knows one hunter who was drawing a bead on a deer moving through the scrub oaks when suddenly smoke began to emanate from about the ears of the buck. Quick investigation revealed that the deer was moving under one-man power, and the one man was lucky enough to be smoking a vile corncob pipe at the time.

Today, getting out a buck is seldom a one-man effort. Most hunt-ers have at least one partner with them in the woods; often there are plenty in the party to get out a deer with a minimum of effort. One buck, which the author killed away back in the dense laurel and scrub-oak lands between Wolf Pond and Westbrookville, never touched the ground after he was once lifted, until we reached the road, about two miles from the spot. I had made a two-pole carry of this buck and, with eight men in the bunch, a fresh pair were always at hand to relieve the two boys with the deer. In this type of country, right in Sullivan County's heaviest covers, it's almost impossible to drag a deer for any distance. The ground is rocky, the trails are narrow and twisting, with dense scrub oak and laurel clutching at the hunters' clothes and the buck's antlers at every few steps.

The easiest way out is to get the deer above ground, above the level of tearing underbrush and off the sharp rocks. There's a simple way to do this and it is *not* to sling the deer on a single pole, to sway and lurch at every step the two porters make. Rather we take *two* poles, heavy and stiff enough so that they won't spring to the rhythm of the hunters' steps. Between these two poles the buck is lashed, belly up, with each leg firmly lashed high up and as close to the poles as the body can be made fast. Then for further support the rope is passed under the deer, one slung under the withers, the other under the rump. With the buck in this semirigid position between the poles a more comfortable carry can be made. There is no back-breaking sway to the carcass; the head is supported be-

TWO-MAN
CARRY

RUMP
PACK

KNAPSACK
PACK

tween the poles by lashing an antler to either side. From the hunter's point of view, the load is distributed equally on either shoulder and both men can walk in an erect position. We have taken out many a buck in this way through rough, brushy cover, rapidly and with a minimum of discomfort.

Of course there is no way by which a buck can be taken out of the woods in comfort. At best it is hard work. A dead deer, while not too heavy for a man of normal strength, can be a loose, slippery, almost liquid bundle. The hair is slippery, the antlers flop around on a loosely hanging neck, the feet stick out almost yards away, it often seems. But we must get him out and that in good condition. No man worthy of the name sportsman will kill his deer and then neglect to bring it out without expending every effort to protect both hide and meat.

Up in the Oakland Valley one of my old deer-hunting outfits had a dandy setup for bringing out the bucks. Through the club's grounds, right past our sleeping quarters, ran a single spur railway. It wound up through the valley from Valley Junction, following the Neversink River till it passed our place, then on up the Bushkill toward Hartwood and St. Josephs. The double line of steel ran conveniently along the base of our mountain, making any point on our hunting grounds not more than a half-mile from the tracks. When any of the boys killed a buck near one of the firelines we'd drag him down the slope the shortest way to the rails. Then a runner would dig out Old Bert Ogden, our caretaker, and Bert would haul out the old "pumper" from the shed. He'd pump the old handcar up the tracks to the deer, we would load him on, then away to camp, a mile below. Within minutes our latest kill would hang from the camp deer rack to cool off before heading into town to the cooler. Several times Old Bert would have two or three deer piled on the handy old car, pumping down the track for dear life, while two or three of the boys would tag along behind to help hang the bucks at camp. Altogether a most satisfactory method of "getting out your buck."

My friend John Shufelt of Northville, in the Adirondacks, some-times uses a novel method of bringing out his buck. John does a good bit of deer hunting along the rugged slopes bordering Stony Creek up in Hope Valley. Quite often he will down a buck several miles up the creek, away from the nearest road. Rather than drag or carry his deer John lashes him to a short pole and heaves him into the fast running clear waters of the creek. He follows along the bank with another, slender pole and pries the buck loose whenever it comes up against a boulder. John says that he'll never carry out a buck if there is a fair-sized stream near by, heading in the same direction he's going.

In every situation the hunter must "cut his garment to fit the cloth," in getting his buck to camp or car. In really open country a lone hunter could rig the buck between two springy saplings, lashing him well up to the poles. Then he could get between the "shafts" and drag out his deer by the old Indian squaw "travois" method. The springy ends of the poles are left to drag on the ground, supporting the deer and taking the shock of uneven ground from the hunter's shoulders.

Many hunters who kill their deer near farm lands can often obtain the use of a horse for taking out a buck. The buck can be thrown across the saddle and the legs cinched tight to the saddle rings. Then the head should be pulled up and over the pommel of the saddle and lashed fast. Under no circumstances should the head with sharp antlers be allowed to swing free. A horse carrying a freshly killed buck is inclined to be skittish and a few jabs from sharp antlers are all that's needed to throw him into a frenzy of bucking and kicking. For those remembering this and exercising such precaution, packing out a deer in a saddle is one of the easiest ways to bring out the venison.

A lone hunter in a wilderness area may not care to tackle the job of carrying his deer to camp, particularly if the end of daylight is near. Normally, it's safe to hang your buck overnight in the woods in the wilderness sections, but in deer country with a normal complement of hunters — never! That is a pretty easy way to lose a deer. But if circumstances make it impossible to bring out your buck alone, then prepare to hide him for the night. When you finally realize that you will need help to get your buck out, hang him with the bent sapling and crotch-pole system so that he will cool thoroughly and drain out well. Stay with him until there is just enough daylight for you to make your way to camp safely, then haul him down, cover him with brush and leaves and blaze out a trail to the nearest landmark. It's wise, too, not to blaze your trail too near the deer thus giving away your hiding place to any possible prowling hunters. Strange as it may be, in heavily hunted areas it pays to trust no one where a whitetail buck is involved. There are many hunters who would cheerfully return to you a well-filled wallet, but these same men would just as cheerfully steal your buck.

The author knows of one man who returned home after dark with his deer loaded on the car. He parked his car in the driveway, then went in to rouse the family and give them the good news. Going out to the car en masse, they found each and every fender without deer. Some of his hunting brethren had decided that stealing this man's deer was easier than killing one for themselves.

The wilderness hunter will be quite safe in leaving his buck until next morning; there's little possibility of another hunter making off with it here. He does, however, need to hang the buck high enough to keep it away from night-prowling wood scavengers, and, in addition, must make certain that he marks well the spot for his return trip. Several trees should be blazed, facing to each of the four compass points, and a clear trail should be marked either by blazing or breaking branches on his way out. As an added precaution it's a good idea to leave a cap, handkerchief or even a shirt tied fast to the carcass. Wild creatures, with the possible exception of a black bear, will seldom bother a deer contaminated by odors from the hated and feared man-animal.

As to the hunter's equipment for dressing and hauling out a deer, this needs to be nothing more than a pair of heavy rawhide, high-top laces and a small, narrow-bladed sheath-knife. For many years the rawhide laces have filled the bill for this writer, but if a hunter feels that his buck should be hung for dressing than let him carry ten feet of light nylon cording. In a pinch even the laces will do this job, just as they are wholly adequate for either dragging out a buck or lashing him between two poles for a carry.

A deer hunter's knife never needs to be a fearsome weapon such as the tenderfoot hunter carries. There is no use whatever, on a deer hunt, for the six- to eight-inch, wide-blade knives that we see every year, dangling in a sheath halfway to a man's knees. Such blades are too cumbersome for dressing a buck, and are even unhandy for the final skinning-out. Conceivably, such a heavy knife might be used for chopping down saplings, but if a hunter feels this job is too much for a small knife, he will be better suited with a tiny Marble's pocket-ax.

With the buck at last in camp or at home, the body cavity can be swabbed clean and dry. Many hunters have a phobia about touching a buck's carcass with water in any form. I believe that this is all foolishness, provided that the carcass and body cavity are thoroughly dried after the washing. It has always seemed most logical to this writer to clean off the carcass and wash off the excess blood, both outside and within the body, if it seems required. Certainly there is no logic in allowing intestinal juices and thickly matted blood to remain within the animal's body to harden and dry. Better to wash the mess off and then dry all thoroughly, using rags, paper towels, dry moss or whatever absorbent material comes to hand. Washing has never in any way harmed a bit of this writer's venison. I doubt if it will do harm to any other deer hunter's buck.

In warm weather the deer hunter's big problem in saving his venison is to keep the meat away from blowflies. Unless the carcass has every body opening thoroughly screened, these flies will crawl into the body cavity and deposit eggs in every moist pocket in the flesh. Within two days the entire body cavity will be teeming with squirming maggots. At the same time, the carcass should not be so tightly covered as to exclude the all-important circulation of air. Of course the best method to escape a "blown" deer is to keep him in a screened shed or, best of all, in the refrigerated cooler. But in camp neither of these is possible.

The camping hunter will provide either several yards of cheesecloth or the porous cloth tubing used in meat-packing houses. A few yards of this tubing will completely cover a buck, screening out the flies and at the same time permitting circulation of air. The cheesecloth or tubing means only a little extra weight to a hunter-camper and it may mean the difference between saving a fine chunk of venison and giving it up to the maggots.

Normally cool weather in camp will keep a deer in the hide in good condition for days. Hang your buck in the shade, well off the ground, head up if he is not yet completely drained, keep the body cavity well aerated and free from flies and wiped dry until the drying action of the air forms a hard shell all over the inside. Then, indeed, will you have good venison for your locker to carry over the winter months.

8 / The Deer Hunter's Camp

LUCKY is the man who can take his deer hunting in large doses; who can get off into the woods for a full two weeks or a month in close association with his quarry and, in a sense, become a part of the country he plans to hunt. These hunters extract the keenest possible enjoyment from the sport and in time will prove to be the most adept woodsmen and the best deerslayers. There is no substitute in hunting for a close association with the territory one hunts and the game living therein. The hunter-camper who has the interest and courage to pack his duffel into the deer country, set up his camp and stay until he bags his buck, is a most self-sufficient individual. He willingly divorces himself from the cloying taint of civilization, temporarily at least, and once in the woods unconsciously becomes an environmental part of the scene.

In true wilderness areas — in the back country — a man must set up camp if he would kill one of the truly wild whitetails found in such territory. And for the man who loves the wilds and who will kill his buck by no method other than still-hunting, this is the only answer to the urge which creeps into his veins with the coming of the first frosts. Few of us who hunt deer will have the opportunity to make such a trip, but no man can know the fullest satisfaction to be gained from deer hunting until he takes a prime whitetail buck under full wilderness hunting conditions.

It hardly seems necessary for a writer to compile lengthy information as to equipment and camp procedure for the hunter who takes to the woods, making his home there until he takes his buck. These hunters must of necessity have a background of woodcraft and experience which precludes the necessity for any advice. But there is a new generation of coming hunters who may not be completely woods-wise in cold-weather camping, yet who have the craving for a wilderness hunting trip. It is to these men that the following hints are directed — the old-timer knows them all.

First of all, although a sportsman may have wide experience in summer camping, his approach to a hunting and camping trip must be quite different. "Roughing it" in a camp may be a thrill for a day or two, but unless the camp has been carefully planned, it can be a dismal hunting trip and a sad, unhappy hunter who bolts for home after sleepless, freezing nights in an uncomfortable bed, eating greasily unpleasant food and tramping the woods in sodden clothes.

To do the job right, choose your spot and make a pre-season visit, if this is at all possible. Plan the location well sheltered from prevailing winds, with a good supply of running water and firewood near by. It's a good idea to cut your supply of firewood well in advance of your hunting trip, for this is a chore that will take plenty of time from your hunting. The site should be well drained, not at the foot of a steep sidehill where the first rainfall will sweep your tent floor. Keep the location in good sunlight to eliminate a damp tent, and be sure that no dead limbs will drop from a near-by tree in a heavy blow to crash through your tent roof.

Unless the hunter is a seasoned woodsman with much experience in building the right lean-to shelter, a good tent is a must. For a small group of four to six men, a 14 × 16 wall tent is the answer. A two-man party can get along with a small miner's tent or one of the surplus army two-man tents. But such small shelters can hardly be provided with inside heating, and a warm tent is a great comfort after a long cold day in the woods. It will pay even a two-man party to pack in a 10 × 12 wall tent, unless the trip will be only for a couple of days. It is a nice thing to be able to recount your experiences in a makeshift shelter to your friends after the trip is over, but for honest-to-goodness comfort, nothing compares with a roomy wall tent and a little collapsible sheet-iron stove for inside heating. Your cooking will be a pleasure in a warm place, rather than struggling over an outside open fire; food can be kept warm and the eating itself will be much more comfortable, taken within the cheery snug harbor of a heated tent. The novice never fails to express his surprise at the warm comfort of a tent heated with a tiny sheet-iron stove, even in the bitterest weather.

With the tent selected, plan well beforehand the room needed for sleeping, cooking and equipment storage, so that the position of the stove can be fixed and the hole cut for the pipe. Collapsible sheet-iron stoves with built-in ovens and telescoping pipe can be obtained, and are just the ticket for the deer hunter's camp. Of course, you can make one yourself from sheet iron, but it hardly pays — they are quite inexpensive. With the hole cut in the tent for the stovepipe, you can insulate the tent material in one of two ways: the simplest is to wrap the pipe with several turns of sheet asbestos, at the point of contact with the tent; the other way, and a more permanent one, is to cut a hole large enough for the pipe in two sheets of asbestos and rivet them together, with the tent wall between, directly over the hole.

It must always be borne in mind that the camp stove offers a certain amount of fire hazard; but if you take proper insulation precautions and keep the stovepipe opening away from inflammable evergreen branches, there will be no trouble.

The deer hunter's tent will need no floor; in fact the floor is a disadvantage because, with the inside stove, insulating material will have to be used to prevent burning it out, and it serves no useful purpose.

Of all the necessary equipment for a comfortable camping trip, a good bed is the most important. For such trips a sleeping bag is a must. Never depend on providing a bed from nature's materials found on the spot. No material found in deer territory will provide a comfortable, warm bed. A man might get by with a moss or balsam bed in summer weather, but for fall hunting this is out. Nothing will do the job as well as a good down-filled sleeping bag, placed over an air mattress. With this outfit a hunter can sleep in comfort on a stone wall, and it is light to carry, easy to clean and dry out. The Army is turning loose many thousands of these as surplus material, so there is little excuse for a camper hunter to be without one. In the absence of an air mattress a camper can make up a bed by rolling up two six- or eight-inch-diameter logs, laying them parallel about three feet apart and filling in the space with first a covering of newspaper or tarpaulin next to the ground, then a thick pile of dried ferns, leaves, balsam tips or any other soft material found near the campsite. If he carries a few gunnysacks with him, he can stuff these with the same material and use them for a mattress, rather than have the loose stuff strewn around the tent. But none of this works as well as an air mattress and nothing else sleeps as comfortably; makeshifts are feasible for a temporary stay, but for a hunting trip of a week or two, the air mattress and sleeping bag are the answer to a deer hunter's prayer.

With the tent, stove and sleeping equipment decided upon, the campers should get together and make a list of all other items of equipment, planning meals for each day and providing enough food for each man for every meal in camp. This might seem like a childish procedure, but for campers short on experience it will pay off in comfortably full stomachs instead of tight belts on the last day in camp. And it might be well to add 20 per cent for the increase in normal appetites when the gang has spent a day in the woods.

I well remember a little incident which illustrates the tendency of a new deer hunter to consume huge portions of food after a day in the woods. One of my friends, a traveling man and bachelor to boot, decided he'd like to spend a week at our deer camp for his initiation in the gentle art of whitetail deer hunting. For a number of years he had been overweight, subject to stomach disorders if he overate, and had been on a rigid diet. He had some misgivings about living on camp fare, but after I assured him we would provide and cook for him any of his special foods, he decided to take a chance.

On the way up to camp we stopped off and bought his list of special cereals, rusks and other assorted dainties. The first meal in camp that night found him eating a rugged bowl of milk toast; next morning we prepared him a hot cereal, with which he ate a dried rusk or two. He passed the entire day in the woods without lunch, refusing our offer of sandwiches because his diet forbade eating at midday. I must admit he was a willing hunter — he took part in every drive and never offered a complaint even though he must have been leg-weary and footsore by the end of the day.

We came into camp that evening with a nice buck and, after hanging him on the camp rack, we set about getting the evening meal. The night before I had skinned out six cottontail rabbits — part of the supply we brought in for camp food — and these, together with three pounds of hot sausage and half a dozen pork chops, had been simmering in Italian spaghetti sauce on the big camp range since noon. To get together the meal I had only to boil up four pounds of spaghetti and put the two big pots on the camp table — one of spaghetti, the other filled with meat and tasty tomato sauce. In the meantime I had put up our bachelor friend's special meal of cereal and light cream.

Our gang of eight had a little trouble in polishing off all the rabbits and spaghetti. If memory serves me there remained in the pot about one whole rabbit carcass, a couple of links of sausage and a single pork chop, but the other pot held a fairly good-sized wad of spaghetti. Now and then our new friend would glance over hungrily at this surplus food; finally, his resistance broke and he asked, somewhat timidly, if we'd mind his taking a taste of the rabbit. Promptly the two big pots were pushed his way and for half an hour this diet-ridden victim of general inertia fed his face in a way that would have delighted any chef's eye. In the end there was little, if anything, to throw out to the skunks. For a week this chap ate our food, enjoyed it tremendously, and went home, alas, minus deer, but feeling in fine shape both physically and mentally. His special cereals, breads and other light fodder were cast aside that night of the first day's hunt and were never mentioned again. Beware then of a meager supply of food for your deer hunting and camping trip!

The food supply will be dictated by the personal preferences of the camping group, but it should include staple items of flour, sugar, salt, baking powder, eggs, bacon, prepared pancake flour, cooking oil or fat (unless plenty of bacon is used), canned or dried milk, dehydrated soups, canned or fresh staple vegetables such as carrots, dried beans and some canned or dried fruit. If the supplies must be packed in, canned goods must be kept to a minimum, substituting dried foods and dehydrated items wherever possible, to save weight. For an extended stay don't try to get along on fried foods for every meal; it palls on the appetite and soon the gang will be wishing for a home-cooked meal. Add fruits and vegetables liberally to the diet if you would keep the crowd healthy.

Bake fresh biscuits in a reflector oven or in your collapsible oven on the sheet-iron stove, or, if you prefer, fill your frying pan with a prepared biscuit dough or flour-and-baking-powder dough and bake over your fire. The hot biscuits and pan-baked bread are always welcomed with open arms. Start your evening meals with a pot of hot soup made from prepared package mixes, follow it with a rugged hunter's stew of beef, venison, rabbits or any other available red meat smothered with carrots, potatoes and onions and thickened with a little flour. Top it off with stewed prunes or canned pineapple and you will have a contented, sleepy bunch of happy hunters, ready to turn in early, sleep well and be on deck next morning ready for the day's hunt. Next to a comfortable bed and a warm, dry tent nothing adds to the pleasure of a camping-hunting trip like good food forming a balanced diet. It is no more trouble to prepare sensible meals in a well-organized camp than it is to throw a gooey mess into a greasy frying pan and expect the boys to enjoy it.

* * *

When the time for the trip arrives give yourself plenty of time to get into camp *early* in the day, even if it means starting a day sooner. Have your grub list completely filled and your equipment list checked by every member of the party before leaving home — don't depend on picking up food or duffel on the way. Something is certain to be forgotten. It is far better to lay out every item at home and check each off the list before packing it for transportation. When you at last arrive at the chosen spot you'll need at least half a day to get the tent properly set up, the drainage ditches cut, a rough table and benches put together and the stove up or reflector fireplace built, as well as cutting firewood and getting ready the sleeping quarters.

As far as the tent is concerned no poles need be carted along. Cut a ridgepole in the spot and make it long enough to project through both ends of the tent, even if holes must be cut to permit its passage. Cut two pairs of fairly long, stiff poles to be used as "shears" for supporting each end of the ridgepole, then wire them together near the top like the letter "A" and lay the ridgepole on the wire-crossed joint. Set the stakes for the guy-ropes and tighten the whole tent by pulling tight the guys and shifting the ends of the shear poles together. Use of shear poles rather than the conventional end poles under the ridge permits easier passage into the tent and at the same time makes a more stable job. If you like an open fire — and what camper doesn't? — build a rough stone fireplace six or eight feet from the tent flap and back it up with a reflector of green logs, piled up on each other and wired fast to a pair of stakes driven in the ground. Complete the job by cutting two crotched stakes for either side of the fireplace and laying across them a pole to support stew kettles or a roast. Such an open fireplace makes a good medium for starting the evening meal. In our camp one of the boys would come in at noon and roll a couple of good red-oak logs on the fireplace and hang up a big kettle of stew or a roast to simmer until evening. Then when the hungry crew would begin to show up at camp after the day's hunt, dinner would be a matter of simply taking off the stew or roast, putting on the coffeepot and sitting down to the meal.

The author would like to re-emphasize that it is of the greatest importance to set up camp completely before any thought is given to hunting. In setting up camp there is no time like the present to take care of all the little jobs that go to make camping a comfort. The member of a party who grabs his rifle as soon as the tent is unpacked "just to take a look up on the ridge" while the rest of the bunch do the job of making camp will most likely wait a long time for another invitation. A deer hunters' camp is a community effort, and each man should have his job to do and carry it through to completion. For example, one of the author's camping parties would select an experienced man for the job of cooking, but he was not expected to gather wood, tend fires or wash dishes. These little chores were divided among the rest of the group and the stay in camp was always pleasant, with no bickering or argument as to just who would do what.

The job of setting up camp can be made much simpler by adding a bit of extra equipment. A hammer, handsaw, nails and a roll of soft iron or copper wire will go a long way in providing extra comforts in the form of stools, drying racks and extra benches. In a well-organized camp nothing in equipment or food is left on the ground. Racks and benches will be provided for everything and the supply of firewood will either be covered with a tarpaulin or placed under an improvised lean-to before the rain or snow gets to it. In such a deer hunters' camp, the hunting trip will be fun and every man will be comfortable, healthy and happy — unless he misses a big buck.

In a permanent camp there are few problems, other than the establishment of rigid rules for the personal safety of the group. In regard to the handling of firearms, the author's Buck Mountain outfit enforced a strict ruling: *All firearms* were to be *loaded* and *kept loaded* while in the camp building. It was agreeably surprising how this simple rule kept the men from picking up and fondling someone else's weapon at odd moments. The wall rack was always full of rifles and at no time was a rifle passed around the circle for casual inspection. Many times it is this odd-moment inspection of weapons which leads to camp accidents.

It's also a good policy for a fairly large group in a permanent camp to employ a cook fulltime, preferably a man who likes cooking and not hunting. If you can locate such an individual, pay him well and treat him with the respect due his position — that of filling the inner man. The hunters will still be expected to provide firewood and wash dishes after the evening meals but this is little enough to give in return for good camp meals served on time. It never works out well in a large group of hunters to have one of them do the cooking for the rest of the gang. The cook will want to get in just as much hunting as the rest of the party and this is hardly possible if the bunch is to be well fed for at least two full meals a day.

As to utensils for camp cooking: The hunters who set up their camp will be interested in saving as much room and weight as possible. Nested aluminum pots and pans are the only solution for the tent-camper and these can be had with folding handles to carry in pack-sack or pack-basket. But for making griddlecakes nothing does as well as the old-fashioned rectangular heavy iron griddle. These are worth every effort necessary to get them to camp, even if you must hang one around your neck with a rope.

For a permanent camp an unlimited number of utensils can be used. Generally there is no transportation problem to the fixed camp building, so a camper can take just about what he likes. However, the most useful article in camp-kitchen hardware ever conceived is a large pressure cooker. These magic vessels will turn out a big stew or a heavy pot roast in one third the regular time and the food so cooked seems to be tastier.

Fully as important in a hunters' camp as good equipment and know-how is the individual attitude of each man toward his fellow camper. Each man must take care that his personal belongings are kept in his allotted space, not strewn around the tent and mixed in with his comrades' stuff. Again he must be willing to do his share of the work. If the cooking is to be done by the hunters themselves, let each man take his turn at the task and give no thought to hunting until the work is done. Beware also of handing out good advice to your brother hunters — no man likes to be criticized for his handling of firearms or his methods of hunting. If your system seems to work the rest of the gang will follow suit quickly enough. Keep your stories of hunting experiences to a single telling — don't bend your campmates' ears with the same tale over and over again.

The proof of a man's worth as a camp companion will not be highly apparent on the trip itself, but in retrospect his co-operative qualities and good common sense, his willingness to share equally in labors and discomfort, will shine in the golden light of memory when the next fall season finds Jack Frost painting his landscapes.

9 / Sportsmanship and Safety in the Woods

SPORTSMANSHIP is an ethereal quality, an intangible character-istic existing in the minds of many thousands of hunters and displayed by their conduct for all to see. It is the highest type of hunter who congratulates a brother hunter for taking a fine buck, with a genuine warmth, not the dark looks of envy; the man who, although a com-plete stranger, will help you trail your wounded deer, even finish him off, then help you to get him out of the woods. He is the man who will offer you his last smoke or sandwich, who will put you on a better stand than his own, hoping to get you your shot. He handles his firearm forever with extreme caution, and when his rifle cracks out he *knows* that his sights are on legal game.

Sadly enough, we have with us in much greater numbers his complete opposite — the obnoxious character who rushes to the best stand, heading off the rest of the party; the conservationist who shoots (or shoots at) any deer coming to his post, ever hopeful that one might have legal antlers. This is the ever-alert man who will pounce like a hawk on another man's wounded or dead deer, franti-cally tying on tags before the trailing hunter comes into view. It is he who sneaks into the woods at the beginning of another party's drive, then leeches his way into the most desirable place for cutting off the oncoming deer. This too is the same man who rocked your boat when you were bass fishing or who stood up in your canoe while making a fast water run, but now, in deer-hunting time, he shoots at the noises in the brush.

Perhaps the author paints too dismal a picture of the unsports-manlike type of hunter we find in the deer woods, but his clan is in-creasing in numbers every year. Deer hunting in many areas becomes a highly competitive sport; the prime objective here is to intercept a buck before the next fellow sees him, blast him down and tie on the ownership tags before some other hunter gets to the downed deer and performs this little task. Personally, I cannot quite understand just what measure of satisfaction a man can feel in taking out of the woods a trophy killed by someone else — yet it does happen, and frequently. If a man is meat-hungry we can understand some of this attitude, but we who hunt deer never hunt for meat alone. The venison is but a final complement to the thrill and satisfaction of a successful day or week in the woods.

One of our Oakland Valley club hunters had an amusing experience with a pair of these deer thieves some years ago. Charlie was one of the older men in our group and had been advised by his doctor to give up deer hunting. For years he had been treating Charlie for a weak pump, and he felt that the heavy exercise and excitement of the hunt could easily finish him. But Charlie had spent too many deer seasons in the woods to give up that easily. As he put it, "I'd just as soon they'd plant me if I have to give up huntin' deer. Not much use of livin' if a man can't hunt." (As it turned out, the Doc was right and one year we carried Charlie out of the woods, never to return, but that doesn't concern this story.)

Our bunch made it a habit to come down off the mountain each midday for lunch and a hot cup of coffee. Charlie, with his bad ticker, couldn't take the climb twice a day so he would carry a lunch and eat it while the rest of us would go down to camp. One day, just as we hit the grub-shack, two shots cracked out near the top of our little mountain. It could be no one but Charlie, we thought, so we decided to grab a quick bite and get up on the mountain to see if he needed help.

Perhaps an hour later we came up to Charlie, sitting by a nice six-point buck. He was visibly agitated, much more so than he might have been from simply killing a deer, so we questioned him.

"Well, sir, I never seen anything like it," he said. "Here this buck had just sneaked out from that laurel over-top the ridge, prob'ly gettin' out after you fellas had left for camp and things had quietened down. Anyways, I knocked him over — hit him both times — and he dropped right here. I got over here and opened 'm up and dumped his guts out, 'cause I knew you boys wouldn't be back for a while to help me. So then I figgered I'd find me a spot to set down and eat my lunch. I went up the hill there a bit an set down by a stump, where I could watch the deer.

"Pretty soon," he went on, "I heard sunthin' over near the fire line and there was two guys sneaking up this runway, here, and lookin' all around, pretty cautious-like, so I got behind that big stump just to see what was goin' on." Charlie's eyes were twinkling now in anticipation as he unfolded the story. "These two birds must have heard the two shots and come over from the next club to see what was goin' on.

"Well, anyway, they come on up the runway a bit and then one spies the deer layin' on the ground. He puts his finger up to his mouth and grabs the other guy by the arm and points to the deer. Then they both look all around very careful to see if anyone was comin', but they don't spot me hidden behind that stump. They didn't look at the deer very carefully either or they'd 'a' seen his guts were out and the tags on his legs. Guess they was excited a bit. They were havin' a conference now to figger out what to do. I could hear 'em mumbling to themselves and one of 'em was shakin' his head at what the other guy was sayin'. Finally the little one went back a ways toward the fire line and stood there; then the other one points his gun up in the air and fires a shot. Then he hollers as loud as he can for the other guy, 'Come on over Bill, here's the buck we was followin'!!' So the other hollers back, as loud as he can, 'Hey, did ya find 'im?' Then they both got together, about thirty feet from the deer, and looked all around again.

"'Bout this time," said Charlie, "I was gettin' a little mad. These birds was figgerin' on dragging that deer over across the fire line and claimin' it. So just as they was starting for the deer, I stuck my rifle over top o' that stump. Just as one of 'em was reaching down to grab the buck's horn I yell out, 'The first man touches that deer *dies!!*' Brother, you never saw two scared guys get the hell out of there and back across the fire line in such a hurry!

"Here these birds figgered they had found a buck that somebody had wounded — they'd heard my two shots — and they just sneaked over here on the chance that the deer was wounded and might come runnin' down on that crossin'."

Undoubtedly Charlie was right in this instance, and regrettably there have been, and will be, many more such instances. The author once killed a large buck that had been missed several times in a flurry of shots by two other hunters. After I made a quick examination of the buck and the tracks in the snow behind the deer, I was satisfied that only my two bullets had scored; accordingly I tagged the buck and was about to dress him, when two hunters came through on the buck's back trail.

Seeing I was alone, they put up an argument that they had hit this buck first, intimating that the deer was dead, or nearly so, when I had come up to him. However, I stood off a bit with rifle ready and invited them to look over the buck, then examine the snow for evidence of a hit prior to my shooting. Neither of them wanted any part of this; they simply wanted to talk me out of the deer. One lad reached over and, lifting the buck's head, moved its lower jaw from side to side. "Sure," he said, "this buck's jaw is broken, we must have hit him in the head." Of course, the buck's jaw wasn't broken any more than theirs or mine; every deer's lower jaw swings loose.

Fortunately, and preventing any unpleasant scene, one of my friends, Miles Winner, happened to come along; he broke up the discussion by taking each of the two men along the deer's back trail through the snow to where they had done their shooting, while I stayed with the buck to dress him.

I had been tracking this buck and had driven him right up to these two hunters as they sat together on a big rock. The deer had walked up to them within thirty yards, and both men had emptied their weapons, a .30–30 carbine and an autoloading shotgun, without touching a hair. Both these men knew right well, after following the deer in the snow for a quarter of a mile, that they hadn't touched him; but seeing that I was alone they hoped they might scare me off. Such incidents are, at the least, unpleasant, and detract immeasurably from the joy and thrill in taking a whitetail buck.

Sportsmanship involves many things in deer hunting. It is the ungrudging willingness, among other things, to share equally in deer drives with no grousing when a less-favored stand is drawn; every man on a deer drive has almost an equal chance to kill his buck. The element of luck in deer drives is an all-important factor, and this can never be pre-ordained. But besides it is the willingness also to give up to its rightful owner any deer which you may stumble on, or have stumble over you, badly wounded and dying. It's true that possession is ten points of the law in deer hunting, but a good sportsman will yield his desires for a buck to the man who inflicted the fatal wound, brushing aside the legal aspects.

In most club and group hunting the unwritten code of sportsmanship delivers the deer to the man making this first vital wound, even though another hunter may be called upon to stop the deer. Hunting deer in open lands is another story. Here the hunter must get to his deer first if he would keep it. There will never be a satisfactory answer to the problem of a hunter who trails his wounded deer and finally comes upon a man or two dressing it out to carry off. The solution lies not in law but in the heart of every man who takes to the woods for the deer hunting season.

We have with us now, and ever shall have, the "sob sister" who bewails the taking of deer by hunters as a cruel, bloodthirsty slaughter of innocent wildlife. Yet each and every one of these paradoxical individuals never hesitates to sink a fang into a succulent lamb chop, veal cutlet or tender porterhouse steak. They refute such argument by stating blandly that such animals are raised for slaughter and are intended to be eaten by man. Obviously true, but so are the deer raised by Nature (and the eternal vigilance of Conservation Commissions) for just such a purpose; and in addition, to enable man, with the fundamental human impulse of the chase, to express his individuality in taking to the forests to kill himself a buck on more equal terms than are provided for slaughterhouse animals.

Whitetail bucks have a much higher incidence of survival than all the millions of cattle, sheep and hogs raised for meat. No one, unless he be a strict vegetarian, can justly object to the taking of deer, or any other of Nature's creatures, for food and sport. This provided that the taking is cleanly done and merciful.

It has long since been proved that in order to have deer in abundance the taking of a normal number of deer each season is a prime necessity. The hunter forms the controlling factor, and an important one, in game management. Deer that are permitted to propagate and exist year after year, unchecked, are their own worst evil. Disease and starvation soon combine to decimate herds to only a shadow of their former peak abundance. The so-called nature lover who objects to the hunting of deer must decide in his own mind whether it is more sportsmanlike to harvest a reasonable crop of deer each year by orthodox hunting methods or permit them to die lingering deaths by starvation and disease. And there is no alternative, for deer either must be controlled by sensible hunting or Nature will step in and take a hand.

It is, however, up to the hunter to make his killing of the game as sportsmanlike as possible. He must make sufficient study of deer anatomy to make a clean, quick kill. He must spend such time as is necessary to develop shooting skill of a kind to hit the vital areas. Most important of all, when he at last sees his buck in the woods, he must make doubly sure of his shot. There is ever an urge to "take a chance" on hitting a buck somewhere in a spot that will down him.

But irrespective of the great power lying within the hunter's bullet, few if any kills will be made unless the shot is directed to a well-chosen spot. This is not only common sense, it is an all-encompassing obligation on the part of every hunter who cares to wear the banner of true sportsmanship.

A deer hunter should use the weapon of the greatest power that he can shoot well. Certainly nothing less than a rifle in the .30–30 class can be depended upon to effect clean kills under average white-tail hunting ranges. A higher-power rifle will be even better if the hunter can shoot it with the necessary accuracy, always bearing in mind that these heavier calibers induce a greater degree of flinching.

The man who subconsciously fears the recoil of his rifle will seldom hit his deer and, even hitting it, will just as often fail to make a clean, merciful shot. Many of the more experienced hunters are going to the .300 Savage as a better deer killer. Possessing a greater degree of shock than rifles of the .30–30 class, it *is* a better deer killer, but only in the hands of the man qualified in its use.

We can carry this excess of power too far though. We can reach a point in rifle and cartridge selection where too much power is involved. The .270 Winchester, for example, when loaded with the lightest bullets, not only kills the deer but mangles a wide area of meat and tissues. If the bullet be directed through the neck or into the chest cavity, this is of little matter, but if the shot happens to hit the back or the hindquarter area, much meat will be lost. Logically, it is far better to recover your deer by using such rifles of excessive power even though much meat may be ruined rather than have the buck stagger off and die unrecovered. In this case not only is a small portion of the meat lost, *all* of it is lost.

The modern sportsman tries to strike a happy balance between his own shooting abilities and the killing effect of the rifle and cartridge he will use. No one but the hunter himself can make this selection. But he owes to the laws of good sportsmanship and the future of his own hunting pleasure the making of a wise choice.

Sportsmanship and safety in the woods are each to some degree dependent upon the other. A good sportsman is a careful shooter; under no circumstances will you find him letting off a shot until he is certain of his target and equally certain that none of his party are in line of fire should he miss. Likewise he will reserve his shooting, in deference to other hunters, for deer only. It never assists any man to kill his deer if hunters are shooting at squirrels, partridge, foxes, hawks, or owls, plus the fact that any rifle bullet directed into a treetop at a squirrel or nest has a pretty good chance of traveling for a couple of miles to a farmhouse or a village. Most of these stray shots we read about during the deer-hunting season come from this kind of foolish negligence. Such shooting is poor sportsmanship as far as the other fellow is concerned and downright dangerous in settled communities.

Probably such carelessness and thoughtlessness has induced much of our legislation against the use of rifles in many sections. Certainly it seems obvious that any bullet fired at deer level within the woods will not travel too far before spending itself in brush or solid timber. It won't require many of these high stray shots in any settled area before sizzling letters from irate farmers and villagers begin to fill their assemblymen's mail. So the deer hunter who prefers to continue to kill his deer with the rifle must use all discretion in shooting and devote all his shooting in the deer woods to legal deer.

High on the list of sportsmen's qualifications rests the burden of trailing and recovering wounded game. Not only does each wounded and unrecovered buck represent a dead loss in conservation figures, but it represents an unfilled license which still gives its holder the right to kill more deer, to say nothing of the lingering torment to the animal involved. If a buck is badly hit, trailing is no problem. A bright trail of blood will lead the hunter very shortly to his dead or dying deer. But what of the deer hit through flank and paunch, deer which bleed only little and, after a short time, fail to bleed at all? And then there are the bucks that are seriously wounded and yet fail to bleed directly after the shot. Many of these are chalked up by hunters as a miss — a clean miss, even though they might examine the ground for blood where the buck stood at the shot.

Often a deer will fail to bleed in any amount for trailing until he has run off for fifty yards or more. A solid hit will not always down a deer, nor will he show any evidence of being hit. The old rule of the buck's dropping his flag when hit has been proven wrong so often that it can be disregarded as a rule. More positive evidence of a hit is the presence of hair on the ground at the point where the shot was made. It's almost impossible to hit a deer anywhere without clipping off some hair. It may be only a tiny bit, but an observant hunter can find it if he will spend the time to look. Once he knows that the deer has been hit, he will take up the trail to examine for blood.

When blood is discovered, note the quantity and nature of the signs. If much blood can be found on both sides of the trail, there is evidence that the buck has been shot clean through and is carrying a highly fatal wound. He should be dead not more than a hundred yards away. If blood signs are small and dark in color, the possibility of a soon-fatal shot is remote. This deer should be allowed to lie down and stiffen up for an hour before you take his trail. If the follow-up is made too soon, the deer will get up and leave without giving the tracker time for a finishing shot; worst of all the wound will close and no more blood trail will be there to guide the hunter.

There is one safe rule for tracking these wounded deer. If you have followed his trail for a hundred to a hundred and fifty yards and your deer is not yet down, then give him an hour before taking the trail again. A solidly hit buck will seldom move far if he is not driven. He will go downhill to heavy cover or head toward water to lie down and rest after taking a drink. To keep on the trail of such a wounded deer will only serve to keep him moving farther and farther away. Meanwhile the blood flow becomes less and less until it disappears entirely and the hunter loses another buck. It is all right to follow a buck immediately only when the blood shows, in its great quantity and bright color, that the buck will be dead in a matter of minutes.

To continue tracking a deer that shows no sign of heavy arterial hits is to drive him into the waiting arms of another hunter. In heavily hunted areas this dilemma of trailing, or not trailing, your wounded buck will always be a problem. But good judgment will indicate that only if the deer is badly hit and bleeding profusely will it be advantageous to make an immediate follow-up. If the deer is lightly hit or paunched, shown by the small dribbles of dark blood, the only possible procedure is to wait out the deer, giving him that chance to lie down and stiffen up. If the buck has been wounded near the end of the day, mark the place well by blazing trees near by and come back at daylight the next morning before taking up the trail. Chances are that you'll find him then not too far off, either dead or incapable of movement.

With snow on the ground trailing the wounded deer becomes much simpler. However, the snow exaggerates the quantities of blood coming from a wounded deer and the hunter may be tempted to make a follow-up much too soon. On snow of course a wounded buck will resort to a few tricks to making tracking difficult. He may head for the nearest brook, wade up or down the stream, then leave it with a tremendous leap into a brushy spot to cover his tracks. Or he will head into a herd of other deer, hoping to cover his tracks by mixing in with the rest of the herd — and quite often doing so, particularly if the blood-flow clots and ceases altogether.

It's a tough job for any hunter to control his urge to chase a wounded deer before giving him that necessary time to lie down, particularly if there are many other hunters in the woods. But it must always be borne in mind that nothing will be gained by driving the deer except to give him up to someone else. Most often chasing such lightly though fatally wounded deer results in *no* one making the recovery.

In club and group hunting good sportsmanship calls for some equalization in dividing the spoils at the end of the season. Much argument and hard feeling can be avoided if some rule is stipulated before the hunting period begins. In one of the author's clubs our rule was fixed and essentially fair, so much so that almost every club in our section of the state has used it for many years. To the hunter who killed the buck went the head and the hide; the carcasses were divided at the end of the season and equally distributed among all the men in the club. If a guest was brought in for a few days' hunting, at the stipulated daily fee, the same rule applied. In this way each hunter saved his trophy and the hide, yet each man was equally rewarded in meat for his part in driving and getting out the venison.

Safety in group hunting involves proper procedure on the drive. The drivers themselves should carry either a crow call or a whistle, both to maintain proper distance from their pals in the drive and to make known to all that their movements are not of deer. The standers should be placed on definite posts, known to *all* the men involved, and should stay there until picked up by the drivers coming through.

I remember hearing of a case where a hunter accidentally killed one of his own hunting partners, simply because one of the men had failed to keep his stand. The accident was inexcusable, but it is easy to see just how it could happen.

Both men were on watch, and next to each other. Separating them was a heavy thicket of white birch and laurel. During the drive a buck came out to a point between the two men and about forty yards off. The hunter fired, dropping the deer, which fell into some heavy ferns and other cover, screening it from view. Shortly after the deer dropped there came a movement in the brush right at the spot where the deer lay, so he fired again, thinking that the deer was getting up, even though he couldn't tell that it was a deer making the movement. When the drive came through, the hunter left his stand and walked over to find his buck and also his hunting partner, both dead. A tragic accident, but one that could have been prevented in the first place by the victim's staying on his stand.

Old Abe Wycoff had a good system for locating stands for his hunters on the Buck Mountain Club. Abe would arm himself with a box full of metal house numbers and nail them to a tree in the right location for each watch. On the wall of the club shack hung a crudely drawn map showing each of these locations with the corresponding number of the stand. In this way each man knew precisely the location of each stander, materially assisting safe procedure on the drive — provided, of course, that every man stayed where put. It goes without saying that every man both on the watch and on the drive would hold his fire if he could reasonably expect one of the bunch to be somewhere in line.

As a matter of cold fact and contrary to general public opinion, deer hunting is one of the safest participant sports in the country. For example: During the season of 1946 in New York State, something over 350,000 hunters took to the woods for the deer season. Of this number there were 26 casualties due to firearms, and only 6 were fatal. Of the 26 deer-hunting accidents in which firearms were involved, 8 were self-inflicted because of careless handling of the hunters' own weapons.

Such carelessness is responsible for the greater part of our accidents. Not carelessness in mistaking hunters for deer, but sheer carelessness in handling the weapons. Last season the author spent the eve of the opening Adirondack date in Perc Flewellin's hotel in Northville. Both I and my buddy were in deep slumber when suddenly we were aroused by a blast from the next room. Sleepy, we were both not too curious at the time as to the cause and went back to sleep. Next day we learned from the proprietor that one of our next-room neighbors had accidentally discharged a revolver. Luckily the bullet struck the hollow steel post at the foot of the bed and lodged within. Conceivably the bullet could have missed and passed through the thin sheetrock walls to inflict injury either to my partner or myself as we lay sound asleep, in a place presumably safe from careless hunters. Had anyone been injured as the result of this incident, another accident would have been charged up to the dangers of deer hunting.

Here is another incident which points up the foolishness of some hunters in gun handling. One of my friends has been for many years the peculiar type of individual who believes that the best spot for watching on a deer drive is high up in a big tree. On a certain day this chap had the good luck to be in the right spot to intercept a nice buck driven out with a herd of does. He happened to pick a big oak tree for his stand and had climbed up to the first big limb, on which he stood throughout the drive. By chance this big oak stood right on the runway and, as the frightened deer ran through directly below him, he began to shoot at the buck. He hit and killed the buck well enough, but as the deer passed below, still on the run, one of his shots blasted a ragged hole through the top of his left foot. Automatically the leg crumpled beneath him and he spilled to the ground. By great good luck he didn't break any more bones, but the bullet-torn foot kept him on crutches for many weeks.

This business of hunting from a tree has all the earmarks of prime foolhardiness. For the little bit of extended vision it grants, the hunter pays the price of limited movement, exposure to the wind, the swaying of the tree deflecting his aim, and the more important hazard of falling out when he does get a shot. I met a hunter just entering the woods one day, carrying a .348 Winchester. The rifle was a new model then, so I stopped him to ask how he liked it. He hadn't shot it much, he said, but he'd bet it would sure kill a deer. No doubt that Winchester kicked just as hard then as these .348's do now. At any rate he passed me on his way out later that day, carrying the action in one hand, the stock in the other. When I looked him over carefully I noticed that his face and hands were badly scratched and bleeding, so I questioned him.

"Well sir," he replied, "to make it short and sweet, I was up a tree watching that run over by King Swamp. A little while ago a damned big buck walked out of the swamp and I took a shot at 'im. And that damned big cannon knocked me right to hell out of that tree. Skinned me all up and busted the gun right in half." He was mad clean through, but he never stopped to think that he could have broken a leg or an arm or have fractured his skull in falling out of that tree. He was mostly concerned because he not only missed the deer but wrecked his gun in the process.

One of my fishing pals had this habit of climbing a tree to watch deer crossings, carrying a pair of linesman's spurs to facilitate the job. During an exceptionally warm, drowsy day he dropped off to sleep and promptly fell out. Not in the least disturbed, he returned to camp, gathered himself a piece of rope, climbed back in the tree and tied himself fast. I believe that he still carries the climbing spurs every season, but I hope for his sake that he doesn't ever forget the rope.

However, statistics tend to show that hunting in the deer woods is just as safe a place to be as in your own home, in week-end traffic or visiting your mother-in-law. The author has a good deal of pity for the man who will not take up or who gives up deer hunting simply because of the "danger" involved. The New York State figures cited here are borne out pretty well for deer hunting throughout the nation. The author has the figures on hunting accidents for all the major deer-producing states for the last ten-year period and can find no excuse for listing them all here. Suffice it to say that the incidence of danger in deer hunting has been highly exaggerated.

Normal care in selecting the proper clothing will help to give a hunter some measure of self-protection, yet strangely enough all these accident reports from various states indicate that a large number of the injured hunters wore red garments or caps. Some hunters feel that wearing red in any form makes too good a target for the man who will shoot blindly, without determining first that his target is not a deer. These men prefer to take their chances with neutral colors in clothing and depend on the law of averages to give them protection. In any event it seems foolish for a man to wear or carry anything white in color while deer hunting, even a white handkerchief.

One of my younger hunting friends was hunting in Delaware County a number of years ago, in a section where the hills and valleys are high and deep. All morning long he had been watching the opposite hillside, several hundred yards away, but had found no deer moving. About noontime he was sitting upon a big stump somewhere near the top of his ridge, to eat lunch. During his long vigil toes had become a little frosty, so he swung his legs vigorously, banging his heels against the stump to restore some much-needed circulation. In a moment there came a ripping thud into the stump at his feet, followed instantly by the crack of a rifle from the far side of the valley slope. Scared and angry, he dropped quickly behind the stump and poured a gun load into the hillside across the valley. He promptly scared out the would-be assassin but he traveled much too fast for my friend to catch. He deduced later that the white-topped long hunting socks, shining out over the tops of his boots, had been the innocent cause of a near accident.

Another friend and my next-door neighbor had his Remington autoloader knocked off his knees as he sat on a watch near Rio in lower Sullivan County. He had been sitting since daylight and had decided to light a cigarette. Sitting calmly and quietly in peaceful contemplation of the valley crossing below him, his rifle was suddenly and violently knocked from his knees, splashing him with bits of bullet and at once ruining the weapon, for the bullet struck the side of the receiver. As I recall the story he told me he had just pulled out his handkerchief — a white one — and was about to lift it to his nose when the blow fell.

Certainly both of these men were in rather plain sight, but the flash of white was all that was required to touch off a hasty trigger-finger. Perhaps the day will come when every man in the woods who hunts deer will be sure of his target before shooting, but at present such a Utopian situation doesn't exist. Thus, to gain the fullest measure of protection, no deer hunter should wear white in any form of garment and it seems wisest to wear red even if it is only a red cap. Even though hunting accidents are rare in proportion to the number of men in the woods each season, it will be best not to flaunt possible danger by wearing a type of clothing that can in any way be mistaken for deer.

Although red is traditionally the coat of arms for deer hunting, and several states compel hunters to wear it, it seems to me that it is not the ideal color for best visibility in the woods. Every season red-garbed hunters are shot at by their brethren during the deer hunting season in spite of the obvious — that no deer wears red other than the reddish-brown summer coat of the whitetail. It's apparent that, for some hunters at least, even more vivid contrast in color is necessary. It is also true that in early morning or late afternoon light, and on cloudy days, red changes to more somber shades.

Scientific experiments in color visibility by highway commissions and the armed forces conclusively prove that a bright yellow is the most visible of all shades of color, at least to the human eye. With this in mind the author managed to extract one of the long-peaked, white swordfishermen's caps from Jim Deren's Roost. After immersion for the specified time in Putnam's yellow dye, the cap was ready for a trial in the woods.

I wore the yellow headgear first in the Adirondacks. On the first day of the season, no less than ten hunters, all strangers to me, commented on the long-range visibility of the cap, even in heavy cover. Down in the Catskills I received the same comment, so much so that I began to ask hunters just how far off I could be seen in the woods. Distances varied, of course, depending on the cover involved, but all estimates indicated that the yellow showed up to at least 50 per cent greater advantage than the conventional type of red hat. This is certainly food for thought for the future, and I am certain that the first capmaker who offers hunting headgear in a bright chrome-yellow shade will have plenty of takers.

Aside from the fact that a man who injures a brother hunter will forever be an outcast among the deer-hunting clan, it is no longer possible to escape scot-free from the penalties of such carelessness. Law courts no longer look upon hunting accidents as "acts of God" and the wanton perpetrator of these sanguinary acts will often find himself convicted of criminal negligence and placed in the position of supporting the victim's family for years to come. The hunter who keeps this forever in mind will think twice before permitting an itchy trigger finger to send a bullet into an unknown target.

As anyone knows, a mixture of alcohol and hunting is not only incompatible but downright dangerous. A "hungover" hunter is far from a cheery, alert companion in the woods. His head aches, his nerves are jumpy and jittery, and he is far more likely to do the foolhardy thing with his weapon than the man who basks on his stand in sobriety. Liquor is a wonderfully heart-warming tonic, but must forever be used with discretion by the hunter, particularly the camper hunter. Good sportsmanship decrees that each man in a deer-hunting group be willing and able to start out at daylight, with a clear head and steady hand, to take part in each drive and be alert to kill the buck driven to him. After a tough "night before" no normal man can do justice to his pal's expectations of him, nor to himself. No one enjoys the lift of a good shot of Old Grandad after a hard day's hunt more than the author, but not to such an extent that getting up at dawn for a day in the woods becomes a hardship.

Success and safety in the woods is to a great degree dictated by the hunter's personal comfort. He must be warmly and properly clothed from head to foot, have a good morning meal under his belt and a long night's rest behind him. "Roughing it" in a deer hunters' camp does not need to include uncomfortable beds and skimpy meals. No man can really enjoy the grand sport of deer hunting to the full unless he himself is physically and mentally in shape every day.

Most important to the personal safety of every deer hunter is the ability to find his way around the woods in strange or wilderness territory without wandering off and losing his location. A lost, fear-crazed and panic-stricken hunter is a pitiable sight. With his sense of location gone and the fear of a long black night in the woods curdling the blood in his veins, he goes completely crazy, "blows his top." We picked up one of these men a few years ago in the scrub oak and laurel bush between Wolf Pond and Westbrookville, late at night. When we at last located him he was a gibbering wreck, clothes ripped off to his waist, pants in shreds, rifle and ammunition gone — lacking even rudimentary human sanity. He had wandered off from the rest of his party in country that he didn't know and when darkness caught up with him he was several miles from the rest of his group. But when we found him he was no more than half a mile from a well-traveled highway and a fairly large river, each of which could have brought him out to safety if he had taken the trouble to study a map of the area. Even without a compass he should have been able to find either the river or the highway, for the weather was clear. Just a few minutes' walk into the setting sun would have brought him to the road, but this victim of ignorance and inexperience couldn't manage to do it.

In marked contrast to this experience I remember the time that Old George Drake, one of our own outfit, succeeded in losing himself in the woods. George was a man of a lifetime in the woods, but at his advanced age his hearing was far from acute and the old eyes were dimming with the years. On this occasion he had gone off by himself to sit out until sundown on a runway, and had inadvertently fallen asleep. He roused himself at last, into pitch-blackness, and in the momentary confusion he forgot the lay of the trail. Meanwhile our whole outfit was pretty much alarmed, thinking, not that he was lost, but that he had passed out from a heart seizure and might be lying out helpless and freezing to death. We scouted all his known haunts without success, and were almost ready to give up when a single shot sounded faintly behind a ridge about a mile from camp. We made a beeline for the spot, and just before we arrived another shot rang out.

We found George sitting near a little fire, with a big pile of dry wood handy, calmly smoking his cracked briar. He was glad to see us of course, and a little bit ashamed at pulling such a stunt, but he apologized for having kept us up so late looking for him. As a matter of fact he had decided to spend the night there, but after thinking it over and knowing that we would be out looking for him, he sent out a shot or two to guide us. Didn't like to do it though, he said, too damned much shootin' in the woods as it was. Besides he didn't like to waste any ammunition, not unless he was shooting at deer.

Any man, irrespective of his experience, should never enter large hunting areas in strange territory unless he first arms himself with a simple compass and a detailed map of the territory. The U. S. Geological maps are ideal. They show all the physical characteristics of the land — streams, swamp, lowlands, ridges, cliffs and mountains. With one of these maps in his pocket and a compass to give a constant directional beam, any hunter, even a rank greenhorn, will have little trouble in placing his location. He must of course have some rudimentary knowledge of using the compass with the map.

One of my early deer-hunting pals showed the typical tenderfoot's reaction to the compass. We had been still-hunting all morning and in the process had covered a couple of miles through an area which was new to him. When we stopped for lunch at midday, we sat down on a big log for a little rest and to compare notes. As we chewed the rag about the morning's hunt he suddenly discovered that we were lost — at least he was. Then, struck with a thought, he reached into his shirt pocket and pulled out a beautiful floating dial compass. Carefully he placed it on the log, waited for the dial to settle, and then asked, "Well, there's the new compass; what do we do now?"

"Nothing, of course," I told him, "you haven't looked at the thing all day until just now, have you?"

"No; didn't think it was necessary. I thought you could tell just by lookin' at it where you were s'posed to go."

After the laughter had died away I explained that the compass was useful only if he referred to it frequently on his way into the woods, using some landmark for orienting his position at each change in direction. Then, with this information catalogued mentally, he could reverse his direction, to find the way out. "And that's about all there is to using a compass," I told him.

Actually this is all that's required if the hunter is making a short foray into strange country. If he leaves his starting point and heads

into the woods due west and maintains that course until he is ready
to come out, then logically he needs only to reverse his direction to
come back to the starting point. However, if he intends to make a
wide sweep through new forests and ridges such a simple system
fails to be of any help. In this event he will begin his travel by taking
a fixed direction to some visible landmark — a lone pine on a ridge-
top, an outcropping of rock or something else equally distinctive.
Then, when he changes his directional movement, it will be at this
easily remembered point; he will strike out in a new line, checking
always with his compass, for another landmark, continuing this
procedure throughout the day's travel. Then, when the sun begins to
close off the day he will retrace his steps in opposite directions to his
incoming path, switching his directional travel at the familiar landmarks.

Such a trip requires a keen memory for cataloguing the directions
and the landmarks in their proper order. If the directional changes
are too varied the hunter will be wise in not trusting to his memory
but will make notes as he travels. Best of all, if he has a topographical
map, he can make the notes and line of movement directly on the
map and never at any time will he be in doubt as to his precise location. This procedure may seem to be a good deal of trouble to a new
hunter, but it is this practice in compass and map-reading, as it re-
lates to the terrain, which will be invaluable to a deer hunter for the
rest of his days. Such training forms the basis of true woodsmanship,
and can only be acquired in this or a similar way. Few men are born
with a keen directional sense, but every normal man can acquire
enough of it within a few years of hunting to carry him safely
through any tight spot.

Experienced hunters and woodsmen who are somewhat familiar
with the areas hunted never need a compass when the sun shines.
A good man in the woods can tell time to within a quarter of an
hour by a quick glance at the sun's position. From this he can plot
any point of the compass. In a pinch a watch can be made to serve
roughly as a compass if the sun shines. Simply hold the watch level,
point the hour hand in a direct line with the sun; then due *south* will
lie directly between the hour hand and the figure twelve. Knowing
south, or any other compass point, the woodsman can plot his course
in the required direction.

Carrying maps may not appeal to the average hunter, and it is not
vitally necessary that a map be carried, provided that the hunter has
a good retentive memory and can fix in his mind a picture of the

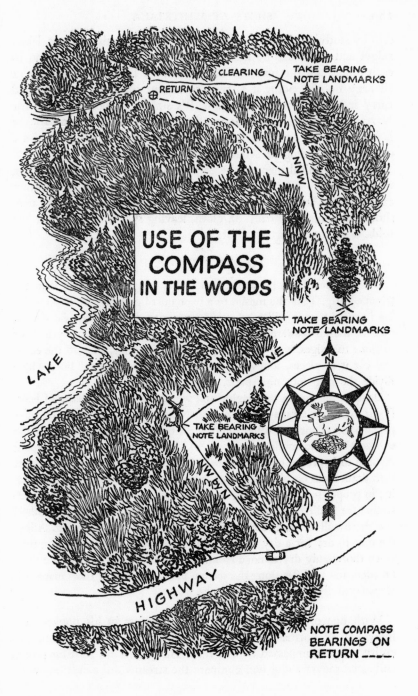

area by studying the map before taking to the woods. Streams, lakes, ridges and roads can be memorized as to direction and relation to each other, and the map can be left behind. But if the hunter is at all hazy on this point it is wise to mount the map properly and carry it right along on the hunt. It's simple to mount a map for carrying, and once this is done a hunter will be reluctant to leave it behind, if for no other reason than that its presence gives him a comfortable feeling of security in a wilderness area.

A topographical map can be carried as is, that is just as it comes, folded like any other piece of paper, but in a short time constant exposure and handling will ruin it. To do a permanent job the map should be mounted firmly on cloth, leaving spaces to allow for the folds. This is one way to do it:

TO MOUNT A MAP

Get a piece of muslin about two inches longer and wider than the trimmed map. Tack the muslin to a wide board or an old tabletop, bearing in mind that it will take a day or two to dry the map. Be certain that the muslin is stretched tightly both ways, using tacks every inch or so along the edges. Now take your topographical map, trim off the edges and cut it in pieces, following the longitudinal and lateral lines which divide the map into nine parts.

Dampen the muslin thoroughly and work into it a thick paste of laundry starch, then scrape off the excess. Next apply a heavy coat of wallpaper paste (flour and water) and work this in well, smoothing off the excess. With the muslin prepared, take your nine map parts, keeping them in their proper order, and soak them for a minute or two in water, then drain them on blotting paper. Now lay them on the prepared muslin, in proper sequence, leaving a good quarter-inch space between each section for folding. Don't attempt to lay the sections touching each other, else there will be no room for folding the map for the pocket. Allow the map to dry for a day or two, after smoothing out the sections, then when thoroughly dry remove from the board, trim off the outside muslin edge, and fold flat along the section lines. Any one of these maps will serve faithfully for many years in the woods.

With one of the maps and a good compass in his pocket any individual of normal intelligence can find his way throughout the entire area encompassed by the map. He will fix his starting point, and as he moves along will compare the streams and elevations with the map outlines. He can easily note landmarks and in time will be able to calculate distances quite accurately. A little of this study adds much to a hunter's overall knowledge of woodcraft.

In spite of all advice on the subject, every year some deer hunters will be lost in the woods, at least for a short time. If a man uses a little natural sense, such an incident, while uncomfortable, is not necessarily a calamity. Some hunters have no ability in orienting themselves, nor will they take the time and trouble to learn such rudimentary woodcraft. These men should hire a guide for their deer hunting and depend on the guide's experience and woodsmanship to keep them in hand at all times.

When a hunter does find himself lost in a strange territory he must follow a definite procedure if he would retain his health and sanity. First he should sit right down and take stock of the situation, fighting off any feeling of panic and trying to assemble in his mind all his moves prior to becoming lost. He should console himself with the thought that he cannot be far from familiar ground and perhaps by clear straight thinking he may be able to figure his way out of the situation. He should try to remember the general lay of the land; main ridges have a tendency to follow uniform lines. By thinking back he may be able to discover that this new strange spot is merely parallel to the next ridge which he followed on his way in. He must try to locate the compass points from the location of the sun and time of day. Lacking sun, it's pretty tough to do this. The old cliché "moss on the north side of trees" hardly works out well in heavy timber — it is not at all reliable as a guide.

Next, if all his best thinking cannot point to a solution he may make a small foray to find a logging road or skidway or even a small stream. Following a running stream will in time bring him to civilization, though it may prove to be a long way off. At any rate there is little need for a lost hunter to become so panic-stricken that he runs crazily in circles, terrorized by the silent loneliness of the big timber and the eerie blackness of the night. Far better than this is to decide right then and there to spend the night in the woods and allow ample time for preparations.

The first step will be to find a naturally sheltered spot; a rock ledge, an overhanging boulder, a big downed log or even a heavily thatched evergreen tree. If the hunter has a small ax or heavy knife he can throw up a couple of sloping poles and quickly thatch them over with evergreen branches, forming a tiny lean-to. His next problem will be to gather together sufficient wood for starting a fire and to keep it going.

In virtually every deer-hunting area plenty of burnable fuel will be found, both for kindling a fire and for keeping it going throughout the night. The dead under-branches of all kinds of conifers and both white and yellow birch, as well as beech, can be broken off readily and cracked up for starting the fire. In wet weather a fire can be started by peeling off the loose bark from yellow, white or paper birch; even damp, these resin-filled scrapings will ignite at once and start the fire. Likewise, the lower dead branches of evergreens make the best fire-starters in damp weather. However, the primary function of this small stuff is to get larger wood burning, and the real fire, once started, with proper tending can be maintained throughout the night even in a steady rain, provided some sort of overhead shelter is selected for the spot.

In starting an overnight fire, build it against some sort of reflector — a big log, rock, or bank. Lay the tinder and place on it a handful of the small under-branches. When the flame catches, feed it more of these branches until the blaze is going. For the heavier firewood, scout around until you can pick up several down-branches or windfalls. Never use stuff that has been lying flat on the ground; capillary action will make this wood damp and dozy and it can be kept afire only by constant addition of more kindling. But in every forest area good firewood can be had just for the picking and there is no need to use an ax for chopping the wood into short lengths, whether or not one is at hand. When the blaze is going the ends of the heavier branches can be laid on the flames and as the wood is consumed the limb is moved up for a fresh bite. By shifting up the logs and branches as they burn, a warm bright fire can be maintained without ever using an ax. The best woods for the all-night emergency fire will be maple, oak, beech and birch. Any of these woods will burn green, particularly in the fall, once the fire is well started, but a hunter without an ax will have some trouble in breaking off limbs from the living trees. It will be easier to look a bit farther for dead timber than to wrestle with the live stuff.

When the lost hunter has made certain he will have enough fuel and a reasonably secure spot for the night he can begin to fire signal shots to aid possible searchers. The standard signal is three shots, spaced ten to fifteen seconds apart, but here again the temptation to burn up all one's ammunition in a hurry should be subdued. Such warning signals can be fired off every half-hour or so but not oftener. It will require at least this length of time for searchers to move out of earshot of a rifle report, so more frequent firing than this is unnecessary, and a hunter's supply of ammunition is not too extensive. The most important step is for the lost hunter to remain in *one place*, giving the searchers an opportunity to locate him.

If a hunter should be so unlucky as not to have a supply of matches for starting a fire, this is no cause for alarm. Everyone who carries a firearm can start a fire quite readily in this way: Prepare the birch bark tinder and small stuff for starting the fire, then take a cartridge and pry out the bullet between two stones. Pour most of the powder onto the tinder, then tear off a piece of a handkerchief or shirt tail and wad it into the mouth of the cartridge case. Fire the cartridge in the rifle, and when it spurts out of the barrel, smoking, pick it up and blow on it until it glows, then drop it on the spilled powder in the tinder and it will burst right up in flame.

One of the handiest fire-starters a hunter can carry is an ordinary candle, household size. With one or two of these stuck in the recesses of his hunting coat he can start a fire quickly with little or no tinder and in damp rainy weather. For igniting damp wood or bark the candle can be lighted and the drippings allowed to flow over the tinder. When the flame is touched to the tinder a prompt fire results. Nothing in a hunter's equipment for fire making will give such positive, quick results for the room it takes up in his pocket.

Any hunter with a small amount of woods sense will never get into any real trouble in the woods. First of all he'll seldom get lost — and if he does, he will sit down and take stock of the situation calmly before blowing up into a panic. As the realization dawns that his hunting pals will be on the lookout for him shortly, he will prepare to stay right on the spot until his signal shots bring help. No man will ever move so far in a day's hunting that he will be out of the hearing area of a rifle report, unless he drops into a ravine. In the daytime he can build a good big campfire and throw up a smoke screen with evergreen branches. These smoke signals won't go unnoticed for long in any hunting territory.

To be on the safe side, the wilderness deer hunter should carry the following items: Map, compass, knife, matches in waterproof case, a small roll of twine, a few chocolate bars and perhaps a small pocket-ax. With this equipment he can spend a full night in the woods with little actual discomfort. He may lose some sleep and will be mighty hungry when he gets out, but that's about all.

A woods compass needs to be only of a simple type. The floating-dial and heavy-needle types are the best as they are not so sensitive to changes induced by outside influences. And in using a compass never hold it near your rifle, knife or other magnetic metal. Set it on a rock or stump, back away from it until the dial settles, then check the readings. There is seldom a need for a highly accurate compass in deer hunting but there is a definite place in every wilderness hunter's pocket for a simple instrument that will furnish constant direction.

A good sportsman will take all the time necessary to acquire such knowledge as he needs to follow successfully the grand sport of whitetail hunting, to the increase of his own personal satisfaction and the everlasting gratitude of his friends and brother hunters. No man must be a blood brother to the Indian or a direct descendent of Dan'l Boone to pursue successfully and safely the whitetail deer, but he must use much the same good judgment that he would to drive his car on a crowded highway. He must forever be alert to his own mistakes as well as to the other fellows, tempering every move with basic common sense.

For some obscure reason, many a man in the woods becomes a different personality. At home he may be a good neighbor and a fine friend but this same man can become thoughtless, selfish, greedy and downright dangerous while deer hunting. To such a man, bringing home the trophy is of paramount importance, whether or not it involves good sportsmanship or regard for the normal human rights of others. Fortunately, almost all of these men grow up mentally after a few years in the woods, to the eternal betterment of their own sport and the safety of the ever-growing fraternity of the deer-hunting brethren.

10 / *Buck Fever*

WHITETAIL HUNTING embraces many variables, in its numerous phases, but none is more mysterious than the strange malady known as "buck fever." The term has come to mean, through the broad usage of many years, any foolish thing a person may do under stress of high emotional tension or excitement. Originating in the deer woods it now is loosely applied throughout the entire field of sporting pursuits, both fishing and hunting. If a fisherman regales us with a long sad tale of the big trout which escaped his landing net at the critical moment, does he accuse himself of having had trout fever or fish fever? No; always it is the admission, if any such explanation is offered, that the unlucky angler must have had a bad case of "buck fever."

Is there such an affliction, which can be honestly termed "buck fever"? I believe not. "Buck ague," "buck fever," call it what you will, has a much greater implication of emotional unstability than the simple term which sweepingly groups all hunting thrills and excitement into a malady of narrow limitations. Probably a more exact terminology would be possible only for a student of individual psychology; certainly the author would never attempt to give it a more precise name. Perhaps careful analysis of a hunter's probable reactions to the emotional drive of deer hunting will give a better insight to the problem. And in many cases it is a problem; one that is far more dangerous and pitiable than humorous.

There seems little doubt that the buck fever victim is, at the moment of his travail, an entirely different character from the pal who shares your camp roof and venison stew. All during the long weeks of waiting for the opening day, through the nights of planning and preparation, right up to the moment of his actually seeing deer, he shows normal enthusiasm. Perhaps he is inclined to ply the more experienced hunters with a greater-than-usual number of questions, but in all other respects he is just another eager hunter, carrying high hopes and expectations, along with the rest of the party.

With the coming of opening day, this man is given a good post to watch the drive. Halfway through, the drivers jump a fine buck and, as so often happens, he heads directly for the new hunter's stand. In a few moments there may be a hurried flurry of shots or perhaps only a single report or none at all. When the drivers come through they find a shaking, palsied hunter, pale of countenance, sweat oozing from every pore; but no buck. The forthcoming explanations may differ in minor details, but they all follow a familiar pattern. The end result is the same — the buck gets away. This is the situation which is humorous for all the party, other than the unhappy victim. Fortunately, this is the usual result of a buck fever attack, but now and then a victim will become so emotionally out of hand at missing, or failing to shoot at a buck, that he may take a crack at the coming driver, when movement shows through the cover. This is the tragic side of the buck fever picture.

Let's analyze the shooter's reactions, if we can, throughout the whole period, up until the time his buck vanishes from sight. It may give us a better understanding of the problem and help to stave off possible future attacks. First of all it is most likely that the buck fever victim has yet to kill his first buck. It's true that now and then a hunter will be gripped by the seizure with his second, third or fourth deer, but it is not quite so likely to occur as with the first deer.

Starting then with a virginal deerslayer, we follow his approach to the hunting trip. Undoubtedly the urge to hunt deer has been implanted by the sight of his friends coming home with a nice buck or two on their cars. He reads of Tom, Dick and Harry bagging their bucks the first day of the season. He learns from his outdoor magazines that deer are on the increase throughout much of the whitetail's range; young lads and old-timers alike are bringing home their buck each season. He visualizes also a wide-spreading trophy hanging over his fireplace or mantel. One of the boys in the office belongs to a hunting camp in the Catskills and, in a moment of largess, invites our hero to spend a week-end trip during the early part of the season. Until now, the victim has been more or less content to spend his autumn week ends with the scattergun and cottontail rabbits. But with Opportunity knocking at his door, his heart leaps with enthusiasm into the spirit of deer hunting. He buys unlimited quantities of new equipment — extra-warm clothing, comfortable boots, heavy long underwear, knife, compass, *et al*. Then, after consulting the circle of his hunting friends and the oracle of the outdoor magazines, he buys, begs, or more often borrows, a "deer rifle." But that which is most important to the success of the hunt, and which he cannot obtain with mere cash, he neglects to obtain — familiarity with his weapon and the development of a certain degree of shooting skill. He may go so far as to spend an afternoon with his office friend just to "try out" his newly acquired weapon, but as for practice with the rifle — he'll wait until he sees his deer. That'll be time enough.

The week preceding his trip to camp is spent in a frenzy of activity. When the day of departure at last arrives, all his friends and his patient mate are glad to see him off. But in fairness to the poor fellow, we must admit that such enthusiasm is a large part of any deer hunter's trip. Anticipation is often greater and more pleasing than realization. Arrived in camp, the new lad is introduced to the rest of the bunch and he sits in on the evening bull session with ears wide open, firmly endeavoring to glean such deer lore as he is able to extract within the next few hours. He learns then that deer are forthright creatures, with minds of their own; that no one knows precisely what to expect of a whitetail buck in the woods. He listens avidly to the tales of bucks, large and small, which have outwitted the gang through season after season, and a creeping doubt, dormant for weeks, but now fully aroused, fills his mind.

Next morning, with the new dawn gray in the east, the standers make their way to the posts. A last-minute huddle outside the camp has formed the quick decision to put the new lad on the watch nearest camp. Deer seldom hit for this run, but at least the boys won't be scouring the woods for a strayed stander instead of hunting.

On the watch the new man is carefully instructed as to where the deer will most likely appear; then the party passes on, leaving him to his thoughts. For a time he enjoys himself; he sits on a smooth stone, back to a big beech, and snuggles down within his new warm clothes, shaking off the early morning chill. The rising sun casts a pink glow through the bare treetops canopying his stand and momentarily he wonders at the dead stillness of a forest sunrise.

Suddenly a lone acorn spats noisily on the crisp dead leaves. Nervously, he glances that way and then checks his rifle to make sure the cartridge is in the chamber and the action is cocked. He shifts the safety off and on experimentally, wondering why it now seems to click so stridently. For a time all is quite still until vague scratchings, followed by a rapid *crush, crush, crush* in the dry leaves, raise his back hair and start his pumper to thumping. Cautiously, he strains his head to peek behind the tree from whence this new disturbance arises. At first nothing is changed in the woodscape, but still the noise persists — quiet rustlings increasing in tempo, then subsiding to a faint murmur. At last, when his mental agitation is at the bursting point, a ghostlike gray tail appears from behind a big oak — only a gray squirrel. With a sigh almost of relief, the hunter once again leans back against his beech tree and attempts to regain his composure.

No sooner has his breathing slowed down to normal with his heart pulsing away at its normal smooth rate than, with a quiet swish of wings, a blue jay swings into a tree near by. With a great show of efficiency he announces the hunter's intrusion in a series of raucous cries which echo interminably throughout the hills. *Damn!* our hero thinks, *every deer in the world will know I'm here!* But getting no results, apparently, the blue jay flutters off, still shrieking, until the cries fade away in the distance. By this time the waiting hunter has a firmly entrenched case of nerves, and at this precise moment deer will inevitably be headed toward his post.

At first our hunter is not aware of their approach. He has heard numerous strange noises during his short wait, and none of them have culminated in the appearance of deer. The faint rattle of brush and tiny rustle of leaves which presage the appearance of deer fails to inflict itself upon his senses. So far he has gathered himself into a tight knot at every new sound, but now he resolves to wait for the appearance of the buck himself before again getting into such a state of funk. Therefore, the sudden appearance of a sleek pair of does directly in front of his stand gives him, to put it mildly, quite a turn. As his eyes first come to rest on the deer a mighty hand clutches at his heart, giving it a quick, thorough squeeze, sending a tingling fluid — hardly blood — through every nerve and muscle within his body. His mouth flies open as he clutches for more breath and, deep within this oral cavity, his ticker clicks with increasing tempo, like a recalcitrant metronome.

Vainly he looks for horns, and, as the graceful does float by, he glances down at his rifle to check the mechanism once again. He looks at the safety, and in his new terror cannot for the life of him remember whether it is off or on. Again he tries it and, satisfied, he clicks it off and looks up once more. As his eyes adjust themselves to the new focus, he finds himself staring directly into a face wearing a high rack of gleaming antlers. Now he is in a fix. Directly before him, head high, ears erect, stands the object of sleepless nights; of many day dreams; of many weeks of preparation and endless planning. Trees and saplings obscure most of the buck from his view; only the proudly erect head and white throat-patch appear vividly before his gaze; the rest of the sleek body is buried behind natural barriers.

Does our hero bring his rifle slowly to rest against his shoulder, carefully cheeking the stock and bringing the front sight up to the gleaming white throat-patch, gently squeezing off the shot that will anchor his prize in a flurry of flailing hoofs? No, he does not. Instead a new fantastic fear freezes his blood — not enough of the deer is visible for him to hit. His palsied hands can never direct the front sight to that white throat-target. His fevered brain now knows that his shooting ability is not that good, and with each fleeting second the buck is nearer to flight. In sheer desperation he throws up the rifle, only to have it catch under his arm, before coming to shoulder. *Dammit!* He'd forgotten to try the rifle when he had the new hunting coat on. But with the first quick movement the deer is away, bounding down through the tall white birch, gay flag flying defiantly. Hurriedly the sights are put together, but in the early morning light the front sight seems dim.

A shift of the head brings the front sight into clear view; now the rifle is poked ahead of the running deer and the shot blasts out, followed by repeated reports until the deer is out of sight. Shaking and weak the hunter comes slowly back to earth, to the grim realization that his deer is still bouncing brightly along, with never a hair disturbed and suffering only the indignities of hurried retreat.

This is the classic example of the seizure known universally as "buck fever." Many times it is evidenced in different ways — the hunter may fail to fire even a shot at the deer, or he may pump every cartridge through his rifle action without firing a single one. But in all cases the end result is the same: the buck escapes. From a purely selfish point of view this is an excellent state of affairs. If buck fever and buck ague were a non-existent malady, few bucks would be left for the rest of us. Almost every man who saw his deer would be shortly carrying it home, to the distinct alarm of conservation officials. However, nothing that this writer, or any other, has to say on the subject will change the condition; my observations are purely rhetorical.

Any man who spends the greater part of his lifetime in the hunting of whitetail deer is bound by the law of averages to encounter some mighty humorous situations, with buck fever as the principally underlying cause. Most of the failures with hunters so afflicted is the direct result of ignorance in handling their weapons and their normal human cupidity to grasp and retain that which is not yet rightfully theirs. Only by careful pre-seasonal preparation can a hunter overcome the ravaging effect of the nervous palsy or rigidity induced by buck fever. The deer hunter must be guided by a great singleness of purpose, a firm resolve to match physical qualifications with emotional stability.

At least on one occasion I had the opportunity to get firsthand information on the influence of buck fever — one might say I was right in the middle of the situation. Here is how it came about. For several days my group of hunting pals had been trying to drive a nice buck out of a valley swamp. Early in the season, one of the boys had missed this buck and since that day we were convinced that he hid away in the safe recesses of the swamp. Cover was good and the surrounding ridges were densely thatched with laurel, scrub oak and jack pine. It was difficult to drive out the deer to a stander, for his path could cover any one of many routes, all of them through thick terrain. Our group was limited in numbers so we were perforce required to stand three men and drive only two. On the morning I have in mind three of us had taken stands along a wood road which paralleled the edge of the swamp, but some few hundred yards above the swamp on a little ridge. The two drivers worked through the low ground, then came up the ridge through tangled cat-briers and laurel clumps, but without starting any deer.

We had made this drive early in the morning, and as the season was well advanced, the boys weren't in any sweat to make the next drive. Accordingly it was agreed to go back to camp, about a quarter-mile away, and have a fresh cup of coffee before beginning the next drive. The two drivers started off for camp, leaving my two companions and me standing in the wood road. For several minutes we talked together in hushed tones, planning new strategy to kill this swamp buck; then we, too, made off for camp. Quietly we moved along the wood road, one young lad leading the way, another bringing up the rear.

As we passed some thick clumps of white birch and cat-brier the man ahead suddenly stopped, pointing down into the white birch through which the drivers had just come. Almost at the same instant the lad behind me whispered "It's a buck!" At the moment my view of the deer was obscured by a clump of big oak trees, but I took one step backward and peered down into the heavy stand of white birch. True enough, there stood a buck, quartering away, with his head turned over his shoulder and looking directly toward us. With a single movement I unslung the short-barreled Krag, swung it up and, as the front sight appeared through the rear peep against the buck's flank, I squeezed off the shot. At once the deer floundered to the ground, and as I was about to send in a finishing shot, both my companions jumped over the stone wall, directly in the line of fire, toward the deer. Meanwhile the buck had risen from the ground, but only moved off a few feet before expiring. This was indeed luck, for I should never have had another shot at him without risking the life of either one of the two men with me.

At any rate, we killed the buck and after we had him in camp, both the boys who had been with me began to lay me out for not giving them a chance at the deer. This was absurd, for both men had seen this buck several moments before I had, yet they seemed to be frozen at the sight. It has always been the author's aim to kill a buck as quickly as the opportunity presents itself, but evidently my companions had suffered a slight touch of that well-known malady at the quick wraithlike appearance of deer where deer had no logical right to be.

Such experiences are common in every deer-hunting territory. There is no way to counteract the thrill attendant on first sighting a whitetail buck, nor should there be. Such a thrill is the primary reason for hunting deer, and without it, a man might better sit home by the fire and recount the experiences of youth, when heart-stopping thrills were still a part of his existence. Any sportsman who can kill his deer without the tingling spine, the quick clutch at his heart, the delicious trembling of nerve fibers when the game is finally down, has no place in the deer woods.

11 / The Archer
Deer Hunter

SCATTERED throughout our broad expanse of deer-hunting territory is a select group of highest-quality sportsmen. In singles, pairs or small groups they take to the woods each year, garbed in conventional woods garments but carrying the primitive weapons of a bygone age. Around each hunter hangs the traditional aura of Robin Hood and the American Indian, for these are the modern-day archers who prefer to take their game under the most exacting of all hunting conditions and with weapons, that, although wholly adequate, are certainly not a most efficient method of destruction.

It might be difficult for the nonhunter to visualize the reasons for bow-and-arrow hunting; but for men who love the outdoors, the sweeping roll of timbered ridges, the stark-white stands of birch and the quiet gray halls of beech, the bow and its silent but deadly missile may become a logical choice. Certainly it will never be the weapon for a man who must kill every buck he sees; neither will it be the choice of the hunter who cannot bear the ridicule of his hunting partners or friends. No, far from this, the bow and broadhead shaft are the weapons of the true nature lover, the hunter who above all things dislikes the discordant crash of gunpowder rending apart the holy silence of the forest. Then too, the man who takes his buck with the longbow and feathered shaft feels a far greater physical intimacy in the act than the hunter who squeezes a trigger, thereby releasing the storehouse of energy which lies within the brass cylinder in his rifle chamber. The killing force of the arrow is the direct result of the archer's muscular effort in compressing the bow, then releasing this force to speed toward the quarry.

Any man who takes up the bow as the weapon for bagging his whitetail buck will realize full well the great handicap under which he will hunt. For many hunters who are surfeited with killing deer with the rifle, archery offers a welcome change in values and results. The kills will be few in number but the experiences will far outweigh those of the rifle shooter. Successful deer hunting with the bow demands by far the greatest skill in woodcraft and stalking, plus the most intimate knowledge of the personal habits and characteristics of the game.

The great, widespread increase in archery deer hunting is a heartwarming indication of the greater sporting trend of a new generation of hunters. The archer hunts not for meat, not for the trophy, but for the sheer, pure joy of matching wits and endurance with that clever animal, the whitetail buck. It is apparently the renewal of the dauntless pioneer spirit, the heritage of Americanism, that prompts this new crop of archers to meet the challenge offered in taking deer with the bow and arrow.

Many states, recognizing this new surge of esthetic endeavor, have gone along with the archer in establishing special seasons or setting aside hunting preserves for archery alone. Here he will be in company of his own choosing and will enjoy a greater feeling of comradeship and sympathy with his fellow hunters. No archer likes to feel that his already slim chance of bagging a buck will be unfavorably influenced by the presence of rifle-toting sportsmen in his hunting grounds.

Leaders in the movement to promote archery hunting have been Michigan and Wisconsin. In Michigan the entire state is open for taking antlered deer from October 1 to November 5 inclusive, and in Allegan County deer of either sex may be taken. In 1946 the State Commission set the special Allegan County season to extend from October 1 through December 15. This liberal archery deer season was excellent for week-end hunters throughout the entire fall. The warm weather hunters had their chance to bag a deer when the air was balmy and the more serious hunters were able to take their hunting trips when the deer were moving in cold weather and on snow. Past experience shows that in Allegan County the best period for archers is during the first two weeks in November, and it is during this period that the annual Archers' Jamboree is held.

Wisconsin's archers have done a creditable job, not only in promoting the sport, but in really taking deer. The 1945 season was one of the most successful in the entire country. Roughly 3500 archers took to the field and bagged 160 deer with the bow and arrow — 69 bucks and 91 does. The state's special archery provisions are highly favorable for the archer hunters — they are permitted to hunt throughout a 45-day period in 49 counties, and during this period 1 deer of either sex, over yearling size, may be taken. The outstanding archery preserve is the Necedah Wildlife Refuge, 40,000 acres in Juneau County, which was opened to archery hunters in 1945 after being closed to all hunting for 6 years. Wisconsin also is unique in that it publishes a complete report in its Conservation bulletin on the deer taken the preceding year, giving sex and weight of deer, county in which taken, weight of bow used, whether the shot was running or standing and how far the deer traveled after being hit.

As far back, comparatively speaking, as 1938 Wisconsin had a keen interest in the hunter archer. The Commission's report for that year shows about 600 archery permits issued with 6 hunters only bagging their bucks; this low average of success in those early years of archery indicates that it was even rougher going than today to kill a deer with the bow and arrow. In deference to these "pioneers" in archery hunting and for the further interest of new archers, the author is listing the circumstances of each kill as published by the Game Commission:

1. Howard L. Thrapp, 215 North Allen St., Madison
   Date: October 15, at 11:30 A.M.
   Location: Columbia Co.
   Shot: Deer standing at 66 feet
   Weight: 191 pounds dressed
   Points: 10
   Bow: Osage orange, rawhide back, 72-pound draw
   Arrow: Birch, 26½" barbless broadhead
   Fall: Deer traveled 30 yards after shot

2. Walter O. Widner, 928 Humboldt, La Crosse
   Date: October 15, 2:00 P.M.
   Location: Buffalo Co.
   Shot: Deer standing at 60 feet
   Weight: 278 pounds dressed
   Points: 10
   Bow: Lemonwood, 45-pound pull
   Arrow: 28" barbless broadhead
   Fall: Deer traveled only 30 feet after shot

3. Clayton M. Sweo, 609 Allen Street, Rhinelander
   Date: October 15, 5:00 P.M.
   Location: Iron Co.
   Shot: Deer standing at 90 feet

Weight: 190 pounds dressed
Points: 8
Bow: Osage orange, 65-pound pull
Arrow: 28″ barbed broadhead
Fall: Deer traveled 400 yards after shot

4. Lester Shore, 1314 Hoven Court, Madison
Date: November 1, 11:30 A.M.
Location: Columbia Co.
Shot: Deer running at 60 feet
Weight: 200 pounds dressed
Points: 10
Bow: Cuban lemonwood, 75-pound pull
Arrow: 28″ birch barbless broadhead
Fall: Deer traveled 500 yards after shot

5. Frank J. Parker, 2560 North Eighth St., Milwaukee
Date: November 5, 10:00 A.M.
Location: Columbia Co.
Shot: Deer running at 45 feet
Weight: 245 pounds dressed
Points: 8
Bow: Lemonwood, 55-pound pull
Arrow: 26″ barbless broadhead
Fall: Deer traveled 100 yards after shot

6. Wallace J. Bowman, Madison
Date: November 12, 11:55 A.M.
Location: Columbia Co.
Shot: Deer turning at 60 feet
Weight: 125 pounds dressed
Points: 4
Bow: Yew, 60-pound pull
Arrow: Cedar, 28″ barbless broadhead
Fall: Deer traveled 150 yards after shot

Each of these six deer were killed with a single shaft and in addition no deer were lost that year by archer hunters, due to failure of the arrow to kill, although two or three of these archers had a fairly long chase to recover their buck.

Seventeen states, at this writing, provide either special archery preserves, special seasons for archers, or both. New York State has so far done little to promote archery throughout the state other than opening Westchester County, just outside New York City's limits,

to the archer deer hunter. During the 1945 season a total of just ove
30 deer was taken by the archers almost within sight of Manhattan'
skyline. There is, however, a new movement underway to open u
additional and more desirable areas to the deer-hunting archers fo.
coming seasons, in New York State.

To become a good deer-hunting archer, not only must a sports
man change his mental attitude to be in tune with the present clar
of successful bow-and-arrow men, but he must prepare to spen
months in patient practice with the primitive weapons before h
steps into deer country. Even then he must reconcile himself to going
deerless for a few seasons, unless exceptional luck is on his side
The archer, by the very nature of his weapon, will never become
threat to our supply of deer, but his rewards in satisfaction, thrill:
and excitement will be far greater when he does connect than any
that ever come to the rifle hunter.

An archer need not be the world's best shot in order to kill hi:
deer. It is a rare buck that is killed at a distance as great as fifty yard
and with only a short practice period in shooting a normal individua
with good equipment can score regularly on a deer target at this
range. There are many more important deterring factors in shooting
deer than the ability of the archer to hit his target. Every man who
has hunted whitetails knows how seldom it is that a fairly open shot
can be had and what we usually term an "open" shot in rifle shooting
can still be an impossible chance for an archer. An arrow needs only
to touch a small twig, either at its head or anywhere along its
length to be deflected far off its course. And the chance of hitting
such overhanging twigs and branches is pretty high in whitetail
deer cover.

With the rifle, a hunter needs only to have a small opening, say
about four inches in diameter, through which he can poke his bullet
and nail his buck. At deer-hunting ranges the trajectory of the bullet
will seldom show a curve greater than one inch above or below
the line of sight. With the bow and arrow this curve is greatly
exaggerated; and the lighter the bow weight the greater the curve
in the line of flight as the arrow travels to the target, even at fairly
short range. Therefore, the archer must have a nominally high vertical clearance in order to direct his shaft above the target that it will
carry up to the desired range. Then we must have sufficient horizontal clearance as well, for when the arrow leaves the bow it "flirts,"
weaving from side to side at the feathered end, until it stabilizes itself in flight. This amount of "flirt" or "whip" varies with the stiff-

ness of the shaft, the cast of the bow, the width and length of the fletching. The larger the feathers, the less of this tendency is evident; but there is a limit to the size of fletching that can be used, and it cannot be fully corrected.

This is the archer's greatest hunting problem: to find his deer through a large enough opening and to be able to drive the arrow through to the target. Just the slightest touch from an intervening branch in the path of the arrow will cause a dismal miss and often a lost arrow as well as a lost deer. Much of this high arching trajectory can be lessened by use of a heavy, fast bow as strong as a man can pull, and arrows that are stiff enough to withstand the shock of the release with a minimum of "flirt."

The layman, and many deer hunters as well, ridicule the killing effect of a broadhead arrow driven from a heavy hunting bow. A number of years ago I was making up a hickory-backed Osage-orange hunting bow when one of my deer-hunting pals dropped into the shop. I was tillering up the bow, shaping up the bends in each limb, and my friend made a remark about my coming into a second childhood, seeing that I was playing with toys. It so happened that a chestnut board, about six feet long, ten inches wide and an inch thick stood against the rear wall of the shop, so I decided I'd demonstrate that modern bows could hardly be called toys. I picked up an old handmade broadhead shaft from the workbench, nocked it and let drive at the chestnut board. By sheer luck the broadhead blade struck close to the center, with the blade upright, and the plank promptly split full length into two halves, each piece rattling to the floor. When my friend's hair had uncurled, I walked over and after five minutes' work with a pair of pliers, managed to get the shaft free of the wall, which it had penetrated freely after splitting the long plank. This of course did not demonstrate any effective killing power, but I am certain that my friend never again thought of an archer as carrying toys.

It has been demonstrated over many years that the broadhead shaft, driven from a hunting bow, has remarkable powers of penetration on even the largest game. The late Arthur Young killed every species of North American game, including the tremendous Alaskan brown bear, with single shafts from his ninety-pound bow. Modern archers who kill game the size of deer find that just as often as not the arrow will pass completely and cleanly through the animal on broadside shots even with the one-inch-wide steel broadhead. The broadhead, of course, unlike the rifle bullet, kills by hemorrhage rather than shock. But any deer solidly hit anywhere in the body area has little chance to escape. The bleeding effect of arrow wounds is prodigious; usually a hit anywhere in the body cavity will bleed the animal to death within a few minutes. A keen-edged broadhead shaft will sever every nerve and blood vessel in its path, giving virtually the effect of a broadsword pushed through the body. The trailing of arrow-wounded deer at once becomes a simple thing; bleeding is not only extremely free, but the shaft within the wound prevents its closing to shut off the blood trail.

A hunting arrow simply has no shocking effect, unless by chance it strikes a nerve center within the spinal column. But a heart-shot buck will invariably come to earth quicker with a broadhead wound than if he were struck with a standard .30-caliber Soft Point. Rifle bullets have a tendency to mangle tissue, contributing to quick clotting of blood and the cessation of a blood trail, unless the hit is highly mortal. With the broadhead blade, nerves, tissues and blood vessels are severed cleanly and thoroughly, making a wound which fails to clot up. Even in a lung-shot the arrow will cause a more quickly fatal wound than the rifle bullet; for with the entry of the shaft, air reaches the lung areas and both lungs collapse as a pricked balloon.

My personal experiences with the bow are not extensive enough to prove of any value, but my first buck was struck in the left flank as he quartered away, the shaft passing through the diaphragm and emerging behind the right shoulder. The arrow penetrated beyond the feathers, out of sight in the flank, and as the buck made off through the white birch, the forward end of the shaft snapped off against the trees. When I came up to the buck, a hundred yards away, there was no sign of an arrow visible, so I concluded that the shaft had passed completely through. However, when I dressed him out, my fingers soon found the shaft, lying diagonally within the body cavity and almost through the center of the diaphragm tissue. This buck bled out most thoroughly within one hundred yards of being hit. When I turned him over after making the belly incision, what seemed like a waterpail-full of blood poured out. I have never seen a more completely drained buck nor one which expired more quickly to a raking shot from the rear with conventional deer rifles.

In selecting his hunting equipment the archer will be wise to get the fastest wood in the heaviest bow he can handle. This means either laminated split bamboo or Osage orange; yew is a wonderful bow wood but it is so soft it damages readily under hunting conditions. The bow should be short, for easy handling; backed with some tough material like silk, nylon or fiber for both increased cast and strength and protection to the bow wood itself, and this backing should be dark in color, otherwise any buck will be alarmed at the light flashes when the bow is raised for the shot. However, in selecting the hunting bow it is not wise to go overboard in drawing weights; many men cannot pull, hold and smoothly release a shaft from a bow weighing over sixty pounds. A fifty-pound bow certainly has enough power for penetration, but it does have a slightly higher trajectory than bows of heavier weight and quicker cast. Therefore, as in all other hunting problems, a happy medium must be chosen.

Arrows must be carefully matched with the bow. Heavier, faster bows will require a heavy arrow shaft for stiffness. Usually a bow pulling over 60 pounds will require a 3/8-inch shaft to prevent buckling or "whipping" at the release. Lighter bows, down to 50 pounds, will be best-suited with smaller shafts, about 11/32 inch in diameter. Feathers should be large enough to support the shaft in flight; probably a minimum size for hunting would be 4 inches long and 1/2 inch wide. Large-diameter shafts with heavy broadheads will require even larger feathers than this. In any event, the fletching on a broadhead arrow should be slightly spiraled on the shaft, or the head will cause "planing" through the air. If the arrow spins in flight, in a way similar to the rotational spin of a rifle bullet, very little, if any, of this "planing" effect will show. Few archers, however, will begin the hunting game by making their own arrows, so when hunting arrows are ordered from the manufacturer the bow length, weight and material should be specified.

Broadheads are still the subject of much discussion and experiment. Roughly the head should be three times as long as it is wide, of light spring steel and without barbs. The barbed head does nothing that the barbless cannot do to kill game, and from the conservationist's viewpoint it is not as desirable, for it will not work out of the wound should a light hit be made. Another thing, the barbed heads continually catch on the top of a quiver as they are withdrawn and often will give an archer a jab in the finger if he makes a full, quick draw.

The most important problem for the inexperienced hunting archer is how to get the right kind of shooting practice for deer hunting. Orthodox target shooting will teach a hunter the proper methods of holding, aiming and releasing, and these fundamentals should be first well-established on the target range. For hunting, however, a different technique is required. The lessons learned in target shooting at specified ranges and with target arrows will be of little benefit in the hunting field. First of all, the switch from light, slender target arrows with pile heads and tiny feathers to the solid, thick hunting shaft with its long fletching and broadhead point will throw the archer's point of aim way low and at the same time will show a much higher trajectory curve over the usual hunting ranges, that is, up to fifty yards. To get sensible practice at hunting ranges and with arrows which will shoot exactly like the hunting shafts the archer should order with his hunting broadheads a matching set of roving arrows, preferably with hardwood footings. Then with these arrows he can spend some time on the target range, learning the new holds for the different trajectory at various ranges. With this knowledge fixed in mind he will spend some time in the field, just wandering, shooting at random targets such as tufts of grass, rotted stumps or anything that comes to his fancy, all at various unknown ranges. Only in this way will he prepare his shooting skill for the deer-hunting season. No rule can be laid down for trajectories and sighting for the archer, as there can be for the rifle shooter; each man, each bow and each set of arrows is a law unto itself and the archer must work out the problem under the best simulated hunting conditions.

It is advisable to perfect a somewhat different draw for the roving and hunting field than is used by the target shooter. Almost every target shooter holds a draw low under the chin and either sights well below the gold over the tip of the arrow, or uses a properly adjusted bow sight to correct for this low draw. But with the heavy hunting bow and the premium on accurate work at unknown ranges up to fifty yards, the line of the arrow's flight must be held as close to the eye as possible. This offers the least change in holding at unknown ranges up to the limit of the bow's point-blank range. Today's best field archers draw to the corner of the mouth or to the angle of the jawbone, rather than under the chin, tipping the bow slightly to the right and inclining the head in the same direction. This brings the arrow more or less in line with the shooting eye and brings the nock end close to the line of sight. Practice with this method in the field at odd ranges will soon prove its worth over the conventional head-erect, low-under-chin draw found on the target range. When the archer has developed a degree of shooting skill that holds most of his arrows within the red ring of a regulation target at forty yards, he is ready to take to the deer woods with the knowledge that should a fair chance at a buck present itself he will at least have the necessary know-how to connect.

How to hunt with the bow and arrow is much more of a problem than it is with the rifle. Orthodox still-hunting methods will seldom get an archer a sufficiently close shot to score. The best method seems to be patient watching on runways at the edge of heavy cover, where the deer will approach the archer's stand close enough to afford a shot. Best of all, if the archer has the opportunity he may stand a regulation deer drive. Organized group hunting will give him his best chance at a buck, but human nature being what it is, archers are seldom welcome among the ranks of rifle-shooting groups. All in all, the archer has a tough row to hoe in the deer-hunting field, but to a man who loves the sport this will never be a deterrent.

The best course for a man who feels the blithe spirit of the archer in his veins, is to seek until he finds a stouthearted companion of kindred spirit. Only the most rugged individualist can follow the archer's way of life alone. But with the understanding and sympathy of a friend or two, archery in the deer-hunting field can be and is one of the most exciting, satisfying and spiritually gratifying sports that a hunter can pursue. New legislation will foster and nourish the growing sport until within the next decade archery will assume a major place in the deer-hunting field. For as one of our modern pioneer archers has said, "So long as the new moon returns to the heavens a bent, beautiful bow, so long will the fascination of archery keep hold of the hearts of men."

12 / *Venison for the Table*

MANY YEARS before the Catskill deer herd had approached its present proportions, one of the nuclei herds in the Southern area was enclosed within the comparatively narrow limits of the Chapin estate in Sullivan County's Mongaup Valley. As this herd began to increase in leaps and bounds the overflow spread throughout this area of the county. Deer hunting was at that time just beginning to come into its own as a major sport for Eastern hunters.

Of this time and this locale Bert Sauer tells a little story in connection with venison. For a number of years Bert and his gang had been hunting their deer along the fringes of Chapin's estate. They had no organized club or camp buildings — just a few interested hunters who would get together each year for the short open season, staying at a near-by farmhouse. Each year their farmer host would raise a young bull calf, fatten it well and slaughter it about two weeks prior to the opening day. When the gang arrived he would have a well-hung, tender young beef for filling stomachs emptied by long hours in the woods.

But one year, what with chores and one thing **or another** keeping him busy, he'd forgotten to slaughter his bull calf in time for proper aging of the meat. In the last-minute rush, he disposed of the job only the day before the gang arrived, bringing with them two young tenderfoot hunters. That night when the gang had assembled around the poker table for the usual deer hunter's bull session, their host called Bert to one side and explained the situation. He suspected that there might be a complaint or two emanating from the ranks after the first few mouthfuls of young bull were consumed, so he decided it would be best to anticipate the reaction. Bert laughed it off, then suddenly was taken with an idea — why not let the two greenhorns get the first crack at the new beef?

Next morning, in the blackness of pre-dawn, breakfast was under way. The host's eldest daughter, in on the plot, sneaked out to the woodshed and sliced two long, tough, stringy slabs of meat, right off the shank. These two choice morsels were thrown into the big skillet and fried as rapidly as the huge, wood-burning kitchen range could turn them out. Slyly yet casually were the two big plates of beef, piled-high home-fries and thickly sliced home-baked bread slipped onto the table before the two new men.

We must credit them here with rugged determination. For many minutes each one bravely sought to hack off a mouthful. This accomplished, more minutes were spent in vain mastication, until in desperation the lump was swallowed whole. Bert noticed that after each had manfully disposed of several mouthfuls the remainder was left severely alone. Each lad tackled the potatoes and bread — but no more of that meat!

Breakfast over, Bert collared the pair. "What's the matter with you boys. Didn't you like that venison? I didn't see you eatin' much of it."

"Gosh, Bert," spoke up the older of the two, "we didn't know that was venison. You can bet if we'd 'a' known about it we'd have et a lot more of it!"

This quite accurately sums up the layman's opinion of venison as a food. And until recent times we could include a great proportion of deer hunters too, in this category. Better legislation and wider education in meat handling has done much to improve this picture with present-day hunters. Not so long ago most states made it illegal to possess venison for any appreciable length of time after the closing day of the season. Extensions of possession time could sometimes be had by applying for, and paying for, a special permit. This was too much trouble for many hunters — they would eat it all or give it away before the end of the short grace period. Such venison had barely time to cool properly, to say nothing of aging. Normally such meat, whether venison or not, is hardly ready for the table. Our best packing-house meats are all well-aged, sometimes for several months, before coming to our tables — why not give our venison similar treatment if we would really enjoy it?

It is decidedly unfair to venison as a food to compare it with best grades of beef. Top-grade beef is the result of many years of carefully selective breeding for the best meat types, careful feeding from infancy and grain fattening before slaughter. Directly before slaughtering every effort is made to keep the animals quiet and comfortable. And of course the slaughtering and butchering is done under conditions which effect complete blood drainage and no damaged meat. Likewise, good beef is slaughtered at certain periods when the animals are in the best physical condition; then rigid inspection permits only the best to reach the market.

This is not an apology for venison — merely a small explanation to mark the distinction between beef and the flesh of the deer, often compared unfavorably with the flesh of the prime steer. To eat good venison a hunter must treat this meat in a special way; must be able to discern the good from the poorer animals and make the necessary adjustments to produce tasty venison dishes. It is perhaps unfortunate that a hunter has little choice in taking his venison. Usually he takes the first antlered deer to come before his sights and merits plenty of praise for making a clean kill. As a matter of fact there is no way to determine how well a buck will eat until he is killed and dressed. I have killed spikes and fork-horns — apparently the best eating of the male deer — and have found one or two which were less prime meat than a heavy old buck of many summers.

It is an unavoidable fact that virtually all bucks should not be hunted until after the rutting season has passed, or is at least well on its way. To kill off a large number of bucks before mating takes place would cut down the fawn crop for the following season. Most conservation departments accede to this theory and adjust the open seasons to give the bucks sufficient opportunity for mating.

Yet it is this factor which produces lean venison, and lean meat of any kind cannot hope to be as tender as that which is well-larded with fat. All other things being equal it is the fattest deer which produce the finest venison, both as to quality and flavor. This has nothing to do with the age of the buck. Young bucks which should be good eating will often run off all their fat during the rut. When the mating fever is full in their blood they neither rest nor eat to any extent until this fire has subsided. A young buck taken just after this period will show the ravages of the reproductive urge in lean hips and protruding ribs.

A fat, senile old buck, passing his prime of vitality, will retain a large proportion of his premating good condition and almost always will be tender and well-flavored. Two of the best eating bucks ever to grace the writer's table were such deer. Heavy in body, with wide-spreading antlers, each of these deer was the "hermit" type, feeding cautiously after dark, hiding away in daylight hours and, so far as I could tell, never associating with the does. Both bucks were blanketed in layers of fat, with thin layers marbling the flesh. Venison of the best!

Conditions under which the buck is taken have a decided influence on the quality of meat. Deer which have been horribly wounded, then trailed for miles before being recovered, show the effects of such killing. The meat will be darkened with diffused blood and much of it will be blood settled near the wound; these parts can be discarded in the butchering but the flavor of the venison throughout will be impaired by such unconventional slaughtering. Any buck so killed will never compare with the deer taken by a clean, quick kill.

In any case we must make the best of what we have. It's seldom that any buck will be in such poor condition that proper handling cannot procure good venison. But the hunter must be able to discern these qualities in his game and take the necessary steps to condition it.

Let's assume that you have a nice little fork-horn buck. When you dressed him out in the woods you noticed strings of fat clinging to his intestines. His kidneys were buried in fat strips, clinging to each rib; plenty of this same fat could be seen lying under the hide along the flanks and over the chest. With such a prime specimen you can strip off the hide, cut a steak and throw it on the broiler as soon as the body heat has cooled — and you'll have good eating. The same goes for a big deer or a small one. If the fat is there the venison will be tender. Not too often, though, do we kill such prime deer. The run of the mill will be somewhat leaner, perhaps much leaner — these are the problem deer, the deer which should be hung in the hide for ten days, three weeks or a month.

No fast rule should be made in regard to handling deer; each must be treated as an individual. Almost every deer will be improved in flavor, if not in tenderness, by hanging in a refrigerated cooler or in a protected building if the weather is uniformly cold. Ideal temperatures for aging venison are somewhere between 36° and 42° — not freezing. Freezing your buck will not age him, for freezing hinders the breakdown of the muscle cells. It is in order to freeze your venison after butchering and after it has been aged, but not before.

The exact period of time for aging venison is by no means fixed. A prime fat buck need hang in the cooler no more than a week; lean, rangy deer, impoverished by the ravages of the rut, can well hang for a month. A light coating of fuzzy mold will form on the inside of the body cavity after a week or more, but this is of no concern. It can be wiped off readily and the meat below will be mellow and tender. Any deer in the hide, properly cooled after dressing, will remain edible for a long period of time in a cooler, provided the temperature is kept constant. Any "high" odor that develops will be from the flank meat or thin edges of the abdominal cavity. When this is cut away the remainder will be sweet and tender.

A buck hung in the hide will cure well and rapidly, not drying out in the process. If the carcass is skinned, then allowed to hang, the whole outer surface will harden like rock and in time will get some of this "high" odor. This does not mean that the meat is spoiled. Simply slicing off this hard "case" will reveal good venison below, but these air-dried deer are never as palatable as the venison cured in the hide.

It's true that some degree of curing will be gained by skinning out your buck, butchering into the proper cuts, then quick freezing and storing in the locker. This is fine for prime venison, but for the less fat animals such treatment stops far short of proper aging. Only a prolonged period in a refrigerator cooler at about 40° will make such deer tender and flavorful. After the curing process, if you still want your deer to hang a bit more, it can be hung in a freezing compartment and frozen solid. Needless to say any buck so frozen will remain in good eating condition almost indefinitely until ready for the final skinning and butchering.

When your buck is ready for eating, get him home from the locker plant and allow yourself a full evening for skinning and butchering. If you plan to have the meat processed and stored in a locker, get the proper wrappings from your locker owner. If you'll make venison sausage — and by all means, do — get a dozen one-quart ice-cream containers either from your locker plant or the local drugstore. Have your small-bladed skinning knife sharp, and borrow a meat saw from your butcher. Together with a short piece of manila rope, your oilstone, an old sheet of oilcloth and a short, heavy club, you are ready to get out your venison.

Bring your deer into the woodshed or even down into the cellar, anywhere there's a good solid beam for hanging him. If the carcass has been frozen you'll need to wait until the juices begin to flow inside the body cavity before you can get the hide started. First, disjoint or saw off all the legs, then slip a short piece of rope through the gambrel of each hind leg. Throw your rope over the beam and pull up the deer while someone gives you a hand to get the carcass clear of the floor. Tie this one leg fast, then make the initial cut from the shank right down to the straddle. Make fast the other leg-rope at a point two or three feet from the first tie, spreading the hindquarters to make the skinning points more accessible at the beginning. Now make the second cut, down the inside of the other leg, meeting the end of the first cut in the straddle.

Pull the skin down on each leg, using the knife only to separate the tissues, until the tail can be skinned out. Run your knife under-side the tail from its root to a point halfway to the tip of the tail-bone, peel down the skin until you can get your fingers between the tail-bone and the hide, then with a sharp, downward pull, slip the tail-bone right out of the tail.

If you are to mount the head now is the time to mark the hide all around the shoulders and across the brisket, bringing the cut over the top of the withers (as outlined in the taxidermy chapter). It will be much easier to determine just where the hide should be cut while it still is on the buck, then no mistakes will be made after the hide is completely off the deer. Also at this point the cut should be made from the top of the shoulders to the midway point between the ears. This greatly facilitates removal of the neck skin, rather than trying to pull it down over the neck as a tube. For some reason the neck skin clings tightly to the flesh and if the hide is not slit at the top of the neck line the whole job of skinning will be lengthened.

From this point, getting off the hide is merely a task of strength. The hide is pulled down, rather than cut loose from the carcass. The knife will be needed only to keep the separation going and at tight places along the sides and the middle of the back. Much of the hide can be pounded loose with the short club, your fist or the butt of the skinning knife. Considerable weight will be exerted on the hide to get it loose, so be certain that the deer is solidly hung, close to the beam and with a strong rope. When the forelegs are reached make the same cuts from the shank end, down the inside of each leg and meeting behind the point of the brisket. If you have made the preliminary marking cuts for mounting the head, the fore-leg cuts can be brought out to meet these cuts, just behind the brisket.

Of course it is not necessary to remove this much hide for mounting the head unless a shoulder mount is desired, but even for a neck mount, better be safe and allow plenty. If the head is not to be saved an opening cut can be made from the junction point of the ribs, through the brisket and up the underside of the neck to the lower jaw, thus opening up the neck for easier skinning.

When the skinning progresses to a point just behind the buck's ears, feel for the axial joint either with your fingers or by inserting the knife point. This joint marks the connection with the spinal column and the skull. Cut through the flesh completely around this point, then simply twist off the head; it is never necessary to saw or chop off a deer's head to get it free.

Now with the butcher's saw begin to cut the carcass in half, first cutting out the tail to clear the path for the saw. Facing the deer's body cavity, start the cut and continue down through the straddle, taking all pains to keep to the center of the spine. It will facilitate making a straight cut if the flesh down the middle of the back is parted first with your knife. Continue the cut right down through the entire spinal column, sawing through the rib cartilage, until the entire carcass is split in two equal halves. Take one half the carcass down from the beam; lay it on your oilcloth-covered table, keeping the body cavity side down.

With your knife and meat saw divide each of the halves of the deer as outlined on the chart. Wrap each portion separately in the locker paper or in wax paper. If you steak the hindquarters, wrap each steak separately. In any case, do a neat workmanlike job, cutting off all scraps and pulling or cutting off external tissues. You can now quick-freeze all the better cuts for roasts, steaks and chops, saving the less desirable portions – shanks, flank and neck – for making venison sausage, meat balls, mincemeat or stew.

As far as the author can see, there is no single part of the animal which should be, or need be, wasted. There are many ways to make use of each portion. Shoulders, loin, saddle, rump and ham will all go to make roasts, chops and steaks; even the neck of a fat deer, boned out and rolled, makes a fine pot roast. Even the toughest part of a tough deer will be tasty and flavorful if the buck has been well hung and the less choice portions stewed or pot-roasted in a pressure cooker. But for greatest utility of these portions give me venison sausage every time. Nothing in pork sausage compares with it, either for flavor or texture. Here is the way the author makes it, and finds it always good:

MEAT CUTS

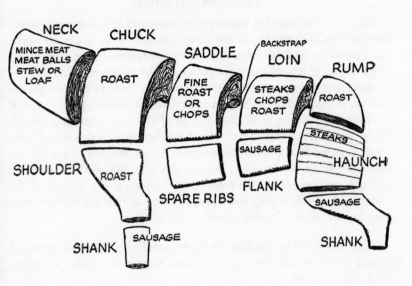

NECK — MINCE MEAT MEAT BALLS STEW OR LOAF

CHUCK — ROAST

SADDLE — FINE ROAST OR CHOPS

BACKSTRAP

LOIN — STEAKS CHOPS ROAST

RUMP — ROAST

STEAKS

HAUNCH

SHOULDER — ROAST

SPARE RIBS

SAUSAGE

FLANK

SAUSAGE

SHANK — SAUSAGE

SHANK

SKINNING THE CARCASS

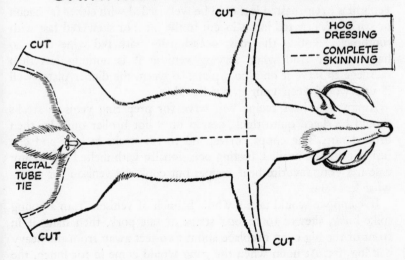

CUT

CUT

HOG DRESSING

COMPLETE SKINNING

RECTAL TUBE TIE

CUT

CUT

VENISON SAUSAGE

Take the two front leg shanks; bone them and strip out the tendons. Do the same with the shank end of the haunch (after steaks have been cut); throw in the flank meat, first making certain that none of this has a "high" odor. If any of this meat does have this odor, under no circumstances use it for sausage or anything else. Now remove most of the excess fat, if any, and if you want a large batch of sausage, put in some of the lower shoulder or neck meat. Cut all of this into cubes small enough for grinding. Take this to your local butcher shop, weigh it and have your butcher add one third this amount of pork fat-back. Then let him grind the whole works twice, but not too fine. Add sausage seasoning and one teaspoonful of powdered ginger for each five pounds of the sausage. Mix well, adding just enough water to free the sausage from your fingers while it is being mixed.

This can now be packed in your containers, quick-frozen and stored in the locker; but first try some next morning for breakfast with buckwheats!

In preparing any of the choicer cuts, much the same procedure is followed as with beef. There are two noticeable differences, however. The meat is somewhat drier, though fine in texture, and the fat is similar in characteristics to lamb fat, almost like tallow. When venison is oven-roasted it should be well-larded with either fat bacon or salt pork, inserted into slits cut in the meat or skewered fast with toothpicks. Basting the roast occasionally with red wine does no harm either! And when serving venison it is nothing less than sacrilege to serve it on a cold plate, so warm the dinner plates well if you would keep your gravy liquid.

Almost any beef recipe will serve for preparing venison; steaks should be sliced quite thick, seared on a hot broiler quickly, then broiled rare. The chops correspond to rib steaks in beef and can just as easily be broiled, basting occasionally with melted fat. In any case use your favorite beef recipes but cook the venison for somewhat less time.

In camp we would take a whole haunch of venison from a young spike-buck, skewer to it long strips of salt pork, then hang it in front of the big open fireplace about two feet away from the heavy oak log fire. At noon when the gang would come in for lunch, the leg would be turned around, more salt pork stuck fast and another log thrown on the fire. After sunset, with a tired, hungry bunch of hunters sitting around the table, that roast leg of venison would disappear like a fog in a breeze. Of course, hungry hunters will eat almost anything; but often I can find myself drooling at the thought of one of those crisply brown, open-hearth haunch roasts.

Certain recipes have become traditional for preparing venison; among these is a venison *Sauerbraten*. For this famous venison party dish, take a solid chunk of the rump and immerse in the following sauer-pickle for 48 hours:

Mix 2 parts (at least) water to 1 part vinegar. Sweeten with brown sugar to remove the bite of the vinegar, tasting as you mix the ingredients. To this add several slices of lemon and raw onion, sliced clove of garlic, two tablespoons of mixed pickling spice, and a stick of cinnamon. The bath should be just enough to cover the meat, and the meat must be turned frequently during the process.

When pickled, brown the meat in a heavy Dutch oven in hot fat. After browning, cover and pot-roast slowly, allowing 30 minutes per pound, but not over 4 hours total. During the roasting baste frequently with the pickling liquid and when the piece is done make gravy, using this pickling liquid instead of water. Add to the gravy half a pint of cream and simmer. Serve with potato dumplings and sauer red cabbage.

Among the author's pet recipes for venison dishes is pan-roasted venison chops.

Take four or five of the rib chops, sliced thick (one to a rib). Roll in seasoned flour and brown quickly in a heavy iron pan. When browned, lay a strip of bacon on each chop, baste with Burgundy or Claret and cover, simmering for half an hour. Thicken gravy with flour and add Worcestershire sauce.

The number of ways in which venison can be prepared is endless. Each section of the country has its favorite recipe: Venison Stew, Venison and Spaghetti, Venison Swiss Steak, Venison Paprika and hundreds of others. The author could list many more recipes for venison cookery, but in the end would add but little to what may be found in household cook books. The only points to bear always in mind are the natural dryness of the meat and its richer flavor. There is no magic in preparing properly handled and cured venison, but it does require a magician to serve appetizing venison dishes if the animal has not been properly treated from the moment of its taking — through hog-dressing, cooling, curing and proper butchering – for only through the most careful, intelligent handling will venison be meat fit for the banquet table.

In camp the successful hunter will want to eat some part of his deer almost as soon as he kills it. Bear in mind that the meat should never be eaten until the body heat has thoroughly cooled out. Usually this will be a matter of twelve or more hours, for the heavy hair forms a most effective insulation for retaining this heat. However, there are two parts of the animal which are fit for almost immediate consumption – the liver and the tenderloins or "backstraps." The liver should be sliced carefully, not too thick, not too thin, roughly about three-eighths of an inch thick. Fry it quickly in good bacon fat until the blood just ceases to ooze. The "backstraps" are the choicest tidbits in the deer. These long tender strips of meat lie along the backbone on the inside of the body cavity, just above the kidneys. Most of the time they can be pulled right out with the fingers. Slice these across the grain in thick chunks for pan-frying, leave whole for broiling. In even the leanest, stringiest buck these backstraps will be tender no matter how prepared.

Sometimes liver "flukes" – liver worms – will be found in a deer's liver. These don't harm the liver in the least if it's properly cooked; remove them and cook liver as usual. Both the heart and kidneys are saved and eaten by venison-hungry hunters; heart should be split, tissues removed, parboiled for fifteen minutes, then fried. Kidneys are split, washed thoroughly or soaked in weak bicarbonate solution, then broiled or fried. All of these parts can be eaten almost as soon as the hunter returns to camp with his deer, but for the rest of the venison, proper aging in the cooler will produce the best meat.

Clayton B. Seagears, Director of New York State Conservation Education, has a simple recipe for an unusually good and different venison ham. Here it is just as he has put it down:

Take your haunch of venison and very carefully separate the muscles so that the connective tissue or membranes can all be stripped off. This will allow the "curing paste" to come in direct contact with the meat. Now mix about 2 lbs. of salt with 5 tablespoons of ground cinnamon (some use allspice) and the same amount of black pepper. Plaster the meat with this. If it won't stick, wipe meat with salt brine. Next hang the coated raw chunks *outdoors* on hooks or string under a shelter so that rain will never touch them. The wind and sun will do the rest. In about 4 or 5 *weeks* cut off some thin slices and holler for your doubting pals.

To this I add "Amen."

Venison can be pickled, smoked, dried and canned. For hunters who have no access to commercial refrigeration all of the meat can be preserved in this way. For *pickling*, cut the meat into long strips; soak in a salt brine heavy enough to float an egg, for twenty-four hours. Remove from the brine and hang up to dry; when dripping ceases lay strips on board or tray and dry in a slow oven. *Smoked venison* is delicious and easy to prepare: soak long strips in salt water for an hour or two, drain and hang on a wooden slat over a slow fire of green wood or corncobs. Sawdust also will create a good heavy smoke. An old barrel makes a good smokehouse for this job: if of metal the fire can be built right in the middle. In a wooden barrel, build a tiny fire on a sheet of metal or an old washing tin, placed in the bottom. The fire should be kept very low and small; only little heat should be generated but it should produce plenty of smoke. After four or five days of intermittent smoking the venison is ready. For *dried venison* hang the strips over a low fire, away from the smoke and flame; no presalting is necessary for the dried venison.

Canning is perhaps the most commonly used method of preserving venison if refrigeration is lacking. The methods used are almost identical with home canning of vegetables; meat can be cold-packed or it can be cooked and then packed. The latter method produces the tastiest venison. The first step is to remove the bones and all the excess fat and stringy tissues, cutting meat into pieces conveniently sized to fit in the canning jars. Pan-broil the meat in salt pork or bacon fat, seasoning with salt and pepper while cooking. When nicely browned pack in sterilized jars to within an inch of the top. Add a few spoonfuls of drippings to each jar, then screw on the lids tightly, wipe off tops and place in pressure cooker. Cook at fifteen pounds pressure for about an hour. Such canned venison makes excellent Swiss steak and venison stews.

Venison can also be kept in other ways if commercial cold storage lockers aren't available. The meat can be wrapped in individual sections for cooking, then frozen in the freezing compartment of the household refrigerator. Then it can be packed in a barrel of sawdust and left outdoors or in an unheated building; such packing will keep the meat in good condition throughout normal late fall or winter weather. Better still, the meat can be frozen and packed in a barrel with cracked ice and sawdust, storing it outdoors in a spot protected from the elements and never touched by the sun.

Another important precaution to remember is not to allow the once-frozen meat to thaw until ready for use. Thawing and re-freezing adds nothing to the quality of the meat and will usually hasten spoilage.

Of all the useful portions of a buck's body none is more abused than the hide. Most hunters discard the hide entirely or give it away. At the city near which the author spent the greater part of his life tons of deer hides were thrown on the dump, to be eaten by the hordes of rats infesting those places. Certainly a disgraceful waste of prospective buckskin, a wonderful leather for garments, surpassed by no other for beauty of texture, softness and durability. If any hunter doesn't care to use his deer hide he should at least give it to someone who will, even if he must be browbeaten into it by his wife. Beautiful gloves, shirts, jackets, and other garments can be made up from a few deer hides at a fraction of their usual cost, if the hunter supplies the hides.

As a matter of fact it's a simple matter to tan your own buckskin. Once tanned, garments can be cut to standard patterns and sewed by a shoemaker or by any dressmaker who uses a heavy machine. To tan a deer hide the hair is first removed. Some hunters will have a hide or two tanned with the hair on, but this makes a messy skin, useful only for a wall ornament. It can never be used for a rug; the hollow, strawlike hair continually breaks off and in time the rug will be an eyesore in the room — if the Little Woman can live with it for that long. There are many ways to remove the hair from a prospective buckskin. Here are two simple methods: Soak the green hide in a strong solution of milk of lime. Leave it in for a short time, then pull on the hair. The solution frees the hair from the hide so that it can all be pulled out easily. Another method: Pour two gallons water, one quart slaked lime and one quart wood ashes into a wooden tub or crock. Immerse hide and leave for twenty-four hours or more — until hair slips and can all be pulled out. After either of these treatments, the hide must be thoroughly rinsed, to remove all traces of the solution.

TO MAKE BUCKSKIN

Five gallons of water
Three pounds of salt
One pound of alum dissolved in hot water

Put the salt in the water, then add the alum solution, stirring until all is dissolved. When the solution is quite cold, immerse the hide and allow it to remain in the bath for a week, stirring it daily. At the end of the first day, take out the hide and hang it to dry. When still moist, go over the entire flesh side with a dull knife or scraper, removing all flesh and fat, then place back in the solution for the remainder of the tanning period. (The salt and alum solution is perfectly safe even if the hide is left within it for more than the prescribed time. It can safely remain for several weeks without any danger of overtanning.)

Now remove the hide and rinse it thoroughly, first in a weak washing soda solution, finally in clear water, until all traces of the salt leave the hide. (Taste it to check this.) Then hang the skin for a few hours to drain completely, then roll up for overnight. Next day, begin to work the skin by pulling and stretching it. If it has dried too hard, dampen lightly with warm water. Put a short length of thin board in a bench vise and work the skin over this until it begins to soften appreciably.

At this point the skin is ready for oiling. Oil lightly with neatsfoot oil, lard, cottonseed oil, bacon grease or any animal oil. Indians oiled the skin with the brains. Whatever the oil used, apply warm to the flesh side of the hide and rub it in well. Let it hang after oiling for a day or two, then soak in a bath of strong soapy water for a few days. Again take out the hide and work it over your board, pulling and stretching until it is completely "broken." This part of the job is hard work, but it requires only time and effort. During this "breaking" process keep the hide moist, not dripping, and permit it to dry betweentimes. Finally the hide will reach a point where it will no longer stiffen after drying; it is now finished buckskin. However, to do a real job and make the hide almost waterproof, close the pores by smoking it over a slow fire of green hardwood.

This smoking does wonders for the hide, making it a better leather for outdoor wear and at the same time turning it to a pleasant dark gray color. It is now ready to be cut up and made into durable garments or gloves, any of which are a joy to own and a pleasure to wear: velvety to the touch, yielding to every movement of the body, quiet in the woods and almost impervious to wind and water. Truly ideal garments for the woodsman!

Let none of your buck be wasted. Eat the venison, tan the hide, tie bucktail lures from the soft tail hair, bass fly-rod lures from the coarse, hollow body hair. Mount the head for your den, make a hat rack or gun rack from the feet. Make or have made a pair of gloves, a new buckskin shirt or a pair of moccasins. Yes, brother hunter, the whitetail deer is a magnificently bountiful creature.

PART TWO

The Mechanics of Deer Hunting

13 / *The Weapon and the Load*

ANY WRITER, however well-informed and widely experienced in the field of hunting, approaches such an important chapter as this with deep humility. That, in a deer book, such a chapter must be written is self-evident, but the problems facing the writer are of great breadth and subject to many qualifications. Many deer hunters, given such an opportunity, would rise to the occasion with high enthusiasm, leaping into the discussion with little regard for the tender toes of the existing millions of deer hunters. The selection of the deer hunter's weapon has always been, and will ever be, the never-ending source of argument and discussion, theory and superstition. No one — writer, gun editor, gunsmith or clairvoyant — can hope to pick a rifle for the experienced hunter, and it would be presumptuous of this author to make an attempt.

Experienced hunters *have* their rifles — they have made successful kills year after year; they handle their weapons with the ease born of long familiarity. No one needs to advise such men on the selection of the proper weapon — this they know, and know thoroughly. On this note, we can leave the experienced hunter and turn attention to the many thousands who have not yet killed their first buck and to those who may have killed one or two deer and have missed or lost all the rest — this latter group are the most inclined to change rifles after each unsuccessful season. They flounder in a welter of confusion, becoming more discouraged with passing seasons.

The author will not launch into lengthy discussion of various calibers and types of actions, citing hundreds of instances to prove the efficiency of outstanding deer rifles. Such information has already been made public through the hundreds of thousands of words already written in the pages of sporting magazines and books since deer hunting first became the sport of the common man. To rehash such information would simply add to the general confusion in the

minds and hearts of many, many hunters who take to the woods
each year. Rather we'll approach the subject from a little different
angle — the capabilities of the shooter himself, not the high degree
of excellence of certain cartridges and rifle actions.

Let's admit at the beginning that there is no *best* rifle for whitetail deer hunting. All center fire rifles, ranging from the tiny .22
Hornet through all the multitude of increasingly larger calibers
and loads to the mighty .405 Winchester and .375 Magnum, can be
and are good deer rifles in the hands of the right man — the shooter
who, by years of training, study of deer anatomy and *physical temperament* can extract from any selected caliber its most efficient performance on game.

The writer has, during the past two decades, been fortunate
enough to have hunted deer throughout a wide area in the Eastern
states. Much of this same period has been spent behind the gun
counter as salesman, gunsmith and firearms mentor to many thousands of deer hunters in the most heavily hunted section of New
York State. The sum total of these experiences indicate that most
hunters select a weapon by the record and reports of other successful hunters and not by examining their own qualifications to handle
such a weapon. It's wise, of course, to pick for yourself a rifle performing well in the hands of your hunting friends, but such a selection is not conclusive. There are many variable personal factors involved in fitting the weapon to the man.

By and large, today's deer hunter is not a skilled hunting rifleman.
I say *hunting* rifleman in the effort to make a clear distinction between the hunter and the target shooter, for there is a marked difference. If we glance at the records of licenses issued to deer hunters
last year and compare with a year, two or even three years ago we
require no Holmes to deduct that hundreds of thousands of new
hunters have been added to the growing ranks in a short time. The
majority of these new men are not *hunting* riflemen of any marked
degree of rifle skill even after a lifetime of deer hunting. These new
hunters, then, are most in need of a word or two of advice in selecting the rifle to match their own degree of hunting skill and their
psychological make-up.

It would be simple indeed if we could pick one type of rifle action and caliber, fitted with a fixed setup of sights and loaded with
one type and weight of bullet, then place it in the hands of each beginning deer hunter, saying to him, "This is the One and Only
deer rifle; it is the *Best* for every range and for every type of shot

you'll get, whether it be broadside, head-on or quartering away, whether your deer is at twenty yards in heavy laurel or two hundred yards off in an open pasture lot. It will kill your deer at the first shot no matter where you hit him, and the sights are so efficient that you will forever be able to see them against the game at any legal hunting time of day, in sunlight, rain or snow and in any kind of cover. The cartridges are loaded with just the right design and weight of bullet to shoot through heavy timber and screens of evergreens, carrying true to your aim; when the game is struck the bullet will penetrate completely and expand just enough so that it will not pass through, but will lie against the hide on the far side of the animal." *Ah! Utopia*, you say, and you would be right, but no such rifle, cartridge, bullet design or sighting combination now exists or can ever exist. Yet I know of many among my deer-hunting friends who are convinced that they themselves own such a rifle, and fearlessly recommend it to the new hunter who searches for the ideal weapon.

Back in the '20's when the writer first took to the deer woods — at a tender age — deer hunting was limited to certain small groups of hunters. At that time we enjoyed no such widespread distribution of whitetail deer as we do today. Deer hunters, in order to hunt deer, joined deer-hunting clubs. Most of the hunting was done on private lands, heavily posted and club-owned; in the more exclusive outfits with limited membership, a new prospective member had to wait several years for a member either to drop out or die, before the new man could gain entry. Under these conditions, new deer hunters had somewhat easier going in weapon selection than today. They were in immediate contact with men of good hunting experience who were well able to give the fundamental advice requisite to killing their buck. Again, the choice of weapons was not quite as wide as it is today, tending to lessen the confusion somewhat when the greenhorn picked out his rifle. He took the Winchester carbine in .30–30 or .32 special; the Savage 99 in either .30–30, .303 or .250–3000; or the Remington 8 or 14, in .30, .32, or .35-caliber — and stuck with the one of his choice until he could handle it well. The deer he would kill in successive seasons would be a clear criterion of the increase in his hunting and shooting skill.

Likewise, such new hunters, in the constant company of men who were killing deer season after season, would gain most helpful first-hand observations in the performances of various rifles and cartridges. There is no substitute for on-the-spot observations of rifle performance in building up a hunter's confidence in the efficiency of his own weapon. Such bolstered confidence goes a long way to improve a new hunter's faith in the rifle he carries; psychologically, this is of the greatest importance to deer-hunting success as far as the weapon itself enters the picture.

Today's new hunter begins his search for a deer rifle under somewhat different circumstances. Most often he will have neither the time, the money nor the inclination to join an established club. Deer hunting today is of great scope. No longer is it limited to the private lands of limited forest areas. Deer today are everywhere, in farm lands, near metropolitan areas and in every part of the land where cover and food exists. New hunters today can find deer within easy driving distance of their homes; gone is the necessity to join a club and spend a week or two each year in hunting the same grounds season after season. Today's deer hunter can seek new fields each year if he so desires; there is no limitation other than the time at his disposal.

Thus it is that today's new hunter often lacks the comprehensive guidance of old and tried deer-hunting pals. Often he hunts with a small group of friends many of whom are hardly more experienced than himself. He must depend on the wealth of controversial literature extolling the virtues of this or that rifle over the balance of the wide field of weapons, then attempt to make an intelligent selection.

But often, perhaps most often, the friendly guidance of friends is not enough. The hunter must himself search his own background of shooting experience, his emotional stability or lack of it and his general knowledge of deer anatomy if he would make a suitable compromise in weapon selection. The author will attempt to point out some of the variable factors affecting the new hunter's reactions in handling his rifle and from these perhaps will be revealed some glimmer of light, some hint to implant or restore confidence in one's selection of the means to bring out of the woods the prize of the hunt.

To establish some sort of starting point for self-classification in the hunter's mind, the author would divide the entire deer-hunting fraternity into five large general groups, all of which are faced with similar hunting problems and shooting backgrounds. The groups would line up something like this but not necessarily in order of skill:

Group (a) would be new hunters with no experience in the shooting field, other than some .22 plinking or an occasional foray after rabbits with the scattergun. It might seem strange to establish such a group as a member of the deer-hunting clan, but it is this group which offers a large potential increase in the added number of hunters each year. To this group deer hunting is not yet a way of life but it offers sufficient glamour for many men who have never hunted before to be now seeking deer. The game is large enough to be highly desirable as a trophy and for its food value, and is now well enough distributed for finding lands inhabited by deer to be no serious problem.

Group (b) comprises the many new deer hunters who have a wide background of small-game hunting with the shotgun, but who have only in the past year or two hunted deer. Many of this group have had indifferent success with the rifle even though they possess a good grade of shotgun shooting skill and general hunting ability.

Group (c) would include that substantial number of city-bound men who have a good background of deer-hunting experience but little time or opportunity to practice with their pet rifle. Most of this group clean up their weapons a day or two before the season opens and pack them away in the hall closet the day after the season ends. This group usually has a majority of small-game shotgun shooters in the ranks.

Group (d) is the simon-pure target shooter who may be a member of a metropolitan rifle club. He is an excellent shot on inanimate targets, well-versed in ballistics and firearms technicalities, and lacks only the acquisition of woodcraft and deer-hunting experience to bring him into the expert class.

Group (e) is the last select, highly skilled group of hunters, small in percentage numbers, who possess an intimate knowledge of woodcraft, an abundance of hunting skill, the ability to hit their deer in the proper spot and the general groundwork in all types of shooting which makes them deadly with almost any type of rifle. These hunters invariably have a wide experience in shooting from early childhood; they have a deep affection for their favorite rifle and treat it as a warm, personal friend.

It is with the first three groups that the writer is primarily concerned. The two latter groups can give most sporting writers cards and spades and still come out top men on a deer hunt.

In order to clarify a situation so controversial as selecting the deer rifle, the author would like to state at the beginning that the weapon in his mind will be used only for whitetail deer hunting in normal Eastern covers. Similarly, the same rifle would be equally correct for such hunting in Michigan, Wisconsin, Minnesota or any other area throughout the country where the type of cover to be hunted so limits the hunter's vision that shots over one hundred yards are a great rarity. This is not to say that whitetail deer are *always* killed at such ranges — there are some exceptions. Occasionally we hear of a hunter who shoots his deer from a platform high in a lone pine tree, overlooking a wide expanse of scrub oak or low laurel. Then in some sections of Pennsylvania deer hunters sit the ridge-tops in rocky, low-brush areas. Here the shooting will be at deer moving along adjacent ridges. But this type of long-range shooting is somewhat special in the deer-hunting field and cannot be considered an important factor to the Eastern whitetail hunter. Deer hunters who go for this long-range work will equip themselves with a flat trajectory, high-intensity bolt-action rifle and mount it with the best hunting 'scope they can afford. Likewise, we will make no mention of rifles that are a compromise between deer hunting and vermin shooting. Such rifles are, at best, a compromise and are not best suited to whitetail deer hunting. Whitetail deer hunting has assumed such a status in the field of sport that the weapon should be selected with deer only in mind. No one in his right mind would pick a shotgun for duck shooting and then use it for woodcock shooting; neither should we select a weapon for deer and expect it to perform properly on woodchucks, coyotes and crows. And it is just as illogical to select the deer rifle when we have moose, elk or mountain sheep in mind. The deer hunter who may someday make an expensive trip for any or all of these larger animals might better wait until the day arrives and then buy a weapon suited to this type of hunting. The added cost of the new rifle will certainly be but a small percentage of the whole outlay for the big-game hunt.

The men in group (a) — new deer hunters — are faced with the toughest problem of selection. Many of this group do not yet own a rifle. When deer-hunting time grows near they beg or borrow either an old hog leg .38–55, a beaten-up, rusty old Krag, or even worse a "souvenir" German Mauser or Jap Arisaka shipped home by G. I. Joe. Any new hunter carrying such a weapon has two strikes on him before he sees deer country. First, he unconsciously fears the rifle, knowing that he'll get a belt in the jaw when he touches it off; secondly the sights on any of these rifles are most likely to be the poorest in the shooting field, hardly discernible in good light and hopeless in deer country. We can add to this the fact that this hunter has no background of mechanically fixed shooting skill and no knowledge of exactly where to hold to hit his deer. If a shot at a buck does present itself, he usually misses. If lucky enough to hit the deer it will be most often struck through the "biggest part" — right through the paunch. If the deer goes down to this shot it gets right up and our hapless hunter fumbles with the action, failing to reload in time for a finishing shot; or he may manage to reload but cannot put his sights on the moving deer in time. Thus we add another lost buck to the Conservation Department's headaches.

There is no quick solution to this problem of finding the right deer weapon for the rank beginner. His tendency will be to consult his more experienced friends, where he finds no two men using the same type of action or the same caliber. This adds to the indecision in his mind. Then he reads avidly every magazine article and book on the subject and comes up with the decision to buy a rifle with sufficient power to kill his deer if he can manage to plant a bullet anywhere in the body area. Secretly, he realizes his lack of shooting skill and he is very hazy on placing his shot in the most lethal spot.

Quite often this shooter comes up with a .30–06 or .270 bolt-action, a .300 Savage or Remington, a .348 Winchester or .35 Remington. With the new rifle in hand, oozing confidence in its excess of power for killing deer, he makes a trip to the outlying districts or the nearest rifle range. At first he stands up on his two hind legs and tries to hold the wandering front sight on the target; perhaps he fires a shot or two, resulting in a clean miss. He decides, then, that the prone position will be steadier, so he gets off a few shots from just above ground level. Now if his will power has been good, the first shot should be satisfactorily near the middle of the bull, but for some unaccountable reason succeeding shots are wandering all over the target, even missing the backstop now and then. He decides then that ammo is too costly and hard to get for this kind of practice, so he carts home the new rifle, his confidence severely shaken.

In almost every instance these new shooters are highly sensitive to recoil and muzzle blast. The .30–06 and the .348 are just too much gun, the .300 and the .35 not much easier on jaw and shoulder. The .270 isn't too tough on the shoulder and jaw but the muzzle blast scares the devil out of a man every time he touches it off. Just a bit of this kind of treatment builds up a deeply implanted fear of the rifle's potency in the beginner's mind, to the end that he never will be able to shoot it with any degree of confidence and skill.

Experts in the field of hunting stoutly maintain that a rifleman never feels the recoil of the weapon when he's shooting at game. To this I agree — if we're talking about experts, but experts are sadly too rare in the deer woods. I find that this is the weightiest factor in choosing the beginner's deer rifle. No man willingly admits, even to himself, that he fears the recoil of his rifle. Once stuck with one of these heavy rifles he will cling to it year after year, afraid to admit to himself or his friends, by buying a lighter-calibered rifle, that he is a flincher and will never become a fine rifleman. Unconsciously he is always hoping that what the experts say is true — that under the excitement of seeing and shooting at his buck he will overcome the tendency to flinch at the shot, making another clean miss or a "fluke" hit.

But this is the wrong approach to becoming a good hunter rifleman. The only solution is practice with a small rim-fire — practice week after week on small targets and big targets, on tin cans, matchbooks, anything that can be seen well enough to hold on clearly. Then and only then will the vital importance of trigger squeeze become paramount in the shooter's mind, to the end that he will summon all his will power to control his nervous muscular reaction until the bullet is on its way.

The new hunter must first seek proficiency in shooting with the small rim fire before attempting to use the bigger rifle. Even then, if his temperament shows a tendency toward nervous reaction to the blast and bump of a high power, let him choose a lighter caliber — adequate for deer — and a rifle action selected for its heavier weight, the better to absorb recoil. To go from a 24" barrel .30–06 sporter to a .30–30 short-barreled lever-action carbine will not give sufficient relief to a sensitive shooter. Let him choose a lighter caliber but let it be in a rifle action of good weight. As an example, the .250 Savage in Model 99 R or RS. This rifle has normally light recoil, little blast and is heavy enough in barrel and stock to make comfortable shooting.

A man who has not yet killed his first deer must be primarily concerned with his ability to hit the deer in a vital area, rather than carry a rifle with an overabundance of killing power but one which scares hell out of him to shoot. No amount of power in a rifle will kill deer unless it is delivered into the game with a well-directed shot.

Rifles of the .30–30 class (.250–3000, .32 Special, .303 Savage, .30 Remington, .32 Remington) all have sufficient power to kill white-tail deer and have the greater advantage for the new shooter in that they are more comfortable to shoot than the heavier calibers. There is such a thing as carrying the lack of recoil too far however; no one could sincerely recommend a new hunter to use a .22 Hornet, .25–20, .32–20 or .38–40 simply because these cartridges have virtu-ally no recoil. This latter group of cartridges are effective only in the hands of the best hunter riflemen and then only under favorable conditions, that is short range and a favorable angle for making a vital hit.

The beginning deer hunter will have no mental commitments as to the best type of action. Remington's Model 81 autoloader in both .30 or .32 Remington caliber is good, but the autoloader is not the ideal type of action for a beginner. It contributes to hasty, unaimed firing in the hope that at least one shot will hit the deer. Better than this is the smooth-functioning, rapid-action Remington Model 141 in the same calibers. Or the new shooter may like the feel of the Savage 99 EG, or 99 R in .250 Savage, or the Winchester Model 65; perhaps the Marlin Model 36 — all lever-actions. Any of these models function well and are certainly rapid enough for additional shooting after the first shot is away. The autoloading-actions are very little faster than the pump-; recoil throws the sights off the target anyway and during this period the hunter learns to throw the slide (or the lever, in lever-actions) so that little if any actual shooting time is lost. There *is* a tendency however, for the hunter with the autoloader to machine-gun his shots at deer, usually with little effect.

The bolt-action types are not the best choice for the new deer hunter, much expert opinion to the contrary. There is a nation-wide tendency among the deer-hunting clan to regard bolt-actions as either a purely military weapon or a long-range affair for plains shooting or potting at vermin. This prejudice unconsciously reflects itself in the beginner's choice of a rifle, and the author feels that it is better for the beginner to by-pass this mental barrier rather than try to use a bolt-action rifle in spite of it. Expert hunters are wedded firmly to the bolt-action; first because of its positive functioning under ad-verse conditions, and second, for its better adaptation to strictly modern cartridges. It is inherently more accurate than any other type of action, but in deer hunting this is of little consequence — all our present rifles and cartridges are sufficiently accurate for any whitetail deer hunting.

Speed of fire is of only secondary importance in killing your buck. It seldom happens that a deer is killed readily after being missed by a hunter's first shot. The first shot is always the best, and every effort must be made to make the first shot count for the most. Many times I have thought, after witnessing one of these rapid-fire matches at deer, that the sport would be farther ahead for both the hunter and conservationist if we were all required to use nothing but single-shot rifles in taking deer. Certainly there would be fewer silly misses at close range and undoubtedly fewer deer escaping to die a lingering death. With the single shot none of us would be tempted to take an odds-on chance at a flash-shot; we would be more patient in waiting until the deer moved into a better position for a clean kill. When a decent shot did come we would be doubly careful to pick the right spot for a lightning kill and would be much more careful to hit that spot. Let every deer hunter, beginner or not, concentrate on placing that first shot, and there will be little need for him to worry about how fast he can dump out a magazineful at his deer.

For these hunters in group (a) there is but one solution to success in killing their buck. Select a rifle of ample power in the .30–30 class, picking the action that feels the best in the hands and that one happens to like. A new man at the shooting game will form a liking for a certain type of rifle. Perhaps it is a carry-over from his boyhood, when he admired the lever-action hammer guns used in the Western "horse operas." Maybe he owned a Daisy "pump-action" repeater air rifle and developed an affinity for this type of action. Subconsciously this will be reflected in his liking for present-day high-power arms. By all means let him follow this tendency, for no one will handle a rifle at its best unless he has a sincere liking for it. When the hunter talks about it, it's a "doll-baby" and "some gun." From this point onward the hunter should handle his new weapon at every opportunity until it becomes as comfortable to his touch as a pair of old gloves.

At the same time that he picks his high-power rifle he should order a .22 rifle in its counterpart. If he picks the Model 141 Remington, then he should buy the 121 Remington. If he selects a Winchester, Savage or Marlin lever-action high-power, then he should match it with the Marlin 39 lever-action .22 rifle. If he decides that the Model 81 Remington autoloader is his choice in a high-power, he will do well to buy with it the smaller Remington .22-caliber autoloader Model 241, or the Winchester Model 63.

He'll then give some thought to the proper sighting equipment. The factory sights on his high-power will no doubt bear some changes — perhaps a larger front sight and a good receiver sight with large aperture for the rear. Let him duplicate these also in the .22-caliber model. To complete the job to its final finish he should have a local gunsmith add weight to stock and forearm of the lighter rifle, bringing both arms into the same weight and balance; the same gunsmith can, at the same time, adjust the trigger pulls to a similar weight and crispness.

All this may seem like a bit of trouble and undoubtedly it is, not to mention the expense involved. But for the man who seriously desires to kill a deer next season and for seasons thereafter it may be the only solution. With the .22 rifle he can enjoy cheap rifle-shooting practice in almost any community; the recoil is no factor and before many months he will be able to pick up his high-power rifle and shoot it with the same skill as its smaller brother. Don't underestimate the need for this background of shooting skill in hunting. One of the fundamental requisites in killing game is that the hunter have a background of training which precludes the necessity for remembering the mechanics of shooting and operating his weapon for successive shots. It must be done by rote, without conscious thought on the hunter's part; at this stage of the chase his full faculties are devoted to keeping the game in sight and deciding at just what point he should make his shot.

It is not necessary that a deer hunter be a highly accurate shot on either game or targets. The definite requirement to kill deer is that he be able to keep all his shots within an 8-inch circle at 50 yards, irrespective of his stance or position with regard to the target. Of far greater importance is that he be able to pick up his rifle, mount it to shoulder smoothly yet rapidly, and touch off the first, second and third shots quickly and within this limit of accuracy. Never should he look at the rifle to determine whether safety is on or off, nor should he look directly at any part of the action or sights. His gaze must be kept always directly on the target and the other operations of shooting must fall into line.

Experts in the hunting field will be inclined to scoff at such elementary advice; yet every man who has gained any degree of proficiency in hunting has, in the beginning, passed through almost this exact procedure. It takes time to achieve smoothness and facility in simply aligning sights; even more time to inure the nervous system to the blasting *pow!* and jerk of recoil as the cartridge explodes. And until this stage has been successfully passed a new hunter should not yet take to the deer woods. It not only may mean a heartbreaking trip for himself, but might result in a badly wounded deer left to die, unrecovered.

The author is fortunate enough to have spent almost all of his boyhood on a farm, in good small-game country, although at that time deer had not yet been seen in any numbers in the area. My parents are both city born and bred and were horrified at the idea of my wanting a rifle. But somehow, along about the age of nine or ten I managed to get hold of a little single-shot Remington .22 — a Model 6 I believe — with a flat, folding tang peep-sight. In a short time I could knock a starling off the barn ridge without too many misses — .22's were pretty scarce in my young life. By the time I reached my middle teens I had acquired a Stevens drop-block .25–20 single-shot with a vernier tang peep-sight. This outfit was tough medicine for gray squirrels in my neighborhood, not to mention the hundreds of woodchucks that fell before the little 86-grain Soft Point bullet. One fall along about the time when I was sixteen I decided that I must hunt deer. My dad co-operated to the extent that he furnished transportation to the nearest deer woods, but there the co-operation ended. Nothing daunted, I sneaked into the woods, following an old wood road, using the same methods I'd use to stalk a gray squirrel feeding on fallen hickory nuts. I hadn't yet seen a deer, either in the woods or on a game preserve, but I was certain I'd recognize one if I bumped into it.

With the confidence of youth and inexperience I walked the trail quietly for about a mile. Suddenly I heard a slight noise off to my left — a crackling of twigs and rustling of brush and leaves. Thinking that it must be another hunter I waited for him to show himself, but instead, out into the little white birch walked a nice, fat little buck. He stopped to look me over, turned his head away just once, then as his eyes swept back to me my little .25–20 bullet ripped through his neck. To be sure, my knees shook horribly and my heart thumped so loudly I was sure the deer could have heard it, but my rifle training kept my mind and hands co-ordinated up to the moment of the kill. There was no magic in killing this deer as my parents seemed to think, it simply was the result of early, thorough training in rifle shooting. So it must be with every man who would kill his deer quickly and neatly.

The foregoing more or less sums up the major problems facing the group (*a*) deer hunters. Hunters in group (*b*) show much the same tendencies but are not quite as sensitive to recoil, owing to the fact that this group takes small game with the shotgun. They lack the primitive fear of the high-power rifle but they too, through constant use of the shotgun have acquired a habit of jerking their shots. The reason for flinching may not be the same but it results in just as many misses on deer. This group as a whole are not rifle-trained and most of their failure in deer hunting rests either with the trigger-jerking habit or lack of familiarity with the strange rifle. It is seldom indeed that we find an expert with the shotgun who is also an expert rifleman. The two methods of shooting are so widely opposed, not only in a mechanical sense but as they affect the shooter's temperament. Good wing shooting with the shotgun requires that the gunner determine at once — before the first movement to throw the gun is made — just what line of flight the flushed bird will take. With this fixed in his mind the gun is thrown to shoulder; taking this line of flight, the muzzle is pointed to swing under and past the target. Then when the eye signals the brain that proper lead has been established, the trigger is abruptly jerked and the follow-through continued.

The rifle shooter is much more deliberate in his actions. When the target is seen in a favorable position for the shot, the rifle is brought smoothly to shoulder, the cheek pressed firmly to the comb to steady the eye with relation to the rear sight. Front sight is aligned on the target and in the same semiconscious movement is aligned with the rear sight. Then the shooter stops all movement momentarily as the shot is squeezed off, with the sights held as nearly as possible in the desired spot.

Of course, there is much more detail to rifle shooting than this, but the author merely wishes to emphasize the difference in movement between the two types of shooting. Shotgun shooting is a picture of rapid movement, lightening calculation, instant action with the slight inaccuracy caused by jerking the shot lost in the pattern spread and the short range. Here the premium is on speed and accuracy in determining length of lead and angle of target to gun — a blended, rhythmic action of gun pointing.

The premium in rifle shooting is on pin-point precision of aiming, a momentary hold when all movement is lost, and the final last squeeze — *smoo-oothly* done, holding everything until the recoil blots out the picture.

The shotgun shooter must meet the challenge offered by this

change of pace in rifle shooting and conquer it, if he would kill his deer. The quick transition from wing shooter to deer hunter with the rifle often finds the hunter unfamiliar with his strange, new weapon and still a shotgun shooter in mind and reflexes. Many times, faced with the sudden, startling appearance of a whitetail buck, he handles and shoots his rifle as though it were a shotgun. He throws rifle to shoulder, points at the game and slams off his shot — following the same action pattern he would use in taking a rising woodcock over the tips of the alders.

Particularly noticeable is his reacting to his rifle as though it were his more familiar pet shotgun when he tries for his second shot, if he either misses or fails to down the deer with his first. Here again the stress of excitement leads him to attempt to operate his rifle as though his favorite scatter-gun were in his hands.

I recall quite clearly an incident that illustrates this tendency. About ten years ago one of my new deer-hunting buddies was on a watch next to mine, as we stood a drive at the feet of the Shawan-gunk Mountains in lower Sullivan County. We were about sixty yards apart, both facing into a short, narrow swale, spongy with peat moss and piled with tangled cat-briers, rhododendron and blown-down, rotting tree trunks. Shortly before we took these stands one of our gang had jumped three deer off the ridge behind us and had taken a snap at a buck, just before they disappeared into the swamp. We had elected to drive the little swamp in the hope that the deer might still be there, hiding away.

Taking my partner figuratively by the hand I placed him in a favorable spot at the base of a huge red oak, right at the edge of the swamp and near the crossing which headed up the ridge. He was carrying a brand-new Winchester Model 55 .30–30, with visible hammer and lever action; at that time I had no idea as to his experience as a rifleman although I knew he hunted small game a great deal. This, however, was his first deer-hunting trip.

Shortly after I had moved up to my stand farther along the swamp-edge, I glanced over and saw him raise his rifle, pointing it down into the heavy growth of briers and blowdowns. I waited breathlessly for him to shoot, but he took his time, following the progress of the deer as they worked through to the crossing. Just as the deer came into my view on his far side, he shot, just once. With a great crashing the deer all turned back into the swamp, out of my sight at once. Feverishly my partner was pointing his rifle after them and making strange movements with his right hand, followed by a series of metallic clicks. It came to me finally that he was cocking the hammer and snapping it on the fired cartridge, not once but many times.

At last he lowered his rifle, having actually fired only the one shot, so I walked over to him, wondering what could have happened to the rifle. I thought at first that the empty case might have expanded tightly in the chamber, locking up the action. When I came near I asked him what in the devil was the matter with him; by now I could see that he had the action open and was dumping the cartridges out on the ground.

"Brother," he said, "I never thought I'd live to see the day that I'd do a fool thing like that. Here two bucks — not one, but two, walk out right in front of me at easy range and what do I do but miss the first shot."

"Yeah, I know," I shot back at him, "but how about the rest of that gunload? You've got six more shells in that gun and you should have had a good crack at 'em going down through that swamp!"

"Right!" he says. "But do you know what I did? I kept cocking the hammer and snapping it on the empty. Ask me why and I can't tell you. Guess I must have thought I had my old double-barrel hammer gun with me."

This is *exactly* what had happened. He told me later that he had hunted for many years with a double-barreled hammer gun and had always carried the hammers down. If he missed his first shot, he'd reach up and cock the second barrel for a follow-up shot. In the excitement of shooting at his first deer he fell back to the old habit. In the stress of the new situation he had forgotten the weapon in his hands was a lever-action repeater.

The writer can recall many such experiences among his own friends and deer-hunting acquaintances. All of these incidents point to a general unfamiliarity with the rifle as a hunting weapon. There is no obvious solution or even a concrete recommendation that can be made to cover a whole group of shooters. Only the individual himself can evaluate his reactions or probable reactions when he first gets his chance at the whitetail buck.

Many times the use of a large front sight, mounted on a ramp, and a large aperture rear sight, will so simplify the act of sighting that the shotgun man can more readily change his instinctive style of gun pointing into more precise aiming. But perhaps of greater importance is his selection of a rifle for deer hunting that most nearly resembles in shape and function his own shotgun. If he regularly uses a pump action shotgun, then the Remington slide-action high-power rifle would be a wise choice for deer. Users of autoloading guns for bird shooting will have less personal function-ing troubles with the autoloading rifle.

In each of our first three groups a general unfamiliarity with the rifle as a hunting weapon is the greatest cause of failure. Even group (c) deer hunters, men of considerable hunting experience, seldom spend much time with their weapons aside from the regular hunting season. They may take a quick trip out into the countryside on a Saturday afternoon, take a shot or two at a paper target or a wood-chuck — just to make sure she's lined up. On the way home they rub their jaws and knead their shoulders a bit, wondering why it is that Old Betsy kicked so much harder than she did last year.

It is this type of hunter who most handicaps himself if he decides to use one of the heavier-calibered rifles for deer. The instinct to flinch at the shot and jerk the trigger is well implanted, primarily through infrequent practice and lack of contact with the rifle throughout the year.

Perhaps the reader feels that I place too much emphasis on recoil. It has been my constant impression for many years that not *enough* emphasis has been placed on this highly controlling factor in deer hunting. During my years in the sporting goods and gunsmithing business I had occasion to fire every make, model and caliber of high-power rifle to appear on the American shooting scene during the past fifty years — and to this we can add a number of foreign arms. In the course of mounting hundreds of rifles with new iron and 'scope sights, I was required to shoot them in on the range.

Many times a customer would return with his newly equipped rifle, after I had adjusted the sights, to complain that his shooting didn't seem to improve. So off we would go to the rifle range to take turns in trying out his pet. I would watch his shoulder and arm muscles carefully as he let off each shot, watching for telltale evi-dence of a flinch. If, after his shots had wandered all over the target and past the backstop, I should accuse him of flinching, he would emphatically deny it. Perhaps he himself isn't aware of it, I would think, so I'd load his rifle for him again, carefully mixing in two or three "dummies"; new cartridges prepared by pulling the bullet, exploding the primer, dumping the powder and re-inserting the bullet. Often it is difficult to detect the flinching habit in a shooter firing a high-power rifle. The blast and jerk of the rifle so closely follows the flinch as to appear like a single movement.

But the "dummies" solved this problem thoroughly, both to my satisfaction and the shooter's.

Only a day or two ago I happened to be discussing deer rifles with Ed Buckley, an Adirondack deer hunter of no little experience with high-power rifles. Ed has killed a good many deer and shot many different rifles and he's a fine pistol shot as well. He mentioned that only last fall he had been shooting a Service Springfield with the M1, 172-grain boat-tail bullet — a pretty hot load, incidently. He confided also that after shooting about a dozen of these loads in the prone position he'd had enough — couldn't keep his shots in the bull. He explained — a little sheepishly — that he hadn't shot the "old girl" in so long that she'd taken him by surprise. Made him so jumpy every time he touched her off, he said, that he called it quits for the day. This from a deer-hunting rifleman with worlds of shooting experience. It can and does happen to the best men if they lay off the rifle shooting for a while.

It's equally true that among the deer-hunting clan we find plenty of men with sufficient will power or such stolid temperament that rifle recoil has little effect on their shooting ability. These hunters can and do handle the heavier calibers with deadly effect, but their number is much in the minority. In the final analysis only the shooter can recognize the existence or lack of these qualities within himself and must choose his weapon on this basis.

As to specific choices in rifles for each of the three groups in question — the author hesitates to go out on that controversial limb. Group (a) new hunters will enjoy good hunting results with any of the following: Remington's Model 141 and 81 in .30 or .32 Remington calibers; Savage's 99 EG, R or RS in .250–3000 with the 100-grain bullet; Winchester's Model 65 in .30 Winchester (.30–30) or .32 Special; Marlin's Model 36 in .30–30. I hesitate to recommend any of the carbines in the Savage, Winchester or Marlin lines for I feel that the lighter weight and shorter barrel add to both recoil and muzzle blast.

For group (b) hunters all of the above are satisfactory and to these we can add the .35 Remington caliber in Remington's Model 141 and 81 and the .300-caliber in the Model 81 only. To the Savage list we can add the .300-caliber in each of the models listed. These added calibers are in the "just-to-make-sure" category. Many hunters prefer them for their added shocking power — but watch out for that recoil!

The hunter in group (c) will be guided solely by his personal evaluation as to his qualifications. He will not go wrong in any of the above calibers of rifles listed. He may prefer the bolt-action arm and, if so, the Model 70 Winchester stands well at the head of the list. Suitable calibers are the .300 Savage, .30–06, .250 Savage, .257 Winchester Roberts, and 7 mm.

This is about as far as the writer cares to go in making specific recommendations in a deer rifle. Any choice of a rifle must be tempered by the personality and sensitivity of its prospective user. To make a definite selection for any hunter would involve a search of his experience in shooting, his mechanical aptitude; his psychological reactions to strange situations; his personal liking for action types, his preference in sights; color of hair, age, weight, Grandmother's maiden name, and so on.

The competent deer hunter unconsciously resents any implication that the rifle of his choice may not be highly adequate for the job. During the late 1920's and early 1930's deer hunters were subjected to a huge wave of sporting literature in magazines and books, extolling the virtues of the .30–06 Springfield cartridge and bolt-action rifle. After reading dozens of such articles in his favorite outdoor magazines any hunter would seriously begin to doubt his judgment in keeping the .30–30, .303, .32 Special, .38–55, or whatever happened to be the caliber of his pet weapon. The tenor of most such information indicated that none of these rifles were adequate for deer hunting except at ridiculously close range or if the animal happened, by chance, to be struck in the head or spinal column.

For a period of several years writers went overboard in condemning rifles in the .30–30 class as deer killers — insisting that good results couldn't be expected unless the .30–06 or rifles of similar power were used. I remember reading, along about that time, an article by the late Captain E. C. Crossman, discussing the merits of various rifle for deer. Crossman said in effect that the .30–06 was far too much gun for a "flea-bitten whitetail buck weighing not over 125 pounds." He added that the .30–06 had been used in taking African lions by his friend Stewart Edward White with a high degree of success and that this fact might impress the deer hunter with the efficiency of the cartridge on whitetails. He stated, with typical Crossman humor, there is a great deal of similarity between the savage lion of Africa and the Eastern whitetail buck — each had a leg on the same corner. But there, he thought, the similarity ended.

Perhaps no man in the country had a better understanding of

the .30–06 cartridge than Crossman. Certainly no one had more respect and admiration for its wonderful accuracy, smashing power and all-round versatility as a cartridge for larger game animals — witness his excellent volume *The Book of the Springfield*. He was a widely experienced big game hunter, an expert ballistician and, perhaps more than anything else, a down-to-earth practical realist in the hunting field. As much as he admired the .30–06 he felt that this cartridge was just too much gun for whitetail deer.

The author followed Crossman's writings for many years, right up to the time of his recent death. Purely on the strength of his recommendations I bought myself a .250 Savage lever-action rifle. This rifle was my first "high-power" job, and for me it has always been a wonderful rifle for taking whitetail deer. At the time I first began to hunt with the caliber, my deer hunting friends gave me the big raspberry. The rifle was entirely too small, bullet too fast; it would blow up on the first twig it touched — and to top it off it was hardly big enough to more than scare a deer.

Strangely enough, I killed the first three bucks shot at with this rifle. One buck was struck in the neck, the others through the chest cavity; all three dropped as though struck by lightning. Shortly after this I joined a deer-hunting club and meanwhile I had picked up another .250 Savage, the neat, trim little Model 20 bolt-action, at that time the lightest-weight high-power on the market.

All my fellow club members were of the big gun type. Most of them used the .35 Remington, a few carried the .300 Savage, one had a .38–55. The advent of a new young hunter with a tiny small-caliber deer rifle came as something of a shock. Somehow or other I had broken tradition with my pea-shooter. The gang decided at once that the new member would contribute very little to the pile of venison "whacked-up" at the end of the season. Nevertheless I killed the first deer driven to my stand, by a neck shot I'll admit, but still a thoroughly dead deer. The following season I again was fortunate enough to get a shot and again dropped my buck. By this time both I and the .250 were accepted by the gang and never again were any remarks made concerning the infantile appearance of my little weapon.

Somewhere along in this period I sold my original .250 Savage to Bert Sauer. Bert is a grand old-time deer hunter, a charter member of one of the first Sullivan County deer-hunting outfits and a thoroughly experienced woodsman and rifleman. Bert had for many years killed his deer with a .303 Savage but on the eve of the opening day of deer hunting some kind-hearted sportsman had stolen this pet rifle from his car. Bert knew that I had an extra rifle so he came to me and offered to buy it rather than borrow it. Inasmuch as I favored the Model 20 over the 99 G I didn't hesitate to let Bert take it, but after he discovered it was a .250–3000 he cooled off a bit. I reassured him by telling him that I had killed three deer with it and hadn't had much difficulty in the killing, so he decided to "take a chance."

"Anyway," he said, as he left, "I can always unload it next year if I don't like it." This was probably true enough, but as of this writing I believe that Bert still owns and uses this same little .250 Savage. The first four years he owned it he killed four bucks with a total expenditure of six cartridges. "Missed one," he explained, a little sheepishly, "and I had to finish another one off with a second shot. But man, I never saw a deer killed any quicker than that little .250 does the job. I never had such good luck with the old .303."

For many years the .250 has been a stepchild. Born of the genius for cartridge design that was Charles Newton's, the cartridge was years ahead of its time, as were most of Newton's designs. It came into being just before World War I when riflemen were not yet used to thinking in terms of high velocity and the tremendous shocking effect resulting from high velocities. Unfortunately, Newton made extravagant claims for all his cartridges; some were justified, many were not. Sportsmen were urged to use these light bullet high-velocity cartridges on the largest of American big game — bear, elk and moose. Soon big-game hunters all over the nation were condemning Newton's claims for these cartridges — among them the .250 — and logically such a cartridge is not adequate for these large animals. As a result the .250 gathered unto itself a big, black eye which it has not yet succeeded in eradicating.

It is a fine killer on whitetail deer when loaded with the 100-grain bullet. It is even better when hand-loaded with the 117-grain bullet in a 10-inch twist barrel, using increased powder charges. But such a combination is not suited to the average deer hunter; it is not available commercially. Suffice it to say that any hunter using the .250 Savage 100-grain load owns a mighty efficient rifle for whitetail deer. It is a cartridge admirably suited to the man who may be sensitive to recoil and excessive muzzle blast. Of all the calibers suited to deer hunting the .250 Savage is without doubt one of the most pleasant to shoot. It is highly accurate, even in lever-ac-

tions; has very flat trajectory, light report and little recoil effect —
altogether a highly versatile cartridge for deer.

Much has been said about the .250's tendency to blow up in heavy
brush and timber. Perhaps with the original 87-grain Soft Point bullet
this may have been to some extent true. But I have killed numerous
deer with this cartridge in the little Model 20 Savage under all
normal hunting conditions. Never have I been able to detect any
such tendency with this cartridge loaded with the 100-grain bullet —
at least no greater blow-up effect than with any of the other
normally acceptable deer-hunting calibers. Each year for a period of
six years I would leave the rifle with "Sherry" Schuerholz for the
Pennsylvania deer season. In this same period he and other members
of his gang killed nine deer with the rifle, without a lost buck, hunting in the heavy Pike County covers. Surely if there were any defect
in the cartridge's performance some tangible evidence should have
come forth during these years of deer hunting in Sullivan County's
laurel thickets and Pike County's scrub oak and heavy timber.

I believe, too, that much of the talk about bullets blowing up and
deflecting on brush can be charged off with many other deer-
hunting alibis. Years ago when the low-velocity, heavyweight bullets
were the only cartridges available, these heavy bullets would deflect
or "ricochet" quite easily. But today's lighter bullets and stepped-up
velocities create a different effect. The fast drive of the bullet keeps
it steadily on its course, even though ripping, tearing through
leaves, twigs and grass, until its force is spent either in the target, on
the masses of vegetation, or within some solid object. It's a difficult
thing to turn a high-velocity bullet from its intended path. Usually
the bullet will destroy itself or "blow-up" in the process, but this
process involves tearing a path through many yards of heavy thickets
or scrub brush.

It is true, however, that bullets of the highest velocities like the
.220 Swift and the 110-grain .30–06 will blow up after passing
through small saplings or branches. The force here involved is the
one imparted by the high rotational spin of the bullet itself — centrifugal force. When the balance of the bullet is disturbed by passage
through any object which tends to change the bullet's shape the
centrifugal energy within literally tears the bullet apart as it wobbles
through the air. To a lesser degree this is true of cartridges having
lower velocities, but the modern bullet design tends to keep the
bullet from shattering itself by providing a heavier jacket.

A number of years ago I decided to get a bit of firsthand information on this matter of bullet deflections and "blow-up." To reproduce hunting conditions as closely as possible I carted my props up into the deer country; up into the laurel, scrub and birch thicket behind our deer-hunting camp. For a target backstop I used an eight-by-four-foot sheet of "Celotex" board on which I had painted a wide black cross; the target was a regulation 100-yard, 8-inch bull, placed over the center of the cross. The backstop was placed within the heaviest cover I could find and I moved away until I could no longer see the target but could determine its location by plotting the intersection of the wide black bands on the backstop. For the test I used rifles of six different calibers: the .250 Savage, .30–30, .300 Savage, .35 Remington, .30–06 Springfield and the .38–55, with as great a variety of bullet weights as I had on hand. The firing point was at a paced-off range of 80 yards from the target, shooting through the heaviest portion of brush and foliage I could select. Ten shots of each caliber and load were fired, each held in the same way to strike center on the 100-yard target. The results were carefully recorded in my notebook and, to say the least, were a bit surprising.

This is the report just as recorded, in the order of shooting:

.250 Savage, 87-grain pointed Soft Point. 2 clean hits in target; 3 hits in target slightly keyholed; 2 hits just off target to the right, in backstop; 2 hits low in backstop slightly keyholed; 1 bullet missed entirely. Group size 14 inches at greatest spread.

.250 Savage, 100-grain Open Point Expanding. 6 clean hits in target; 2 in bull; 2 keyholed in target; 2 hits just under target in backstop. Group size 18 inches, maximum, all shots in group.

.30–30 Winchester, 150-grain Open Point Expanding. 5 hits in target; 3 just below target; 1 just above target; 1 shot missing. Group size 15 inches maximum.

.30–30 Winchester, 170-grain Soft Point. 2 hits in target; 7 hits scattered in backstop, making group 40 inches maximum. 1 shot, badly keyholed, high and right at 2 o'clock, 42 inches from target center.

.300 Savage, 180-grain Soft Point. 3 hits in target; 7 scattered right, left and low in backstop; group size 22 inches, maximum. 3 shots slightly keyholed.

.35 Remington, 200-grain Express Mushroom. 2 shots in target; group size in backstop 22 inches excepting a wide left shot, which was 28 inches from center of target, badly keyholed.

.30–06, 110-grain Hi-Speed Mushroom. 7 hits in target; 1 just above

target; 2 missing. Target perforated with bits of bullet jacket and lead, either from one or both of the missing bullets. Group size of bullet holes 10½ inches maximum.

.30–06, 180-grain Western Soft Point. 8 hits in target; 2 low in backstop. Group size 15 inches maximum. One of these shots cut off a small poplar sapling about one inch in diameter, 50 feet from the target.

.38–55, 255-grain Soft Point. 2 shots in target, both low; 8 hits scattered in backstop, 3 badly keyholed, one high, the rest low. Group size 30 inches maximum.

Of the 60 shots fired only 4 failed to hit the 8 × 4 backstop; presumably, these blew up on some brush. If we analyze this report we find that about 90 per cent of the shots stayed within 10 inches of the point of aim — and this at 80 yards through the heaviest kind of deer cover. Also there is no doubt in my mind that some of the groups would have been smaller if I could have been certain of holding on the target. At best I could only guess as to the location by checking the intersection of the guide lines on the backstop. Probably my holding would show an error of 4 or 5 inches at this range. After each group of 10 shots were fired, the firing point was shifted just a bit in order to give the next string a new path. Needless to say, the passage of 60 bullets created many scars on the vegetation involved in the test.

Such a performance, however, is not meant to be all-conclusive. Rather it serves to strike a balance between imagination and reality. Many shooters who have exaggerated ideas as to bullet deflection and blow-up could learn much about this hunting problem if they conducted such a test for themselves. The indications, supported by my own observation, are that the slower, heavier-weight bullets do plow through brush and saplings better than the lighter, higher-speed bullets, but show more inclination to wander from the original sight line. But this wandering is not nearly as great as many deer hunters would have us believe. In this test the writer put bullets through more brush and small trees than any hunter would be called on to do if he were actually shooting at a deer, for at no time in this test could the target be seen. Even so, if the shooting had been done at a deer at this 80-yard range, 9 shots of each 10 fired would more than likely hit the deer.

Certainly the writer does not suggest that a deer hunter shoot blindly through heavy cover at his buck without making the simplest effort to find an opening. The implication is that many deer hunters are overworking the bullet-deflection alibi as a substitute for better shooting.

Any selection of a deer rifle is closely knit with the cartridge desired. Many of the more recent new cartridge developments are available only in bolt-action arms; most of the older type, rimmed-head numbers are confined to lever-actions. Selection of the proper cartridge, then, has an immediate bearing on the type of rifle action to be chosen. The deer hunter with a new rifle in mind tends to pore over ballistic tables in the effort to find a cartridge of just the right performance to meet his ideas. Unfortunately, this practice is not of any great value; many factors are involved in cartridge performance on game other than the estimated figures appearing in the factory listing of muzzle velocity, energy and trajectories. The sectional density and rate of expansion of the bullet is by far the most important controlling factor in any cartridge performance.

For example, suppose we select a cartridge in the .30–06 category, the 220-grain bullet with short exposed lead point or the 220-grain Express Mushroom. Here we find a velocity of about 2300 foot-seconds and striking energy of 2800 foot-pounds (depending on which manufacturer's tables are used). We compare this with the .257 Roberts and find a 100-grain bullet driven at 2900 foot-seconds and with a striking energy of 1860 foot-pounds. The natural conclusion, based on the figures alone, is that the 220-grain .30–06 bullet would be much the better choice as a deer killer. Actually the .257 Roberts load with 100-grain bullet would be much more effective, since the design of the bullet would permit more of the available energy to be transmitted to the game.

The heavier 220-grain .30–06 bullet is designed particularly for game heavier than deer. The expansion of the bullet is delayed by its thick jacket design so that great penetration is achieved before the expansion takes place, making it a desirable load for moose, grizzly bear and other large game. Such a bullet would zip through the comparatively small carcass of a whitetail deer with little or no expansion unless the deer were shot through from end to end. By far the greater portion of the bullet's energy would be spent in the terrain on the far side of the deer after passing through. Such expended energy does little to kill your buck.

On the other hand the lighter, higher speed 100-grain bullet of the .257 will seldom pass through a whitetail buck, even on broadside hits. Its open-cavity, thin-jacket design permits it to expand almost as soon as it enters the body cavity, tearing a terrific wound channel and expending *all* of its available energy within the carcass. It is this salient feature of all the lighter-bullet, high-velocity cartridges which makes them deadly on thin-skinned game in the deer class.

But the hunter who selects his new rifle must carefully consider all the elements involved in deer hunting. He must sacrifice some of the desirable characteristics of the highest-velocity cartridges in order to obtain sufficient bullet weight to give good penetration on raking or angle shots, and to carry through scrub oak, laurel and all the other hazards involved in shooting whitetail deer. The cartridge finally selected should have a bullet of sufficient weight, be of such design that the expansion takes place readily, and yet should not be so heavy that it induces flinching from recoil. There are many such cartridges in the field, giving the shooter a wide choice.

Generally speaking the consensus of opinion — if we can say that there is a consensus in such a controversial matter — is to suggest the use of a cartridge having the following characteristics: it should be roughly .30 caliber, shoot a bullet weighing between 150 and 180 grains, driven at a velocity somewhere between 2200 foot-seconds and 2700 foot-seconds; be loaded with a bullet design effecting a high degree of expansion in its forward end and a jacket design thick enough to hold the rear portion of the bullet together for greater penetration. Any cartridge conforming to these specifications will perform well on whitetail deer.

In this connection of penetration on deer I recall a deer shot by one of my fellow club members. This chap had a new .30–06 Winchester 54, traded in on his .32 Special carbine which he had carried for a good many seasons. He had killed a number of deer with the little carbine but he had lost a deer the year before so he concluded he had better get a rifle of more power, hence the .30–06. On one of our drives he took a stand next-man to mine but about two hundred yards below me, farther down the ridge slope. On the drive a fine ten-point buck came quartering up the ridge, eventually passing directly before him. With supreme confidence he waited for the best shot, finally driving a bullet through the buck's chest cavity, broadside. The buck dropped but at once gained his feet. Again my friend plowed one through the shoulders and the deer again came up for more, this time quartering away. His third and last shot took the buck far back and this time it failed to down him.

The moment that these three shots resounded sharply through the peaceful serenity of the Oakland Valley, echoing back and forth across the Neversink River, I shifted my stance toward my partner's post. Seconds later I could see a deer heading my way, hobbling slowly and painfully through the white birches. I knew at once the deer was badly hit even though I could not yet see antlers. He stopped momentarily in a little clump of birches, then loped ahead, finally stopping within thirty yards of me near a large beech tree. To my amazement, he leaned heavily against the tree for support, blood trickling down his foreleg. I quickly dispatched him with a shot through the neck.

After the drive came through, my partner walked up to my stand and together we looked over the deer. Two holes pierced his left side, halfway up and just behind the shoulder; the third shot had entered far back in the flank. We turned the buck over and found two neat holes on the other side of the forequarters, the third hole right behind the last rib. None of the exit wounds showed signs of any great expansion. When we opened up this deer the vital organs were, remarkably, in good condition with the exception of the holes through the lungs and paunch. There was no evidence of the great rupturing effect usually seen in the chest cavities of deer I had killed with the .250 Savage.

Naturally, I wondered what load he had used so I asked to see a few of his cartridges. He handed me several loaded with a long bullet tipped with a tiny bit of lead; as a guess I thought they might be Western's 220-grain short exposed point. My friend didn't know the bullet weight — he had "just bought a box of .30-06's" — but sure enough, when we made camp he looked up the box and they proved to be the 220-grain heavy-jacket, delayed-expansion type of bullet designed for really heavy game. This load is not at all designed for deer or similar game, therefore the bullets passed cleanly through, distributing little shock. Fortunately, he had been able to get in three shots at this buck which no doubt soon would have dropped even had I failed to finish him off. There's little doubt in my mind that we would have had a long chase after this buck if he had been hit only once with this heavy, slowly expanding '06 load. If the better deer loads had been used — the 150- or 180-grain Bronze Points, Mushroom, or Open Point Expanding — the first shot would have in all likelihood produced a very dead buck.

Bullet design has come to be one of the most important controlling factors in selecting a rifle for deer. Within the last decade we have seen new bullet types produced by our manufacturers, engineered to give us the maximum in killing effect. Some of the light bullet, high velocity cartridges have been improved immeasurably by the appearance of the Core-Lokt Remington and Western Silvertip loads, particularly the .250 Savage and .257 Roberts. One of the stock complaints with users of these calibers is that they blow up so readily good penetration is lacking. In the older Spitzer Soft-Points and the Hi-Speed Mushroom there has been a tendency in this direction. But with the advent of the controlled expansion Core-Lokt, Silvertip and similar designs much of this objection has been removed. These bullets expand beautifully at all whitetail deer ranges, yet the jacket design prevents a complete disintegration of the bullet within the animal. Likewise we note the same improvement in these loads over the old .30–30 and .32 Special Flat Point soft-nose, using the long exposed point. The new bullet gives uniformly good expansion in front, yet restrains the rear half for follow-through punch.

The ultimate ideal in bullet design for whitetail deer is one in which, when the bullet is fired from a rifle of good power (the .30–30 class or a bit heavier), complete penetration of the vital organs is achieved in all reasonably taken body shots, the bullet stopping either against the hide on the far side of the animal or some little distance short of this. This means, briefly, that we have driven a bullet past the middle of the animal, "where he lives," and yet have delivered the full force of the rifle's striking energy to the animal's nervous system. No one design of bullet can achieve this result in every instance. For example it's obvious that a bullet designed to blow up in side or short angle body shots will fail to penetrate if the deer is hit from behind. Such a bullet will stop before the vital areas are reached; even though the wound will eventually prove fatal it will fail to drop the deer in a hurry. To make an intelligent selection the hunter must make some sort of compromise. If he selects the more efficient design for quick expansion he must forgo these rear-end shots at deer, if he would make a clean kill. No one in complete command of his faculties will deliberately choose a bullet of high penetration on the odd chance of having to shoot lengthwise through a deer in order to kill it. Yet every year hunters can be found in the deer woods carrying rifles loaded with just this type of ammunition.

One of the most satisfactory loads in this respect, for my use at any rate, has been the 180-grain Remington Core-Lokt bullet in the .30–40 Krag cartridge. I have killed five deer with this cartridge in which the bullet passed through the body cavity and lodged against the hide on the far side, dropping out when the buck was skinned. All of these bullets expanded to about three times their diameter, at the forward end, leaving roughly half the bullet remaining to carry through. Some of the forward end of the bullet disintegrated in the process, but this is an indication of the desirable shocking effect which dropped each of these deer virtually in its tracks. No doubt the .300 Savage with the same bullet weight and design would have performed similarly because ballistically these two cartridges are almost identical.

The deer hunter of today has many bullet types from which to make his selection of the best load for his pet rifle. The list includes regular Soft Points, Hi-Speed Mushroom, Open Point Expanding, Bronze Point, Protected Point, Peters Belted Bullet, Remington Core-Lokt and Western Silvertip; the latter three are all of the controlled-expansion type. Often the deer hunter vacillates in choosing between the Open Point and the Soft Point, shying away from the Open Point. Many stories have been circulated to the effect that the Open Point bullets don't expand readily enough on deer, but in the opinions of the best big-game hunters in the country no bullet design is better than this, provided it is driven with sufficient velocity. Most of the Open Point bullets depend on compression of the trapped air within the cavity to force the sides of the bullet apart, thus upsetting the balance, blowing the forward end of the jacket to pieces and in general making a wound of a highly shocking effect.

To gain this desired effect the bullet must be driven at a fairly good velocity, something over 2000 foot-seconds *when it strikes the game*, not when it leaves the muzzle. Hunters are inclined to think of velocity in terms of muzzle velocity, when they think about it at all, forgetting the loss in velocity involved in the flight to the target. With some cartridges this velocity loss is extremely high in the first 200 yards of the bullet's flight, but for whitetail deer shooting the long-range losses in velocity are not important. But Open Point bullets are not efficient at velocities lower than 2000 foot-seconds, so this must be borne in mind when choosing a load. For example the .35 Remington load with 200-grain bullet starts off at about 2200 foot-seconds. By the time it reaches the 100-yard mark, it has slowed down to about 1850 foot-seconds; and from here on to the 200-yard mark it drops off another 100 foot-seconds or more. Beyond the 100-yard mark then, the Open Point 200-grain load cannot be entirely depended upon to open up rapidly in a deer. It will of course open up at these ranges on heavier game, but for deer there may be some failures.

With these fairly low-velocity cartridges and loads the full long Soft Point bullet is the most dependable; above the critical velocities no bullet design performs any better than the Open Point type. There are variables in jacket thickness among different manufacturers which tends to change the expansion rate of these bullets, but in general this rule is a good one.

Traditionally, when we think of the weapon for deer, it is the rifle which at once comes to mind; but in many sections the rifle is barred. The writer has always been confused as to the legislative logic which bars the use of rifles in one state or county, then arbitrarily enforcing use of the shotgun with its heavy slug or round ball, both of which have greater tendencies to ricochet than a rifle bullet and which are certainly as dangerous at fairly long range. Then in some sections, immediately adjoining those in which rifle hunting is permitted, only buckshot can be used. A highly paradoxical situation which does little to conserve game.

At best the shotgun is an inadequate weapon in the hands of a deer hunter. True, in the Southern states where deer are hunted with hounds the shotgun and buckshot are the only practical combination. Here vegetation is dense, shooting ranges are short and most shooting is at hard running deer. In most deer hunting areas the shotgun man is at a definite disadvantage whether he uses the rifled slug or the load of buckshot. Legislation being what it is however, there are many thousands of men who must use the shotgun if they would hunt deer in their home state or county. The writer's own home county at present permits only the use of a shotgun and single ball or slug, but we solve this problem by hunting in adjoining counties where none of this foolish legislation enforces the use of an inadequate weapon.

Of course the slug load in any shotgun larger than .410 gauge is deadly if the slug can be placed somewhere in the vital area of your buck. With the shotgun this can be a serious problem: shotguns lack any sighting equipment but the most rudimentary type of front sight, making sight elevations largely a matter of sheer guesswork. Then too, double guns have a nasty habit of crossing their patterns, making the right barrel shoot the slug to the left and the left barrel over to the right.

On single-barrel guns, pumps, autoloaders and over-unders the hunting accuracy can be vastly improved by mounting a pair of simple rifle sights. I have fitted a number of guns in this way, with sights easily removable, so that the gun was in no way changed for small-game hunting. Judging from the way most shotguns shoot — or fail to shoot — the writer would state that this is the only satisfactory way to make a deer-hunting weapon from a shotgun. Any shotgun is designed and built by its maker to throw shot, never a rifled slug. Consequently, there is no attempt made to make the gun perform with slugs. Likewise, the rifled slug shoots with greatest accuracy from a barrel having a minimum of choke or no choke, and such guns are seldom found in the field.

Good hunting accuracy can be had with the rifled slug. I have test targeted many guns with slugs after fitting rifle-type sights, and have been surprised at the accuracy of certain guns. One Winchester Model 12, 20-gauge, for example, would consistently shoot 5-inch groups of 5 shots at 60 yards — the recommended "point-blank" range; and I have shot some groups at this range of less than 4 inches. This is exceptional accuracy from a smoothbore, certainly quite good enough for deer hunting. After having put several hundred of these slugs through half a hundred or more guns I conclude that any of them will shoot groups of less than 10 inches at 50 yards. Undoubtedly there is good hunting accuracy in the slug; the problem for the deer hunter is to bring it out, either by fitting good sights or practicing on the target range to determine the peculiarities of his weapon, or both.

As far as trajectory and energies are concerned, both characteristics are well embodied in the slug loads for whitetail deer, at least for ranges up to 75 yards. The figures are something like this:

	Muzzle energy	*100-yard energy*	
12-gauge	1995 ft.-lbs.	1165 ft.-lbs.	1-oz. slug
16-gauge	1600 ft.-lbs.	940 ft.-lbs.	⅞-oz. slug
20-gauge	1245 ft.-lbs.	720 ft.-lbs.	⅝-oz. slug

	Midrange height *50-yard range*	*Midrange height* *100-yard range*
12-gauge	½ inch	2½ inches
16-gauge	½ inch	2¾ inches
20-gauge	½ inch	2¾ inches

The slugs travel quite flat over the 100-yard range, certainly flat enough to eliminate holding over at normal hunting ranges. There is little expansion with the rifled slug after the game is hit, but the large size of the slug gives it terrific smashing effect, certainly enough to down any buck hit in a vital area. Paunch shots are taboo though with the rifled slug and it is these shots which take a heavy toll of deer that are never recovered by the hunter. In general the shotgun and slug load should be effective on deer at normal hunting ranges, but the missing factor in the hunting field is the lack of proper directive equipment — meaning accurate sights. If a hunter *must* use the slug load he will save himself much grief by having his gun fitted with reasonably accurate sighting equipment, adjusted to shoot somewhere between fifty and sixty yards, dead on.

A novel and highly effective addition to a shotgun for use with slugs is the so-called one-power (actually *no*-power) shotgun 'scope. These 'scopes are designed to give quick sighting through wide field of view and have the additional advantage of placing the target and the sighting dot in the same focus — true of any 'scope, also. These shotgun 'scopes have windage and elevation adjustments like the rifle 'scopes and permit the best accuracy to be extracted from a shotgun with the slug loads.

The shotgun and buckshot is a different story, and, in this author's opinion, a mighty sad one. The limitations of buckshot as a deer killer are a realization to only a handful of deer hunters; but unfortunately many sportsmen must use this load if they would hunt deer in their home states or counties. It's true that in those deer-hunting areas where cover is so thick a deer cannot be seen over 35 or 40 yards off the shotgun loaded with buckshot is deadly. As a matter of fact any load driven from a shotgun at close range is deadly. One of my friends killed a buck a number of years ago while partridge hunting, dropping the deer at 40 feet with a load of Number 9 shot through its neck. Yes, the shotgun is a weapon of tremendous power at close range; for many years African hunters have used a big-bore double shotgun to back up their rifles against charging, dangerous game.

The major drawback in the use of the shotgun with the buckshot load is its failure to retain initial striking force for any considerable range; rapid dispersion of the pellets precludes putting enough shot into the game to create killing effect through shock. And the shotgun, to be effective at all, must kill by shock. The individual pellets cause little bleeding unless by chance they happen to sever large arteries; there is no apparent expansion of the pellets in flesh — no tearing lacerations and ruptured tissue, which make the rifle bullet such a deadly killer. In order to kill a buck neatly with the shotgun, then, the hunter must put a large part of the original load into the deer, inflicting enough shock to kill.

But when we take our favorite scatter-gun out to the range for pattern tests we're due for a shock. We may have a fine, full choke gun capable of putting 70 per cent of its Number 6 shot load into a 30-inch circle at 40 yards — a close-shooting gun highly efficient on ducks or wide-flushing ring-necks. Let's say that we load the gun with oo buck and fire it at a 4-foot square of paper at 25 yards. Checking the result, we should find a fairly good pattern, bunched in small groups, but with all 9 shot well within a 24-inch circle. This, we think, should certainly kill any deer it hits; undoubtedly it would and quite suddenly.

Then we move back to the 40-yard range and fire another oo load at the pattern paper. Here is where we get the shock. The same load which gave us a well-grouped killing pattern at 25 yards now has spread all over the paper, with perhaps two or three shot missing entirely. The shot-holes in the paper will be unevenly grouped, leaving wide gaps in the pattern. Quite often this oo buck load at 40 yards will throw shot in little bunches, two in one corner that can be covered with the hand, then far over in another corner a group of three equally close together. But it's the gaps in between, plus the wide dispersal of the pattern as a whole, which make buck-shot a poor killer at such, or longer, ranges. The vital body area of a whitetail deer is not large, roughly 12 × 18 inches; the neck and head area is somewhat smaller. In order to kill a buck and still recover him, a major proportion of the buckshot load must enter this area. If we lay off a 12 × 18-inch rectangle on a pattern board and fire at it over the 40-yard range, we will be lucky to get more than four shot into this area at every try. We will need more than this to be certain of killing our deer, unless the guiding hand of chance puts two or three through the heart or into the spine.

With the single o buckshot load we have three more shot to give an effective pattern. Also the single o buckshot load gives somewhat better patterns with less tendency to group in small bunches and fewer "flyers." But even with this better-balanced load, the patterns will not be good beyond 40 yards. Full-choke guns will not give as good patterns as the modified or more open chokes. The swedging effect of the tighter chokes deforms the shot as it passes through, giving more tendency for the shot to wander away from the center of the pattern spread. Either of these loads will kill deer; it's up to the owner of the gun to pattern both loads at ranges up to 50 yards before deciding whether he will use the heavier pellets of the oo load or the somewhat fuller pattern of the single o buck.

From time to time buckshot shooters have experimented with numerous methods of producing closer buckshot patterns. One of these is to take off the top wad and pour hot paraffin over the shot, then replace the top wad. Thus far I have never heard of any remarkable results from this experiment; ballistically, I fail to see its merit. Another and more practical method is to split each shot open and string them on a silk line, crimping each shot over the line about four inches apart. Then the shot are packed back into the shell, usually leaving out a shot or two to make room for the line. These loads are reputed to shoot much closer patterns than the same load before "doctoring." Some of my New Jersey friends use them exclusively; they say that the much closer grouping is worth all the trouble it takes to "doctor" the load. As a matter of fact, this load is being marketed commercially by a Southern outfit which custom-loads them to order. Certainly it is a step in the right direction, for the hunter who must use buckshot is severely handicapped in taking his deer. Now and then we hear of a freak kill made with buckshot at long ranges, even up to a hundred yards. Not many deer hunters will have the phenomenal luck to bag a deer at such range with a shotgun, but I suppose it is this one-chance-in-a-million odds that will forever urge the buckshot slinger to shoot at deer far outside the range of his gun's effect.

The writer began the preparation of this chapter on deer hunting firearms and loads just before Pearl Harbor hit all of us with such tremendous impact that everything else was forgotten in the interests of the nation's defense. As World War II rolled along with its new developments in weapons and fire power, I had visions of a changed postwar era for the deer hunter. However, as I write this there has been but little in the line of new firearms developments to arouse interest in the sportsman. All the big gun plants are crowding out as many of the prewar models in rifles as production capacity will allow. The demand for firearms is so great that there seems to be little need for the expenditure of development money to create demand for new designs in hunting rifles. All of the arms plants are concentrating production in the few models most suited to supply the greatest need. Stevens-Savage has announced a new light bolt-action .30–30 in the low-priced field, modeled on the older Savage 40 bolt-action. The new rifle is a bit more graceful in appearance than the 40, with flush magazine holding three cartridges, making a four-shot weapon in all. Altogether it looks and handles as a deer rifle should; it will make a highly suitable arm for the young hunter, especially the ex-G.I. with his training in the use of bolt-action arms.

Remington's latest contribution to postwar firearms is an interesting low-price bolt-action high-power rifle which has several new features. Somehow or other this new Model 721A is faintly reminiscent of the old Model 30 Express, which was designed on the 1917 Enfield action. However, this new model comes in several attractive calibers — .30–06 Springfield, .270 Winchester, both with 24-inch barrel, and the .300 Magnum with 26-inch barrel.

A shorter-action design of the above, called the 722A, is built either in .257 Roberts or .300 Savage calibers. The 722A has a shorter bolt-throw and a bit less weight than the 721A, otherwise both rifles are identical.

The racy stock design with a nice, full pistol grip will appeal to the deer hunter who likes the bolt-action type of rifle, as will its comparatively light weight. The 721A rifle will weigh about 7¼ pounds, the 722A a few ounces less. In the design of this new rifle, the 'scope shooter has been kept well in mind: safety is of the side type, not interfering with the low mounting of any type of 'scope; and the bolt handle does not turn up into the sight line to give similiar interference. Receiver ring and bridge are both drilled and tapped for standard 'scope mounting.

Remington has provided, in this rifle, a new adjustable tension trigger, without double draw pull; also an encased bolt head which completely surrounds the head of cartridge, giving maximum protection to the shooter. With these new desirable features, and at a fairly low price, this rifle should prove to be an excellent addition to Remington's top deer-hunting favorites — the Models 141 and 81.

Winchester has promised an announcement of interest to deer hunters, but so far the writer has failed to get any dope on the new rifle. Other than this, Winchester is concentrating production on the Model 70, the .94 Carbine, the .64 Deer Rifle, and the .348-caliber Model 71. Remington of course is turning out the slide-action 141 and the autoloading Model 181, both highly effective weapons for the deer hunter. However, the demands are so great and distribution so thin that many hunters will be without their new rifle when our season opens.

This lack of new weapons for deer hunting will force many men to buy a used rifle if they are fortunate enough to locate a good one. Most of the used rifles of American make now available are good buys; rifles bearing Winchester, Savage, Remington and Marlin trademarks are built to perform satisfactorily for the lifetime of the hunter. The great majority of these will function properly for many additional years if they are kept clean and free of rust. Aside from dents and scratches in the stock and worn spots in the bluing any of these arms may be just as good as a new rifle. However, there are a few points to check before buying any used rifle, and this is a good time to point them out.

First of all, the rifle should show some evidence of having had reasonably good care during its previous ownership; the most obvious indication of abuse is the appearance of rust pits on barrel or action. Such rust can be removed by polishing off with steel wool, but the pits will forever remain as telltale evidence the former owner didn't spend much time in looking after his weapon.

Second, be sure ammunition can be had for the rifle in question. Many calibers are no longer being loaded by the ammunition makers nor do they intend to load many of these in the future: 6.5 Mannlicher, 6 mm. Lee Navy, .256 Newton, .25–36 Marlin (the .25–35 Winchester and Marlin *rifles* are no longer made but ammunition will probably be loaded for many years), .30 Newton, .32 Winchester self-loading, .33 Winchester, .35 Winchester S.L.R., .35 Newton, .40–60, .40–82 and similar old-style black powder cartridges. Likewise a prospective used-gun purchaser must be sure he is not picking up a "wildcat" caliber – a .250 Varminter, .25 Niedner, .280 Dubiel, .35 or .400 Whelen – unless he is fully aware that he either must hand-load his own stuff or buy it from a commercial hand-loader; not the cheapest way to buy ammunition, incidentally.

Sometimes a good American-made weapon will be offered in otherwise good condition but having a small part missing – a hammer, firing pin, extractor or ejector. Unless the rifle is more than fifty years old, its maker will be able to supply parts for it out of stock. But this is true only of American-made arms with the makers still in business. For example, the Standard Arms Company, Wilmington, Delaware, turned out a number of gas-operated and slide-action rifles built to use the Remington rimless .30, .32 and .35 cartridges. Since this company has been out of business for many years, replacement parts just don't exist. This is also true of most foreign arms, with the exception of the '98 German Mauser and the British Enfield. Our own Krag, Springfield and 1917 Enfield can be supplied with parts right out of the National Rifle Association's service department.

Once these points are cleared up, the inspection of the mechanical parts of the rifle is in order. The barrel should be wiped dry before inspection. A light film of oil or grease in a bore will make a badly worn and pitted bore look pretty good; a barrel filled with dust and lint will look much worse than it may be. The gun should be held up to an indirect light for inspection; if the lands are badly rounded off, not sharp-edged in any sense, and the grooves rough and black, the chances are that the rifle has seen all of its useful life. If the lands seem somewhat distinct and the grooves fairly clean, most likely the barrel will, even though worn, give enough accuracy for hunting purposes. Particularly is this true should the last half of the barrel show good condition, that is, right up to the muzzle. No rifle will shoot with accuracy if the muzzle end of the rifling is worn smooth, or damaged. Considerable wear at the chamber end is permissible, but at the muzzle end, never. It is fairly easy to inspect the bores of take-down arms and bolt-action rifles, but solid-frame lever-actions won't permit looking through the bore. To inspect these, insert a bit of white paper into the opened action, and hold this to reflect the light.

Of course the best test of the rifle's accuracy is its performance on the range. If this is permissible, the rifle should be targeted at any desired range up to 100 yards, using a padded rest for the forearm and shooting in the prone position. If all the holes in the target paper appear round with no tendency toward an oval shape, this indicates that the barrel is still good enough to keep the bullets spinning properly. Should the bullet holes show any of this tendency to enter sideways or "keyholed," discard the rifle at once. Likewise, the group size will show some measure of the rifle's accuracy but it's not conclusive unless the tester is a skilled rifleman.

The sights on the used rifle should be examined for damaged or bent front sights or missing screws. Any of these items can be repaired but this must be considered in the deal. The action should be checked to make certain it locks fairly tight; extractor and ejector should be both in place and in working order; be sure that the extractor hook is not broken out. The safety should be tested for positive functioning; the hammer or cocking piece should be forced forward with some pressure, with the rifle fully cocked, to determine the margin of safety in the sear surfaces. Often these used guns have been tinkered with by their former owners and the trigger mechanism is the usual sufferer. Lightening trigger pulls is a delicate job, not in the lightening alone but in the preservation of the flat contact surfaces. Rounding these surfaces will result in an accidental discharge if the hammer or cocking piece be struck or shoved with enough violence to push the cocking sear over the trigger sear. This should be most carefully checked in a used rifle.

A dented or otherwise marred stock should not deter a hunter from buying a rifle otherwise sound. A cracked stock, particularly one cracked through the grip, is not so good, but any stock damaged only by the usual scratches and dents incurred in normal hunting can readily be refinished — dents can be steamed up, scratches sanded off and the whole job done over with an oil finish. The cost will be in labor only, and besides it's good fun for long winter evenings.

The foreign military arms of World War II are far too numerous to mention in detail in this chapter. The country is now flooded with all types — German, Belgium, Czech, Austrian, Italian and Japanese. Most of these are, and should forever be, merely "souvenir" weapons. Many are good for the deer hunter but the hunter is seldom qualified to separate the wheat from the chaff. Unless such rifles can be examined and checked by competent gunsmiths the entire category should be discarded for the American hunting field.

Our own new military rifles of World War II, the Garand and the M1 carbine, are neither suited to hunting nor available to the hunter. The Garand is a highly efficient military weapon of great fire power in .30–06 caliber but is a clumsy, poorly balanced arm in no way suited to sporting conversion. The little carbine with its pitifully inadequate cartridge can never be a rifle for the deer hunter. Some deer will be killed with it, but for each one recovered ten will wander off to die miserably.

In Europe many commanding officers sensibly barred the use of the carbine to soldiers taking European deer for food, permitting the use of the Garand only. This carbine cartridge compares unfavorably with our old loadings in the .32–20, never a deer killer except in the hands of the best hunter riflemen. Many hunters have had visions of picking up a wartime Garand or M1 carbine for little money, planning to use these for deer, whereas at the present time it is illegal to have either of these arms in civilian possession. Furthermore, ammunition manufacturers have been forbidden to offer the .30-caliber carbine ammunition for civilian sales. Generally speaking, this writes *Finis* to the Garand and the M1 carbine for the hunter, at least for the present time. It's conceivable that at some future date the Garand may be offered for civilian sale, but the writer doubts that any hunter will seriously consider this weapon after looking over all our present sporting rifles.

Strangely enough, the lady hunter is appearing with greater frequency in the deer country each season. Last season up at Northville in the Adirondacks the writer noted a sizable number of red-capped-and-coated Dianas. It was inevitable that this should be so, for deer hunting comes within the reach of more people each year. The wider distribution of the game, easier methods of hunting and the glamour of taking a whitetail buck should all appeal to the huntress.

The perfect deer rifle for the Little Woman would be the Savage lightweight 99 T in .250–3000. No rifle of ample power for deer will be more pleasant for her to shoot. Perhaps a heavier caliber will be more in line with her ideas, and if this is selected the rifle can be fitted with the excellent Johnson Muzzle Brake, a highly efficient device for any hunter who is sensitive to recoil. It does increase the muzzle flash and blast, however, so this must be considered in making a decision.

Perhaps a few words about the custom gun should be included in this chapter on weapons. With each year, as hunters and riflemen become more discriminating in their choice of weapons, the truly custom-built rifle is more in demand. This type of rifle should never be confused with the sporting-conversion of military rifles now being offered by many firms throughout the country. These conversions are justly popular with many hunters and in most cases are well-designed and serviceable. The usual practice in building these rifles for the hunter is to take standard military arms — the Springfield, Enfield and Mauser — remove the military sights, shorten the barrel (if necessary), polish the barrel, fit ramp front sights and aperture rear, then provide the rifle with a machine-turned and inletted stock, designed in accordance with the individual maker's ideas. Some handwork is required in final fitting and finishing of the stock; then the action and barrel are reblued. Some models, particularly the Enfield conversion, require additional machinework to remove the rear-sight base and fit the magazine to flush outlines.

All of these jobs make excellent sporting rifles at no higher price than similar rifles of standard design. They do fill a need, at the present time, when gun plants are far behind deliveries. However, the great proportion of these sporter conversions offer little more than the shooter can have with the Remington and Winchester high-power bolt actions.

The custom gun lies in a special field of gunsmithing; it is designed individually for the shooter for whom it is built. Such a weapon is expensive, being built by a skilled craftsman, but it is only in such a rifle that the discriminating hunter rifleman can incorporate his own ideas. Fine wood can be obtained in the custom-gun stock, designed according to the hunter's personal needs — correct drop at heel and comb, Monte Carlo comb, desired pitch and length of butt plate, suitable shape and fit of the cheek piece, special sighting equipment, more comfortable pistol grip, a pleasingly artistic checkering design and a fine finish. Perhaps the shooter wishes a new barrel of a special caliber, not available in the action type he chooses. This the custom gunsmith can supply.

Rifles of this type should be, and usually are, purchased by men who have been in the shooting field long enough to have well-established ideas as to their requirements. A man of abnormal build, or with physical disabilities preventing his using a standard arm, can many times be fitted with a suitable rifle by the custom gunmaker. Nor should any hunter plan to spend money on one of these costly arms unless he has need for special work. Most of our great army of hunters have no fixed ideas of gun design. These men will be suited well with standard arms and at much less cost.

As a matter of fact, true custom-gun work is limited to a comparative handful of gunsmiths scattered throughout the country. It is difficult for the hunter to select the right man for his job, but, to save himself much disappointment and wasted money, he must pick a thoroughly reliable man to perform his work.

Most custom rifles are built on bolt-actions or single shots. For the deer hunter the Springfield, Krag, Mauser and Enfield are all good actions for a basic start. However, there is no good reason why any of the lever-actions, autoloaders and slide-actions cannot be built to fine custom specifications, as are the bolt-actions. Such a sturdy action as the 99 Savage, built with special cheek-piece stock, suitable design of forearm, together with the right sighting equipment and other refinements, can well take its place beside the best bolt-action, custom-built sporters. The emphasis, however, in the custom gun field is on the bolt-action arms. These are best suited to rebarreling with special calibers and are more adaptable to drastic changes in stock design.

Whatever the hunter's choice of action for the custom job may be, let him first fix in his mind the principal design and specifications before placing his order. Let him also consult the gunsmith commissioned to do the work on any of the points which in his mind are hazy. Most gunsmiths are willing to perform work exactly as outlined, even though it may be against their better judgment. In any case the smart hunter will get his gunsmith's advice, recognizing the fact that the gunmaker's wider experience will temper radical design to more practical lines.

During World War II the author was associated with Eric "Pop" Johnson and Bob Owen in the manufacture of the .50-caliber Browning machine gun. Both of these gunsmiths, world-famous in barrel making and stock work, confided that their biggest headache in the field of custom-gun work was connected with either many of their customer's "screwball ideas" or the fact that many of them failed to supply enough accurate information for intelligently building the weapon.

The custom gun will never be a weapon for the masses; rather it takes up where the regular manufacturers stop. It is the only answer for the hunter rifleman who feels he must have a rifle "tailormade" in order to conform to his advanced ideas. Perhaps best of all it is the answer to every man's craving for "something different," a weapon of beautifully graceful lines, artistically executed by a master gun-craftsman whose love of firearms is apparent in his work. In a word, a weapon to cherish, to fondle, to hold close to one's heart as a warm friend and dependable companion in the woods.

In this somewhat lengthy chapter the author has deliberately avoided a discussion of firearms technicalities. It has been written in the hope that the new or less experienced hunter may find in it some hint to explain away some of his failures. No one hunter can find sufficient experience, even in his lifetime of deer hunting, to become the sage advisor whose words are the criterion by which deer hunters must, forever after, live. The writer is merely another deer hunter who has had, through fortuitous circumstance, a bit more firearms experience than the average man who signs a deer license each year.

It should forever be fixed in a hunter's mind that the caliber and design of his weapon are of far less importance than his ability to handle it. With a well-made reliable rifle in hand he must climb the mental, physical and emotional steps up the ladder of experience, until at last his ability matches the accuracy, killing power and reliability of this weapon. If his confidence then matches his ability, he should, with the favorable smile of Old Lady Luck, kill his deer.

14 / Sights—Open, Peep, and 'Scope

THE CONNECTING LINKS between the deer hunter's weapon and his buck are gun sights. Widely discussed among all shooters, always a controversial subject with big-game hunters, metallic rifle sights have made less progress in development during the last fifty years than any other part of a firearm. Accuracy of any rifle is strictly dependent on its sighting equipment, yet many thousands of wonderfully accurate weapons are handicapped with obsolete sighting equipment.

It does seem silly to find a rifle as highly accurate as any good .30–06 equipped with a plain metal bead or blade-front sight and a notch rear sight — equipment that would fail to deliver better than fair accuracy even in the hands of an expert. This same .30–06, with hunting ammunition, is easily capable of putting all its shots into a 6-inch circle at 200 yards, but these crude sights make holding as close as this a physical impossibility. Just take a look through the rifle line-up of any American manufacturer and you'll find new model rifles, even those chambered and bored for the most modern cartridges, turned loose on the shooting clan with sights that were old stuff during the Civil War.

There can be only one reason for this neglect — cost of manufacture. A dollar or less in manufacturing cost saved will make the consumer's price in the final outcome much more attractive. It's also possible that rifle makers have adopted the point of view that many shooters are going to change the sights to their liking anyway, so why jack up the retail price with sights that are going to be discarded? This latter might be a very pleasant thought, but actually it doesn't happen too often.

Now, if these gunmakers could be made to realize just how badly these poor sights make their latest development in rifle and cartridge perform, I'd almost bet that a quick change would evolve in the factory sight equipment. It's true that the last ten years have seen some manufacturers releasing two or three models with receiver or tang peep sights as standard equipment, but on the whole these few models won't amount to more than 10 per cent of the entire line of American-made rifles, speaking of rifles in the deer-shooting class.

There is nothing really new in the entire line of metallic hunting sights. Many hunters seem to think that peep or aperture sights are a recent fad, but actually the use of the aperture dates back to the days of crossbows, hundreds of years ago. The tang peep of Lyman and Marble type has been in use for over a hundred years; in fact, the Lyman tang sight is today virtually the same as the Lyman of a century ago. Why, then, don't more shooters use good sights — we can't call them "modern" sights, because they're not — instead of worrying along year after year with poor equipment? Let's lay the blame on the rifle makers for not educating the shooter and supplying him with good sights, either through negligence or deliberate intent.

Metallic rifle sights fall into two classifications: the open or "notch" type, and the aperture or "peep" style. With both of these rear-sight designs the same type of front sight may be used, so let's go into the front sight situation first, as it's highly important. No matter what type of rear sight your rifle carries, if your front sight can't be readily seen, you might just as well not have sights at all.

The term "front sight" covers a multitude of types for widely varying purposes: small-game hunting, simon-pure target work, "plinking," long-range big-game hunting and quick, accurate work at fairly short range in heavy cover. In whitetail deer hunting we can short-cut through all these different styles right down to the last mentioned, because all of our whitetail shooting is done at ranges less than a hundred yards, in most cases, and in close cover where backgrounds are not well adapted to easy visibility. For this hunting, then, we need a front sight easily seen in any light, durable enough to stand hard knocks and of a type permitting a fair degree of accuracy in a hurry, for snap shooting at moving targets.

First, the size of a front sight. Regardless of the style of sight or material used in its make-up a front sight for whitetail shooting should be *large*. The only possible reason for using a small front sight under any shooting conditions is to obtain a greater degree of accuracy on small targets, and by no stretch of the imagination can a whitetail buck be called a "small target" at all normal hunting ranges. In some instances, the barrel length of your rifle will determine the size of the best front sight, for it's self-evident that a $\frac{3}{32}$-inch bead will look larger on a 20-inch barrel carbine than on a 26- or 28-inch barrel rifle. If we can make any definite statement as to a minimum front-sight dimension for deer shooting, it would be this $\frac{3}{32}$-inch size, and under some conditions of poor visibility and deficient vision on the hunter's part a $\frac{1}{8}$-inch bead is a big advantage. Sights of this size are sometimes listed by the makers as "semi-jack" sights, but don't be fooled into thinking that they're only for night shooting. These big sights are highly accurate on deer at all hunting ranges, and are a necessity under all adverse sighting conditions.

The medium beads, measuring about $\frac{1}{16}$ inch, with which most rifles are factory equipped, are just a bit too small for good results on whitetails. These sights are intended as a compromise, to be used on game and targets of all sizes from chucks to big game, but if any deer hunter wants to mount a front sight for deer hunting only, better let it be one of these larger sizes.

Now as to shape of a front sight: The round bead is almost universally used and is conceded to be as good as any for all hunting purposes. Some hunters who have been trained in shooting at targets will prefer the military type square-top post and for some eyes this sight will give better holding for elevation. The squarely cut off top of the post makes a clear line of demarcation against any target and will eliminate the tendency of the top of the sight to blend into the background, which sometimes happens with the round bead. This writer prefers the square-topped sight for all hunting purposes for this reason, as there is never any doubt as to the position of the top of the front sight in reference to the target. This is drawing the point a bit too fine for deer hunting though, and we can consider it of minor importance for all whitetail hunting.

One point in front sight shape that is important, however, is to have the face of the bead perfectly flat. Many round beads are made up with round or almost round faces and with this type of sight we will encounter the condition known as "shooting away from the light," caused by light reflection distorting the shooter's view of the bead. Sunlight striking this type of bead from the side will cause that side to look larger than the other, throwing the bead center out of line, or "away from the light." This objectionable feature is particularly noticeable with large front sights, so to correct it, or prevent it, use nothing but a flat-face bead. The flat face will reflect light uniformly and give true holding under all angles of light reflection.

Developed along the lines of better illumination by light reflection is a hunting front sight made by King called the "Reflector front sight." This sight incorporates a built-in chromium reflector in the base, which picks up light from overhead and throws it on the bead. The principle is good, certainly it is quite new, and it makes this sight outstanding for all hunting under poor light conditions.

Materials of many kinds have gone to make front sights: pure gold or silver, "German silver," copper, bronze, ivory and various plastics in different shades. The selection of the best material for a front sight, which determines the color, is largely a matter of backgrounds and cover to be encountered as well as the season of the year. The clear, dead-white of an ivory bead is fine for all conditions except when snow covers the ground. Then it may be hard to find, just when you need it most. It does stand out well against the green of spruce and laurel, or the brown and black of the late fall hardwood covers. The silver bead is equally good under these conditions, but neither of these should be used if the country to be hunted is likely to have a blanket of snow. Some deer hunters will compromise on a gold bead, as this can be seen well against any background, and it has the outstanding virtue, common to metal beads, of durability. Probably the best bead color that can be chosen, for any and all conditions, is red. It stands out sharply against evergreens, dead leaves, tree trunks and snow, not forgetting the gray-brown of a deer.

The only weak point in all these plastic or ivory beads is their fragility. Sometimes just a mere touch against a stone, a tree trunk or frozen ground will crack them off and the hunter is out of luck for the rest of his trip, or for that day at least. The smart thing for the deer hunter to do, if he's at all careless with his rifle and makes a habit of breaking off ivory sights almost every season, is to use a silver or gold bead for strength. Then, if he encounters snow during the season, he can blacken the front sight by smoking it with a match, resmoking it as often as it happens to rub off. When the snow runs out, the original silver or gold can be renewed by polishing the bead with some fine steel wool. Don't try to smoke an ivory or plastic sight because you may learn to your surprise that it's made of celluloid — and before you know it, you'll need a new front sight. Ivory sights that have turned yellow with age can be bleached to their original whiteness by exposure to sunlight, but if they're smoked in any way by the shooter, they will never again be white.

No discussion of hunting front sights can be called complete without mention of the front-sight ramp. Hunters who follow the latest trends of rifle makers have probably noted that almost all of these new models are equipped with a special type of front-sight base, called a ramp, in which the front sight is mounted. Some of these are made as an integral portion of the barrel and others are made separately and attached by bands, screws or sweating to the barrel.

These ramps are not by any means a new flight of fancy with the rifle makers. Rather they serve two very definite purposes: quicker sighting and greater strength, not to mention a more artistic appearance. Their practical application in quicker sighting consists in rapidly guiding the eye upward along the incline toward the front sight, throwing the shooter's eye on this sight at once. Many of the older types of rifles, especially military rifles, are equipped with very high front sights (out of necessity), leaving the front sight bead perched way up on the top of a narrow stem. This narrow stem gives no guide to the shooter's eye, slowing down the sighting process somewhat.

These high front sights also are easily bent out of alignment and, as far as appearance goes, they add nothing to the graceful lines of the arm. The use of the long ramp as a base for sights makes possible the mounting of a low sight, much less subject to damage and enhancing the general appearance of any rifle. In addition, most of these ramp sights provide for a hood or sight cover which is a great protection to the sight in transportation. Of course, for deer hunting the hood should be removed, to allow all possible light to reach the sight.

Front sights are made in a tremendous variety of shapes and sizes, each adapted to special conditions. Globe sights, combination sights, reversible sights and aperture sights all have a definite place in the rifle-shooting picture, but certainly not for whitetail deer hunting. What is needed most is a rugged sight, clearly visible against all types of backgrounds and in poor light — a sight that, once properly mounted and adjusted, will stay that way for seasons to come.

Open rear sights have always been a pretty touchy subject with this writer, but just as long as manufacturers keep putting them on their rifles, they must be considered. Many of these open sights consist merely of a flat-topped bar with a small V- or U-shaped notch to center the front sights. And of all the many styles of open rear sights, this type seems to be the lesser evil; it's fairly quick to catch and obscures very little of the target. However, the so-called "buck-horn," "semi-buckhorn" and Rocky Mountain types, found on thousands of hunting rifles, are the worst possible sighting equipment for all whitetail deer hunting. Of all standard factory sights these are the slowest to use, the most difficult to see and the least accurate. For any quick shooting and shots at running deer they invariably cause the shooter to throw his bullets high because the front sight is not pulled down low enough in the notch.

With the flat-topped sight some of this high-shooting tendency is prevented, but even with this type the notch is fuzzy and indistinct, especially in the poor light of the deer woods. In my opinion, there is only one good open rear sight now being regularly supplied for deer rifles by an American manufacturer. This sight is a slightly concave-top rear sight with a vertical white line in the center of the face; the notch is eliminated entirely. To align this sight properly all that is necessary is to catch the front bead over the top of the rear sight in line with the vertical white line, and the hold is right. There's very little chance to hold too high, because the bead just rests on the top of the rear sight, and windage alignment is quickly made with the center line. There is no notch to "fuzz" and no possibility of holding "too fine" or "too coarse" unintentionally. This rear sight is listed by Savage Arms Corporation and is regularly supplied on their 99 T model in connection with a red bead front sight, making as good a set of open sights as can be had for deer hunting. The red of the front sight makes a startling contrast with the white line of the rear sight, giving rapid, positive sight alignment. This combination of sights can be had on any of their regular models if specified, and can also be adapted to a great many other makes of rifles.

Redfield makes a flat-top replacement rear sight using the white line principle in connection with a notch. Marble's and King also have similar rear sights, using a white diamond in place of the line, with the point of the diamond ending at the bottom of the notch. In these three different makes of rear sight, the notches and white line, or diamond, are made up as a separate insert, giving the shooter the choice of either V-shaped or U-shaped notches by simply reversing the insert. In addition to the flat-topped style of sight all these manufacturers make similar sights in semi-buckhorn and buckhorn styles, but of the three, the flat top is by far the best for all shooting.

Any and all types of open rear sights offer certain sighting difficulties to the shooter. They must be mounted at least fourteen or fifteen inches away from the eye, for optical reasons, to be seen at all clearly, thus shortening the sighting radius of the rifle with resultant increase in sighting errors. For the same reason, unless the hunter is very familiar with his rifle, the sight being placed at this distance from the eye makes it slow to pick up. Then for quick shooting, or when light is poor, the shooter either won't take time to pull the front sight down in the rear notch or he won't be able to see it if he does get it down where it belongs. In either case his shot will go high, and if he's using a buckhorn type the high "ears" on each side of the notch will further induce this high shooting tendency. Add to this the fact that the outline of the rear sight itself obscures a large part of the target, and anyone can readily see that such open sights are hopelessly inefficient.

In many cases the hunter himself can make small changes in his regular sight equipment, materially aiding its efficiency in the woods. If his rifle happens to be mounted up with a rear notch having high sides, these can be filed flush with the top of the notch, thereby gaining the advantage of the regular flat-top sight. Shooters who like the easy visibility of the ivory bead can make an effective substitute by adding a drop of white lacquer to the face of the regular bead sight. This lacquer can be carried in a small bottle in a recess in the stock under the butt plate, and applied with a pin or matchstick. To remove it when desired simply scratch it off with a fingernail or a knife blade. The filing of the rear sight will, of course, leave the metal bright, so it should be reblued to avoid possible light reflection. The chapter on gunsmithing will treat this process in detail. Front sights that have the rounded or oval-faced bead can be filed flat to eliminate the "shooting away from the light" fault, but it does require some care to keep the surface perfectly square.

Many times during the past decade and a half this writer has gone out on a limb in recommending the use of peep sights to deer hunters, both seasoned veterans and novices alike. With but a single exception, in all these years every one of these new peep-sight users has been better suited than with the open sights he had used formerly, and this one hunter was finally fitted up with a good 'scope before he was satisfied.

*　　*　　*

It has always been a deep mystery to me as to just why there is such a widespread prejudice against the use of peep, or aperture, rear sights among the great army of deer hunters. Surely the peep type of sight is infinitely more accurate, faster to use and easier to see than any other type of metallic sight, yet not more than one deer hunter in ten is willing to give it a tryout. The optical advantages of such a sight are self-evident — longer sighting radius; rear sight closer to the eye; better view of the target. There is no possibility of holding a high front sight in relation to the rear sight, no focusing on the rear sight necessary, and better sighting under poor light conditions.

Use of the peep sight is ridiculously simple; so simple, in fact, that the shooter is not even conscious of it in his shooting. The peep hole becomes an open window through which we see the front sight and the target very clearly. No effort should be made to *see* the rear peep ring, much less to try to *focus* on it. One of the major reasons for mounting the peep close to the eye is to discourage any attempt on the part of the shooter to focus his eye on the peep ring; with the ring so close to the eye it is impossible to focus on it, which is just as it should be.

Now in the effort to clarify some of the confusion in regard to use of the peep sight in hunting let's compare the sighting processes of peep and open sight. With open sights the shooter first brings his front sight into his line of vision, then he settles it in the rear notch, being careful to have it centered in the notch and neither too high nor too low. This process takes a certain amount of time and concentration, even though the act may be unconscious on the part of the hunter. He then must swing the front sight on the target in the proper spot and squeeze off the shot. The peep-sight user has only to look through the peephole at the front sight, then swing the front sight on the target and touch off the shot when the sight comes to rest in the right place. Of course, the trained rifleman, in either case, does not look directly at his sights. He prefers to keep his gaze focused on the target and let the sights fall into line as they will, even though they will be somewhat out of focus.

It's an optical truth that the eye can focus at only one distance at any given time. Use of the peep necessitates concentration on only two points, the front sight and the target. With the open sight some attention must be paid to the rear sight in addition to the front sight and the target. It seems to me that the benefits of peep sights would be of great advantage to the new hunter, the inexperienced rifleman, who must pay more attention to sight alignment than the skilled shooter. A good shot knows almost unconsciously just when his sights are in the correct relative position and he can concentrate on the target exclusively.

Beginners at the rifle shooting game have the bad habit of trying to look directly at their sights, first the front, then the rear; finally they shift their vision to the target. We all know that the eye cannot change its point of focus abruptly; it takes a fraction of a second for the shooter's vision to clear up on the target after he has been watching his sights. Often, in this brief instant, his buck has disappeared or shifted his position, requiring an entire sighting procedure all over again. I should like to emphasize that with the experienced hunter, this is not a major point, for reasons already pointed out. He can shift his aim readily and quickly as occasion demands. But for the uninitiated, this slower sighting process often means complete failure to make a kill or even a hit.

This, then, is the major advantage of the peep sight in deer hunting: it requires less concentration in sighting than the open type sight and leaves the shooter free to watch his game directly. The aperture is usually large enough so that the entire target can be seen within it, none of it is obscured by high sides or the flat bar of the rear sight as with open sights; the front sight stands out clearly and alone in the center of the aperture and gives the shooter greater latitude in holding.

Why, then, the great prejudice against the peep sight? For prejudice there surely is, at least among the deer-hunting fraternity. Frankly, it rests in ignorance and inexperience on the part of the hunter, and a certain amount of reluctance in changing to something new. Deer hunters usually claim that they're "used" to the rear sight of open type and that they can't find the front sight in a hurry through the peephole. This, of course, is due to the condition I've already pointed out — they try to look *at* the peep rather than *through* it. They fail to realize that the less attention they pay to the rear peep the more natural and rapid their sighting will be. Complaint number two is that they can't get the front sight bead in the center of the peep, whereas it actually is very difficult to hold it anywhere in the peep ring *except* in the center. Fortunately for all of us our eye, normally and very naturally, will align and hold the front sight in the center or approximate center without any effort on our part. I might add too that there is no crying need to have the front sight held in the *exact* center under any hunting conditions. Slight errors in holding of the front sight with relation to the rear peep will not make any appreciable difference in results on the target. The reason for this also must be obvious to the shooter; the rear peephole, although relatively small in size, appears extremely large to the shooter, because of its close position to the eye. Therefore, any error in centering the sight large enough to cause considerable inaccuracy is immediately detected and corrected unconsciously by the eye, because of this magnification in appearance.

We need not concern ourselves, then, about centering the front sight in the peephole; merely looking through it in the natural act of sighting will give extremely good alignment for both windage and elevation.

Some years ago I made a practical test under actual shooting to find just how much this "off center" influence would have in throwing bullets out of alignment. I used a Springfield sporter mounted with a receiver peep, carrying a disk with ⅛-inch hunting-style aperture. At 75 yards, shooting in the prone position with a padded rest, I fired 4 groups of 3 shots each, holding each group of 3 shots with the front sight held as far out of the center of the peephole as I could and still see the sight clearly. Group 1 was held to the top of the circle, group 2 at the bottom, groups 3 and 4 to the right and left of the peep ring, which should show the maximum amount of error to be expected from the most extreme hold.

Results on the target were gratifying; I had made a more or less square group with a maximum spread of 12 inches, measuring between the widest shots. This would very definitely indicate that as long as the front sight could be seen at all in the peep ring the bullet would strike not more than 6 inches from the point of aim at 75 yards. Very few hunters who roam the deer woods each fall can hold any better than this in the normal offhand hunting position. And then, for most all deer hunting we can shorten this 75 yards by half, giving the effect of not more than 3-inch inaccuracy in any direction due to holding the front sight out of center in the rear peep. Bear in mind also that a deliberate attempt was made to make the group as far out of alignment as possible, and still results were in the effective "killing circle" at whitetail deer ranges. This in itself should be convincing enough to any hunter concerning the accuracy possibilities of the rear-aperture sight.

This writer does not want to create the impression that only peep sights are effective on deer; many more deer are killed each year by hunters using the open sight than are taken with peep-sighted rifles. But the cold fact remains that peep sights of the right kind will materially aid the novice hunter and even the veteran whose vision may be failing. To a very few deer hunters sights are not at all important; they can kill their buck almost without seeing sights. Years of constant practice and use of the same rifle have made them so familiar with the feel of the stock against their cheek that they can shoot well enough to kill deer without paying very much attention to the sights.

Just a few years ago a white-haired old hunter came into the shop with a .351-caliber autoloading Winchester, equipped with the regular factory sights. He confided that his shooting had been falling off lately and he'd missed a deer or two because he couldn't make out just where the sights were any more. His problem was poor vision and I recommended a good scope for his rifle. This idea didn't seem to be in accord with his ideas, though, for he had in mind the mounting of a straight shotgun rib on the barrel in place of the regular sights. He was certain that this rib would be all he needed to kill a buck, so I accordingly mounted a shotgun rib in line with his ideas.

The following spring he was back again with the rifle, looking for suggestions on different sighting equipment; but he didn't want "one of those new-fangled telescopes." The only alternative for this old-timer was a set of peep sights, so I mounted a ⅛-inch ivory bead on the front and a tang peep rear equipped with a hunting disk of ½-inch outside diameter and having ⅛-inch aperture. After we had sighted up the rifle properly, old-timer used it for 'chuck hunting that summer and then proceeded to kill his buck with it that fall, and he has used the outfit just as is ever since. Needless to say, the combination suited him very well, but regretfully I must add that he has since passed on to the Happy Hunting Grounds, where sights are no problem.

About five years ago I had occasion to fit up a friend with a set of peep sights, but only because I had been hammering at him for a couple of seasons to give them a tryout, knowing that they would improve his shooting. This chap and I were members of the same hunting club at that time and I had had several opportunities to watch his shooting effectiveness on deer. He made many misses of what we can call easy shots. His eyes were normal enough, but he never seemed to take time enough to line up his sights properly; just the instant his rifle touched his shoulder he would start throwing lead, most of it high over his buck. He was using regular factory sights, a plain bead front sight and a semi-buckhorn rear. I was convinced after hunting with him long enough that his trouble was sights, because he was a fair enough shot to be able to kill deer with little trouble.

After plenty of persuasion I was allowed to mount up a good rear peep on his rifle along with a red bead front sight of good size. He used this setup throughout the summer 'chuck season with good results; in fact, he almost doubled his average on woodchucks; but just a few days before the opening of the deer season he suddenly developed a bad case of cold feet. He rushed to the shop with his rifle and asked me to put on an open rear sight similar to the original factory job, simply because he was afraid to take the peep sights into the deer woods. It so happened that I was unable to supply him out of stock on hand so I wired at once for the sight. It arrived just too late to catch the first day of the deer season, but I called him up that night after his first day's hunting, to give him the news. You can imagine my surprise when he told me that he'd just that day killed a dandy buck with his outfit and he wouldn't change sights again for anything. He's been using these same sights ever since and to date has a pretty good record of bucks killed.

In the line of aperture sights suitable for hunting purposes we find three types: the tang sight, the receiver sight and the cocking-piece sight. Of these three types, the cocking-piece sight is little known and not in general use. Lyman makes one for various bolt-action rifles including the Krag, Springfield, Newton and Mauser, to be mounted on the end of the cocking piece or bolt, placing the sight relatively close to the eye, and this is its only advantage. Against this, we find that this type is difficult to mount properly, has no adjustment for windage, and its weight often slows down lock speed, causing misfires. To remedy this latter condition a heavier mainspring must be installed. Altogether, the cocking-piece sights have little merit, so we can eliminate them from this discussion.

The tang peep has two distinct advantages; its position is close to the eye, making for quick sighting, and it is easily mounted on hunting rifles. Almost all lever, slide and autoloading rifles of American make are drilled and tapped to take some type of tang peep sight. These holes are filled with dummy screws by the factory so in most cases all that's necessary to mount them is to remove these dummy screws and screw the sight base in position, using the screws that are furnished with the sight. In the Winchester lever-actions you'll find two screws in the "tang" — the metal strip in the rear of the action on top of the grip. The rear screw of these two is an action screw, which fastens the action to the stock; the front screw is a dummy. Furnished with tang sights for these rifles is one long action screw and the regular forward-sight base screw; it's simple to remove the action screw and mount the sight in place. Savage lever-actions have two dummy screws in the top tang just behind the hammer indicator; the Remington slide-action has two of these dummies in the rear of the action placed side by side; and in the Remington autoloader the single dummy screw is in the middle of the upper tang, just behind the receiver wall. Both Lyman and Marble's make tang sights to fit all these rifles, each to be mounted by the shooter if he so desires. The Lyman line of tang sights is made in two styles, Number 1 with built-in turn-down peep, making two sizes of aperture readily available; and the Number 2 series, to be used with disks of any size that suits the hunter's fancy. The Number 1 style cannot be used with a disk, as it is not drilled and tapped for it, so for best all-round purposes the Number 2 style is probably the better of the two, as various sizes of disk and aperture make the sight better adaptable to varying shooting conditions.

Of the three available types of rear aperture sight this writer prefers the receiver sight, rigidly mounted on the rifle receiver and having good windage and elevation adjustments. The past decade in sight design and manufacture has seen more attention paid to this type of sight than to any other in the metallic sight field and with good reason. Receiver sights, properly mounted, become almost a part of the rifle itself; they are seldom knocked out of adjustment by a hard blow and they are easily sighted-in at any hunting ranges. They are the best type of aperture rear sight adapted to bolt-action arms and are equally well adapted to lever, slide and auto-loading actions. In all respects except one they are superior to the tang type of sight and this one point is that they cannot be mounted quite so close to the eye as the tang sight. In the face of other advantages this is but a minor detail and is far outweighed by the receiver sight's ruggedness for hunting purposes.

All types of receiver sights are, of course, mounted on the receiver, usually necessitating the drilling and tapping of two holes, sometimes three. There are a great many rifles that are turned out by the manufacturer already drilled and tapped for receiver sights exactly the same as for tang peeps, among these the Winchester Models 54 and 70, the Savage Models 40 and 45 and the Remington Model 30 Express. On the whole though, we find many more rifles which can be fitted with tang sights by simply attaching to holes already placed there by the manufacturer than is the case with receiver sights. Winchester, Marlin and Savage lever-actions must all be drilled and tapped for receiver sights, either by the shooter himself or by a gunsmith. The chapter on gunsmithing will give details on this job as in most cases it's well within the capabilities of the hunter himself.

In any type of rear aperture sight it's important to have adjustments for elevation and windage that can be securely *locked* after the rifle is sighted in at the proper range. Without such locking features your rifle is constantly subject to subtle sight changes in the hands of well-meaning friends or hunting partners. Many of these individuals simply *must* fiddle around with sight adjustment screws every time they pick up a strange rifle, and if you happen to be the victim, your next shot at a buck might be three feet away from your holding, all through no fault of your own. This then, is one of the strong points in favor of the receiver sight over the tang sight; almost every model has some means of securely locking both windage and elevation adjustments so that they can't be moved with prying fingers; neither will a hard blow move them.

This feature of easy adjustments for elevation and windage is also more or less exclusively true of receiver sights. Few tang sights have any adjustment for windage and if so, they can't be locked in position. Elevation with the tang sight is obtained by turning a knurled sleeve, which is threaded to the stem, raising it or lowering it as desired, but such adjustments are very coarse. Add to this the lack of windage adjustment in these tang sights and we can appreciate the fact that these sights are not too easy to adjust. The receiver sight incorporates a movable slide for elevation, with definite graduations clearly marked and with a graduated windage scale. This makes sighting-in a simple matter, and adjusting sights for different loads and ranges equally simple.

For all deer-hunting conditions, though, rifles should be adjusted with one chosen type of ammunition and one definite range. The sights should then be locked in that position and very severely left alone. Why then the need for accurate adjustments? In the first place, the initial sighting-in is simplified and the sights can be adjusted accurately. There is no need to fiddle around with paper shims and hammering the front sight this way and that before a satisfactory adjustment is reached, with a colossal waste of ammunition. Very often a shooter is tempted, in desperation, to let it go as "good enough" even though the sights may not be quite as they should be. With good adjustments there is no excuse for this

practice. Secondly, deer hunters like to change front sights occasionally, or change the bullet weight in the cartridge they're using.
With sights easily adjustable, this little task is a pleasure, but with
the tang type of peep having no windage adjustments or a coarse,
non-locking elevation adjustment, it becomes too much trouble for
most hunters and with good reason.

In making your decision on a receiver sight you can choose from
Lyman, Pacific, Redfield and others. Of all these various makes,
Redfield has some outstanding features. Most Redfield sights are
designed so that very little wood, if any, must be cut out of the
stock to inlet the base, and several of their designs enable the shooter
to attach the sight without drilling and tapping additional holes.
Their windage adjustment is of the opposing screw type, permitting
very accurate and easy adjustments and, perhaps best of all, complete
adjustments for elevation and windage can be made with a coin or
washer; there is no need to carry a screwdriver. This latter feature
of course applies to their Number 102 line of hunting sights and
not to their line of micrometer sights.

Micrometer sights brings up another point in receiver-sight design.
These micrometer sights are primarily designed for target shooting,
as they allow positive adjustments for windage and elevation at all
ranges. Each click of the elevation or windage screw moves the
point of impact a very definite distance — quarter inch, half inch,
inch and so on, depending on the make of sight and the shooting
range. These sights are all excellent in design, positive in adjustment and very durable. They are fine for all hunting purposes, but
they cost just a little bit more than necessary for hunting use. Their
very fine and accurate adjustments are wasted on the deer hunter,
because all he needs is a sight that can be readily adjusted for his
shooting conditions, then locked in position until he either wants
to change front sights or his "point-blank" range, and this might be
a matter of months or years.

No, the micrometer receiver sight is designed for the target
shooter, who must be able to make accurate changes in his sight
adjustment every time he visits the range. The hunter, of course, can
use these sights to good advantage, but he will be paying two or three
times more for adjustment features that he does not need and will
seldom, if ever, use.

Choosing the best type of receiver sight usually means going
through all the manufacturers' catalogs, selecting from each the
model and design of sight that will best apply to your particular

make of rifle. Look for rugged design which will add to rather than detract from the appearance of your rifle; make sure that there are good windage and elevation adjustments and make *doubly* certain that these adjustments can be positively locked after all necessary sight adjustments have been made.

One additional point in the use of the aperture rear sight: If you find that the use of the peep disk, even with large aperture, seems to slow down your sighting, don't hesitate to remove the disk and use the stem hole only for sighting. This might seem to be a very wide peep hole at first glance, but rest assured that very accurate shooting, and the very fastest shooting, can be done with the peephole only, without disk. The peep outline will seem fuzzy and indistinct and the hole so large that the entire front sight, sight base and forward end of the barrel will be seen through the peep, but if you look through this ring, not *at* it, and hold your front sight on the target, you'll do a good job of hitting your game.

It seems hardly necessary to point out that in all cases where peep rear sights are used, the middle open, or barrel, sight should be removed. Every now and then we run across a hunter carrying a rifle mounted with a good peep sight but still having the rigid open sight still in place — something like trying to walk with an extra leg. The peep rear and front sight are the only two points needed for accurate alignment and the middle sight is just up there in the way, slowing down sighting speed and obscuring half of the target. There is a good point in using a folding middle sight in place of the regular open sight, but this should be kept folded down out of the way when the peep is used. Then if any need arises to check the alignment of the peep sight, the folding sight can be snapped up and the check made by glancing through all three to make certain that they are lined up. This folding sight is especially useful when a tang peep is used as these tangs are subject to slight changes caused by falls or hard knocks either in the woods or in transportation. The folding sight affords an instant check-up and a means of re-aligning the peep sight, if it should be out of adjustment, without the necessity of shooting the rifle in on the range.

Recent developments in the rifled shotgun slug, plus new legislation prohibiting rifles in certain states and some areas in other states, has brought about new interest in possibilities of the shotgun for deer hunting. These rifled slug loads are remarkably accurate in all gauge shotguns for deer hunting at normal ranges, meaning from 50 to 75 yards.

As has been pointed out in the previous chapter, the rifled slug load will group closely enough to the point of aim to make vital hits a certainty at these ranges, so all that remains is to equip the shotgun with suitable sights to bring out this accuracy and make close holding a possibility. Good sights, even of the simplest type, will make an effective weapon of the shotgun for most deer-hunting conditions, and some hunters are using them today rather than going to the expense of a new rifle just for deer hunting. A great many sportsmen can only spend a few days in the deer woods each year and some of them feel that this hardly warrants the purchase of a high-power rifle, if the shotgun can be made to do the job.

As a matter of fact, any shotgun can be used just as is, with the regular front sight and no rear sight, but we can't expect much in the way of accurate holding with this outfit; certainly we can't bring out the accuracy of the slugs with such crude sights. Each year a goodly number of deer are killed with just such equipment, but much better results will be had with good sights. Any gunsmith worthy of the name can adapt rifle sights to most shotgun models, using screws for attaching them, making it possible to remove the sights after deer hunting and put the gun back in service for small game.

My own practice with double guns is to mount a standard front sight of low height just behind the regular factory sight, screwing the sight base to the rib with small fillister head screws. The sight base is first sweated to a thin steel block and this block is drilled with a drill large enough to just permit passage of the 6 × 48 size screws. Then the rib is spotted and drilled with a Number 31 drill and tapped with a 6 × 48 tap. After screwing the sight and its base in position, a low folding leaf sight is selected for the rear, and a dovetail filed in a quarter-inch piece of steel of a width to suit the rib, and the sight base fitted in place. The steel block is then drilled and screwed in position at a point which will place it about fourteen inches from the shooter's eye. The gun can then be tried out on the range and the rear sight can be adjusted by moving it sideways in the dovetail. Elevation on the first trial will probably be too high, so the base should be filed off and tried again on the range, repeating this until the sight is correctly aligned.

This setup of shotgun sights permits their easy removal at any time, and the holes can be filled with dummy screws; it requires only five minutes to mount them again when the shooter is ready to use the slug loads. A great many variations in sights can be selected for shotgun use; even receiver sights and tang peeps can be adapted to repeating shotguns with good results, but it must be remembered that if a rear sight is fitted, either of open or peep type, a new front sight must also be mounted because the regular front sight, although suitable perhaps from the hunter's standpoint, will be much too low to be used with the rear sight.

Every hunter has heard the term "point-blank range." Some of them know what it means; most of them don't. The idea most often circulated among the deer hunting fraternity is that the point-blank range is the greatest range at which a rifle will "shoot flat." As a matter of fact, no rifle shoots flat, but many have much flatter trajectories than others. This is particularly true of modern high-velocity cartridges whose trajectory over a 200-yard range is so low that the bullet seems to drop not at all.

Generally speaking, the point-blank range of a rifle is the exact range at which the bullet will strike the line of sight on the target. For example, if we're shooting a Springfield .30–06 it's customary for deer hunting to adjust the sights so that the bullet strikes at the point of aim at the 100-yard range. Then, at 50 or 60 yards the point of impact will be slightly above the line of sight, only an inch or less, but still above. At 200 yards the bullet will strike about 5 inches below the point of aim, using a game bullet of 180 grains. The point-blank range then, with this sight setting, is actually 100 yards, although it could be changed to 50 yards, 200 yards, or even 300 yards, simply by changing the elevation of the rear sight.

Under most hunting conditions though, the term "point-blank range" means that particular sight setting for any rifle which will give the least error in impact over the greatest range without changing the hold on the target or changing the sight setting. With the .30–06 using the 180-grain bullet this setting would be about 200 yards, because with this setting there will not be more than 4 inches variation from the point of aim at any range up to 250 yards. In other words, with the rifle sighted at 200 yards the rise in bullet flight at 100 yards will only be about 2 to 3 inches above the point of aim; at 250 yards the bullet will still only drop 4 inches below the point of aim. So with a .30–06 rifle sighted at 200-yard point-blank range we can hold on a buck's shoulder at any range from 25 yards up to 250 yards with a reasonable expectation of making a vital hit, even though we make the same hold at any range.

With rifles having a higher trajectory than the .30–06, a shorter "point-blank range" must be used. Rifles in the .30–30 class should be sighted at 100 to 150 yards for best results over their effective range. For example, if we sighted a .30–30 in at 200 yards the rise in bullet flight at 50 yards would be 3 inches and at 100 yards it would be 4½ inches. On neck shots at deer this would be enough variation to cause a high miss, so it's best to shorten the point-blank range for this caliber. To obtain maximum efficiency with rifles in this class, the 150-yard range is the most effective. Sighted-in at this range, we find that the bullet rises no more than 2 inches at any range up to the point-blank distance, which is close enough for all practical hunting purposes.

The charts showing the trajectory curves of two popular calibers will give the shooter information enough so that he can make his own choice in deciding what the point-blank range of his rifle and cartridge should be. There is a big variation in the comparative flatness of trajectory in these two different calibers and each has a different point-blank effective range.

Every hunter who is at all interested in bettering his shooting performance has at some time or another pored over the ballistic tables issued by various ammunition makers; to most hunters the information has little value because they don't know how to apply it to their pet rifle. For instance, let's suppose that we have a rifle using the .300 Savage caliber and we decide to use the 180-grain bullet for all purposes.

Glancing over the trajectory table we extract the following information: mid-range height at 100 yards, .84 or approximately ¾ inch; at 200 yards, mid-range height is 3.76, or about 3¾ inches; at 300 yards we find the height is 9.64 or about 9½ inches. This means that if we decide to sight our rifle in to hit center at 300 yards, at the 150-yard range our bullet will strike almost 10 inches above the line of sight. This is entirely too high for hunting purposes, unless most of the shooting is to be done at ranges over 200 yards.

Dropping back then to 200 yards we note the fact that, with the rifle sighted at this range, the bullet will strike only about 4 inches above the point of aim at the halfway distance, or 100 yards. This is much better, but for very accurate work on small targets it will still be a bit high. We go on, then, to the figures on the 100-yard trajectory and we find that at 50 yards the height above the sight line is less than an inch. So for deer hunting, where ranges are almost always less than 100 yards, we sight the .300 in at this

TRAJECTORY CURVE OF .30–30
(170-GRAIN BULLET) AT VARIOUS RANGES

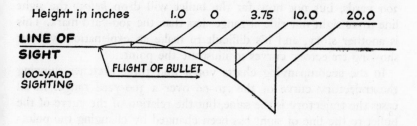

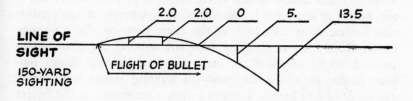

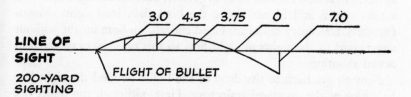

Each point on the trajectory curve represents 50 yards of range. The trajectory curves are somewhat exaggerated in proportion for the sake of clarity. The curve of course remains the same at all ranges; only its relative position changes with each change in "point-blank" sighting.

range, knowing that at all ranges up to 150 yards our bullet will travel within 2 inches of our line of sight, disregarding any change in range.

Now what these trajectory tables do *not* tell the shooter is how much the bullet will drop beyond the 100-yard range, provided our rifle is sighted-in for that distance, or for any other range. They tell us how high our bullet will go *above* the sight line at 100, 200 or 300 yards, but not how far the bullet will drop *below* the sight line if we sight our rifle at ranges less than the 300-yard mark. This is another story, and it's difficult to make an explanation without showing trajectory curves to illustrate the point.

In the accompanying charts you'll find three sketches showing the trajectory curve of the .30–06 over a 300-yard range. In all cases the trajectory is the same, but the relation of the curve of the bullet to the line of sight has been changed by changing the point-blank sighting range. Here are the mid-range trajectory heights for the .30–06 loaded with 180-grain bullet, just as taken from the manufacturers' tables: At 100 yards, height at 50 yards is .62 inch; at 200, height at 100 yards is 2.80 inches; at 300, height at 150 yards is 7.20 inches. Now let's look at the chart showing the trajectory curve. On the curve showing 100-yard sighting the chart shows 50-yard height of about .25 inch; 200-yard sighting shows 100-yard height at 2.5 inches; 300-yard sighting shows a height at 150 yards of 6.75 inches. There is a slight discrepancy in the figures which is accounted for by the fact that the line of trajectory starts about 1 inch lower than the line of sight, although this distance varies with different rifles and sights. For instance, with telescope sights the variation would be even greater, because the sight line with a telescope is still higher above the bore than iron sights. Manufacturers' trajectory tables are based entirely on bore height without any regard to the sights or sight line, so this must be considered in actual shooting.

Now to get back to the drop of the bullet beyond the sight line let's look at the 100-yard trajectory. Here, although the bullet has risen the prescribed distance above the sight line at the halfway mark (allowing for the height of sights above the bore) we find that at 200 yards the bullet has dropped 5 inches below the line of sight, and at 300 yards it has dropped 18 inches below the line of sight. This, of course, at 100-yard point-blank range.

By changing our sighting to 200 yards we get a different picture. Our mid-range height is still just about what it should be at the

TRAJECTORY CURVE OF .30-06
(180-GRAIN BULLET) AT VARIOUS RANGES

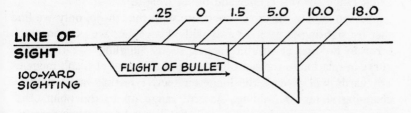

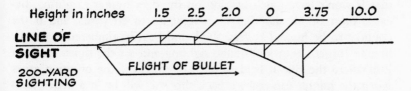

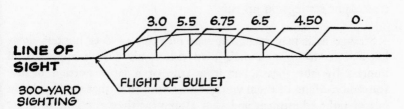

*Each point on the trajectory curve represents 50 yards of range.
The trajectory curves are somewhat exaggerated in proportion
for the sake of clarity. The curve of course remains the same
at all ranges; only its relative position changes with each change
in "point-blank" sighting.*

100-yard mark — 2.5 inches — but our drop at 300 yards has been reduced to only 10 inches. If we go still further and sight our rifle in at the 300-yard mark, we will get a rise in bullet flight of the amount given in the table, about 7 inches at 150 yards. This is a little too much error in sighting for game shooting, so we finally decide on the 200-yard distance as being the most effective point-blank range for this caliber and bullet weight.

We can follow the same procedure with the .30-30, only we find that by sighting-in at 200 yards with this caliber we get too much error in holding at shorter ranges, so by juggling our trajectory curve in relation to the sight line we find that a point-blank range of 150 yards will give us the longest effective hitting range without changing sights or holding. At any range up to the point-blank range of 150 yards, the rise of bullet will not be over 2 inches and at 200 yards it will still be only 5 inches low, meaning that with this sighting we'll have to hold just a bit high at this longer range.

Perhaps I have placed too much emphasis on this problem of choosing the best point-blank range for the hunter's rifle. It's true that it won't have much bearing on the deer hunter's sighting, because most of his shooting is done at 40 to 60 yards, and if the country to be hunted is very thick and heavily timbered it will be best to forget about long-range sighting and set the sights to shoot just where the rifle is held at 50 yards; then, if the occasion arises when the hunter can make a neck shot, he will be in a better position to do so. However, there are many times when a deer hunter will want to use his rifle for "varmint shooting" to keep in practice; and much of this shooting is done at ranges from 100 to 300 yards, so it's important for every sportsman to know something about these sight settings on his rifle.

Strange as it may seem, the vast majority of deer hunters don't know *how* to sight-in their own rifles; this doesn't apply to all hunters by any means but it is true of a large portion of the fraternity. Many of them worry along with rifles that are hopelessly out of sight adjustment and year after year they continue to make the most unaccountable misses on easy targets. Too many deer hunters use their rifles only during the deer season; they never take them out in the field or on the range until they're ready to go hunting and this seems to be a bit too late most of the time.

During the past fifteen years I've had occasion to do this little job for hundreds of hunters with every conceivable type and caliber of rifle, not to mention a multitude of different kinds of sights, from the coarsest of military sights to the modern 'scope. In all but a very few instances the hunter himself could have done the job just as well as I, perhaps better, for then he would have the sights adjusted to his particular method of holding and his own peculiarities of vision.

It might seem decidedly elementary to go into details as to just how sights should be moved to achieve the desired results on the target, but we must remember that not all hunters, in fact very few of them, are technical riflemen. It is second nature with experienced riflemen to check their sight alignment whenever they are ready to do any shooting, and to make necessary corrections. Deer hunters, on the whole, don't take the time to acquire the information, and even if they do most of them hesitate to take a chance on putting it into effect.

I hunted deer for a couple of seasons with a bunch of old-time deer hunters, all of them wise in deer lore and skillful enough with their rifles to bring home the bacon. During my third year with them one of these men had a little tough luck during the first few days of the season — he missed three bucks very cleanly, all at easy killing distance. After his third miss I had the temerity to suggest to him that his sights might be out of line, but he assured me that they hadn't been touched for ten years and he'd always done good work with them before. Nevertheless, I persisted until he offered to let me try out his pet — an old Winchester .38–55 with a long octagon barrel, fitted up with plain bead front sight and a wide-V rear notch.

As I picked up the rifle and glanced over the barrel it seemed to me that the rear sight was perched 'way out to the left, but I thought I'd shoot it before making any comment. My only available target was a fair-sized white rock about sixty yards from the camp, so I fired one shot, holding for the center. This first shot passed out to the left of the rock, missing my hold by at least a foot. I tapped the sight over a bit to the right with a small hammer and tried again; this time I hit the rock, but still to the left. After a few more wallops with the hammer and some more shooting, the sight was finally aligned and is still doing service in the deer woods. I'll never forget the look of amazement on the owner's face when I lined up the sights so easily, just by tapping the rear sight over with a hammer. He had an idea that adjusting sights was some deep dark mystery performed in the hallowed recesses of the gun factories and should never be attempted by the layman. In his case the rifle had very likely been dropped or given a hard blow in transportation, just hard enough to move the rear sight in its dovetail slot.

"Sighting-in" a rifle is essentially a very simple operation. All that we must first do is form a mental picture of the sight line and the line of fire. Just visualize two imaginary lines, one running through the rear sight and over the center of the front sight, forming the sight line, and another line running through the center of the rifle bore, following the exact path of the bullet's flight. Viewed from above and behind the rifle the sight line should be superimposed on the line of fire, or exactly parallel to it. If we change the relative position of either of these two lines the rifle will shoot either to the right or to the left.

For sake of illustration, let's take a lever-action rifle that is fitted with regular open sights: a metal bead front and a notch rear sight. Assume also, for the sake of illustration, that the rifle is correctly sighted with the sight line directly over the bore. Now to see what happens when we change the position of the rear sight, let's take a heavy needle and scribe a tiny mark on the barrel and a corresponding mark on the rear sight base. Then we take a small hammer and a copper drift punch and tap the rear sight over to the left about $\frac{1}{32}$ of an inch.

Now what has this done to our sight line? The rear of the line, starting at the rear notch, has been pushed over to the left, so that the line of sight passing over the front sight now looks out to the right of the line of fire, just below it. We fire the rifle now at a target, being careful to hold just below the center of the bull's-eye, and squeezing the shot off carefully. We check on the shot and find that it has gone some distance to the left of the bull's-eye, indicating that the rifle now *looks* to the left even though our lines of sight was held directly for the center of the bull's-eye. Now our problem is to bring the shot back into the center of the bull, meaning that the shot must be moved toward the *right*. To achieve this result we must tap the rear sight over to the right — in the same direction that we want the shot to move — and keep on firing at the target until the sight is moved over to the proper distance, bringing the point of impact into the center of the target.

If our rear sight were moved to the right out of alignment, in a like manner, our shots would pass to the right of the target and we should have to move our rear sight toward the left in order to bring our point of impact toward the left and eventually into the center of the bull. The only point to remember is that the rear sight must be moved in the *same* direction as we wish the point of impact to move.

Again, we find a similar condition in changing sight adjustments for elevation or "range." If our rifle is shooting high we must lower the rear sight; if it is shooting low, we must *raise* the rear sight. The same rule of directional movement remains the same, the rear sight must be moved in the *same* direction that we want the shot to go. Viewing this process from the side, for purpose of explanation, we find a bit of difference in the two lines, the line of sight and the line of fire. Here our sight line is still a straight line, passing through the sights and out to the target, but our line of fire is now curved, caused by the trajectory of the bullet. These two lines, from the standpoint of elevation, are not parallel, nor can they ever be, because we must elevate the bore just enough so that the bullet will carry up and out to the point where our line of sight strikes the center of the target at the desired range. In other words, even though our sight line may be exactly level and parallel with the ground, the line of the bore will be lower at the rear than at the muzzle, giving the bore an upward tilt just enough to compensate for the drop of the bullet. When these two lines are fixed in their proper relation to each other, so that the bullet strikes the target exactly at the same point as the line of sight at the proper range, we will have "point-blank sighting" at that range. Now to get a clearer picture of what happens when the sights are raised or lowered, we must visualize the raising of the rear sight as having the effect of dropping the rear end of the bore, further tilting the line of fire above the target and causing the shot to go high. Lowering the rear sight brings the rear ends of our two imaginary lines closer together, lifting up the rear of the bore, so to speak, and tilting its angle of fire downward, giving a lower point of impact.

That's all there is to adjusting sights, provided that adjustment can be made with the rear sight, as it always should be whenever possible. However, under some conditions (changing to a light-bullet, high-speed load) we find that our rifle still shoots high, even with the rear sight dropped to its lowest position. We find then that we can't raise the rear end of the bore line any closer to the sight line to effect a lower point of impact, so we must make our change in the front, or muzzle end of the bore line. Our problem is still to lower this bore end below the line of sight, dropping the angle of the bore which in turn will give us a lower shot. The logical solution then is to change the front sight, but in what way? Some hunters' first thought would be to file off the front sight, but this makes the rifle shoot still higher. The answer is, of course, to mount a *higher* front sight giving us the effect of spreading apart the line of sight and the line of fire at the forward end of the rifle. Now if we use the line of sight as a base line, or constant, we can readily see that the effect of this higher front sight will be to throw the front or muzzle end of the rifle lower, giving us the desired effect of dropping the angle of fire.

With all rifles having open rear sights mounted in dovetail barrel slots, the problem of sight adjustment is not quite so easy as if the rifle were fitted with an aperture rear sight having definite graduations for windage and elevation. The only method that we can follow under these conditions is to first scratch the scribe line on the sight base and barrel and make the necessary adjustment for windage by tapping the sight in its slot either to left or right as required. The purpose of the scribe line is to give us a definite starting point in the operation and we can check with it as we go along, using the "cut and try" method, tapping the sight a little, and then shooting at the target, checking results and repeating the process until the windage is correctly aligned.

With most open sights elevation adjustment is made with a step; a notched piece of metal resting under the base of the rear sight notch. Sliding this step further under the rear notch base raises the sight until the desired elevation is reached. This method is very crude and quite often fails to give the exact elevation requirements. As we go along with our sighting in, raising the step notch by notch, we'll finally reach the point where our last adjustment will be too low and the next step too high. This can be remedied by carefully filing off the bottom of the step, trying it from time to time until the correct elevation is reached.

With the receiver-aperture sight, sighting-in is simplified. This sight will have a graduated windage scale, each graduation moving the point of impact a very definite amount, although this varies with the manufacturer. There is no necessity to use a hammer on this type of sight, because windage movement is obtained by screws as a general rule. The same goes for elevation, and after the rifle is properly sighted, the point-blank or "zero" screw can be tightened and the elevation slide locked in position.

The principles of sighting are very simple and when once grasped by the shooter will always be firm in his mind. Any problem involving different types of sights can be solved by applying the

ELEVATION ADJUSTMENT

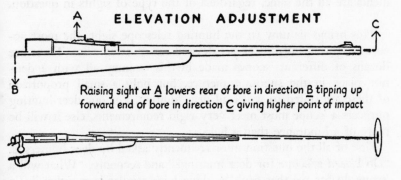

Raising sight at **A** lowers rear of bore in direction **B** tipping up forward end of bore in direction **C** giving higher point of impact

WINDAGE ADJUSTMENT

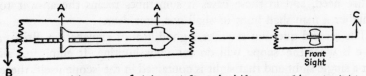

Front Sight

Movement of sight to left at **A** shifts rear of bore to right as **B** since front sight is fixed, throwing impact toward **C**

Line of sight on Line of Fire

Movement of sight to right at **D** shifts rear of bore to left as **E** and, since front sight is fixed, throws impact to **F**

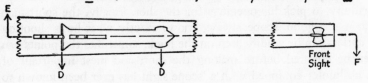

Front Sight

SIGHTING-IN ADJUSTMENTS

principles just outlined. The movements to obtain requisite adjustments are all the same, regardless of the type of sights in question.

This brings us now to the hunting telescope sight, the most accurate sighting instrument yet devised for sporting rifles. There are dozens of different 'scopes made in this country all with a definite place in the shooting picture, but only a small proportion of these are suited to whitetail deer hunting. For our deer-hunting purposes a 'scope must meet very rigid requirements, else it will be more of a hindrance than a help.

First of all the question most frequently asked by deer hunters is, "Do I *need* a 'scope for deer hunting?" and secondly, "What will a 'scope do for me that can't be done with regular iron sights?" To answer the first question honestly, I must say that in most cases a 'scope is not a necessity, but it can be a big help. Only in those instances where a shooter's vision is extremely impaired is the 'scope a dire need, and in these cases it sometimes means the answer to whether a man shall hunt or shall not hunt deer.

The second question requires a good deal of explanation. Briefly, here is what the 'scope will do for your hunting. It eliminates all but a single sight and that sight is contained in the 'scope itself; there is no worry as to whether two sights must be properly aligned on the target, for with the 'scope sight both the target and the sight are in exactly the same focus. Next, it permits shooting, and good shooting, under light conditions so poor that neither iron sights nor the target would be seen at all. It brings the target closer to the shooter, by its magnification, allowing much more accurate placement of the shot. And in heavy cover, when shots are always taken through timber and brush, it uncannily picks out obstructions that would stop or deflect the bullet, giving the hunter a better opportunity to pick his openings for the shot. Finally, the sportsman who uses a good 'scope always knows exactly what he is shooting at; antlers can be readily seen on the buck, sometimes the points can even be counted before making the shot; and most important of all, no hunter equipped with a 'scope sight has ever been known to kill or injure a fellow hunter by mistaking him for a deer.

Understand, though, that not all 'scopes will give us these desirable effects. Low-priced instruments with poor optical qualities and narrow field of view are worse than nothing at all, so the sportsman who contemplates a 'scope for deer hunting must know what to look for. About fifteen years ago I had an amusing experience that shows the need of selecting the right 'scope for whitetail deer hunting.

Along some time in the early fall an elderly gentleman of my acquaintance approached me over the gun counter with reference to a 'scope sight for his deer rifle. He confided that the old eyes were going back on him, and the boys were starting to rib him a bit about the misses he had been making during the preceding year or two.

At that time there were very few American-made 'scopes on the market that I could recommend to him for deer hunting. I happened to be using a good quality imported 'scope then so I suggested that he buy one of these and I would mount it on his rifle. Somehow or other the imported 'scope idea didn't hit him just right, so he said that he'd pass it up for the time being. Not long after this he dropped in again waving a Lyman circular which extolled the virtues of a certain 5A telescope. He explained to me that it was his understanding that the 5A was the best 'scope Lyman made (at that time) and it should be good enough for him. In vain I tried to explain to him that this was a target 'scope and not for hunting purposes at all, but he couldn't be swayed.

According to his wishes, then, I ordered the 'scope, mounted it on his rifle, and with a heavy feeling of remorse I delivered it to his hands. I heard no more from him after that until the deer season was well past, when one day he dropped in again. My first question to him was, "How did the 'scope work out?"

"Oh — " He waved his hand. "That d——d thing; I knocked it off with a rock." He went on to explain that two bucks had come to his stand during the first two days of the season; he put his rifle to his shoulder and try as he would, he couldn't find them in the field of view, so he never did fire a shot at either of these two. At an extreme moment, some time after the second buck had walked off, he found a good-sized rock and calmly proceeded to knock the 'scope off the rifle. He finally killed his buck, using the front sight alone, because I had removed the rear sight in the 'scope-mounting job.

This 5A 'scope, while an excellent model for target use, had not a single feature that would adapt it to deer hunting. Its five-power magnification was too high, its field of view — about 18 feet at 100 yards — much too narrow. The "reticule" was a fine cross-hair, and the light-gathering power left plenty to be desired; it was mounted in fragile mounts, having delicate adjustments, and was so mounted that the 'scope tube slid forward from the recoil of each shot, making it absolutely necessary to pull the 'scope back into shooting position after each shot. In a word, everything about it was wrong from a deer hunter's point of view.

Here, then, are the points we must demand in a 'scope for deer hunting:

It must have good light-gathering power or illumination, so that the game can be seen even under the most adverse sighting conditions encountered in heavy coniferous timber and at early morning or late afternoon.

The field of view must be wide; wide enough so that running deer can be easily "picked up" by the hunter. This field of view is the amount of landscape that can be seen through the scope in normal shooting position. Most manufacturers list the field of view by stating the width of vision encompassed by the 'scope tube at 100 yards. For example, Noske lists the field of view of one of his 'scopes as 38 feet, meaning that if we sight through this 'scope at 100 yards we will be able to see 19 feet to both right and left of the target as well as above and below it. This makes for very quick sighting even at moving targets.

Another most important feature in a hunting 'scope is a low power, for only with low power can we get good brilliance and wide field, still keeping the weight and length of the 'scope down to proper limits. It's only with a low-power glass that we can hold the rifle steady enough for offhand shooting, because the "wobble" of the shooter's hands is magnified in direct proportion to the 'scope's power. Even though the rifleman can actually hold his weapon just as steady with a 10-power glass as with a 2½- or 3-power instrument, the psychological effect is so damaging that poor shooting results. A 3-power glass is definitely the highest magnification that should be used in a hunting 'scope for whitetails, and less than this is better.

Still another necessity in the 'scope is long eye relief — the distance the shooter's eye must be held from the eyepiece in order to see the fullest field of view. In high-power rifles this eye relief should be long enough to prevent the 'scope from striking the hunter's skull when the rifle recoils; add to this the danger of fogging the lens with the breath during cold weather if the lens is too close to the face. In connection with long eye relief, a hunting 'scope should have a noncritical eye relief; that is, the shooter must be able to take a quick, clear sight even though his eye is not in line with the exact center of the 'scope tube. There should be a latitude in hunting 'scopes of about ¼ inch, giving the hunter accurate sighting anywhere within this radius. Then, when he throws his rifle to his shoulder hurriedly, he will be better able to see both target and 'scope sight immediately, without the necessity of changing the position of his head to the right or left, high or low, before he can see the full field of his scope. To incorporate this feature, 'scopes should have listed somewhere among the makers' listed specifications a notation as to the size of the exit pupil. The size of the exit pupil controls, to a degree, the amount of light admitted through the 'scope as well as this noncritical eye-relief feature.

Choice of the sighting device within the 'scope tube, usually called "reticule," is important too. This should be heavy enough and coarse enough so that it will stand out well against any background and in dim light. Popular and very efficient styles of reticule include the sharp picket post and the flat-top picket post, and either of these can be obtained with a single lateral cross-hair. Of the two styles the flat-top picket will give the best definition for all deer hunting as the cleanly cut-off top gives definite holding for elevation under all conditions. The lateral cross-hair, which is a single fine wire extending horizontally across the 'scope field, crossing just below the top of the post, is a good check to prevent canting of the rifle. Normally, though, it isn't necessary because it's easy enough to hold the wide post in a fairly upright position, at least accurately enough for all purposes. There are many other varieties of reticule available on both American and foreign-made 'scopes, but either of these two will perform properly for deer hunting. Cross-hair reticules, pin heads, narrow-taper posts and other target styles of reticule are not designed in any sense for whitetail hunting, so they should never be considered for this purpose.

In the 'scope sight for hunting considerable emphasis must be placed on windage and elevation adjustments. These should both be internal, or contained within the 'scope tube, permitting a rigid, nonadjustable mount to be used with the scope. Adjustments in the mount itself seldom prove satisfactory for hunting purposes as they will not hold their zero for any appreciable length of time. Hunting 'scopes need not have quite as close adjustments as target types, but they should be graduated to within an inch at 100 yards. For the same reasons as outlined for receiver peep sights, they should be capable of being rigidly locked in place once they are sighted-in at the required range.

Lastly, a hunting 'scope should be short, light in weight and rugged in construction; it should be fixed focus and so streamlined that there will be few if any projections from its contours to catch in brush or clothing. The 'scope complete with its mount should add no more than a pound to the weight of the rifle, particularly if the rifle is to be carried all day in rugged country.

A great wave of postwar development has made available to the deer hunter a wide choice of highly suitable optical devices for sighting. Prior to World War II, we had a limited field of American-made 'scopes of high quality. The Lyman Alaskan and the Noske were the only two makes which could compare favorably with the best imported glasses. The Weaver line included the 330 and 29S, both excellent value in their price field, but lacking wide field and best light-gathering power.

At the present time there are no less than ten excellent makes of low-power scopes suited to whitetail hunting on the market and more are in the development stage. All of these possess the qualifications required of a big-game 'scope to a greater or less degree, dependent upon the price involved. Some of these 'scopes have desirable features setting them apart from the rest; but in general, any one or all of them will prove to be highly satisfactory to the deer hunter.

To clarify some of the confusing details involved in selecting a hunting 'scope, the author has made up the following chart — listing each of the 'scopes in order of price range as this is written; some of the salient points of excellence are also listed, to aid the hunter's choice.

Make of glass	Power (Actual)	Field Ft. at 100 yards	Exit pupil Diam. in.	Eye relief
Lyman Alaskan	2.16	38	.36	4¾ in.
Noske	2.35	32	.30	4½ "
Norman Ford Texan	2.0	42	.35	4¼ "
Leupold	2.25	35	.30	3¾ "
Bear Cub (Stith)	2.25	35	.32	4 "
Maxwell Smith G88	2.25	36	.29	4¼ "
Maxwell Smith Zicon	2.50	34	.26	3½ "
Weaver K 2.5	2.1	39	.38	5 "
Maxwell Smith Vectra	2.6	32	.26	3¼ "
Weaver J 2.5	2.1	33	.28	4¼ "

Price range of these 'scopes begins with the Alaskan at $70.00 and goes down to $22.50 for the Weaver J 2.5, all without mounts.

Certainly this price range gives the deer hunter a wide choice in selecting a glass suited to both the hunting and the pocketbook. All of these scopes have internal adjustments for windage and elevation with the exception of the Bear Cub. This model has adjustments for elevation only and must be provided with a mounting which will permit the required windage adjustment.

There is no great variation in weights or lengths of any of these 'scopes. The Alaskan is the heaviest at 11 ounces, the Bear Cub the lightest at 5½ ounces. The longest model is the Bear Cub measuring about 11¾ inches; the shortest is the Noske at 9⅝ inches. One of the interesting departures from the conventional can be noted in the Leupold; this model has no projecting knobs for sight adjustment. The entire tube is streamlined, with rotating sleeves being used for windage and elevation changes, making a smooth-looking job.

The hunter making his choice from the above list will bear in mind the important points in the hunting 'scope: wide field, good light-gathering power (large diameter exit pupil), sufficient eye relief. The higher-priced models generally give most of the best, in this respect. It is safe to say that if a deer hunter wants the best in a hunting 'scope he will choose the Lyman Alaskan. If he wants the most for his money, dollar for dollar, the Weaver J 2.5 is without an equal in this field.

Mounts for the hunting telescopes have enjoyed even greater development than the 'scopes since the war. It is a truism that any 'scope is worthless unless the mounting holds it firmly and rigidly, not only from shot to shot but over long periods of time. But we now have such a multiplicity of mount designs that a deer hunter will be more confused than ever before in making a good choice.

With few exceptions, there is no need to select a mount which gives windage or elevation. With the exception of the Bear Cub no American-made glass for deer hunting needs such adjustment. This makes for rigidity and simplicity in the design, for the mount can be made to become almost a part of the rifle. With such a simple type of design in mind the hunter will now decide whether he needs a fixed, "semi-fixed" or "quick-detachable" model for his hunting.

Among the fixed types are the Weaver line of side and top mounts — the Type N, the Type Q and the Type U — also the Redfield Senior mount. This latter mount is desirable for use with a heavy scope on a rifle of heavy recoil. Many deer hunters, however, will not like the fixed type of mount since it is not removable and replaceable without careful re-sighting. Conditions sometimes make it necessary to remove the 'scope and go over to iron sights, and it is here that the detachable type of mount proves its worth.

An old and tried favorite in this category is the Griffin and Howe double-lever mount. The author has had one of these on a .256 Newton for over fifteen years, and has many times removed and replaced the 'scope with no apparent change in sighting. This type of mount also leaves the top of the rifle "clean" for use with regular open or aperture sights. The Redfield Junior is also a highly popular light mount which is "semi-fixed" but it can be removed easily and will retain its zero when replaced on the rifle. However, with this type, part of the base remains on the receiver bridge and will interfere with replacing an aperture sight.

In my mind one of the best of the new mounts at a low price, which permit easy removal for use with the iron sight, is the Echo. This is a side mount which slides on a half dovetail base firmly attached to the receiver, much the same as the G. H. Mount and the Noske. It goes back on the rifle right to its original zero, and removes by unscrewing two knurled nuts. This mount is somewhat less costly than either of the other two mentioned and thus far works fully as well.

The Williams "easy-detachable" mount has great appeal to the whitetail hunter. In this mount we have a fixed base on the rifle which screws fast to the mounting rings on the 'scope with two large knurled screws. The 'scope can be removed rapidly by unscrewing the mounts off the bases, with the fingers, and a neat aperture sight installs instantly in the rear base making a quick conversion job for the hunter who encounters unfavorable 'scope hunting conditions.

Then again we have the "swing out" mounts by Pachmayr and Burton. In each of these the entire mount is hinged to permit the 'scope to be swung to the left and out of the way for use of iron sights. However, these mounts place the 'scope low on the receiver, so that for instant change-over in sighting an open rear sight must be used. It is not possible to retain the aperture rear sight in place with the 'scope in position.

Stith's mounts will appeal to many hunters who want to install their own mount and 'scope. These mounts can be had to go directly on the Winchesters 54 and 70, or the Savage 99s, without drilling additional holes. Also this mount is desirable for use with the Bear Cub 'scope, since it has an excellent windage adjustment feature.

In selecting any mount the hunter must first decide what features he needs for his hunting conditions. The best mount is one in which the design is simplest, permitting strong construction and eliminating moving parts which can be tinkered with by one's hunting partners. It is desirable, however, for whitetail deer hunting where we are quite liable to encounter all kinds of weather, to have some means of changing over to iron sights conveniently, then back to 'scope sights without the necessity for re-sighting.

Besides the mounts listed here, there are many others now on the market and new designs constantly appear. Each of these has merit, but each must be carefully examined in the light of whitetail hunting conditions. Once again the hunter must call upon his own background of experience in order to make a wise choice, but the factors mentioned here should influence that decision.

Thus we cover, for the deer hunter at least, the field of gun sights. Again, I must emphasize that sights are the link between the hunter and his game and only by proper selection of sights can he hope to enjoy good hunting — which means, first, last and always, not only hits, but clean kills. Only by experiment can the hunter work out the problem for himself. No two individuals are exactly the same in vision, in co-ordination, or in ability to handle their weapons. In gun sights, more than in any other branch of shooting, "one man's meat is another's poison." Sights must be chosen to fit the individual and, when once the happy combination is reached, he should stick to it until physical or mental changes signal new experimentation.

15 / Gun Work for the Hunter

ALL SHOOTERS can be roughly divided into two classes: those who should, under no circumstances, attempt any repair or remodeling work on their firearms other than routine cleaning and oiling, and those who possess enough mechanical skill, ability with their hands and an abundance of patience to perform the simpler gunsmithing jobs that may be done at home.

Usually it is safe advice sweepingly to advise all shooters to leave their guns strictly alone and trust incidental repairs and changes to the hands of a competent gunsmith; many fine rifles have been almost irreparably damaged in the hands of their owners. Eventually these damaged rifles must be either sent to the factory or to a gunsmith, who in turn must not only make the original repair but correct the mistakes made by the owner — often a costly procedure.

On the other hand, many repairs and alterations are easily made at home. Often it is inconvenient, sometimes impossible, to find a good gunsmith in the owner's neighborhood; it may be equally inconvenient to send the rifle to the factory for repairs — and many alterations desired by gun owners will not be handled by the factory; finally, the shooter may not be able to afford professional charges for all the work wanted. Add to this the fact that a great number of the shooting clan have a hidden but overpowering desire to "tinker" with their weapons, particularly on long winter evenings when there is nothing to be done in connection with their sport but looking ahead until next season, so far away.

Only the shooter can properly classify himself. He alone must decide whether to leave his pet rifle severely alone or, if he is willing to take the time to learn exactly how the desired job must be done, whether to purchase necessary tools and materials, and patiently carry the work through to completion. Most sportsmen have the "hurry" complex. If they start a job they want to rush it through because they just can't wait to see how it will look when it's finished.

Just a few months ago, to illustrate, I completed a re-stocking job for a friend on a bolt-action rifle, using French walnut of good figure and applying a nice oil finish. There was no checkering on this stock, as he felt that this work would place the price of the job somewhat above the limit of his pocketbook. A few weeks later he dropped in to inquire whether I thought he would be able to do the checkering work himself, if he had the tools. I encouraged him to attempt the job, warning that he would need to spend quite a bit of time in practice on either his old stock or other scrap pieces of wood offering a rounded surface. I cautioned him also to proceed very slowly and carefully, taking at least three weeks for the job, which in this case I felt was a safe minimum.

The very next morning he was back again to return my tools, telling me that he had completed the whole works, pistol grip and forearm, the night before. He admitted, though, that he'd had to stay up a bit later than his usual bedtime to finish it. I didn't quite have the heart then to ask him how the job looked, but about a week later I saw the mess myself. Needless to say the stock was completely ruined, at least in appearance. Very little attempt had been made to keep to the proper spacing of the lines; the angle of the cross lines was all wrong, and none of the lines were deep enough to be called checkering. Rather the surface of the wood on grip and forearm was covered with a series of hideous scratches. To effect a repair on this job would mean the complete removal of these scratches, using scraper and sandpaper; then complete refinishing of the grip and forearm and a new checkering job. This work would easily cost this chap twice the price of checkering alone.

I am satisfied that this shooter had enough ability to perform the work properly, but he was so obsessed with the desire to complete it in a hurry that he rushed it through to the end, making a mess of the whole works.

Here are some of the gunsmithing jobs that easily can be done at home by the shooter possessing a certain degree of mechanical skill and an abundance of patience: fitting of new sights; stock changes for better fit; rebluing of metal parts; altering trigger pulls; fitting of sling swivels and slings; re-bedding of rifle barrels for better accuracy; remodeling of military rifle stocks and applying wood finishes. All of this work can be done with a minimum expenditure for simple tools and materials obtainable from hardware dealers in small communities. In this chapter all work will be outlined as performed by simple tools even though special tools would be more efficient but more difficult to obtain, and more expensive. We cannot consider the use of these special tools as a timesaver, for it's assumed that the shooter will have ample time to perform any and all operations.

Perhaps the most commonly attempted alteration of the sportsman's rifle is the addition of new sights. As we have seen, factory sights are seldom satisfactory to the discriminating deer hunter. Some changes are almost always in order to better suit the rifle to the owner's vision and the country to be hunted. Our chapter on sights will give some aid in selecting the correct sighting equipment, so we will deal only with the operation of fitting and adapting these sights to the rifle.

First, the front sight. Almost all factory rifles are fitted with front sights driven into dovetail slots; a few are mounted with the blade-type carbine sight, held in place with either a pin or screw. It's a simple matter to remove the old front sight from a dovetail slot by driving it out from the *left* side of the barrel toward the right, using a drift punch of copper, brass, fiber or hard wood. For this operation the barrel should be held in the jaws of a substantial vise, padded with leather, lead, or soft wood, to prevent marring the barrel. Never try to drive the sight out with a hammer directly. This will not only deform the sight base, but there is a possibility that the sight stem will be struck and bent out of shape, making it worthless for possible future use.

The new front sight must be selected not only to fit the slot but must be of the *same height* as the old sight. Otherwise, the elevation will be changed, necessitating a change in the rear sight. If an aperture receiver or tang sight is to be fitted also this is not so important, as accurate adjustments for elevation can be made in the rear sight, but at least some attempt should be made to have the new front sight of the same approximate height as the old one.

Drive the new front sight in place, using the copper drift, from the right side toward the left. These dovetail slots are all tapered for a tight fit, so this must be remembered in removing and replacing sights. The front sight should be centered as accurately as possible, using the eye alone, then the rifle must be sighted-in, following the suggestions in the chapter on sights.

Blade-front sights are somewhat simpler to replace, because the position is fixed and with the new blade pinned or screwed in place no further sighting-in is needed, provided of course that a sight of the correct height has been chosen.

Open rear sights, fitting in barrel slots, are handled in just the same way, driving out the old sight from the left and driving in the new sight from the right. It will help in replacing the new sight if a scratch is made on the barrel at the forward point of the old sight before removal, marking the location. The new sight is then driven in until it is aligned with the scratch mark. Sometimes this can be done with enough accuracy for the rifle not to need further sight adjustment. If the rear sight should prove to be a bit too high, the sight elevator (step) can be filed a bit on the bottom until the correct adjustment is reached.

The mounting of peep or aperture sights is a bit more detailed than this, but all of these can be mounted if reasonable care is used. Most American rifles other than bolt-actions are already drilled and tapped for some type of tang peep sight. If your rifle is one of these, remove the dummy screws and attach the sight with the screws furnished. Then check the alignment by glancing through the peep and aligning it with the front sight and middle barrel sight. If, as is almost always the case, the tang sight has no windage adjustment, it will be necessary to shim the base with paper or thin strips of metal to bring it into proper alignment. Better than this, remove the sight and carefully file off the base to bring the stem into proper alignment. This gives very close, permanent windage adjustment if the filing is done carefully.

With bolt-action rifles, and in those instances where a receiver sight is to be mounted on other action types, the job is not quite so simple. Some of our bolt-action models, notably the Winchesters 54 and 70, the Remington 30 and the Savage 40 and 45, are already drilled and tapped to take standard receiver sights. On these rifles mounting means only attaching the sight with the screws furnished and inletting the sight base and/or slide into the stock.

To do this properly the action should first be removed from the stock, the sight screwed in place and the action then placed in position in the stock. With a scriber or sharp pencil mark the stock to the outlines of the sight base, then measure down the side of the stock to the approximate depth of the base. Saw out this section with a fine-tooth saw or hacksaw and remove the wood with a flat chisel. Coat the bottom of the sight base with a mixture of red oil tube colors and light oil. Place the action back in the stock and tap the sight base lightly with a wooden block, just enough to make an impression on the wood. Remove this wood until the base goes into position, taking care that no gouges are carelessly made. With the base in place, relieve the sides of the cutout by removing wood with the chisel so that there is a slight gap about the thickness of a playing card on each side of the base and the bottom. This clearance is to prevent loosening of the sight from recoil. No shims are necessary under the sight base to achieve alignment as such adjustments are made in the windage adjustment itself.

Owners of the Krag, Springfield, Enfield, Newton and other related foreign-made arms, such as the Mauser and Mannlicher, must drill and tap the receivers for mounting these sights. This is also true of most lever, slide and autoloading arms of American make, if receiver sights are to be used. This shouldn't discourage the owners of these rifles because mounting of such sights is rather simple, and perfect results can be expected if the proper steps are followed in the procedure.

If a receiver sight is to be mounted, the primary step is to order the proper size drill and tap with the sight. Most sight screws are not standard and taps will not be available locally, so get these from the sight maker. (Most sights are mounted with a Number 31 drill and a 6 × 48 tap.) With the sight in hand go to your nearest hardware store and purchase a drill that will just enter the holes in the base. A Number 29 is usually right but there is often some variation in base holes, so buy the size that will just pass snugly through the hole. This will be your spotting drill, used for locating the tap-drill holes in exact center.

Set up your action in the vise between the padded jaws; then set the base on the receiver, aligned with the iron sights. Clamp the base in this position with a small "C" clamp. Now with the spotting drill, drill into the receiver through one of the base holes just deeply enough to center the tap drill. Then with the tap drill go right through the receiver, but be sure to change the spotting drill for the tap drill first. Many times a shooter has forgotten to change to the tap drill after spotting the hole, making an oversize hole through the receiver that could not be tapped for his sight screw.

With the base still in position, start the tap, first wetting it with turpentine. Proceed very gently, making a quarter-turn at a time, backing up the tap after each quarter-turn to free the chips. Now go right through with the tap, taking care to keep the shank properly centered in the base hole. Remove the tap carefully and screw the base down tightly with the sight screw. Repeat the operation with the other hole, still keeping the base in position. This is important, for the base acts as a drill jig, giving properly centered holes.

As an additional word of caution in mounting sights, make certain that base screws are kept tight at all times. When the sight base is screwed fast as tightly as it can be done by hand, set the screwdriver in the slot and tap it with a hammer. This will often permit an extra quarter-turn to be made on the screw, setting it up tight.

On the Krag, Springfield, Enfield and other military rifles the owner will often find casehardened receivers. This casehardening is a hard outershell, only a few thousandths deep, caused by the absorption of carbon during the heat treatments. It is too hard to drill, so this outer surface must be ground off on an emery wheel before the drill can be started. Simply mark through the base holes with the sight in position to determine the location, and grind two small spots, just large enough for the drill to go through; then proceed with the drilling and tapping as outlined. The job is then completed by inletting the sight base into the stock as previously described.

In all cases where an aperture rear sight is mounted the middle open sight should be removed. This slot can then be filled in with a slot-blank or with a folding middle sight. If you don't care to go to the expense of either of these, make a blank from the old rear sight by filing off the sight and front projection, leaving only the base to fill the slot.

Cocking-piece sights, mentioned in the chapter on sights, are a mounting job for either the factory or a skilled gunsmith; the gun owner himself should not attempt to mount this type of rear sight, as it necessitates the annealing of the cocking piece and milling in a dovetail slot at exactly the right angle.

With the great increase in telescope sighting equipment during the last few years, many riflemen will want to mount these themselves. However, this writer cannot conscientiously recommend this to any but the most experienced shooters and mechanics. It requires a considerable degree of skill, and knowledge of sighting principles to properly apply the hunting telescope to a high-power rifle. This had best be left to the 'scope maker himself, or to a gunsmith of established reputation.

The alteration, remodeling and refinishing of rifle stocks offers perhaps the best opportunity for the shooter himself to make necessary changes to better adapt the weapon for his needs. Unfortunately, most American rifles seem to be designed for that unhappily nonexistent individual, Mr. Average Man, with the result that factory stocks actually fit very few hunters. Not that any of these rifles cannot be properly handled, but many of them can be better adapted to the individual's requirements, making them more suitable for his purposes. Slight changes in the shape of the butt plate or its angle, size and height of the comb, and shape and position of the grip all will make the rifle point more accurately for the hunter, an important requisite for quick, accurate shooting.

Most work on gun stocks requires little equipment. A saw, a few chisels, a rasp, files and sandpaper will perform almost any stock alteration, even to the building of a complete new stock. With these tools, pistol grips and higher combs can be inset, stocks shortened or lengthened, and pitch of the butt plate can be changed. Military rifles are good subjects for this kind of work as almost every military rifle stock is wrong in most respects for sporting use.

Let's suppose that we have a Krag carbine, as issued, to be converted to better stock dimensions for improved fit and handling. The Krag, of course, has a very low comb and no pistol grip, and the stock is a bit too short for most hunters. The first step in raising the comb will be to lay out on the sides of the old stock the proper lines for cutting off the comb. Start at a point about 1 inch below the top level of the grip. Then measure down from the top of the butt about 1½ inches and from this point, draw a line connecting with the bottom of the first line drawn. Saw to these lines, which should make a right-angle cut on top of the stock.

Select now a piece of walnut about 2 inches thick, giving enough surplus for finishing on the sides, and high enough to give enough height to the finished comb.

Square the ends of this block and plane the bottom to a true square surface. Rub this surface all over with carpenter's chalk and spot it to the cutout on top of the stock, removing the impressions made on the old stock cutout with a chisel and flat file. When a good bearing has been obtained, and no light shows through the joint, we are ready for the gluing. For this nothing works better than Casco waterproof glue.

Mix up a small quantity of glue and size both sides of the joint, letting it dry for a few minutes before the final application. Coat the joint well with glue and place the two surfaces together, clamping tightly for about twelve hours. The comb can now be shaped to the desired form, first reducing it on top just so the bolt will

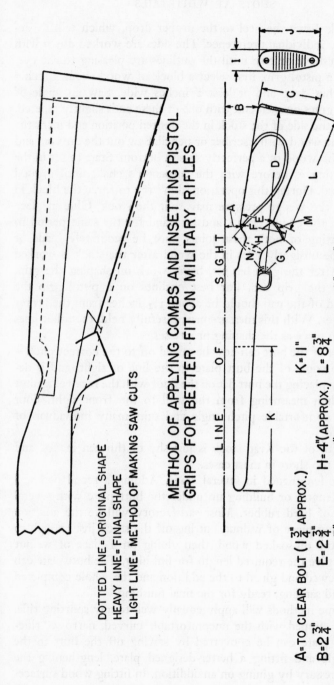

DOTTED LINE = ORIGINAL SHAPE
HEAVY LINE = FINAL SHAPE
LIGHT LINE = METHOD OF MAKING SAW CUTS

METHOD OF APPLYING COMBS AND INSETTING PISTOL
GRIPS FOR BETTER FIT ON MILITARY RIFLES

LINE OF SIGHT

A=TO CLEAR BOLT (1¾" APPROX.)   K=11"
B=2¾"   L=8¾"
C=5"   H=4"(APPROX.)
D=13⅝"   I=1½"
E=2¾"   J=5"
F=7⅜"   M=GRIP CAP 1⅞"×1⅛"
G=3⅝"   N=4¾" TO 5¼"

TYPICAL STOCK DESIGN FOR DEER RIFLE

clear. Work down the heel to the proper drop, which will be determined by individual preference. The sides are worked down with plane, spokeshave or rasp until the outlines are pleasing to the eye.

To inset a pistol grip, first select a block of wood about 4 inches long, 3 inches deep and at least 2 inches wide. Saw an angle of about 20 degrees on each end with one of these ends slightly tapered. Lay this on the side of the stock in the desired position and mark the angles on the wood with a scriber or pencil. Saw out the dovetail and chisel out the wood to a perfectly square bottom. Start to set in the block, spotting as before with the carpenter's chalk until a good fit is obtained. During this operation, don't try to force the block in position or the wedge pressure may split the stock. Glue in place just as with the comb, clamp, and let stand for the same period to set. The fitting of both these joints must be accurately made or there will be unsightly gaps in the wood after the stock is worked to shape. After the glue has set, begin work on shaping the grip, first fitting the grip cap. For best outlines on a pistol grip the forward end of the cap should be about 3½ inches from the center of the trigger. With this measurement carefully held, the other lines will fall into place as the shaping progresses.

The angle of the butt can now be sawed off to the correct pitch — pitch is the angle of the butt plate to the line of sight, and is determined by placing the butt flat on the floor with the receiver against the wall, then measuring from the wall to the front sight. Four inches is a comfortable pitch angle and suits many individuals of normal build.

The length of the Krag stock is just shy of thirteen inches, and this will be too short in most cases.

It can be lengthened in several ways. Adding a recoil pad will give extra length, or building up under the butt plate with several thicknesses of hard rubber. Most satisfactory will be the addition of a matching piece of walnut, cutting off the stock just enough to get under the oil-soaked wood, then gluing on a piece of walnut which will give the required length for finishing. The butt plate can then be screwed and glued to the addition and the whole completed by filing and sanding, ready for the final finishing.

These same methods will apply equally well to any sporting rifle. Any arm equipped with the uncomfortable curved, narrow, "rifle-type" butt plate can be converted by sawing off the butt to the proper angle and fitting a better-designed plate, lengthening the stock if necessary by gluing on an addition. In fitting wood surfaces that must be glued, always use carpenter's chalk for spotting rather than a mixture containing oil, for oil will prevent the glue from adhering to the joint.

Any work of this nature necessitates the complete refinishing of the stock. Many hunters would like to refinish their rifle stocks, even though no other changes are contemplated. The standard varnish or lacquer finishes found on factory arms are certainly not durable, and a few days in the woods with such a rifle finds it covered with unsightly scratches that cannot be removed or easily covered up. The solution to this problem is an oil finish, and nothing in gunwork is simpler than this, for it requires only linseed oil and hand rubbing.

The first step in refinishing is to remove the old varnish. This can be done by wetting the surface with paint remover, using an old cloth or a piece of cotton. Allow it to stand until the varnish begins to curl; it may require more than one application if the stock is an old one, but two or three applications will do the job. (Of course for any work of this nature the stock should be removed from the action, for the protection of the metal parts.)

After the varnish is removed by scraping, go over the whole stock with coarse sandpaper, then wet the wood to raise the grain. Dry the stock over a quick heat — a gas flame is about right — after which you'll note that the grain has raised up in the form of tiny splinters. Cut these off with steel wool, then sand the stock with medium sandpaper. Continue these alternate wetting-and-dryings and sandings until the grain will no longer raise, then finish the stock with very fine cabinetmaker's 6/o paper, sanding always *with* the grain of the wood.

At this point, there will be a number of tiny pits or depressions noticeable in the now smooth surface. These are the pores of the wood which are normally filled with sap in the living tree. In American black walnut these pores are very noticeable and they should be filled before the application of the finishing oil. In foreign walnuts these pores are not so large, and they can usually be filled by the action of the oil itself. Another perhaps more important point in the use of wood filler is to prevent the penetration of the oil from darkening the stock to the point where all grain and figure will become obliterated. In dark American walnut this is an objectionable feature in oil finishing, but in the lighter woods it tends to add beauty. Only the owner of the arm himself can decide what type of finish will best suit him, but it is advisable to use the filler on all dark woods of attractive figure.

To achieve the darkening effect on light woods while still using the filler to fill the pores, first apply to the bare wood a mixture of turpentine and raw linseed oil. This will penetrate and darken the wood with each successive application until the desired shade is reached, whereupon this treatment is stopped and the filler applied.

Use a paste filler mixed with benzine or turpentine to the consistency of cream. It should be applied with a brush and rubbed in across the grain, then allowed to set about an hour. The excess must then be rubbed off across the grain, using a heavy rough cloth like burlap. Several applications should be made over a period of several days, allowing each to dry thoroughly before more is put on. The final coat should be thinned with turpentine and allowed to dry very hard. It may then be sanded smooth with the fine cabinetmaker's paper.

The stock is now ready for the oil finish, which merely means the application of raw linseed oil with the hand. Only enough oil should be applied to make the rubbing easy; rub until the stock becomes warm and dry to touch, then put it away to dry. This first coat will dry and harden in about a day, when another coat should be applied as before and again put away to dry. It should be borne in mind in this process that no further oiling of the wood should take place until the previous application has dried fully, or oxidized, else further rubbing will only remove what has already been applied. As the finish is built up a longer period will occur between applications, until the final coats will require a week or more to dry depending on temperature and weather conditions. After a heavy coat has been built up, filling all slight blemishes and presenting a dull lustrous finish, the stock can be rubbed down with rottenstone and sweet oil, using a felt rubbing pad. This brings out a fine smooth finish that is durable enough to last for the life of the gun, its luster improving with handling. Small scratches that occur from time to time in use can be rubbed out with a new application of the raw oil, so that the stock will always look as good as new. This oil finish is waterproof, untouched by changes in temperature or weather, and is the most beautiful finish that can be applied to a gun stock.

One of the vague mysteries resting in every gun owner's mind is the process used to achieve the dull blue or black finishes on the metal parts. Many believe this is painted on the steel, somewhat on the order of stain or lacquer; but rebluing is simply a chemical rusting process which produces a blue or black rust rather than the common red rust. It is a straight oxidation process, induced by action of the proper chemicals, and it's really a simple thing once the principles are outlined. Old rifles and shotguns, with bluing faded away by many years of handling and use (perhaps a little abuse), can be made to look just like new again with a little effort and expense.

The double purpose of bluing firearms is to protect them from rust and to dull the surface of the metal sufficiently for light reflections not to scare away game. Originally, bluing was called "browning" and the old-time arms were all finished in the deep nut-brown stain that we now see on only the "Damascus" barrel shotguns of half a century ago. Some bluing processes still leave the metal a deep brown, which is subsequently changed to blue by the action of linseed oil, but today these old formulas are seldom used, as they require quite a bit of time for their application.

As in many other processes, the success of a bluing job depends entirely on the preparation of the metal before the chemicals are applied. This means complete removal of all the old bluing using a fine grade of Aloxite or emery cloth. Barrel, receiver, trigger guard and all metal parts must be carefully brought to a high polish with the abrasive cloths, for it is only with a high polish on these parts that a deep, rich blue can be had.

With the barrel and action polished, prepare two hardwood plugs for the barrel. The solution must be kept from entering the bore — otherwise, it may be rusted beyond repair. Turn these plugs so they will make a tight fit in the bore, leaving enough of each plug to project so that it will act as a handle for the work. During the bluing process nothing must be allowed to contact the barrel until the bluing is complete, so these handles are important.

Materials needed will be a tank of sheet metal for boiling the parts; this tank to be made of sheet iron, galvanized, about 6 inches wide, 6 inches deep and 40 inches long. It should be at least long enough to take the longest barrel, together with receiver, that will be reblued. You can have this made up by a local tinsmith or you can buy the sheet metal yourself and bend it up, then solder the ends. At the same time get a box of fine steel wool, and have your druggist make up the following formula:

FORMULA

250 grains (avoir.) potassium chlorate
300 " " potassium nitrate
100 " " sodium nitrate
100 " " bichloride of mercury
35 " " copper chloride (cupric)
75 " " iron chloride (ferric)
50 cc. niter (sweet spirits)

BLUING

Heat 400 cc. of distilled water to about 125 degrees Fahrenheit, add all chemicals except niter, stirring thoroughly until all are dissolved. After the mixture is absolutely cool, add the sweet spirits of niter and pour all into a colored glass bottle. Let this stand for a day or two before using, as the chemicals must amalgamate.

Now place about 2 inches of water in the tank and set it on the stove to boil. Immerse the barrel and action in the water together with the other metal parts — trigger guard, magazine and so on. These small parts should have wires attached so that they may be handled easily. Now add to the water a good handful of lye and bring it to a boil; then boil the parts for about five minutes. This dissolves all oil and grease, making the steel receptive to the bluing solution. At the end of five minutes or so, remove the barrel and lay it on a pair of wooden blocks prepared for the purpose, resting it on the wooden plugs; the metal parts can be hung from a nail in the wall or beam to prevent their touching anything that might dirty the surface.

Dump the lye out of the tank, wash thoroughly in hot water and also wash off the barrel and other parts in hot water, using a clean cotton cloth to remove any lye residue. Again pour about 2 inches of clean water in the tank and bring the parts to a boil. Now take a wide-mouthed glass jar, and wire it fast in one end of the bluing tank; pour into the jar about 3 or 4 ounces of your bluing solution and let it heat with the water in the tank.

You are now ready to start bluing. Take a short piece of dowel and lace on a clean swab for applying the solution; keep this in the solution during the bluing process, right up until the moment of application. Now take out your barrel and allow the heat of the parts to dry off the metal. Small drops of water forming on the barrel can be removed by blowing on them. Apply the solution to the barrel in long, lengthwise strokes as though you were painting it. Cover all of the barrel and action, allow it to dry from its own heat, then place back at once in the tank. Permit it to boil for about five minutes, then remove it from the tank and set it up on your wooden blocks.

Now you'll note that the entire barrel and action is covered with a dark rust; remove this gently by brushing off with the steel wool. As soon as you have carded off the rust, place the barrel back in the tank to bring it up to boiling temperature. Again remove the barrel and coat with solution, then place back in the tank and permit it to boil for a few minutes. This process must be repeated until the desired dark color is obtained. On ordnance and regular high-pressure steel, about eight applications will be enough; but for some nickel steels and other alloys as many as twenty applications will be needed to produce the proper color.

On bluing the smaller parts speed is essential; the solution takes best only on heated steel, so it's important for the solution to be applied the instant the part is removed from the tank and the water dries off. On very thin pieces such as stamped trigger guards and magazines it helps in the process to hold the piece over the source of heat as soon as it is removed from the tank to dry off the water before applying the solution. It is equally important to allow the solution itself to dry, forming the rust, before being placed back in the tank. This drying of the solution on the metal causes the required oxidation.

After the proper number of coats have been applied to the parts, remove and brush off the final rust with the steel wool; then while all the parts are still hot, apply raw linseed oil liberally and allow them to cool for a few minutes. Meanwhile, heat equal parts of turpentine and beeswax over your fire and rub down the barrel, action, and all metal parts with this mixture. This brings out a high gloss, rubbing out all the linseed oil, which, if not removed, would harden on the metal, making a messy appearance.

Occasionally the sportsman will want to reblue small parts such as front sights, sling swivels, sight bases, screws and pins rather than a complete firearm. For this work there is a much simpler process than the above, giving equally good results with much less labor.

Obtain from your druggist these chemicals: one pound sodium nitrate, one pound potassium nitrate, one quarter pound manganese dioxide.

Heat these together in a heavy iron pot until they melt together and begin to bubble. Prepare the parts by polishing as before, and remove oil and grease by washing with alcohol. Attach wires to the parts so that they may be suspended in the solution off the bottom of the receptacle. Hang the parts in the pot, and allow them to remain for about 15 minutes. At the end of that period examine for color; if not dark enough, place back in the solution until the proper color is reached. Then remove the parts and place in hot water (not boiling) for a few minutes. Remove and dry off in sawdust or with cotton cloth, then oil with a light oil, allowing the oil to remain until the parts are quite cool.

This nitrate bath attains a temperature of about 750 degrees during the bluing process, so care should be taken not to drop any water or oil into it, otherwise it may spatter badly. In like manner, no springs or hardened parts should be blued by this method as the heat attained is sufficient to affect the temper of the parts.

This, substantially, covers all the bluing work that the sportsman himself will need in his repair and remodeling work. There are literally hundreds of formulas in use, all very good, but none are simpler or more effective than the above. This method of barrel rebluing is especially to be recommended for the sportsman because it is rapidly done. Many of the rusting processes of bluing cover a period of from ten days to three weeks, usually with no better results than this quick method. This solution will take on all kinds of steel, with the possible exception of casehardened receivers, and these require special treatment, as follows: All Krag rifles and early Springfields have casehardened receivers which are difficult to blue by any method. However, if the receivers are carefully brought to a high polish and treated with raw nitric acid, the surface will readily take the bluing. Simply take a splinter of wood, wind it with some cotton cloth for a swab, and rub the raw acid over the surface until it sizzles and turns black. If the metal will not respond, heat it over a gas flame, then apply the acid as before, washing the parts in hot water before the bluing process.

At present there are a great many commercial bluing preparations on the market; all of these work well if manufacturers' instructions are carefully followed. The important point to remember in all rebluing is to prepare the metal so that it is not only physically but chemically clean, and to keep it that way during the entire bluing process. The parts should not be touched with the fingers, with woolen rags, or allowed to contact any foreign object for each of these will leave its mark on the surface. Likewise, the steel wool used in brushing off the rust should be kept in a dry, clean wooden box. If these points are religiously followed there is no reason why perfect results cannot be obtained on your first attempt. As a last thought: City water is sometimes treated with chemicals which often streak the metal in the bluing process. If this is observed, try to obtain spring or well water or, best of all, rainwater.

All fairly recent models of military rifles have attracted much of the sportsman's attention during the past decade. This may be due to increased interest in the bolt-action type of repeater, a search for greater accuracy, the demand for more powerful cartridges, or a greater appreciation of the more positive functioning under adverse conditions of this type of repeating rifle mechanism. At any rate, this interest has been influenced greatly by those manufacturers who are making it easier for the sportsman to convert his military rifle to a suitable sporting arm, himself. Easily fitted ramp sights, a wide variety of butt plates and other fittings, good aperture rear sights, and, most important of all, rough-turned and rough-inletted sporting stocks are readily obtained in sufficient variety to meet almost all needs.

This field of converted military rifle accessories gives the hunter almost all the advantages of a truly custom-built weapon at less cost than a standard factory-made repeater, provided that much of the work is to be performed by the owner. Our Krag, Springfield and Enfields all offer fine strong actions which, once rebuilt, give us the best in sporting rifles for big-game shooting. All of this remodeling work can be performed very nicely by the shooter himself with a minimum of expense for tools, but it necessitates much patience, care and time.

Let's assume that we have a Krag rifle — the long-barreled variety, not the more popular carbine — that we would like to convert to a sporting rifle. Unfortunately, the Krag rifles are no longer available from government sources as the supply is exhausted, but all of us can remember when about fifteen years ago every hock shop and "Army and Navy" store sold these at prices varying from two to five dollars. However there are still plenty of these grand rifles in the hands of sportsmen throughout the country. These actions are without question one of the smoothest bolts ever manufactured, and are the quickest and easiest of any repeater to load. Simply snap open the hinged magazine cover, dump in a handful of cartridges, bullets pointing forward, snap the cover shut and the rifle is loaded

— speedy and simple, especially if fingers are half-frozen. Its only drawback from an ultramodern viewpoint is the fact that the Krag is built to handle rimmed head cases only, and the bolt has only one locking lug, which eliminates it from the class of really up-to-date rifles. However, the action is more than strong enough for the .30–40 cartridge, itself well suited ballistically to all whitetail deer hunting. It is my opinion that these rifles will become more and more sought by hunters as the years go by, for nothing that we have now approaches its smooth operation and ease of loading.

The first operation in converting the Krag to a sporter is to dis- card the stock and top hand guard, removing the bayonet band and the forearm band. The barrel too, now thirty inches long, will have to be cut to a length for quicker handling and better balance, but before cutting the barrel we'll decide on the type of front sight to be used. Most logical choice is the barrel band style of ramp ob- tainable from either Lyman, Redfield, Pacific or others. This ramp slips over the end of the barrel, is tapped into place and held in this position by either a pin or pointed set screw. It's advisable not to cut the barrel to length until the ramp has been driven into place as there is some variation in the diameter of these barrels.

Before the ramp is finally set some attempt should be made to square it. In the gunsmith's shop this is done with a surface plate and proper gauges, but the novice can obtain good results by setting the barrel square in his vise, using a level on the bottom of the magazine from below. The sides of the ramp can now be squared by using the end of the level, bringing it as closely as possible into true square with the eye. It is remarkable how this work can sometimes be accurately done with the eye alone; if it isn't absolutely square, don't worry about it. Proper adjustment of the rear sight will take care of any slight error.

With the sight in place, mark the barrel about ¼ inch ahead of the ramp with a three-cornered file, then saw it off as accurately as possible with a hacksaw. In the shop this work in done on the lathe and the muzzle is crowned at the same time time with a form tool. However, with reasonable care this facing can be done with a flat mill file, testing for squareness with a carpenter's or toolmaker's steel square. We won't crown the muzzle on this job for this is more or less a matter of appearance. It *is* necessary to counter- sink the rifling at the muzzle. Do this by placing the barrel level in the vise and, with your rose countersink in a bit brace, carefully bevel the inside of the bore to a depth of about $\frac{3}{32}$ inch, keeping the brace centered with the line of the bore as much as possible. The barrel as now finished may not come out to an even number of inches because of the position of the ramp, but this is of no consequence if it is of approximately the right length — 24 inches is the accepted standard.

Now, to obtain the required accuracy of the muzzle it must be "lapped in" perfectly square with the bore. To do this get a small brass ball from your hardware dealer — the type used in valve ball seats. Sweat this to the end of a short piece of quarter-inch cold rolled steel, using soft solder. Plug the bore of the barrel just below the muzzle with a wad of cloth. Coat the end of the ball with lapping compound or valve grinding paste and with your bit brace begin to lap in the end of the bore. It will require quite a bit of labor to make a perfectly true seat, but it is vitally important to the best accuracy of your rifle. This operation is easily and rapidly done with a crowning tool in the lathe, but lacking a lathe we must use the ball method to obtain the same result.

If a receiver sight is to be used this is now mounted; for a job of this type the Number 102–K Redfield is admirable because it requires no drilling and tapping of the receiver. If an open sight is desired a base must be filed out, drilled to fit the screw-holes in the barrel and the required rear sight fitted to this base. The aperture sight, however, is infinitely more satisfactory on such a converted sporter, and if it is so decided upon, the screw-holes in the barrel should be filled. We can use the regular sight-base screws, cutting them off to a point just above the barrel surface. They should then be peened down flush and filed smooth.

With the barrel cut and sights all mounted we turn to the stock for the next consideration. Rough turned and rough inletted blanks for this and other rifles can be had from a great number of firms who advertise in the sporting magazines. Write for catalogs and compare designs until you find one which meets with your ideas in a sporting stock. All of these stocks are made somewhat oversize, so they can be worked down to individual measurements in most cases. Probably the points that will most influence your choice will be in the shape and style of cheek piece, the height and shape of the comb and the drop at the heel; but by all means order the cheek piece style of stock. If you decide later that you won't want it, it can be quickly shaved off with a draw knife.

The choice of wood will depend on your pocketbook. Plain

American walnut is the cheapest, plain French walnut next, crotch- and feather-grain walnuts are higher in price, and so on. Plain walnut stocks can be had for all our conversion purposes for about seven dollars and for a first attempt it is wise to use this type of blank.

With the blank in hand, remove the bolt, magazine box and trigger mechanism from the action. Set the blank firmly in the padded vise jaws and prepare a mixture of red or black oil tube color and a light oil for your spotting-in work. Don't use linseed oil for this as it will harden on the action and cause inaccurate fitting as well as being difficult to remove. First compare the new blank with the old stock, noticing the cutouts for magazine, receiver, trigger guard and barrel.

Now set the action in the stock and note where it touches the wood, for the chances are that it won't even start down into the inletted portion. Remove the action and note the impressions left on the wood by the red fitting paste. Remove these portions with a flat chisel, taking great care not to remove more wood than is needed.

From now on the work is simply "cut and try." The action must be frequently coated with the red paste to determine the contact points; these are removed with the chisel and the process repeated. Particular attention must be paid to the cutout at the rear of the magazine box. This is the recoil shoulder, and a perfect bearing must be held against this throughout the entire inletting — otherwise the action will be set back in the stock from recoil, possibly splitting it beyond repair.

As the barrel begins to enter the groove, coat with the spotting mixture and remove the contact points with a wide flat chisel, making the cuts straight down and parallel with the sides of the barrel. If only a small amount of wood is to be removed from the channel use a half round file for all this work, being careful at all times to remove only as much wood as is indicated by the impressions. A perfect bearing must be kept at all times along the full length of the barrel; the receiver also must have a perfect bearing on all sides and the bottom.

When the receiver and barrel have been inletted to half their depth in the stock, assemble the trigger mechanism and the magazine box. Inlet these as before, taking care to leave no unsightly gaps in the wood that will show when the stock is completed. Relieve the trigger cutout on the inside so that the mechanism works freely.

As the action begins to enter the blank it is advisable to set in the trigger guard screws from below, catching them in the proper holes before tapping the action down to make the spotting-in impressions. This will keep the action properly centered in the stock and keep it at right angles with the sides of the blank. If this is not carefully watched during the inletting work, the guard screws will not meet the holes in the action at the final stages.

If you are satisfied that the action is in place or nearly so, begin to inlet the trigger guard, using the guard screws to keep it centered. Apply your fitting paste on the bottom of the guard and tap it lightly to secure the outlines; remove this wood carefully and as the guard enters the cutout, coat the sides as well as the bottom to secure the side bearing. Be careful in fitting the guard not to go too deep with the mortise or you will not be able to pull the action up tight with the guard screws.

In this work proceed very slowly and carefully. Don't attempt to rush it, otherwise a serious or unsightly mistake may be made. Resign yourself to removing only as much wood as is indicated by the impressions made with the fitting paste and strive for perfect bearing at all points, particularly along the sides of the barrel and around the receiver. Proper bedding of the barrel is very important to your rifle's accuracy and ability to hold its zero, so spend as much time as necessary to achieve results. Many different types of tools can be used in this inletting job but the only real necessities are flat chisels of different widths and half round or round bastard-cut files. Small gouges will aid in making the various radii, for example, at the ends of the trigger guard, but they are not essential to a careful workman.

The final step, after all parts are in place, the receiver and barrel inletted to half their diameters and the trigger guard and guard screws in place, is to relieve the wood at the tang or extreme rear point of the action. A tight fit at this point forces the action back from the recoil with a wedge effect, eventually splitting the stock through the grip. With a radius gouge or half round file remove the wood behind this tang leaving a gap not less than the thickness of a playing card; slightly more than this may be better, depending entirely upon how accurately the rest of the fitting has been done.

Shaping on the outside of the stock can now begin. Start by measuring from the trigger to the center of the butt, marking off somewhere between 13 and 14 inches, allowing for the thickness of the butt plate. The angle of the butt plate, or pitch, should be determined with the line of sight and this line laid out on the sides of the butt stock. It's best to make the stock a bit longer for the first cut than necessary. If too long it can be shortened after trial. Cut down the comb now so the bolt will just clear and mark off your drop at heel, which should be somewhere between two and a half and three inches. Draw a line connecting these points and plane this flat, to the line. Lay out now for the pistol grip, measuring first from the top of the comb down to rear edge of the grip, which should be about 3 inches. Measure now from the center of the trigger to the front edge of the grip, which should be between 3½ and 3¾ inches. Using the standard length of 1⅞ inches for the length of the grip-cap, the bottom of the grip can be determined by shifting these measurements to coincide. The butt should be at least 5 inches from heel to toe, so by connecting this toe-measurement with the rear of the grip-cap we obtain the outlines of the butt stock. The point of the comb should be about 2½ inches from the end of the tang to give good outlines. With these measurements made, the stock can be now worked to shape, using draw knife, spokeshave, rasp and coarse files.

During all this shaping the stock should be brought to the shoulder frequently to determine its fit and feel. Fit the butt plate before the work has progressed to the final stage, because this may influence the final finishing. The forearm can be shaped while the work is proceeding on the butt; any length or style can be used depending only on the owner's personal tastes. Strive only for graceful lines, blending in well with the outlines of the butt stock and the action. A good length for the forearm is 11 inches from the front of the receiver, although this again will be determined by personal tastes.

Unfortunately we are limited in dimensions by these rough turned stocks, but most of these can be properly worked down to good proportions if a little forethought is used. The butt plate, as indicated, should be wide and rather deep, either perfectly flat or slightly concaved, as this style helps to distribute recoil over a wider shoulder area, lessening its effect.

After final shaping is completed the stock should be given a thorough sanding to remove all toolmarks, sanding always in the direction of the grain. Finish this up with medium paper, and prepare the stock for the oil finish as outlined previously in the chapter.

Before the final finishing takes place some means must be provided for fastening the forearm to the barrel. This can be done in two ways: first choice is to obtain a barrel band with a stud and screw, which passes through the forearm and secures the barrel tight to the wood. Or the shooter can use the original stock band that held the military stock to the barrel, fitting it during the shaping operation. This should be made a tight wedge fit and can be held in place by a small pin driven into the forearm just in front of it. The barrel band and stud is much neater in appearance, however, and is to be recommended.

With the major remodeling work now complete (with the exception of rebluing), we now can attend to refining the trigger pull, as this is directly related to accurate shooting. A hard, creepy pull with three or four "bumps" in it is far from conducive to good shooting. Shooters who have had some experience with military rifles have probably noticed the long-creep or "double-draw" pull common to this type of firearm. To fire this rifle the long slack must first be taken up before the final stage of the trigger let-off is felt. This double-draw slack is entirely out of place in a sporting rifle and some means should be taken to eliminate it. Primarily, the result to be achieved is the prevention of the return of the trigger sear to its high position in front of the cocking-piece sear. In other words, we must prevent the trigger from coming forward too far after it is released, following each shot.

There are several methods used to block the sear in the proper position. The simplest and most positive is to drill and tap a hole for a small screw in the front of the trigger guard. Drill this hole about ¼ inch from the front end of the trigger slot, so that a small plate can be screwed in position, so set that the trigger will rest against it, thus being blocked in its forward travel. To obtain proper adjustment the plate should be drilled with four holes of the screw size, set in line to touch each other, then filed out to make an elongated slot. Then, by shifting the position of the plate against the trigger and tightening down with the screw, the trigger can be blocked in the proper position to remove the preliminary or double-draw pull. Stoppage of the trigger should take place just as the hard part of the trigger pull is felt. The plate need be only a small one, about ⅜ inches wide, ¾ inches long and not over 1/16 inch thick.

It has been suggested to grind off the top of the sear, shortening it enough to eliminate the slack, but this is decidedly unsafe. In most cases when this is done the shooter forgets that there is a great deal of lost motion in the cocking pieces of these rifles, and when the rifle is cocked it can be fired simply by pulling up on the cocking piece, allowing the sear to ride over the top of the trigger sear. This one treatment is responsible for a number of shooting accidents every year. Better leave it alone.

Of course, when such a plate is used in removing the double-draw pull it will have to be inletted into the stock under the trigger guard. However, this can be done at any time during the final operations on the rifle.

This brings us to the problem of the trigger pull itself. Almost every high-power rifle made, with the exception of the Winchester Model 70, comes through now and then with a hard, rough pull; and military rifles are especially annoying in this respect. Most hunters will do their best work with pulls of four to five pounds, and these are entirely safe. Factory rifles many times are turned out with pulls of eight, ten, even twelve pounds, none of which help the hunter to hit his game. The only thing lacking in these factory arms to produce good pulls is hand labor and the time involved necessary to perform the job. We must admit, though, that in the hands of a certain class of hunters such pulls are hardly safe enough. But the shooter who appreciates the niceties of good shooting qualities in his firearms will most certainly want to make some changes in his weapon.

The only tools needed are the proper-shaped slip-stones. Only two oil stones are essential, one threesquare stone and one double knife-edge stone in ¼-inch diameter and medium grit. Add to these the same size and shape of stones in the "Hard Arkansas" type for final polishing; your local hardware store will get these for you on short notice.

The first step is the inspection of the contact surfaces on the trigger sear, and hammer or cocking-piece sear. Very likely you'll find an uneven contact on both sears, with a few ridges showing on the surface — this causes the roughness in the pull. Carefully stone both these surfaces perfectly smooth and flat until good contact is made. It will help in this operation to hold the parts in a small vise to prevent "rocking" the stone, resulting in a rounded surface. With the surfaces smooth, assemble the action and test for evenness of pull; you'll find a big improvement already. The pull will still be a bit too hard, so dissemble the action and begin to stone a small radius on the nose of the trigger sear. For testing the pull during this operation a small spring scale, weighing by quarter pounds, is very handy. The regular hook can be removed from the scale and replaced by a long piece of thin drill rod hooked to the proper angle to contact the trigger.

The lightening operation will require many trials before the required pull is obtained, but a clean, sharp pull on your rifle is worth far more than the little time spent in obtaining it. The main points to remember are to keep the contact surfaces square to prevent creep in the pull; stone very carefully to prevent lightening the pull too much all at once.

On bolt-action rifles, after the contact surfaces have been stoned square and smooth, the pull will still be too hard. To reduce this begin to stone a small angle on the cocking-piece sear on the inside, that is, so that the angle slopes toward the rear, shortening the contact surface. In most cases this will lighten the pull, but sometimes the angle must be stoned to slope back and down toward the outside of the sear rather than the inside. This will depend on the shape of the trigger sear, and can be determined only by trials. If you have difficulty in determining the contact surfaces, coat each with a bit of Prussian blue before you test the pull, and the high spots will at once show up.

On hammer guns, where the hammer travel is an arc with the hammer pivoting on a fixed stud rather than traveling in a straight line as in bolt-action rifles, the stoning of the sears is just a bit different. In these actions, the trigger sear comes to a sharp point and it engages in a deep notch. Pressure on the trigger causes a slight camming action against the tension of the spring, causing the heavy pull. To eliminate this, both sears must be stoned to an angle which is at right angles to the radius of the hammer fall, preventing the camming action.

After the pull is smooth and reduced to the required weight or nearly so, stone all contact surfaces very carefully with the "Hard Arkansas" stones. These stones are used only for this final polishing as they do little, if any, cutting of the metal. In trigger stoning operations great care must be used to keep surfaces square, otherwise a hard blow or knock is liable to cause an accidental discharge of the gun. Proceed very slowly, trying the trigger after each step to obtain an idea of how the work is progressing. Rapid, roughshod stoning may ruin the parts, necessitating replacement before the rifle can again be used.

On certain rifles it is inadvisable to attempt removal of the double-draw pull. These are the models which use the trigger sear as a bolt stop, preventing the bolt from being withdrawn from the receiver at the rear of the bolt throw. A few such models are the Winchester 54, Savage Model 20, Models 40 and 45, and the low-power center-fire Models 23 B, C, and D. In such actions the high position of the sear is quite necessary and any removal of this slack will permit the bolt to be jerked out of the bolt channel in rapid fire. Fairly good pulls can be stoned in these actions by following the suggestions as outlined for bolt-action pulls, but the long preliminary creep must remain.

Fitting of suitable sling swivels now completes the remodeling work on the Krag. As with many other gunsmithing operations, the method of attachment will lie with the tastes of the owner, but for sake of simplicity we will outline two methods that will be in order with our Krag remodeling job.

If a barrel band and stud have been used for the forearm attachment, it is only necessary to use a swivel attaching screw in place of the regular forearm screw; in this way the swivel will serve the double purpose of fastening the forearm and holding the sling. If a sling is contemplated for the converting job, by all means order from the supply house the barrel band, stud and front swivel bow as a single unit. If this has not been done, or if the military stock band has been used as a forearm attachment, than the amateur gunmaker should purchase a swivel bow equipped with an escutcheon. This is a round, fluted nut which is inletted into the inside of the forearm, taking the swivel screw. In either case mounting of the butt swivel is the same. A hole is drilled at right angles to the bottom line of the stock and about 3 inches from the toe; the butt swivel is then screwed up tight. The standard width for sporting rifle sling swivels is ⅞ inch, but if the regular army sling is to be used, 1¼-inch swivels are required.

Polishing the bolt and oil-finishing of the stock now completes the remodeling work on the Krag. Bolts can be nicely polished with fine Aloxite cloth, saving the almost worn-out pieces for the final high finish. Or the rifleman may prefer to blue the bolt during the rebluing operation. If so, the bolt must be polished anyway, so it's only a matter of deciding whether a polished bolt or blued bolt is more attractive. As a word of caution in polishing bolts — don't polish the locking lugs in any shape, manner or form. Any removal of metal from the lugs, however slight, may cause uneven distribution of pressure or excess headspace. When we remember that correct headspace is only a matter of two or three thousandths of an inch we can also realize that even light polishing on the lugs may affect the safety or accuracy of the rifle.

*   *   *

SOME GUNWORK JOBS

ADJUSTABLE STEEL PLATE

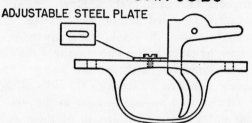

METHOD USED TO BLOCK SEAR, REMOVING DOUBLE-DRAW PULL IN MILITARY RIFLES

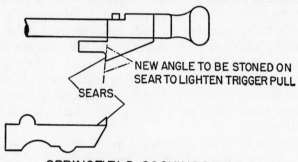

NEW ANGLE TO BE STONED ON SEAR TO LIGHTEN TRIGGER PULL

SEARS

SPRINGFIELD COCKING PIECE AND TRIGGER SEAR

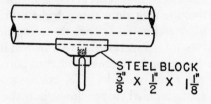

STEEL BLOCK $\frac{3}{8}" \times \frac{1}{2}" \times 1\frac{1}{8}"$

ATTACHING SLING SWIVEL BY SWEATING BASE BLOCK TO BARREL

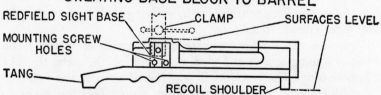

REDFIELD SIGHT BASE

CLAMP

SURFACES LEVEL

MOUNTING SCREW HOLES

TANG

RECOIL SHOULDER

METHOD OF SETTING UP SIGHT BASE FOR DRILLING AND TAPPING SPRINGFIELD RECEIVER

The suggestions for converting the Krag rifle apply equally well to the Springfield, Enfield and others. However, on these rifles the magazine is centrally located and should be inletted with the trigger guard from the bottom of the blank, as it is tapered in that direction. Great care must be taken in this operation that the magazine enters the well on the underside of the action. This is a close fit, so be sure to keep the magazine square with the sides of the blank — also holding its relative fore-and-aft position in the stock. This is the only difficult operation in the inletting of these actions, so some forethought and care should be given before making the cutouts. It will help, before beginning the work, to assemble the action with the magazine in position and screwed up tight with the guard screws, without the stock of course, so that the situation may be studied thoroughly before mistakes are made. Also, on these actions the recoil shoulder is in front of the magazine and is located in a little well in the stock. Keep a tight bearing on the wood at the rear of this flat portion throughout all the inletting work, and you need have no future fears of your stock splitting from recoil. In these, as in all high-power bolt-actions, the tang must be relieved just as outlined for the Krag.

To illustrate how important is this recoil shoulder in stock construction let me tell of a little incident that happened last season. A young chap brought into my workshop a nicely remodeled Enfield — well-figured stock, carefully checkered and finished, but, unfortunately, split from the tang right through the grip into the comb. I dissembled the stock and noted at once the complete absence of any recoil shoulder. My questions revealed that he had inletted the stock himself, but he had completely removed that portion of the blank which formed the recoil shoulder. His excuse was that he didn't have a narrow enough chisel to get down into the cutout forming the recoil shoulder, and he thought it didn't matter anyway, so he had just chiseled it out completely. On the first half-dozen shots the stock had split because lack of support had allowed the recoil to drive the action back into the stock, wedging the tang into the grip with force enough to split it.

Repairs to this stock necessitated the insertion of a new recoil shoulder — using screws and glue, then refitting the metal to make a firm bearing. The stock itself was forced open at the split and Casco glue forced into the break. Then a stock-bolt was made, to pass through the stock between the rear of the magazine and the trigger cutout, binding the parts together, and the whole firmly clamped. After drying, the stock-bolt head and nut were counter-bored and inlays were glued into the holes, then the sides of the stock refinished. A costly mistake; but we were able to restore the stock to good shooting condition.

Owners of Enfield rifles should remove the rear-sight base on the rear bridge of the receiver. This can be done by hacksawing, grinding and filing to a nice contour, leaving a wall thickness over the bolt channel of about $\frac{3}{32}$ inch. Then a receiver sight can be mounted on the right side, just as with the Springfield. This Enfield action is identical with the Remington Model 30 sporting rifle, so if the owner can examine one of these in his dealer's shop, he will get some ideas in shaping the contour of the rear receiver bridge. The Enfield has a barrel just a bit too long for sporting use, so this should be cut off and faced, just as with the Krag, after the ramp sight is placed.

The Springfield barrels are the right length as issued, so a ramp can be installed without cutting off the barrel. If a ramp is not wanted a sporting front sight can be fitted, using the standard front base. Redfield makes a nice model for this; they call it the "Full Block" sight, and it is furnished in both round and square gold bead, and round ivory beads, in $\frac{1}{16}$-inch and $\frac{3}{32}$-inch sizes.

The sportsman who contemplates purchase of a military rifle for conversion to a sporter should have some ideas as to the comparative excellence of various models. Any of the Krags, Springfields and Enfields are good; some of the Enfields come through with barrels slightly over bore diameter, but this won't affect the hunting accuracy to any great extent. Excellent rifles also are the German Mauser model 1898, the British Lee-Enfield, the Canadian Ross, the Austrian Mannlicher, Spanish Mauser, Belgian Mannlicher, and others — but rough-turned and rough-inletted stocks are not generally available for these arms other than the Mauser, so we cannot consider them for conversion purposes by the novice.

Each of these military rifles has its own good and bad points. The Krag has a smooth bolt and a magazine easy to load, but it has not so strong an action as the others designed for rimless cases. The Springfield (a modified Mauser action) and the Mauser itself are distinctly high-quality arms, making up into the best of sportsters; the Enfield is a bit heavy, but it has a handy safety on the right side and it permits low mounting of 'scope sights without alteration of the bolt handle, a necessary change in the Springfield and the Mauser. Also the Enfield can be procured at a low price, making it a suitable subject for the beginner's experiments.

There are a great many other repair and alteration jobs that the sportsman may be called upon to do — broken stocks, making replacement parts, pins and screws, and so on; but space prohibits any further explanation of this work in one chapter. The really interested shooter can find complete books on this subject dealing with a wide variety of the technical details that are so much a part of the gunsmith's work.

One of the simpler additions that the deer hunter may want to make to his rifle is a set of sling swivels. Use of the sling is becoming more popular each year, for a good reason. Slinging the rifle over the shoulder now and then during a day's hunt will relieve the cramped sensation caused by carrying the rifle for hours at a time. If country is rough and steep ravines and hillsides must be climbed frequently, the use of both hands is a decided help. Aside from this the sling permits the hunter to carry his rifle while using both hands to bring out his trophy, usually quite necessary in the deer woods. Some hunters, while liking the sling for these reasons, object to encumbering the rifle with a sling in heavy brush and scrub oak, maintaining that it catches on every other branch. The solution to this problem is the quick detachable sling swivel, by which the sling can be removed instantly and carried in the hunting coat. The method of attaching these is just the same as with the standard type of swivels, but they are quite a bit more expensive.

On factory-made arms of any type, the attachment of the rear butt swivel is made simply by drilling the proper-size hole, which should not be larger than the base diameter of the screw (the thickness of the screw, less the threads) or the threads will strip in the hole. It is with the forward sling swivel that we are concerned, for this offers many problems.

In rifles having ample wood in the forearms the escutcheon type of attachment should be used, inletting this into the inside of the forearm, just behind the tip, then catching the swivel into the threaded escutcheon, pulling it up tight. All bolt-action rifles can be fitted in this way, as can some of the Savage lever-action models. Lever-action Savage models with short, thin forearms must be handled differently. Most satisfactory is to make a block of half inch cold-rolled steel, filing in the barrel radius with a round or half round file, spotting it to the barrel for fit with Prussian blue.

The block is then placed on the barrel in the desired position, its outline scribed on the barrel, and the bluing removed from this enclosed area on the barrel with a small file. This bare spot is then tinned with solder after coating it with "No-Ko-Rode" soldering paste or zinc chloride. The same treatment is given to the block and the two are clamped together and heated with a blow torch or over a gas flame until the solder melts, forming a perfectly sweated joint. The block is now drilled and tapped to take the swivel screw, probably an 8 × 32, and the swivel made tight. If desired the block can be drilled and tapped before the soldering operation to eliminate any possibility of drilling into the barrel.

The Winchester and Marlin lever-actions can be handled in the same way, by sweating the block to the magazine tube, but there is another way this can be done, with less labor. Remove the metal cap over the fore-end tip, drill it with a hole that will take the forearm swivel screw tightly, then insert the screw in this hole and mark it at a point about $\frac{1}{16}$ inch above the hole. Cut this off with a hacksaw, then once again insert in the hole and rivet it down solidly from the inside, resting the swivel on an anvil or heavy vise jaw. Replace the cap on the forearm, removing just enough wood from the underside of the forearm to allow passage of the riveted end.

The Remington autoloader, Model 8, should be handled like the Savage lever-action, by sweating on a base block. However, the slide-action Models 14 and 141 present a problem. These have no means of attaching a swivel other than the magazine band, as the magazine tube moves with the slide handle and attachment here would be unsatisfactory. The logical solution is to drill or bore out a block, filed open at the upper end, which will just slip over this magazine band, then sweating it in place as outlined for other models.

Quite a bit of detail has been given on this work of attaching swivels, for I feel that many hunters are carrying around rifles wishing unconsciously for a sling — in fact, I know this to be so — and lacking one only because they don't quite know just what type of swivels to use and how to attach them to their particular kind of rifle. Much emphasis has been placed, in late years, on the use of the sling with bolt-action rifles, but little attention has been devoted to other types of actions, for which slings are just as desirable. There must be a large number of such rifle owners, for, on a purely mathematical basis, there are many, many more lever, slide and self-loading actions in use than there are bolt.

Finally, we come to the last task of gun ownership, which does not concern the owner's abilities of craftsmanship or patience — but his duty: cleaning his weapon properly. *What?* you say. *Why, there's hardly any need to clean a gun now that we use noncorrosive ammunition!* To this we must say, *No — that's not so. There is every obligation on the shooter's part to clean his rifle.* The difference to be noted with the use of noncorrosive ammunition is that the process can be *delayed*, without causing any damage. But regardless of the claims of the noncorrosive qualities of modern ammunition, most of which are true, we still have moisture in our atmosphere; and we have a certain amount of metal fouling from jacketed bullets.

A good solid steel cleaning rod is the most essential tool for keeping your rifle bore in good shape. With our modern ammunition, cleaning of the rifle can be deferred until we reach home after our hunting trip, so the jointed, more portable rods are not necessary. Rather, get a substantial steel rod, not brass, and keep it in your workshop or gun cabinet. Add to this some patches of Canton flannel, purchased already cut for your rifle caliber, or cut them yourself from a yard of the same material.

The first step is to remove the loose powder solvent; push this out first with a clean dry cloth, not too tight. Next, the powder and primer residue should be dissolved. The very best way is to get hot water through the barrel; hot water is a universal solvent and it works as effectively on powder residue as any commercial preparation. Unfortunately, it can only be used conveniently in rifles that can be cleaned from the breech. To do this, insert a fairly tight patch into the bore from the breech end and set the muzzle end in a pan of boiling water, on the floor. Now pump up water into the barrel, using the cleaning rod as a suction pump, then expel the water by pushing the patch down to the muzzle. Repeat this until the barrel becomes warm, but be careful not to withdraw the patch completely from the chamber end, else the action may be flooded with water. Now dry the bore at once with a couple of dry patches, examine it for traces of fouling, and if it looks bright and clean, run through a patch coated with a standard gun oil.

Solid-frame lever-action rifles that cannot be cleaned from the breech should be cleaned with a commercial powder solvent. For this, use a bristle brush, with which the bore can be thoroughly scrubbed. Now wipe dry with clean patches and oil as before.

If any lumps or patches are noted in the bore after the solvent has been wiped out, metal fouling is indicated. Usually this can be removed by brisk scrubbing with a brass or steel brush. If this fails, thread a wad of fine steel wool through the slotted wiper and scrub with this. Very badly fouled barrels won't respond to this treatment, and in these cases the rifle should be taken to a gunsmith for application of the ammonia solution. I hesitate to recommend that this treatment be undertaken by the gun owner himself, as barrels and actions can be badly rusted if the solution is not intelligently handled.

With rifle barrels in good condition and modern ammunition used exclusively, few hunters will have much fouling trouble. If it does occur, the brush-and-steel-wool treatments will remove it safely. Rusted barrels are another matter, and they require special treatment. If rust can be clearly seen in the bore, don't waste time with hot water, powder solvents or oils. Attack the bore at once with the steel wool first of all, and if this doesn't remove it, take an old brush and wrap it with a cloth soaked in a mixture of flour of emery and sweet oil. Scrub the barrel thoroughly with this, then clean as usual. Unless the barrel is far gone this will restore most of the original brightness.

For badly rusted barrels only a lapping operation with a lead lap will put the rifle in shooting condition. This work also is for a gunsmith as it requires the use of a special lapping rod and a good knowledge of rifle barrels. However, if you have a pet rifle that is badly rusted in the bore, don't junk it until you've had a good gunsmith lap it out. If this won't give enough accuracy for hunting conditions then either buy a new barrel or discard the entire arm.

Some consideration must be given to the choice of solvents and lubricating oils. Stay away from commercial preparations which claim to serve as both solvent and lubricant. Each fluid serves an entirely different purpose and the liquid consistency of each must be different. A powder solvent, to penetrate to all points of the bore, into the corners of the rifling and under metal fouling, must be of a water-thin consistency. Such an oil cannot lubricate properly nor will it serve as a rust preventative due to its tendency to flow off the metal. The lubricating oil and rust preventative must be quite the opposite; it must leave a thin, permanent film of oil on contact surfaces, remaining there for an indefinite period without flowing off, gumming or evaporating. If you must use commercial oils put up in handy cans, by all means select an oil made for guns and advertised as such rather than the multi-purpose household oils. A single two- or three-ounce can of such oil will serve the hunter for at least a year, unless he decides to use most of it for the lawn mower or his squeaky car-doors. Buy a can of regular *gun oil* and use it only for your gun.

To protect the inside of the bore under normal conditions of humidity your regular gun oil will be enough, but it must be renewed about once a month. In hot, humid climates a heavier, semi-liquid grease will be required, or in any case where the rifle is to be laid away for a long period. Many deer rifles aren't used between seasons, so to protect the bores they should be given a thorough cleaning after each season and well covered with a regular gun grease. Under no circumstances should the muzzle be plugged with a cork or rag as this causes condensation of moisture within the barrel, soon rusting it. Likewise the so-called "anti-rust ropes" should never be used. If they are allowed to remain in the bore for any length of time the oil evaporates and the rope will rust solidly into the bore, either ruining it or so plugging it that the barrel may be ruined by its removal.

The external portions of a rifle require little care. If small rust spots have formed at any time, brush them off with steel wool — not an abrasive cloth or compound, as this also removes the bluing. Before a hunting trip, if wet weather is anticipated, rub the metal parts with furniture wax or the melted beeswax and turpentine mixture used after the rebluing process. Either of these will protect against moisture. If the action of your rifle gets soaked during a heavy rain, tie it to the back of a chair, muzzle down, and set it close to a hot fire to dry out quickly. Then oil with gun oil. The best insurance against rust on the external parts of a firearm is an oil-soaked chamois kept in a glass jar in the gun cabinet. Every time the arm is used or handled it can be gone over once lightly with the chamois; and *that* gun will never rust.

In very-cold-weather hunting, use only a little of a light oil for lubricating the action, otherwise it may freeze tight or, at least, the firing pin travel may be slowed down enough to cause a misfire. The best bet for all cold-weather hunting is to use no oil whatever on the action, simply flush it out well with gasoline from a squirt-can. A clean action will almost always function perfectly even without lubrication. At any rate it is much the lesser of the two evils. If the action is new and very stiff, lubricate with kerosene and you'll have no action troubles even in zero weather.

If your stock is a varnished or lacquered job, as most factory jobs are, there is nothing that can be done to remove scratches incident to hunting. Furniture wax may help its appearance, but a new oil finish is the best solution. Oil finished stocks can be brought to original condition quickly, by only the addition of more raw linseed oil, rubbed in with the hand. Age and use merely serve to increase the beauty of these oil finishes, and any hunter who values the appearance and serviceability of his pet gun will do well to apply one.

In a chapter such as this, few technical details have been given. It is not our purpose to write a book on gun work, for there are many such books already on the market which delve thoroughly into such work, far beyond this writer's abilities. We have tried to discuss those points which are of most interest to the hunter who loves his firearms, and who takes pride in his ability to create things with his hands. Much work on firearms is the result of personal fancy — so don't hesitate to carry out any ideas that may seem practical to better suit the arm for your own use. The suggestions outlined here are merely to show the way for the individual of initiative and patience.

In stock work, particularly, only few principles need to be followed; the rest will be dictated by personal needs and taste. We have made no mention of those branches of gunmaking which require special knowledge and special tools. All of the work outlined can be successfully completed, albeit more slowly, with tools found in the carpenter's box or on the garage workbench. Materials in most instances can be obtained locally. Arm yourself with a number of catalogs from various shooting supply houses, decide on the job you want most to do — and jump into it with a mental resolve to work slowly, with patience and forethought; then results will be always in excess of your expectations.

16 / Mounting
the Trophy

THE CULMINATION of all successful deer hunts is the preparation and preservation of the trophy. Any representative whitetail head, gracefully mounted, and hung properly on the wall of his office or den, serves ever to renew the pleasure and thrill of that red-letter day when the Red Gods smiled favorably on the sportsman. Even as I write this final chapter, there hangs on the wall near me, looking out over my left shoulder, the head and huge antlers of the biggest buck it has ever been my good luck to bring to earth. Almost every time I glance that way I can see again the flashing gleam of his two-foot spread bobbing through the pines and over scrub oak in his last desperate dash for safety. These are the memories that make our hunting so worth while, and the trophy itself serves amply to keep bright the thrilling moment that the years may try to dim.

Few hunters ever think of mounting their own deer heads, and fewer still will attempt it; yet deer-head taxidermy is remarkably simple. Modern methods of the commercial taxidermist have eliminated the major part of the messiness and have reduced the requirements of skill to the point where very little real craftsmanship is required to turn out a creditable job. Taxidermy, as a whole, is still one of the fine creative arts; but deer-head work is now definitely out of this classification. All the skilled workmanship formerly required in modeling, shaping and posing the mount is now performed by the artists who manufacture commercial supplies and the sportsman can buy these products at a low figure. With the proper materials at hand — forms, ear liners, eyes and panels — almost any individual can prepare and mount any deer head with the expenditure of very little time and a minimum of effort.

The mounting of game birds and animals always has been shrouded in deep, dark mystery. Taxidermists have jealously guarded their methods from the public and from their professional brethren. This factor of secrecy has obscured the sportsman's general knowledge of the craft, and has certainly done nothing to encourage his attempting the preparation and preservation of his trophies. There is so much pleasure and satisfaction in the work for hunters, however, that I believe it is only fitting that the details should be outlined for those who will want to perform the work as a large part of their outdoors hobby.

Mounting a deer head requires only a small amount of room — just a corner in the attic or basement. There will be no overripe odors to permeate the household and very little debris to clutter up the floors. A garage or workshop is ideal for the purpose, but it's not at all necessary; the work can easily be done in the home without too much objection on the part of the Little Woman.

The first step in preparation, whether the sportsman is to mount the head himself or send it off to a taxidermist, is proper care of the head before shipping or skinning it out. If the head can be shipped by express to reach the taxidermist within a couple of days, or if the weather is cold, then there is no need to skin out the head. It can be shipped whole and the taxidermist will take the necessary measurements before skinning.

The usual precautionary measures should be observed: don't cut the deer's throat or make any incision in the neck skin whatever. Next, be sure, when cutting off the head and neck skin from the hide, to leave plenty of neck skin. Cut it off well behind the shoulders and brisket to give the taxidermist plenty of skin to work with. I've seen some mighty fine heads that were spoiled by cutting the neck skin off too short. The only possible solution, in this event, is to use a whole new scalp, or skin, from another deer, and the taxidermist will be forced to make an extra charge for this. In addition, the head will not have its original skin, although this is not so important, as deer skins look pretty much alike.

Now, if you're going to mount the head yourself, or if there is a possibility that the head entire will spoil in transit should you want to ship it away, it will be necessary to take measurements and then skin the head out. A glance at the drawing will show just what measurements are needed so that the form of correct size can be selected for the final mounting. It's best to take all the head measurements indicated, because some of the taxidermy supply houses have different requirements than others, but the measurements indicated will take care of all needs.

The distance from *nose to eye corner*, and from *nose to point of skull*, determines the head-size of the form. The *circumference around the neck* determines the size of the neck, which varies considerably with different supply houses. When taking the skull measurement, feel behind the antlers on the back of the skull for a little bump, or knob. It is to this point that the skull measurement should be taken. In measuring the circumference of the neck, pull the tape measure very tight, otherwise the reading, taken over the hide and hair, will result in a larger form than necessary.

The *measurements to antler burr and antler points* are essential for correct placement of the antlers on the form. Few taxidermists use these measurements at all, but I find that they save a lot of guesswork in preparing the form. By this method the position of the antlers with relation to the head is definitely established. Measure *from the tip of the nose to the base of the antler*, or burr, and *to the tip of each antler from the nose*. These are all the measurements necessary to correct mounting of the head, so keep them in a notebook as a permanent record.

To give the novice an idea as to what measurements he can expect to obtain, here is a complete set taken from a medium-sized Northern whitetail buck: *nose to eye corner*, 6¾ inches; *nose to skull point*, 12 inches; *circumference around neck behind ears*, 17 inches; *nose to antler burr*, 9½ inches; *nose to right antler point*, 14 inches; *nose to left antler point*, 14¾ inches. These measurements were for a medium-sized, eight-point set of antlers.

With measurements taken and recorded, we can begin skinning-out the head. For this I use a surgeon's scalpel with two-inch blade and a screwdriver with a fairly broad, dull blade. A small pocket-knife will serve in place of the scalpel, but it must be sharp; to keep it sharp during the skinning have an oil stone handy on the workbench.

If the hide has not yet been separated from the neck skin, do this now by laying the hide flat on the bench, folded along the center of the back line. Cut it off well behind the withers (top of the shoulders) and brisket, making the cut straight down from the top through the skin of the forelegs, cutting both sides as they are held together flat on the bench. This gives enough skin to make a full shoulder mount if desired, and it gives us enough extra skin for a margin of safety. Now place the head upright on the bench and, working from behind, start the point of the knife into the skin directly between the ears in the center of the top of the neck. Slice through the skin from this point straight through to the top of the shoulders. This line is easy to follow even if the neck has been completely skinned-out, because there is a line of dark hair running right down the top of the neck between the shoulders; so just follow this line.

Next, start the point of the knife directly behind the base of an antler and cut through to the beginning of the first line; repeat with the other antler, forming a Y-shaped cut on top of the skull. Begin now to separate the skin between the ears, widening the cut until the base of each ear can be seen on the sides of the skull. If the neck has not been skinned-out before, this will have to be done before the ear bases can be reached. In all this skinning take pains not to cut into or through the hide; rather take some of the flesh with the hide, as it can be removed easily after the skin has been salted.

When the bases of the ears can be seen, cut these off from above by slicing straight down with the knife, keeping close to the skull. This leaves the ear completely attached to the hide, to be skinned out later. Be careful in cutting off the ears not to cut the hide when the bottom of the cut is reached, but proceed gently, working the hide around the back of the jaw bones until the ear bases can be completely severed close to the skull without danger of cutting the hide. The next step is to free the skin from around the antler bases, beneath the burr. For this *don't* use the knife, except to make the starting incision, but pry the skin off carefully with the screwdriver. If the head has dried out to any degree, this process will be slow, but continue until the skin is completely freed from under the burrs of the antlers.

From now on continue skinning-out all around the head until the eyes are reached; then to skin these out properly, place a finger in the eyesocket under the back of the eyelid, lifting it up and out so that the blade can slice through between the eyelid and the skull; be careful in this operation not to cut the eyelid in any way. When the front eye corner is reached we find that the skin here is attached to the skull by a firm, hard gristle which makes skinning at this point a bit tricky, but with normal care we can preserve the eyelid and corners. Now, directly in front of the eye corner, we notice that the skin grows down into a depression, or pit, in the skull. This is the tear duct, and we must exercise special care to separate this from the skull without tearing it. Again, by inserting a finger under the skin and lifting up and out we can work the point of the knife down into the skull pit, cutting all around under the skin, freeing it from this depression. This tear duct skin is thin and not covered with hair, so it's important that no cuts should be made through it, as they will show in the finished mount.

Now our task is to peel the skin down until the back corners of the mouth are reached; again insert a finger or two, to lift the lips away from the jaw and slice through the flesh, leaving the lips *entirely on the hide.* Follow around the jaw line in this manner, cutting close to the jawbone, until the skin of the lower jaw is removed.

The nose and nostrils are at this point the only attachment of the skin to the head, so we remove the hide finally as follows: Insert a finger into a nostril until the cartilage of the nasal passage can be lifted up slightly at a point about two inches above the nose. Cut through straight down to the skull at this point with each nostril, leaving the cartilage attached to the nose skin; continue down to the nose, cutting this off close to the upper jaw and leaving all the flesh and lips attached. The head is now completely skinned out and ready for salting, but before doing this we'll saw out the antlers so that the head and skull can be disposed of before decomposition sets to work.

The diagram shows how this cut is made. Simply place the skull in an upright position on the workbench with the nose to the left and the antlers at right angles to the edge of the bench. Take your handsaw (any old carpenter's cross-cut saw) and start the cut at the rear of the skull, just under the skull point. Angle this cut so it will emerge at the top edge of the eye sockets, being careful to keep the saw level as it makes its way through the skull. After the antlers are freed with their little patch of skull, shake out the small quantity of brains that clings to the top of the brain pan. Wash the skull and antlers thoroughly now with hot water and trim off any loose flesh, after which the skull and antlers can be set aside to dry out.

Now we are ready to finish up our work on the scalp before it can be salted, meaning the skinning-out of the ears by turning them inside out. Notice that the base cartilage of each ear is surrounded by flesh, so first we must remove this, starting at the back side of the ear and trimming it off close to the cartilage, but leaving all the cartilage attached to the ear. After the flesh is removed we start to reverse the ear by working our fingers up into the pocket between the ear cartilage and the skin on the back of the ear. This is sometimes a tough job because the cartilage grows very tightly to the skin. Don't use the knife for this operation, just persevere with your fingers and the end of your blunt screwdriver until the cartilage is broken loose from the ear all along the back. There are certain little attaching tendons here that can be severed with the knife, but other than this the knife should not be used. Professionals use what is called "ear-opener pliers" for this operation, which greatly speeds up the work, but it can be done just as outlined.

When the cartilage is loosened about halfway up the back of the ear, it's time to start turning the ear inside out. Work it carefully, separating the cartilage from the skin right down to the very edges of the ear and out to the tip, being careful not to tear the skin at the edges of the ear. It's vitally important to break the cartilage loose right out to the edges of the ear, otherwise the ear liner will not reach to the full outline of the ear in mounting and the edges will wrinkle and curl in drying, making a messy-looking mount. It's a good idea, after the ear is reversed almost entirely, to turn it back again to its original position so that the edges of the ear can be opened up from the cartilage. Do this by inserting your finger and pushing against the edge until the outline of the ear is reached.

With the ears reversed and cartilage showing, we are ready to salt the scalp. Spread it out flat and sprinkle it liberally with table salt, rubbing it in well around the eyes, nostrils and lips. Fold it over and roll it up; then lay it away overnight in a cool place. Next day you'll note that certain juices have formed overnight, so hang it up outdoors to drain off a bit, then resalt it and lay away as before for another day.

By this time the salt will have sufficiently hardened the loose flesh and fat on the hide so that it can be fleshed out, at least partially. Take your small knife and a heavy-bladed hunting knife and trim or scrape off the flesh and fat that is clinging to the hide, paying particular attention to the regions around the eyes, nostrils and lips. It's very likely that you won't be able to remove all the flesh from the region of the nose and nostrils at this time, because the salt will not have affected the flesh right next to the skin. Leave this temporarily and start on the lips. The lips must be split with the knife almost to their edges and the flesh pared down closely, but the lips must *not* be cut off at the edge of the mouth. After splitting the lips and removing some of the flesh, again apply salt liberally to the lips and nostrils and lay away for twenty-four hours, or until the flesh has toughened from the action of the salt.

As an extra precaution I might add that in the first salting the skin should not be allowed to remain for several days without inspection. In this first salting the flesh is not completely cured next to the skin and the skin might start to spoil in the areas around the eyes, nostrils and mouth. Then when the hide is placed in the tanning solution the hair will slip off the hide around these areas, making an irreparable blemish. However, after the hide has been partially fleshed and more salt applied the salt will strike through down to the hide, preserving it for an indefinite period up to a year or more.

The final fleshing should involve only the paring of the flesh down to the skin of the lips, around the eye sockets and the nostrils. In final fleshing of the nostrils the nasal cartilage should be removed and the skin of the nostrils preserved intact at least for an inch or slightly more, because the skin of the nostrils will show in the finished mount. The flesh must be painstakingly shaved from the nose itself, otherwise the nose will wrinkle when the head is mounted and dried out.

The skin is now ready to be tanned, so we will prepare the tanning solution as follows:

Obtain a wooden or earthenware tub (not metal) — a buttertub is just right — and into this pour about four gallons of tanning liquor, made up of this formula:

> One quart common salt (NaCl)
> One gallon water (H_2O)
> One ounce by volume sulphuric acid (H_2SO_4)

Dissolve salt in warm water and add acid very *gradually*, to prevent an explosion. After the solution cools the scalp should be immersed and kept submerged by placing a block of wood on it. Move the hide around in the solution every few days for a period of at least two weeks; it is then completely tanned and ready to mount.

In the interim, while the scalp is tanning, you will have gone through the classified advertising sections of some of the outdoor magazines and sent for a few catalogs from various supply houses. All that remains, then, is to pick out the style and size of mount that suits your fancy. All the big supply houses carry head forms for whitetail deer in various styles: neck mounts, straight, right or left turn; shoulder mounts, straight, right or left turn; sneak mounts in the same order, and shoulder sneaks likewise. You'll decide on the style of mount first, your decision to be influenced by the position it will occupy in the household; but by all means select a mount that is turned in some way, either to right or left, whichever is suited to its proposed location. A turned mount is much more expressive of life than the regular straight mount.

If your buck has rather a large head, a shoulder mount will be in order. The shoulder mount balances up to much better advantage when a large rack of antlers is to be mounted; but again, the size of the room will influence your choice in this respect.

After you've picked the style of mount, take your measurement record and go over the manufacturer's specifications, picking out the form that most closely meets your requirements. If there is any doubt as to your selection when measurements do not coincide with your record, always choose the next smaller size. The hide will shrink down very nicely without wrinkling even if the form is a little too small, but never order a form that is oversize. You'll be able to stretch the scalp to fit it without too much trouble, but when it dries — watch out! The stitches will break up the back, the skin will pull away from the antler bases, the eyes will pop out. So better have the form too small than too large.

With the form, you must order ear liners of the right size, matching them to the size of the head form — small form, small ear liners; large form, large ear liners, and so on. If there should be a doubt in your mind, get the ear liners *large*, then they can be trimmed to fit the ear, although this is seldom necessary.

Perhaps a word here as to the construction of the forms is in order. All commercial head forms and ear liners are made of paper. Layer on layer of the wet paper is glued together inside a hollow form or cast, built up to a thickness of a quarter of an inch or more, making a very strong, light mount for the hide. Inside the top of the form, a block of wood is placed for the antler screws and held there by gluing over it more layers of heavy paper. The ear liners are made in the same way, except that they are not built up to the same thickness. These forms are permanent; they will never sag or lose their shape and they're correctly modeled to the proper outlines. They require only that the skin be stretched over them and sewed; no building up is necessary, as each detail is properly worked out in the form itself.

Here are a few points to look for when selecting your form. Choose the type in which the top of the head, where the antlers are to be placed, is flat. Some forms are made up with a notched top to take the skull section, but these are not quite so easy for the novice to use. Then, the eye sockets should be molded in the form, even to the high crown over the eye, eliminating any necessity to build up this point. The nostrils and nose should be well modeled, and the outlines of the jaw reproduced. As an added point, be sure that the form is fitted with a neck board at the factory; sometimes there is a small extra charge made for fitting these neck boards into the base of the form, but it is well worth it.

Ear liners should be purchased with the bases or butts already formed as in integral part of the ear liner; this eliminates the necessity of building up the ear base with plastic compounds, a necessity when the short type of ear liner is used. The short liner simply fills the pocket between the back of the ear and the cartilage, but does not provide for filling in the space left when the flesh is removed from the ear base. When the ear liner is made up to include this base the setting of the ear is much simplified, especially for the novice.

Perhaps the most important single point in the entire mounted head is the eyes. The eyes are the life of the trophy; on them depends the lifelike expression that is found in some mounts but is lacking in many others. They must be lustrous and correct in color and shape, truly "the windows of the soul." The very highest-quality eyes are the concave convex, hemispherical in shape and hand-painted; these are also the most costly. For all our deer-head work the imitation concave convex are entirely suitable. They are just a little flatter in front and quite flat in back and are also hand-colored. The workmanship on these eyes is fully equal to that of the genuine convex eyes, but the construction is not quite so expensive. They are somewhat better suited for use with the paper forms, as they set back further in the socket because of the flat back, preventing to a great extent the pop-eyed expression common to many mounts.

All deer eyes should be ordered with blue-tint pupils, as this most closely approximates the color of the living eye. The iris should be veined and of a multicolor brown to carry out the color scheme still further. Above all, don't buy cheap eyes; they detract immeasurably from the appearance of the finished head. Sizes in deer eyes are graduated in millimeters rather than inches: 26 mm. for small deer, 28 mm. for medium deer and 30 mm. for very large bucks. These three sizes will cover all variations that any whitetail deer hunter is liable to encounter — although the 28 mm. size is the most in use.

Additional materials that must be ordered with the forms and eyes are needles, papier-mâché, a panel or shield, and a plate hanger for this. Any other incidentals can be purchased locally as needed. Two needles, usually termed "scalp needles," will be required. These are curved, about 3½ inches long, and have three cutting edges. The papier-mâché can be purchased in the dry form to be mixed with water, or already prepared in an airtight can. About a pound will be sufficient for one head. The panel or shield will depend on the taste of the sportsman; it's important though to have it large enough. For medium-sized neck mounts the shield should be at least 13 × 17 inches; for medium shoulder mounts the shield should be 15 × 20 inches or larger. Black walnut and oak are good panel woods; they look well and aren't too costly. Fir is somewhat less expensive, but it doesn't present the rich appearance of either black walnut or oak.

Incidental materials include some oil colors, camel's-hair brush, paraffin, beeswax, linen thread, some spring clothespins and a few 18-gauge wire brads. Some of these items will be available around the house or shop, but if not, their cost is slight.

When we have acquired the necessary supplies as outlined, we are ready to go right ahead with the mounting of the head. The scalp, after its two weeks in the tanning solution, is well cured, so we can prepare it by beaming it down a bit in order to thin the skin at the proper places.

Remove the scalp from the tanning liquor and wash it thoroughly in warm water to which a double handful of washing soda has been added. This will soften the hide, making it more pliable and at the same time the soda will neutralize the action of the tanning solution. Hang it up then for about an hour, letting the water drain off, leaving the hide moist but not slippery. Now we can prepare a small fleshing beam to facilitate the work of thinning-down the hide. Take a piece of 2 × 4 lumber about 2 feet long and with a plane or drawknife round off one of the wide sides so that it presents a fairly smooth-crowned surface. Now bolt this to the bench so that the end will project about 12 or 14 inches over the edge, with the rounded surface uppermost.

Now slip the scalp over the end of the beam, flesh side out and with the nose snug against the end of the beam. Take your heavy hunting knife, or drawknife, and pare the skin down around the eyes, the nostrils, the under jaw, the top of the head and along the lips. Shave the hide so that it is thin enough to conform easily to the contours of the head form. Take care in shaving the lips so that they will not be cut off at the hairline; thin down the hide around the antler burrs as this prevents a great deal of shrinkage at this point.

For this operation it is not essential to have the fleshing beam made up as outlined and if only one head is to be mounted the novice may prefer to beam down the hide simply by laying it flat on the workbench. It can be done in this way, but the use of the rounded beam helps the operation along. After the hide is thinned down to the proper point at the place mentioned, it can be again returned to the tanning solution until the head form is made ready.

Hang up your head form by boring a hole in the upper portion of the neck board and setting it on a large headed wood screw or lag screw, firmly fastened to the wall or a beam. It should be hung at a height that will bring the nose of the form at about chest level.

With a hand drill and a ¼-inch drill, bore three holes through the top of the skull carrying the antlers. These should be placed so that there will be two holes in the front, just between and in front of the antler bases; the rear hole is drilled in the center of the skull, just behind the antler bases, making a triangle with the apex pointing toward the rear of the head. Now countersink these screw holes with a rose countersink or a larger drill so that the anchoring screws will be almost flush with the top of the skull.

Take your measurement chart and place the antlers on top of the form with the antler bases at the given distance. Fasten them in this position with three 2½-inch Number 10 galvanized wood screws, setting them just tightly enough so that the antlers will be in position. Now with a tape measure or yardstick check the measurements from nose to antler points. In most cases this measurement will be too great, indicating that the antlers must be tipped forward somewhat to shorten the distance and bring the antler points into the correct measurement. To do this loosen the screws and insert a small block of wood under the rear of the skull; then screw the skull down once again and check the measurement. You may have to change the thickness of the block several times before it comes out right, but keep at it until the antlers are in the correct position according to your measurements. If the angle of the antlers is too far forward, shims of cardboard or wood will have to be placed under the front of the skull piece in like manner to achieve results.

After the antlers are in place, small gaps may be noticed between the skull and the form, also the contour of the skull will show a gap between the forward end of the skull and the beginning of the flat portion on top of the form. These will have to be filled in and built up with the papier-mâché composition, following the outlines of the form. Then just under the antler burr is a hollow that must be filled out with papier-mâché because at this point some flesh was removed in cleaning off the skull and it must be replaced. If this is neglected the hide will shrink down into this hollow in drying and pull the skin away from the antler burrs, leaving a bare expanse of bone visible. When the papier-mâché has dried hard the form is ready for trying on the skin.

Once again remove the scalp from the tanning solution and hang it to drain off a bit before trying it on the form; it's not necessary to wash it at this stage at least until a fit has been made on the form. Place the scalp, hair side out, over the form in the position it will assume when mounted. Slide the nose skin up over the nose of the form and pull the scalp up to the antler burrs; then fold the skin around the neck, estimating at this point whether or not the skin will completely go around the neck. If so, hold it in this position with one hand and with the other slide the nose skin down over the nose on the form, checking the position of the eye-holes with relation to the eye sockets on the form. If the form has been correctly ordered all these points will be in line, but sometimes the skin, due to handling on the fleshing beam and washing, is stretched out of shape, and it fails to go around the form completely or fails to come out right over the eyes. This is nothing to worry about, because wet buckskin stretches a great deal, and by working the skin over the fleshing beam or over the edge of a board held in a vise it can be stretched in any direction, at least enough to cover the form completely.

When a good fit is made by stretching and manipulation of the skin, we are ready to wash the hide and clean it for mounting. Do this by immersing the hide in warm water with washing soda added, then wash well in soapy water and rinse well in clean warm water. Press out the excess water, but don't wring out the skin — rather lay it on a wide board to drain off a bit.

Poisoning of the hide is now in order, to protect it from attack by moths and dermestids. Arsenical soap can be used for this, painted on the flesh side of the hide, but the following solution will give better results with no danger of infection to the operator:

PROTECTIVE SOLUTION

2 gallons water
1 lb. borax
1 oz. carbolic acid
1 oz. spirits of camphor

Boil water to dissolve borax, then add acid and camphor.

The hide, still damp, should be immersed in this solution and allowed to remain about twenty-four hours; by that time it will be thoroughly poisoned. The scalp should then be removed, excess water pressed out and laid out flat to drain off, ready for the final mounting.

This poisoning solution can be poured into the tub which was used for the tanning solution; the tanning solution should have been dumped out as there is no further use for it in the mounting of the head.

Arsenical soap is, of course, widely used in all mounting work, including deer heads, but as it is highly poisonous, a treated skin should not be handled if there are any small cuts or abrasions on the fingers or hands. Rubber gloves will give adequate protection against the arsenic, but on the whole the poison solution given above will be much more satisfactory.

As a matter of general interest, however, here is the formula for the arsenical soap:

ARSENICAL SOAP

One pound white soap (Ivory)
One pound white arsenic
6 ounces spirits of camphor (by volume)

The soap should be sliced thin and melted over a slow fire, adding a little water. When it is melted add the arsenic, stirring constantly, then add the camphor. Let it simmer until it becomes thick; then pour into a glass jar labeled POISON. To use, mix a small quantity with water and paint on the hide with a brush.

After the scalp has been thoroughly poisoned, the ears should again be turned right side out and the ear liners fitted. First enlarge the openings to the ear pocket by stretching them with the fingers;

they can be pulled just as hard as you please – there's no danger of tearing the hide. The liners can now be inserted in the ear pocket, but if they still go in hard, a little soap applied along the edges will help the process along. With the liners in place, press the cartilage back against them in position and note how they fit; they should come right out to the tip of the ear and flush along the edges. If the cartilage bulges very much the liner will have to be trimmed a bit to make a fit. Do this with a pair of heavy shears, tinsnips, or a sharp knife.

With the liners properly fitted, mix up a little Casco glue and cover both the inside of the ear pocket and the liner. Again insert the liners and hold them in place by clamping all along the edges of the ear with spring clothespins. The cartilage at the base of the ear should be trimmed a bit, and if necessary the base of the liner also, permitting the cartilage to be pulled back into the base of the ear liner.

The scalp and form are now all ready for the final mounting; as a warning at this point let me say that the final mounting, once begun, must be completed while the skin is still wet, so leave plenty of time for the final operation. If a head is left in a half-finished state to remain overnight the scalp will be so dried-out that it will be impossible to give it the necessary manipulations in the setting of eyes, ears and nostrils.

To begin: Take your two scalp needles and thread both of them with a double thickness of heavy linen shoemaker's thread, previously waxed with beeswax. Remove your form from the wall and fit the scalp in position, then lay the head on the bench upright but facing away from you. Look now on the scalp for the areas of skin which surrounded the antler butts; they can be recognized by a more or less ragged appearance at the edges, because this skin was pried loose from the skull, not cut with the knife. Start your first needle from the flesh side at one corner of the antler section; do likewise with the other needle at the other corner, then knot both of the stitches so that each threaded needle will be firmly attached to the scalp. Now bring the scalp around the antler butt, and make your first stitch with each needle to the opposite side of the hide, inserting the point about a quarter of an inch down the edge from the first stitch; then repeat with the other needle. Make about three of these stitches loosely with each needle, then pull on both threads together, bringing the skin firmly around the base of the antlers, just under the burrs. Continue now to sew up the incision, using the two needles, one at a time, inserting the points from the under or flesh side of the hide. (Sewing in this way from the flesh side prevents the hairs from being pulled through with the thread.)

When the end of the first branch of the Y-cut has been reached, tie off the two threads at this point by knotting them together with a square knot; then repeat with the other antler until the end of the other Y-cut has been reached. Now, instead of knotting at this point, continue to sew up the neck cut in a like manner, to a point about three inches behind the ears. Tie the two ends together at this point, again using the square knot.

Now we must take a lump of papier-mâché and work it around the butts of the ear liners, so that they will be well set in place when the mount is dry. After filling around the bases continue to sew up the neck incision until the form has been completely covered right down to the base board, then tie off the threads, but don't cut them off. Leave the ends with needles attached until the head is finished, because we might need to do a bit more sewing after the ears are pulled up into place.

Take the form and place it back up on its hook on the wall or upright; then stand back and look it over. It's a mess. The ears droop dismally, the eye sockets gape, the nose is lumpy, the lower jaw skin hangs down, and the entire scalp is wrinkled. All just as it should be at this stage of the mounting! Each of these points will be shaped and adjusted in its proper order, very quickly and easily.

First the ears must be set. Stand in front of the mount and grasp an ear butt in each hand and pull them toward you, bringing them well up against the backs of the antlers in an erect or "alert" position, facing well forward and slightly out away from the head. They can be held in this position in two ways: the easier of the two is by simply looping a soft rope or strip of cloth around the back of each ear, passing the end around the base of one ear, then over the top of the skull in front of the antler burrs to the base of the other ear, then around this and again over the top of the skull just behind the eyes, tying the two ends together on top of the skull between the eyes and antlers. Pull this rope up quite tight, smoothing the hair down under it so that it won't be ruffled after the mount is dried. This will hold the ear butts well forward and firmly in position.

The alternative method is to take two pieces of $\frac{3}{16}$-inch welding rod, each about a foot long and sharpen an end on each rod. Then,

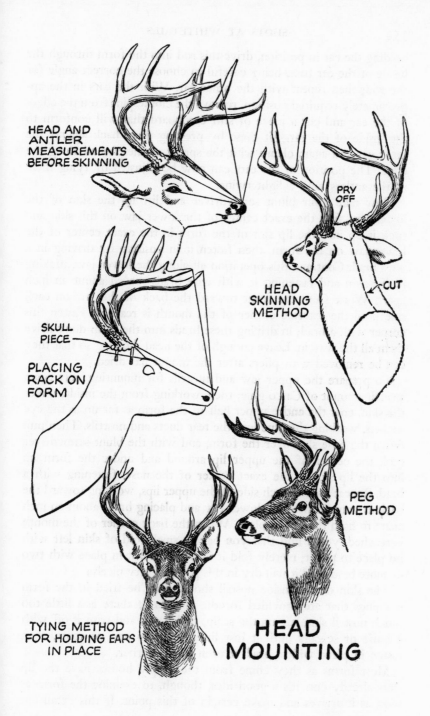

HEAD AND
ANTLER
MEASUREMENTS
BEFORE SKINNING

PRY
OFF

CUT

HEAD
SKINNING
METHOD

SKULL
PIECE

PLACING
RACK ON
FORM

PEG
METHOD

TYING METHOD
FOR HOLDING EARS
IN PLACE

HEAD
MOUNTING

holding the ear in position, drive this rod into the form through the inside of the ear base, being careful to choose the correct angle for the rod; then repeat with the other ear. With the ears in the approximately required position, remove the clothespins from the edges of the ear and cut a piece of stiff cardboard that will conform to the inside of the ear. Fit these by pressing them back against the inner ear and again clamp with the spring clothespins all along the edge. The position of the ears can now be adjusted by tying them to the antlers with a light twine.

Now take your blunt screwdriver and lift up the skin of the lower jaw, find the exact center of the lower jaw on this skin and tuck it up into the lip slot of the form in the exact center of the lower jaw on the form, then fasten it in position by driving in a wire brad. Continue this operation all along the lower jaw, tucking in the skin and fastening it with wire brads spaced about an inch apart. Work from the front toward the back of the jaw on each side until the extreme corner of the mouth is reached. Fasten this corner with a brad; in driving these brads into the form don't drive them all the way in. Leave enough of the head showing so that they can be removed with pliers after the mount has dried.

To prepare the upper jaw and nostrils for mounting, mix again a small amount of Casco glue; then, working from the inside, under the skin, coat the entire upper half of the form as far up as the eye sockets, working the glue into the tear ducts and nostrils. Then pull down the nose skin over the form, and with the blunt screwdriver tuck the center of the upper lip around and under the form up into the lip slot in the exact center of the nose, fastening with a brad. Repeat around each side of the upper lips, working toward the back as you did with the lower jaw and placing brads about an inch apart to hold the lips in place. When the back corner of the mouth is reached, you'll find that you have a small fold of skin left with no place to put it; merely fold it over and nail it in place with two or more brads and it will dry in this position very nicely.

The skin of the inside nostril should now be tried in the form openings that are provided for the nostrils. If there is a little too much nostril skin left on the scalp, pull it out and trim it off with a knife or scissors until it just lines the form and no more, then fasten in place with a brad at each upper corner.

Most forms as they come from the supply houses have the lip slots already cut. It's a good idea, though, to examine the form as soon as it arrives and make certain of this point. If this detail has not been worked out by the makers, then it's up to the operator to cut the slot, using a narrow wood chisel and a hammer. Turn the form upside down and with your chisel cut straight down through the paper form directly between the upper and lower lips, making the cut close to the sides of the lower jaw and in such a way that the cut will be vertical in direction when the head is hung upright. It often helps in placing the lips to widen this slot a bit either with the chisel or a knife, giving more room for the lip skin. This lip skin is very important to successful fashioning of the mouth, so again, be certain that there is plenty left on the hide after the fleshing and beaming operations.

Now the most important detail comes up — setting the eyes. First take a small wad of papier-mâché and line the eye socket for the eye to rest upon. Lift up the upper eyelid and slip the eye under the lid, then bring the lower lid around and over it. You'll note that the pupils are a long oval, so place the eye in such a way that the long axis of the oval is nearly horizontal, with the front end tipped down just a bit. Now take a nail or some other fairly blunt tool and press the skin into the tear ducts in just the same way that they originally grew to the skull. Drive a brad down into the bottom of this tear duct and set it permanently with a nail set — this brad will not be removed from the mount. Now take another brad and drive it into the front corner of the eye and into the front corner of the eye socket on the form. Place the other eye in exactly the same way; it's best to place both eyes before trying to obtain the right expression, rather than setting only one eye at a time.

Stand back away from the head and look at each eye; probably one will be higher than the other or one may protrude farther from the eyelid. Now from a position directly in front of the head push each eye toward the rear of the eye socket, pushing the front corner of the eye in toward the skull. The back of the eye should be covered all around by the skin of the eyelids, but the front corner should show a small triangular piece of the papier-mâché filling. Adjust both eyes together, bringing each into correct adjustment by sliding them and pressing them into the pliable papier-mâché filling.

There can be no given rule for setting eyes in any deer head, because each mount is slightly different. In general, keep the eyes slanted slightly toward the front of the head, pupils tipped forward and down just a little, with the focal point of the animal's gaze at a point about ten feet distant and just below the mount's eye level. The upper lid should be pulled well down over the top of the eye and the lower lid pulled up to an almost flat line; then, when the head shrinks in drying, the eyelids will shrink back away from the eye, creating the proper expression. If no allowance is made for this shrinkage, the eyes will bulge or "pop," giving the mount a frightened expression. Properly set up before drying, the mount should have a decided "squint" in expression, or, in other words, a "sleepy look." The major point to guard against is allowing the eyes to protrude too far from the head; they should project just beyond the contour of the eye socket about an eighth of an inch — no more than this.

The head is now completely mounted except for arranging the skin and cleaning off loose papier-mâché or glue. Sponge off the extraneous matter with a wet cloth, clean out the excess from around the eyes and nostrils and comb out the hair on the head. Check the sewing at the back of the neck incision and take any extra stitches that may be needed, then knot the threads together. Now with an awl or ice pick arrange the skin on the form by sliding it back toward the neck board to remove wrinkles.

When the hide lies smooth and sleek on the form take your box of wire brads and nail the skin down all along the rear of the form, placing the nails so that they will pass through the hide, form and edge of the neck board, spacing them about two inches apart. Take your sharp knife and trim the hide off all around the edge of the form, leaving about a quarter inch extending beyond the edge of the form. Place the form on the wall and spread out the hide and hair all around the base of the neck, brushing it out so that it will lie smooth.

Go over the entire mount with the brush, removing the marks made by the comb, for if the hide dries with these comb-marks they might show up as streaks in the finished mount. A bit more brushing of the ears and the head, and the mount is ready to be put away in a warm place to dry for about a week.

When the head is completely dry and hard, remove first all the wire brads around the mouth and nostrils with a pair of pliers; remove the clamps and cardboard from the ears, and untie the ear butts and ears from the antlers; then go over the entire mount with comb and brush, and lay the hair down with the hands. You'll note that the skin around the eyes and nostrils has a pale appearance after drying out, but this color will be restored with either oil tube colors or colored wax. But first, any small gaps around the nostrils and the front corners of the eye must be filled in with the papier-mâché and allowed to dry.

The proper oil colors for finishing the head are Vandyke brown, Alizarine Crimson and Black. They can be applied with the camel's-hair brush directly, after being thinned with turpentine, but a neater job is effected by using colored wax. Take equal parts of paraffin and beeswax melted together and add a small quantity of the color from the tube, stirring quickly to aid blending. Let us say that you have made up a small quantity of the Vandyke brown in a medium tone. Now while the wax is hot apply it to the eyelids and inside of the nostrils, allowing it to run down into the tear duct, covering this area of bare skin and giving it a natural color. Make up also a small amount of the black wax and paint the nose. Apply it smoothly by keeping the wax hot and holding the brush in the solution right up to the moment of application. Finish up with a small quantity of pink wax made of the crimson in a light tone; apply just a touch to the inside front corner of the eye and inside the nostrils.

If the wax fails to flow just right and does not present a smooth appearance, go over it gently with a small pad of cloth wet with turpentine. This will smooth out all lumps and ridges, making a neat job. However, good results will come by simply painting the parts mentioned, using the regular shades of oil colors thinned a bit with turpentine. If a high gloss is desired on the nose and around the eyes, apply a thin coat of clear varnish after the colors have dried.

If the work has been carefully done on the mouth and lips no filling-in will be necessary; under no circumstances should the lips and edges of the mouth be colored or varnished in any way, for this is decidedly unnatural. Neither should the antlers be varnished — rather give them a dull gloss by applying with a cloth a polish made up of equal parts of raw linseed oil and turpentine.

Your mount is now complete except for the panel. Prepare this by first drilling three holes spaced about three inches apart and roughly triangular in setup, drilling from the front center of the panel with a ¼-inch drill. Now countersink these holes in the back of the panel and attach the plate or hanger. Set up your head, well centered on the panel, and screw it down tight using 2½-inch Number 10 galvanized wood screws — and the job is finished.

You now have as good a mount as can be turned out — a light, durable trophy that is proof against moths and the ravages of time, at least for many years to come. You'll note that no clay or plaster is used in the process, for a good reason. Both clay and plaster placed next to the skin will eventually cause cracks in the mount, ruining both its appearance and durability. This mount is light, well posed and graceful in appearance, making it a constant source of delight to its owner.

Before attempting any work on deer heads the novice should study all the photographs and artists' drawings of deer that he can get his hands on; the outdoor magazines are a good source of supply. If possible, he might visit his state game farm and look over the captive deer in the experimental stations, gathering for himself firsthand information on positions of ears, eyes and so on, and valuable points in expression that only actual observation of the live animal will give.

Many times, my shooting pals have asked me just how long it takes to mount a deer head completely. This varies, of course, with different jobs, but here is a fairly accurate estimate of the time involved in actually performing the manual operations, without considering the lapses of time involved in tanning the hide, salt curing, and poisoning.

Breaking it down into the various steps it reads like this: *Taking measurements and skinning the head,* 1 hour; *salting and fleshing,* 1½ hours; *beaming the skin, washing and poisoning,* 2 hours; *preparing the head,* 3 hours; *finishing the mount after drying and mounting on the panel,* 2 hours. This gives us a total of 9½ hours for the entire job, including all incidentals. The novice will have to add perhaps 5 more hours to this total, to allow for inexperience and possible mistakes; but at any rate the entire job can be done in less than 20 hours of work.

Any sportsman who has already completed his first job of mounting his own trophy is certainly entitled to a feeling of superiority over the average deer hunter, yet there is no sound reason why any man capable of killing a whitetail buck under sportsmanlike conditions cannot also mount his buck, in view of the simplicity of present methods. Any trophy mounted by the sportsman's own hands brings with it and keeps a pleasant feeling of intimacy that is lacking in all other mounts.

With the mounting of the trophy we come at last to the end of this volume on whitetail deer; through life habits, hunting methods, caring for the prize of the hunt; through the mechanics of weapons, loads and sighting equipment. Each and all of these points hang heavily on the scales of deer-hunting success. The author hopes that throughout each of the chapters the reader can detect the ring of sincerity; certainly every paragraph in the text has been done with this uppermost in mind.

Any reader, whether sportsman or not, after wading through this book may conclude that the writer's sole ambition in life is to spend every waking moment in new plans for destroying more and more deer. Nothing could be further from the truth. No one has greater admiration for these grand, graceful wilderness spirits than I myself. Even as I write these concluding paragraphs there are, within two miles of my home, numerous wild whitetail deer. How I envy them their carefree, peaceful existence; their perfect liberty to move when and where they please! It is true that their lives are threatened now and then, but so are we all — not only for two weeks, but for the full fifty-two weeks in every year, to almost the same degree.

It is my aim in presenting this work not only to aid the whitetail hunter in taking his trophy but to implant in him some of my unbounded admiration for these wonderful game animals; to aid him to success in a soul-filling sport whose rewards lie deeper in the heart than the filling of a license. I shall forever wonder how close I came to the mark.

A Note About the Author

Larry Koller was born in 1912 in Brooklyn, but from age seven lived in Orange County, New York. He ran a sporting goods store in Middletown, New York, worked during World War II as a barrel department foreman for two New Haven gun manufacturers, and had been a Catskill guide, gunsmith, and tackle maker long before he became known as one of the country's leading outdoor writers and editors. He was later outdoor editor of *Argosy*, editor-in-chief of *American Gun*, and at his death in 1967 was a staff editor and columnist for *Guns and Ammunition*. He is best known for the FIRESIDE BOOK OF GUNS, TREASURY OF HUNTING, and TREASURY OF ANGLING.

A NOTE ON THE TYPE

This book was set on the Linotype in Janson, a recutting made direct from type cast from matrices long thought to have been made by the Dutchman Anton Janson, who was a practicing type founder in Leipzig during the years 1668–87. However, it has been conclusively demonstrated that these types are actually the work of Nicholas Kis (1650–1702), a Hungarian, who most probably learned his trade from the master Dutch type founder Kirk Voskens. The type is an excellent example of the influential and sturdy Dutch types that prevailed in England up to the time William Caslon developed his own incomparable designs from them.